Lecture Notes in Computer Science 3803

Commenced Publication in 1973
Founding and Former Series Editors:
Gerhard Goos, Juris Hartmanis, and Jan van Leeuwen

Sushil Jajodia   Chandan Mazumdar (Eds.)

Information Systems Security

First International Conference, ICISS 2005
Kolkata, India, December 19-21, 2005
Proceedings

 Springer

Volume Editors

Sushil Jajodia
George Mason University
Center for Secure Information Systems
Fairfax, VA 22030-4444, USA
E-mail: jajodia@gmu.edu

Chandan Mazumdar
Jadavpur University
Department of Computer Science and Engineering
Kolkata - 700032, India
E-mail: chandanm@cse.jdvu.ac.in

Library of Congress Control Number: 2005936358

CR Subject Classification (1998): C.2.0, D.4.6, E.3, H.2.0, K.4.4, K.6.5

ISSN   0302-9743
ISBN-10   3-540-30706-0 Springer Berlin Heidelberg New York
ISBN-13   978-3-540-30706-8 Springer Berlin Heidelberg New York

Springer is a part of Springer Science+Business Media

springeronline.com

© Springer-Verlag Berlin Heidelberg 2005
Printed in Germany

Typesetting: Camera-ready by author, data conversion by Scientific Publishing Services, Chennai, India
Printed on acid-free paper   SPIN: 11593980   06/3142   5 4 3 2 1 0

Preface

The 1st International Conference on Information Systems Security (ICISS 2005) was held December 19–21, 2005 at Jadavpur University, Kolkata, India. The objectives of the conference were to discuss in depth the current state of the research and practice in information systems security, enable participants to benefit from personal contact with other researchers and expand their knowledge, and disseminate the research results.

This volume contains 4 invited papers, 19 refereed papers that were presented at the conference, and 5 ongoing project summaries. The refereed papers, which were selected from the 72 submissions, were rigorously reviewed by the Program Committee members. The volume provides researchers with a broad perspective of recent developments in information systems security.

A special note of thanks goes to the many volunteers whose efforts made this conference a success. We wish to thank Prem Chand, Ernesto Damiani, Patrick McDaniel, R. Sekar, and Vijay Varadharajan for agreeing to deliver the invited talks, the authors for their worthy contributions, and the referees for their time and effort in reviewing the papers. We are grateful to Arun Majumdar and Aditya Bagchi for serving as the General Chairs.

Last, but certainly not least, our thanks go to Vijay Kowtha of the U.S. Office of Naval Research Global and Michael Cheetham of the INDO-US Science & Technology Forum for providing the generous financial support.

December 2005
Sushil Jajodia and Chandan Mazumdar
Program Chairs

General Chairs' Message

It was our great pleasure to organize the 1st International Conference on Information Systems Security in Kolkata, India. Though such conferences are held in different parts of the globe, a conference dedicated to data security issues only has not been organized before in India. That way it is a unique event. It gives us great satisfaction to admit that our colleagues in different countries have extended all possible help in making it a success. As members of the Program Committee, they have extended all possible cooperation. We are very much grateful to our keynote speakers for accepting our invitation and for delivering lectures on frontier topics in the area of data security. We are thankful to the tutorial speakers for providing interesting tutorials. We are also grateful to the authors of the submitted papers for showing interest in this conference and sincerely hope that they would do the same in future years as well. We hope that the participants have found this conference informative enough and would also join in coming years.

In this connection, we take the opportunity to express our great appreciation to the wonderful work done by our Program Chairs Prof. S. Jajodia and Prof. C. Mazumdar. Only because of their untiring effort has the conference achieved an enviable acdemic level in its first year.

We are also very grateful to Jadavpur University for hosting the first conference as part of their Golden Jubilee celebration program. The Organizing Committee under the leadership of Prof. A. Kar has also done a wonderful job.

To organize such an event, we need money. Fundraising is not an easy job. The Finance Chair managed the show very well. We are very grateful to all our sponsors. Only because of their help could we make the conference a success.

Aditya Bagchi and Arun K. Majumdar

Organization

General Chairs: Arun K. Majumdar, Indian Institute of Technology, Kharagpur, India
Aditya Bagchi, Indian Statistical Institute, Kolkata, India

Program Chairs: Sushil Jajodia, George Mason University, Fairfax, VA, USA
Chandan Mazumdar, Jadavpur University, Kolkata, India

Organizing Chairs: Avijit Kar, Jadavpur University, Kolkata, India
Samir Basu, Department of Information Technology, Government of India

Tutorial Chairs: Sarmistha Neogy, Jadavpur University, Kolkata, India
R.T. Goswami, Birla Institute of Technology, Mesra, Ranchi, India

Finance Chair: Mridul S. Barik, Bengal Engineering & Science University, Howrah, India

Publicity Chairs: B.B. Pant, Birla Institute of Technology, Mesra, Ranchi, India
Anil K. Kaushik, Department of Information Technology, Government of India

Industry Chair: Kushal Banerjee, TCS, Kolkata, India

Program Committee

S. Arunkumar	Indian Institute of Technology, Bombay, India
Vijay Atluri	Rutgers University, USA
Mridul S. Barik	Bengal Engineering & Science University, India
Joachim Biskup	University of Dortmund, Germany
Frédéric Cuppens	ENST, France
Ernesto Damiani	University of Milan, Italy
Neil Daswani	DoCoMo USA Labs, USA
Deborah Frincke	PNNL and University of Idaho, USA
K. Gopinath	Indian Institute of Science, India
B.N. Jain	Indian Institute of Technology, Delhi, India
Christopher Kruegel	TU Vienna, Austria
Michiharu Kudo	IBM Tokyo Research Laboratory, Japan
Yingjiu Li	Singapore Management University, Singapore
Fabio Massacci	University of Trento, Italy
Patrick McDaniel	Pennsylvania State University, USA
Sharad Mehrotra	University of California, Irvine, USA

Sukumar Nandi	Indian Institute of Technology, Guwahati, India
Brajendra Panda	University of Arkansas, USA
Arun K. Pujari	University of Hyderabad, India
Indrakshi Ray	Colorado State University, USA
Indrajit Ray	Colorado State University, USA
Bimal Roy	Indian Statistical Institute, Kolkata, India
Pierangela Samarati	University of Milan, Italy
A.K. Sarje	Indian Institute of Technology, Roorkee, India
R. Sekar	State University of New York, Stoney Brook, USA
Indranil Sengupta	Indian Institute of Technology, Kharagpur, India
Shiuh-Pyng Shieh	Chiao Tung University, Taiwan
Shamik Sural	Indian Institute of Technology, Kharagpur, India
Vijay Varadharajan	Macquarie University, Australia
Alec Yasinsac	Florida State University, USA
Bill Yurcik	University of Illinois, USA

Advisory Committee

Prof. A.N. Basu	Vice Chancellor, Jadavpur University, Chairman
Prof. Shyamal K. Sanyal	Pro Vice Chancellor, Jadavpur University
Prof. A.R. Thakur	Vice Chancellor, West Bengal University of Technology
Prof. S.K. Pal	Director, Indian Statistical Institute
Prof. S.K. Mukherjee	Vice Chancellor, Birla Institute of Technology, Mesra, Ranchi (D.U.)
Shri K.V.S.S. Prasad Rao	Chief Controller, R&D (Technical), Ministry of Defence, Govt. of India
Shri A.K. Chakravarti	Adviser, Department of Information Technology, MCIT, Govt. of India
Shri N. Sitaram	Director, Centre for A. I. & Robotics, Bangalore, DRDO, Govt. of India
Shri Pankaj Aggarwala	Joint Secretary, Department of IT, Govt. of India
Dr. M.S. Rao	Director-cum-Chief Forensic Scientist of India, Ministry of Home Affairs, Govt. of India

Sponsoring Institutions

Center for Secure Information Systems, George Mason University, USA
Center For Distributed Computing, Jadavpur University, Kolkata, India
Birla Institute of Technology (D.U.), Mesra, Ranchi, India
INDO-US Science & Technology Forum, New Delhi, India
U.S. Office of Naval Research Global, USA

Table of Contents

Authorization and Trust Enhanced Security
for Distributed Applications

Vijay Varadharajan

Professor and Microsoft Chair in Computing,
Macquarie University, NSW 2109, Australia
vijay@ics.mq.edu.au

Abstract. This paper addresses the issues of authorization and trust in a federated distributed environment. We describe some of design principles involved in the development of authorization service for practical large scale distributed systems. We present the design of web services authorization architecture and discuss its implementation within the .NET framework. Then we discuss the notion of trusted computing and presented our approach and architecture to enhancing the distributed authorization service using trusted platforms technologies.

1 Introduction

Security issues are becoming even more significant in the age of pervasive mobile networked computing where we have different types of information being used by mobile and fixed large scale distributed applications interacting over wireless and wired networks to deliver useful services to enterprises and users, fixed and mobile. (see Figure 1). We also have mobile software agents that move from place to place doing some work on behalf of the applications and users. The applications themselves are varied in their characteristics ranging from simple dedicated ones to large scale applications in finance, telecommunications and healthcare. In terms of computing platforms, we have systems ranging from big and powerful computers to cluster of computers to PCs to PDAs to dedicated information appliances. In terms of distributed middleware, we have technologies ranging from distributed remote programming to distributed object systems to web services and service oriented architecture platforms. Perhaps the key component in Figure 1 is the Users component and the main reason for all these technologies is to provide the users with the ability to perform their tasks more conveniently, more securely and more effectively from anywhere and at anytime.

The heterogeneous pervasive mobile networked computing and information infrastructure outlined above poses many security and privacy challenges. Not only there are different technology components such as computing hardware operating systems, middleware, networks and protocols, databases and applications and users but also there are different platforms in each of these technologies and different providers developing them with different security services and mechanisms. There will also be different security policies and requirements from users and organizations using these

S. Jajodia and C. Mazumdar (Eds.): ICISS 2005, LNCS 3803, pp. 1–20, 2005.

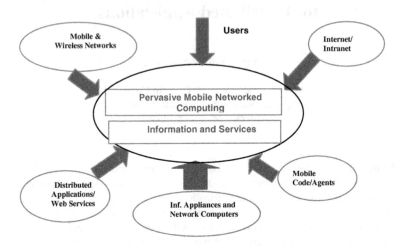

Fig. 1. Pervasive Mobile Networked Computing Environment

platforms and applications are likely to have their own security requirements. Furthermore, nowadays there are numerous standards that relate to security ranging from mechanisms to services to protocols in different networks, systems and applications; compliance and conformance to security standards, though they are claimed by different vendors and developers, are difficult to prove and are not often achieved. All these imply that the design and management of secure systems and applications and their interoperability pose several major challenges both in research and in practice.

One of the emerging areas in the middleware space in this pervasive mobile networked computing that is key to businesses and applications is that of web services or more generally service oriented architectures. Web services provide the pillars for evolving the Internet into a service-oriented integration platform of unprecedented scale and agility. The foundation of this technology lies in the modularization and virtualization of system functions as services that can be described, advertised and discovered using (XML-based) standard languages, and that interoperate through standard Internet protocols. These services aim to use standard formats and protocols to promote interoperability and extensibility among applications and to enable complex operations. Traditionally, distributed computing mechanisms have typically evolved around technical architectures rather than broader problems of application integration. On the other hand, web services have evolved around the problem of application integration using standard open technologies. Web services can pose significant security challenges as they can offer a decentralized architecture and administration with heterogeneous technologies across multiple enterprises in a federated environment. Furthermore, as web services may operate in highly autonomous and dynamic environments, security concerns are more pronounced and challenging in service oriented architectures than in conventional distributed computing architectures.

In general, security for web services is a broad and complex area covering a range of technologies. At present, there are several efforts underway that are striving for the provision of security services such as authentication between participating entities, confidentiality and integrity of communications. A variety of existing technologies can contribute to this area such as TLS/SSL [1] and IPSEC [2]. Security functionality based on XML Signature and XML Encryption standard efforts [3] are currently being done at W3C. There are also natural extensions of these to integrate security features in technologies such as SOAP and WSDL [4]. There is also work as part of XKMS [5] defining interfaces to key management and trust services based on SOAP and WSDL. These primarily target the "transport" level. There are also draft standards being developed in the areas of web services policy, trust and federation. At this stage, they are primarily concentrating on message structures and exchange formats, rather than policy modeling, specification and enforcement. However there are some fundamental architectural and design issues in the areas of distributed authorization, trust establishment and management, which need to be addressed for the development and deployment of secure large scale web services based applications in the future.

In this paper, we will consider some specific research issues in the areas of authorization and trust in a distributed environment. In particular, we will look at the design and management of authorization policies for enterprise wide distributed applications and introduce the notion of trust enhanced authorization to improve security decision making. The paper is organized as follows. In section 2, we begin by outlining some of the design principles involved in distributed authorization. Section 3 presents the design and development of distributed authorization architecture for web services. Section 4 discusses the notion of trust in "trusted computing" and presents our approach to enhancing the authorization using trusted platforms in distributed applications.

2   Distributed Authorization

In a distributed system, when one principal requests a service from another, the receiving principal needs to address at least two questions. Is the requesting principal the one it claims to be and does the requesting principal have appropriate privileges for the requested service? These two basic questions relate to the issues of authentication and authorization. There are also other security concerns such as auditing, secure communication, availability and accountability. The authorization requirements in distributed applications are much richer than the authentication both in terms of the types of privileges required and the nature and degree of interactions between participating entities. In this paper, our focus is on the design and management of distributed authorization and will not address the issue of authentication.

2.1   Authorization Architecture Framework

In general, the authorization architectural framework should be aimed at addressing the needs of several classes of users. These include the developers, administrators, policy setters and the end users.

From a developer point of view, much of authorization security today is still often implemented as part of the programming effort. The authorization logic is written for each application, which is often based on developers' knowledge and skill level. We believe from an architectural point of view, it is important to separate out the authorization logic from the application logic as much as possible. This can be accomplished by defining appropriate authorization attributes and formulating rules that specify how the authorization decision is computed and processed outside the application logic. There are several benefits that arise from this strict separation. An important practical consequence is that it results in a consistent application programming interface across all applications and platforms thereby allowing common policies across them. Furthermore, checking of access rights is abstracted away from a particular application. This enables the developers to concentrate on the business logic instead of reinventing the security portion of the application.

From an administrator point of view, often each application is administered separately. This often leads to custom security processes for administering the required security information, such as user names and privilege capabilities. Enterprise wide security policies are become difficult to implement consistently across all applications and these policies are even more difficult to verify. Certain security tasks require more than one administrator to check the correctness of the task. It will be useful if the architecture is able to consolidate security management. This can provide a consistent view of principals and their privileges for a given application.

From the end user point of view, in large systems, they suffer most from the fact that each system and each application implements its own security mechanisms. When each application provides its own authorization facilities, the user can get confused by the different policies in the application. For example, why is a bank manager's limit in one banking application is $1500 and in a related application it is $2000? It may be necessary for the security related attributes of a user to be consistent throughout the range of similar applications.

Furthermore, policy setters and managers require facilities and tools to ensure that the policies are correctly specified and implemented. Hence there is a need for the authorization architecture to be a way of structuring and grouping principals and resources, establish and manage privileges, check and test for consistency and validate the correctness and completeness of policies.

2.2 Authorization Service Design Principles

The design of any security service involves at least the following aspects: security information used in the provision of the security service, the security mechanisms that are required to support the service and the authorities involved in the management of the service. In the case of authorization service, the security information used ranges from user identities to group identities to role information to location information to actions and parameters associated with the actions. From an architecture point of view, it is important to recognize the characteristics of the different types of the authorization security information. At an informal conceptual level, we can classify the various types of information as follows: Some security information is generic and static in nature. For instance, typically identity based information falls into this category. Then there is security information that is specific but still somewhat static in nature. For instance, role based access information falls into this category. Roles are specific to organizations and they are reasonably static in the sense that they are unlikely to change on a day to day or even on a monthly (or even yearly) basis. In fact, one of the main benefits of access control system based on role based information is to reduce the effect of the changes in the user population on the management of access privileges. Then we have security information that is specific and dynamic in nature. These are specific in the sense they may relate to specific applications or parts of applications or files. They are dynamic in the sense they are prone to changes in system state. Such a characterization of different types of authorization information in turn helps to understand better the requirements on their management. First, the authorities involved in the management of these different types of authorization information are likely to be different. Not only the strategies with respect to when the changes and updates to this information take place are likely to be different but also who are allowed to make these changes is likely to vary. For instance, the specification and changes to the role information in an organization will be the responsibility of a certain group of people who can be different to those responsible for setting the privileges for a specific file or application in a server.

From an architectural point of view, such a characterization also leads to some basic principles for distributed authorization service design. First, it is appropriate to locate the static and generic authorization information in some form of a central server within a domain, which is responsible for a collection of clients and server principals. Second, the dynamic and specific authorization information can be located near or at the target, enabling the target system authorities to be involved in their management. From a distribution point of view, static and generic authorization information (for instance, stored in a central server within a domain) can be "pushed" by the client principal to the target principal. In fact, static and specific information can also be pushed in a similar fashion. Finally, specific and dynamic authorization information needs to be "pulled" at the time of the decision process.

Based on these principles, one can see that conceptually there can be multiple types of trusted management authorities involved. For instance, one dealing with generic and static security information and another dealing with specific and static information, both of which can be architected as centralized servers (say, one per domain) servicing a number of principals (e.g. clients and servers) within the domain. Furthermore, specific and dynamic security information needs to be managed at the target principal (or at some entity attached to or close to the target), as this type of information is often dependent on the state of the application or resource under consideration. Such information may include attributes associated with specific rights in the application. We have used these architectural design principles in the design and management of distributed authorization service which we will describe in Section 3 below.

2.3 Authorization Checks

Another fundamental aspect that needs to be considered in the design of the distributed authorization service is the type of authorization checks and their location. In practice, there are different places at which authorization checks can be made. In general, there are at least the following to consider: (a) A coarse level check determines whether access to the application (or server hosting the application) is to be allowed access or not. The check may be performed by the application or by some component that is a front-end to the application. (b) The function access check is made on the type of function or operation being requested. This may or may not include parameters from the request in the authorization decision. As with (a), this check can be embedded in the application or performed by some front-end component. However, in the case of a front-end component, more sophistication is required for the front-end to recognize one function or operation request from another. (c) The business logic check is not only done on the function or operation but also on the transaction parameters of the request and on the parameters from calculations from within the application. This check is dependent on the business logic and state of the application. With such multi level authorization checks, one can model from simple to complex policies required by the distributed business applications.

2.4 Authorization Service Design Stages

Let us now briefly outline the two distinct stages involved in the design of the distributed authorization service. Conceptually, there are two stages namely the administration phase and the runtime or the evaluation phase. The administration phase involves facilities and services for the specification of authorization policies, updating and deleting of policies and their administration. The runtime phase is concerned with the use of these authorization policies in the evaluation of the access requests. The representation of the authorization policy information can be different in these phases. There are at least two arguments for maintaining distinct representations of authorization information in these two phases. First, there is the information captured by the language that can be compiled out before access decision time. For example, the meaning of inheritance and override depends only on the user and not on the server and transaction attributes. This enables the authorization system to make the access decision faster, by avoiding searching the inheritance hierarchy. Secondly, it is possible to envisage different strategies for replication of the information needed for administration versus the information needed for access evaluation decisions at the application servers. This in turn has implications in terms of interfaces and components required in the authorization service design. For instance, in terms of interfaces, there will be at least two interfaces namely the administration interface used by the administrators and the policy setters and the runtime evaluation interface used by the clients and application servers during access decision time. There will also be another interface used for auditing purposes. For instance, the configuration and the management of the authorization server may require an independent auditor to monitor whether the authorization policy meets the required controls. In terms of components, the authorization service requires an administration component where the authorization policies are entered and stored in one representation, and a runtime evaluation component, which stores the authorization rules at a different representation for runtime access.

2.5 Authorization Policies and Policy Languages

Having considered some of the principles involved in the design of distributed authorization architecture, let us now consider the policies to be supported by the authorization service. A fundamental objective of any authorization system is to enable to represent and evaluate a range of access policies that are relevant and required. These policies capture the authorization requirements of the distributed applications.

Languages have long been recognized in computing as ideal vehicles for dealing with expression and structuring of complex and dynamic relationships. Over the years several languages have been proposed, some mathematical logic based [6,7], some graph based and some programming language based [8, 9, 10]. On the one hand, a language should be sufficiently simple thereby enabling the administrators and policy setters to use the language in specifying their policies, while on the other hand, it should have sufficient expressive and analytical power to represent and evaluate a range of policies used in practical systems. We believe a programming language approach to specification is often more practical in terms of developer friendliness. While in theory a general-purpose programming language could be used to specify authorization policies, often a special purpose language providing for optimizations and domain specific structures considerably improves the efficiency. A language-based approach is useful not only for supporting a range of access control policies but also useful in separating out the policy representation from policy enforcement. Over the years, we have developed some dedicated languages for specifying authorization policies [8, 10, 11]. Naturally, a "standard" policy language is useful for interoperability between different systems and applications. Administrators save time and money because they are not required to rewrite their policies in many different languages. Developers save time and money because they do not have to invent new policy languages and write code to support them. Also good tools for writing and managing policies for a policy language are likely to emerge if the policy language is standardized.

Authorization policies themselves can range from simple identity based policies to complex dynamic and collaborative policies. Hence the need for the language to have suitable constructs to be able to specify the range of required policies. At present, some of the commonly used access policies include the following: identity based policies, group and role based policies [12], delegation policies [13], static separation of duty policies, dynamic separation of duty and Chinese wall policies [14], and joint action [15] and collaboration access policies.

3 Distributed Authorization Systems

Over the recent years we have been involved in the design of large scale practical authorization systems for different distributed environments. I was involved in architecting, designing and developing Praesidium Authorization Service System [8, 16] at Hewlett-Packard. This is a large scale distributed system, involving Distributed Computing Environment (DCE) and Transaction Processing technologies running on top of Unix Operating System used for financial applications. The authorization system was designed based on the above architectural principles. A dedicated policy language, Praesidium Policy Language, was developed and was used to specify a range of authorization policies such as role based access policies, delegation policies, static and dynamic separation of duty policies and joint action and collaboration policies. An Authorization Server per domain (see Figure 2), comprising Administration and Runtime Components together with libraries and interfaces for administrators, users, policy setters and auditor and verifiers. The Praesidium system was released commercially and it was highly successful. Then we designed an authorization service for distributed objects based architecture. We developed a policy language for specifying authorization policies for object-oriented systems called Tower [10] and developed an authorization system for CORBA based distributed architecture [17]. Over the last couple of years, we have been working in web services security. Here we first developed extensions of XACL, an XML based Authorization Language [11] to specify authorization policies such as role hierarchies, static and dynamic separation of duty policies, delegation and joint action based access policies. We also developed a corresponding Extended XACL based Authorization Engine. These were then used to demonstrate secure healthcare application enabling secure access to electronic patient records in a distributed system [18]. This work led to the development of a generic architectural framework for web services [19]. In this section, we will describe the design of this Web Services Authorization Architecture (WSAA) and its integration with the .NET distributed computing platform [20].

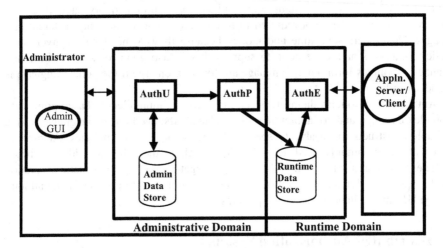

Fig. 2. Authorization Server

3.1 Web Services Authorization Architecture (WSAA)

Authorization services for the web services have somewhat different design requirements as web services present a complex layered system. For instance, a service could be a front-end to an enterprise system and the enterprise system accesses information stored in databases and files. Web services may be used by enterprises to expose the functionality of legacy applications to users in a heterogeneous environment. Or new business applications could be written to leverage benefits offered by the service oriented architectures. We have proposed authorization architecture for web services (WSAA) to provide extensions to the security layers of web services. We also extend the Web services description and messaging layers to provide authorization support for Web services. In this section, we outline the design of the WSAA and describe the extensions required to the Web service Description and Messaging Layers. We also briefly describe the authorization algorithms used by WSAA and outline our implementation of the WSAA in the .NET platform.

3.2 Characteristics of the Proposed Architecture WSAA

First let us briefly highlight some of the characteristics of our proposed architecture.

- Support for Various Access Control Models: WSAA supports multiple access control models. The access policy requirements for each model can be specified using its own policy language. The policies used for authorization can be fine-grained or coarse-grained depending on the requirements. Authorization can be achieved either using the push or the pull model or even a combination of both.
- Support for Legacy and New Web Service Based Applications: Existing legacy application systems can still function and use their current access control mechanisms when they are exposed as Web services to enable an interoperable heterogeneous environment. At the same time, WSAA supports new web service based applications built to leverage the benefits offered by the service oriented architectures. New access control mechanisms can be implemented and used by web service applications. A new access control mechanism can itself be implemented as a web service. All WSAA requires is an end-point URL and interface for the mechanism's access policy evaluation.
- Decentralized and Distributed Architecture: A web service can have one or more responsible authorization policy evaluation (APE) component involved in making the authorization decision. The APEs themselves can be web services specializing in authorization. This feature allows WSAA to be decentralized and distributed.
- Flexibility in Management and Administration: Using the hierarchy approach of managing web services and collections of web services, authorization policies can be specified at different levels.
- Ease of Integration into Platforms: Each of the entities involved both in administration and runtime domains is fairly generic and can be implemented in any middleware including the .NET platform as well as Java based platforms. The administration and runtime domain related application programming interfaces (APIs) can be implemented in any of the available middleware.
- Enhanced Security: In our architecture, every client principal request passes through the web service's security manager and then gets authenticated and authorized. The security manager can be placed in a firewall zone, which enhances security of collections of web service objects placed behind an organization's firewall. This enables organizations to protect their web service based applications from outside traffic. A firewall could be configured to accept and send only SOAP request messages with appropriate header and body to the responsible security manager to get authenticated and authorized.

3.3 Design of the Proposed WSAA

Let us first briefly describe an overview of the proposed architecture (see Figure 3). WSAA comprises an administrative domain and a runtime domain. Web services are managed in the administration domain by arranging them into collections and the collections themselves into a hierarchy. Administration support is provided to manage a collection of web services. Support for the arrangement (adding, removing) of web services within the collections and the movement of web services within collections is also provided. Authorization related components can be managed in the administration domain. Also security administrators can assign a set of authorization policy evaluators (APEs) to authorize requests to web services. To make the authorization process efficient, we have a runtime domain where the authorization related information such as what credentials are required to invoke a particular web service and how to collect those credentials, is compiled and stored. This information is automatically compiled from time to time when necessary using the information from the administration domain and it can be readily used by components in the runtime domain.

The Registry Server located anywhere in the Internet is responsible for maintaining relations between services and their service providers. When a client requests the Registry Server (for instance, UDDI directory) for a specific service, the latter responds with a list of web services that implement the requested service.

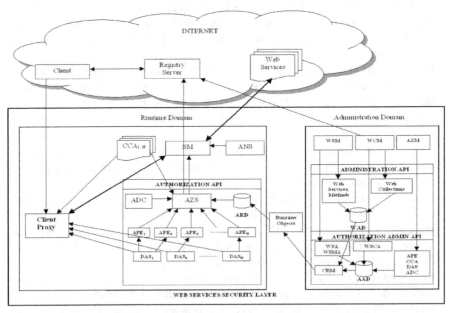

Fig. 3. Web Services Authorization Architecture (WSAA)

3.4 System Components

We define the set of Certificate and Credential Authorities (CCA), Dynamic Attribute Services (DAS), Authorization Policy Evaluators (APE)} and Authorization Decision Composers (ADC) as objects in our system. The Authorization Manager (AZM) for an organization is responsible to manage these components. S/he uses the Authorization Administration API (AA-API) to manage them and the related data is stored in the Authorization Administration Database (AAD).

- Certificate and Credential Authority (CCA) is responsible to provide authentication certificates and/or authorization credentials required to authenticate and/or authorize a client.
- Dynamic Attribute Service (DAS) provides system and/or network attributes such as bandwidth usage and time of the day. A dynamic attribute may also express properties of a subject that are not administered by security administrators. For example, a nurse may only access a patient's record if s/he is located within the hospital. A DAS may provide the nurse's ``location status" attribute at the time of access control. Dynamic attributes' values change more frequently than traditional ``static" authorization credentials. Unlike authorization credentials, dynamic attributes must be obtained at the time an access decision is required and their values may change within a session.
- Authorization Policy Evaluator (APE) is responsible for making authorization decision on one or more abstract system operations. Every APE may use a different access control mechanism and a different policy language. However, it defines an interface for the set of input parameters it expects (such as subject (client) identification, object information, and the authorization credentials) and the output authorization result.
- Authorization Decision Composer (ADC) combines the authorization decisions from APEs using an algorithm that resolves authorization decision conflicts and combines them into a final decision.

The runtime domain consists of the Client Proxy (CP), Security Manager, Authentication Server (ANS) and the Authorization Server (AZS) components.

- Client Proxy (CP) collects the required authentication and authorization credentials from the respective authorities on behalf of the client before sending a web service request and handles the session on behalf of the client with the web service's Security Manager (SM).
- Security Manager (SM) is a runtime component responsible for both authentication and authorization of the client. A client's CP sends the necessary authentication and authorization credentials to the SM. It is responsible for managing all the interactions with a client's CP. It uses the Authorization API to invoke the Authorization Server.
- Authentication Server (ANS)} receives the authentication credentials from SM and uses some mechanism to authenticate the client. We treat ANS as a black box in our architecture as our focus in this paper is on authorization. We have included ANS in the web services security layer for completeness.
- Authorization Server (AZS)} decouples the authorization logic from application logic. It is responsible for locating all the APEs involved, sending the credentials to them and receiving the authorization decisions. Once all the decisions come back, it uses the responsible ADCs to combine the authoriza-

tion decisions. Where required, AZS also collects the credentials and attributes on behalf of clients from the respective CCAs and DASs.

3.5 Authorization Administration and Policy Evaluation

A Web Service Manager (WSM) is responsible for managing the authorization information for the Web services s/he is responsible for. We consider a web service method to be a high-level task that is exposed to clients. Each task (method) is made up of a number of system operations. These operations can be of different abstract types. It is reasonable to assume a WSM knows the set of tasks a Web service under his/her control performs. Similarly a WSM knows the set of operations each of these tasks (methods) perform. Using the APE definitions from AAD (database), WSM associates APEs to web services and their methods. This association is made in the Web Service Authorization and the Web Service Method Authorization objects. WSM uses the AA-API to create and manage these objects. Similarly, a Web Service Collection Manager} (WCM) manages APE and ADC information (using AA-API) in a separate object called Web Services Collection Authorization (WSCA) for all the collections s/he manages. These objects are stored in AAD.

Similar to web service methods, a web service can also have one or more APEs responsible for the web service itself. Web service level policies are first evaluated before its method level authorization policies are evaluated. A web service's APEs evaluate web service level authorization policies. These policies will typically not be as fine-grained as method level policies. A WSM may choose to create a new ADC for one or more Web services s/he manages or may decide to use one from the set of existing ADCs from AAD if it serves the purpose.

Similar to web services and their methods, a web service collection can also have one or more APEs responsible for authorizing access to the collection itself. Collection level policies are first evaluated before a web service's policies are evaluated. A web service collection's APEs evaluate collection level policies. These policies will typically be coarse-grained when compared to the web service and web service method level policies. Every root web service collection has an ADC associated with it responsible for combining the decisions from all APEs involved. The coarse-grained authorization policies for the relevant ancestor web service collections (of an invoked web service) are first evaluated, followed by the web service level policies and finally the fine-grained web service method level policies are evaluated. For example, in Figure 4, when a client invokes WS1's method M1, WSC1's authorization policies are first evaluated by APE1 and APE2, followed by WSC2 (APE3) and then WSC3 (APE4) policies. If APE1, APE2, APE3 and APE4 give out a positive decision, WS1's authorization policies are evaluated by APE6. If APE6 gives out a positive decision, then finally M1's authorization policies are evaluated by APE7 and APE8. WS1's ADC combines the decisions from APE6, APE7 and APE8 and if the final decision is positive, WSC1's ADC combines the decisions from APE1, APE2, APE3, APE4 and ADC WS1. If the final decision from ADC WSC1 is positive, the client will be able to successfully invoke WS1's method M1.

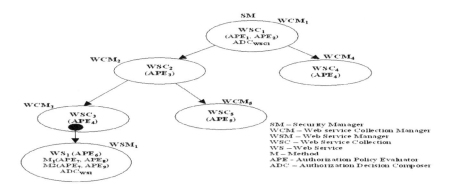

Fig. 4. Web Service Collection Hierarchy

3.6 Runtime Authorization Data

So far we have addressed who assigns (and how) APEs and ADCs for web services and web service collections. The next question is, at runtime, how does a client know (where necessary) how to obtain the required authorization credentials and dynamic runtime attributes before invoking a web service? What are the responsible APEs (and the credentials and attributes they require), CCAs (the credentials they provide) and DASs (the attributes they provide)? How does the Authorization Server (AZS) know what is the set of responsible ADCs for a particular client request?

To answer these questions, we have an Authorization Runtime Database (ARD) in the runtime domain. ARD consists of the runtime authorization related information required by clients and the Authorization Server. Credential Manager (CRM) is an automated component that creates and stores the authorization runtime information (using CRM algorithm) in the ARD. The CRM is invoked from time to time, when a web service object is added to or removed from a collection, moved within a hierarchy of collections or when the shape of the tree itself changes, to update these objects in the ARD.

3.7 Extensions to the Description and Messaging Layers

WS-Authorization Policy statement: We extend WSDL (description layer) to include a Web service's Authorization Policy as well as the location of its Security Manager. WS-SecurityPolicy statement consists of a group of security policy ``assertions'', that represent a web service's security preference, requirement, capability or other property. Similarly, we define WS-AuthorizationPolicy as a statement that contains a list of authorization assertions. The assertions include which credentials (and from which CCA) and attributes (and from which DAS) a client's CP has to collect before invoking a Web Service. WS-PolicyAttachment standard can be used to link the WS-AuthorizationPolicy to a Web Service's WSDL statement.

Security Manager Location: When a client wishes to invoke a web service WS1, its Client Proxy requires its Security Manager's location. Therefore, we need to give this information in WS1's WSDL statement. We introduce a new element SecurityManager to the WSDL document that encapsulates the Security Manager location information required by the Client Proxies.

SOAP Header Extension: We provide extensions to the SOAP header (messaging layer) to carry authorization related credentials and attributes. WS-Security enhancements for confidentiality, integrity and authentication of messages have extended SOAP header (SOAP-SEC element) to carry related information. Similarly we extend the SOAP header to carry authorization credentials and attributes to carry authorization related information. When a client wants to invoke a web service object, its client proxy creates an authorization header object and adds it to SOAP Header before making a SOAP request.

3.8   Authorization Evaluation Algorithms

WSAA supports three types of authorization evaluation algorithms: push based or pull based or a combination of both. Push based model algorithm supports authorizations where a client's Client Proxy, using WS-AuthorizationPolicy, collects and sends the required credentials (from CCAs) and attributes (from DASs) to a Web service's Security Manager. Pull based model algorithm supports authorizations where the AZS itself collects the required credentials and APEs collect the required attributes. The combination model supports both push and pull models for collecting the required credentials and attributes.

An organization must deploy one of these algorithms depending on the access control mechanisms used. If all the access control mechanisms used by the set of APEs are based on a pull model, then the organization must deploy the pull-model algorithm. If all the access control mechanisms used are based on a push model, then the organization must deploy the push-model algorithm. However, when some of an organization's APEs use the pull-model and others use the push-model, the combination-model algorithm must be deployed. A detailed description of the authorization algorithms along with their respective system sequence diagrams can be found in [19].

4   Trust Enhanced Security

Let us return to the basic distributed system scenario we started off with in the beginning. This is whereby an entity A requests a service from an entity over an untrusted network. We had several security services are required to counteract the perceived threats in such a distributed environment including authentication, authorization, confidentiality, integrity, non-repudiation, and auditing and accountability. Provision of these security services require some form of "trusted" authorities to establish and manage "trust" between the mutually suspicious entities A and B over an untrusted network. In the above sections, we considered the authorization service in some detail and considered the various trusted management components, authorization policies and mechanisms for providing such a service in distributed environments. Similarly for other security services, one could identify trusted authorities and mechanisms. In general, these authorities are "trusted" by the entities within a given domain or realm. A typical distributed system will have multiple domains and the relationship between these domains can be peer to peer or hierarchical or a combination thereof.   In this section, let us look at more closely some of the issues involved in the notion of trust and the trusted authorities and the assumptions made and technologies used to derive this trust.

Though trust has been a foundational stone for security, it has been a difficult concept to define clearly. The notion of trust has been around for many decades (if not centuries) in different disciplines in different disguises. In security, the concept of "trusted systems" has been around explicitly at least since late 1970s. Perhaps the most notable one is in the development of Trusted Computer System Evaluation Criteria (TCSEC) [21] in the late 70s and the early 80s. Here trust is used in the process of convincing the observers that a system (model, design or implementation) is correct and secure. A set of ratings is defined for classification of systems and the claim is higher the level, greater the assurance that one has that the system will behave according to its specifications. Then there is the notion of "trusted" processes. These processes are trusted in that they will not do any harm even though they may violate the security policies of the system, which all the other processes are required to satisfy. This notion is still being used in secure systems particularly in the operating system context. These led to the concept of Trusted Computing Base (TCB) which encapsulates all the security relevant components both hardware and software which are necessary to enforce the security policies in a system.

In the above sections, we mentioned "trusted authorities" such as authorization server and authentication server, which are involved in the provision of security services. These authorities are "trusted" by the various parties such as the communicating entities A and B above. We did not explicitly specify the type of trust but in fact assumed complete trust. That is, A and B trust that the Authorization Server will perform all of its functions correctly and honestly. For instance, Authorization Server will keep the authorization policies securely and it will perform the authorization checks securely and correctly and the software of the Authorization Server has been implemented correctly and free from any malicious software. Similar assumptions are made with respect to other security services such as the authentication service. In fact, all of these components require some form of Trusted Computing Base where these security components and mechanisms reside. This trusted base ensures the secure and correct operation of the security components and services themselves.

Another important development in the security field over the recent years has been the notion of "trusted platform" for commodity systems such as the PCs. This notion of trusted platform (TCPA [22], currently known as TCG) was backed by a broad spectrum of companies including HP, Compaq, IBM, Microsoft and Intel and many others. A "trusted platform" is a platform that "contains a hardware based subsystem devoted to maintaining trust and security between machines". A trusted platform has some "special processes", which dynamically collect and provide evidence of behavior. These special processes themselves are "trusted" to collect evidence properly. So there is a combination of social (static) trust on the mechanisms and a behavioral (dynamic) trust based on the information collected. There are also third parties endorsing platforms which underlie the confidence that the platform can be "trusted".

In general, when an entity (trustor) trusts another entity (trustee), one can talk about characteristics such as competency (ability to perform certain actions), honesty (its intentions), reliability (correctness and commitments) and availability (resources) within a context. Also trust has several properties that are somewhat unique. These include non-transitivity (A trusts B and B trusts C does not necessarily imply A trusts C), action dependent (A may trust B for certain set of actions only), time dependent and trust is asymmetric in that it takes a long time to build but can easily be destroyed.

In this section, we will briefly discuss two extensions which could help to make better use of the notion of trust to enhance the security decision making. First, we will consider the ideas behind the trusted platform and propose a way of enhancing the authorization architecture described above with trust to improve secure decision making. Second, we will refine the notion of trust by introducing a hybrid trust model, which can better take into account the dynamic aspects of trust. This could further help to enhance the authorization decision making.

4.1   Trusted Platforms and Trust Enhanced Distributed Authorization

Let us return to the distributed authorization environment where we had introduced an authorization service layer. As mentioned above, we assumed that this layer and its components are trusted and hence they were part of the so called trusted computing base, except that this resided at the middleware level (typically above the basic operating system). Now consider the situation where we have a trusted platform underneath the operating system which contains say some trusted modules such as the Trusted Platform Module (TPM) of the TCPA. Before, we look at how to make use of this trusted module in the authorization decision making, it is necessary to briefly review some of the basic functionalities and properties of the TPM [23].

The TPM is essentially a cryptographic co-processor with special functionality. It is a chip closely bound to a computing platform's main hardware (e.g. soldered to a PC's motherboard). Information in the TPM is resistant to any direct software attack, as the information can only be accessed through well defined commands called TPM capabilities. Every TPM has a unique public key - private key pair (RSA key pair) imprinted in it, called the "Endorsement Key". The private party of this key pair never leaves the TPM and is used only to decrypt certain data structures that are sent to the TPM for very specific purposes. The public part can be retrieved from the TPM but only under certain conditions. The notion of TPM Identities is introduced which allow a user to signify to third parties that s/he is using a genuine trusted platform without revealing its particular identity. For our discussion here, we do not need to go into details here as to how this is achieved.

These trusted platforms are able to reliably measure, store and report their configuration and software state. This is achieved by applying a one-way hash function to software that is about to be executed on the trusted platform. The resulting hash value is called an "integrity metric" which is stored inside one of the TPM's Platform Configuration Registers (PCRs). Hence the integrity metrics reflect software state of the system. This is done right from the beginning, whenever software is loaded, for instance, from BIOS to OS loader to OS kernel to applications. Hence the state of the system can be determined at a given time. This can be communicated to a third party in a secure manner which enables the third party to be confident that the trusted platform's software state is as represented by the integrity metrics and has not been modified. Then the third party can decide whether or not to trust the system for the intended purpose.

Using the above mechanisms, we can see that the Authorization Service Layer (such as the WSAA) can be securely loaded on to a system with the trusted platform. Furthermore, once loaded the correct state of the Authorization Service Layer can be maintained and communicated to other entities both locally and remotely. With this additional functionality available to the entities, the authorization protocols mentioned earlier can be extended to include the signed integrity metrics of the platforms of the different entities involved in the communication. For instance, now when a client wishes to request a service from a server, the client can append to its request the state of its platform in a protected manner. The server can determine whether the state of the client system can be suitably trusted for it to provide the service, before deciding whether to provide the requested service or not and before going through the authorization process. If the server finds that the client state to be not suitable for it to be trusted (trust policy), then the server can decide not to go through with the authorization service process. Similarly, the client can request for the state of the server before accepting the service from the server. Hence we can see that one can layer the distributed authorization service on top the trusted functionality and properties provided by the trusted platform via its TPM, which can help to enhance the authorization decision making.

In general, with the availability of the trusted platform and its characteristics, any two entities wishing to communicate with each other can go through this trust determination phase before performing authorization or at the beginning of the authorization process. For instance, this scheme can be extended to transfer of authorization policies between two Authorization Server Systems in two different domains. We are currently developing such a distributed authorization service on trusted platforms. We are also developing a demonstration of an healthcare application showing secure access to electronic patient records using this trust enhanced distributed authorization service [24].

In addition, the introduction of the trusted platforms also provides an opportunity to reconsider some of the design choices in the distributed authorization architecture described earlier. In particular, the trusted platform can lead to a different way "distributing" the distributed authorization service itself. Previously we had a trusted authorization service provider involved in the decision making of the requests. The trusted platform technology offers a mechanism for logically running the service within its own trust domain that can physically reside within the client requesting the service. One can have an instance of the authorization service running in the client and the relevant authorization policies for the particular client and server and the transaction can be loaded onto the client trusted platform by this instance at runtime after going through a trust verification process similar to the one described above. This instance of the authorization service can go through the authorization checks and determine whether to grant or deny the request. This decision along with the request suitably signed can then be forwarded to the web service provider for the client to access the services if appropriate. The security relies on the trusted platform technology; the web service provider is able to trust the instance of the authorization service running in the client machine only because it is able to verify the state of the client machine and trust the authorization service running there (is able to carry out the necessary authorization checks based on the service provider's policies). Such arguments lead to changes in the design principles of the distributed authorization architectural framework. We are currently working on such scenarios to investigate their suitability and their implication on the design of trusted distributed applications.

4.2 Hybrid Trust Model and Trust Enhanced Authorization

Finally we conclude this paper by briefly outlining another facet of trust that could further enhance the authorization decision making. At the modeling level, I believe there is a need to expand the scope of the trust models, instead of the limited scope that we have seen so far in authentication and access control based "trust" management. For instance, in general the trust relationship should be able to include a set of conditions and properties that allow one or more trustors to trust trustees that they will do a set of actions or have a set of attributes. Such a general structure will enable us to investigate some emergent properties, in addition to the traditional ones such as non-transitivity. We have been exploring such an extended trust model that can capture some of these properties [25]. There is also a need to further develop what we call "hybrid" trust models, which bring together the so called "hard" trust with the "soft" trust into the architecture. By "hard" trust, we mean traditional aspects such as authentication trust captured via certificates and authorization trust captured by attribute certificates and credentials. These types of trust can be explicitly represented and captured using traditional security mechanisms such tokens and certificates. Then there is the "soft" trust, which is based on recommendations and reputations. These are beliefs based on recommendations from multiple entities and are not based on concrete security credentials; they are characterized by uncertainty, are dependent on past behaviors and can change over time. Soft trust can arise from direct experience, from recommendations or from observed behavior or a combination of these. We have developed a hybrid trust model combining the hard and the soft trust, and built a trust management architecture that sits on top of the authorization service layer [26]. That is, the output from this hybrid trust management layer feeds into the authorization service layer and enhances the quality of decision making. We have developed such a combined trust and secure authorization architecture and applied it in the context of mobile agents based applications. Currently we are investigating a similar approach with web services and peer to peer computing applications.

5 Concluding Remarks

In this paper, we have addressed some research issues in the areas of authorization and trust in a distributed environment. We outlined some of the key design principles involved in the development of distributed authorization service. Then we described distributed authorization architecture for web services and outlined its implementation in the .NET framework. Then discussed the notion of trusted computing and presented our approach and architecture to enhancing the distributed authorization service using trusted platforms technologies.

In my view, this paradigm of trust enhanced authorization, which combines the use of trusted platforms underneath and a trust management layer based on a hybrid trust model, offers a promising approach to security in pervasive mobile networked computing. We believe that such a trust enhanced security approach is not only significant in terms of its technical characteristics but also has tremendous potential in terms of optimizing utility and minimizing business risks.

References

1. E. Rescorla, SSL and TLS: Designing and Building Secure Systems: Addison Wesley, 2001.
2. S. Kent and R. Atkinson. Security architecture for the Internet Protocol, RFC 2401, 1998, http://www.ietf.org/rfc/rfc2401.txt.
3. World Wide Web Consortium, XML-Signature Syntax and Processing, http://www.w3.org/TR/xmldsig-core/ , XML Encryption Syntax and Processing, http://www.w3.org/TR/xmlenc-core *(2002)*.
4. World Wide Web Consortium, *SOAP v1.2,* http://www.w3.org/TR/soap12-part1/, Web Services Description Language (WSDL) v1.1, http://www.w3.org/TR/wsdl, 2002.
5. D. Ash, B. Dillaway, D. Eastlake, Y. Elley, J. Epstein, S. Farrell, et al. (2004, April 05). XML Key Management Specification (XKMS 2.0), http://www.w3.org/TR/xkms2/.
6. S. Jajodia, P. Samarati and V.S. Subrahmanian, 'A Logical Language for Expressing Authorizations', Proceedings of the IEEE Symposium on Security and Privacy, USA, 1997.
7. Y.Bai and V. Varadharajan, 'A Logic for State Transformations in Authorization Policies', Proceedings of the IEEE Computer Security Foundations Workshop, USA, 1997.
8. V. Varadharajan, C.Crall, and J.Pato, 'Authorization for Enterprise wide Distributed Systems', Proceedings of the IEEE Computer Security Applications Conference, ACSAC'98, 1998, USA.
9. N. Damianou, N. Dulay, E. Lupu, and M. Sloman, 'The Ponder Policy Specification Language', Proceedings of International Workshop on Policies for Distributed Systems and Networks, UK, 2001, pp.18-38.
10. M.Hitchens and V. Varadharajan, 'Tower: A Language for Role Based Access Control', Proceedings of International Workshop on Policies for Distributed Systems and Networks, UK, 2001, pp.88-106.
11. S. Indrakanti, V. Varadharajan, M. Hitchens and R.Kumar, "Secure Authorization for Web Services" Proceedings of the 17th IFIP Conference on Data and Applications Security, USA, 2003.
12. R. Sandhu et al., 'Role based access control models', IEEE Computer, 1996, 29, (2), pp.38-47.
13. V.Varadharajan, P.Allen and S.Black, 'An Analysis of the Proxy Problem in Distributed Systems', Proceedings of the IEEE Symposium on Security and Privacy, USA, 1991.
14. D. Brewer and M. Nash, 'The Chinese Wall Security Policy', Proceedings of the IEEE Symposium on Security and Privacy, USA, 1989, pp 206-214.
15. V. Varadharajan and P.Allen, 'Joint Action based Authorization Schemes', ACM Operating Systems Review Journal, Vol.30, No.3, pp 32-45.
16. V. Varadharajan, "Distributed Authorization: Principles and Applications", Book Chapter, Coding, Cryptography, Singapore University Press, 2001.
17. M. Hitchens and V. Varadharajan, "Design and Specification of Role based Access Control Policies", IEE Proceedings – Software, August 2000, UK.
18. S. Indrakanti, V. Varadharajan and M.Hitchens. "Authorization Service for Web Services and its Application in a Healthcare Domain", accepted for publication in the International Journal for Web Services Research, Idea Group Publishing, March 2005.
19. S. Indrakanti and V. Varadharajan, "An Authorization Architecture for Web Services", Proceedings of the 19th Annual IFIP WG 11.3 Working Conference on Data and Applications Security, USA, 2005.
20. Microsoft Corporation, ".NET Framework, http://msdn.microsoft.com/netframework/," 2005.
21. Dept of Defense, "Trusted Computer System Evaluation Criteria", (TCSEC), DoD5200.28 STD Dec.1985.

22. TCPA, "Trusted Computing Platform Alliance", Building a Foundation of Trust in the PC, Jan. 2000, http://www.trustedcomputing.org (now known as Trusted Computing Group, https://www.trustedcomputinggroup.org/home).
23. B.Balacheff et al., "Trusted Computing Platforms: TCPA Technology in Context", Prentice-Hall, 2003.
24. V.Varadharajan, "Trust Enhanced Authorization and its Application", In Preparation 2005.
25. W.Zhao, V.Varadharajan, G.Bryan, "Modelling Trust Relationships in Distributed Environments, International Conference on Trust and Privacy in Digital Business, TrustBus04 (in conjunction with DEXA2004), Spain,2004.
26. Ching Lin, Vijay Varadharajan, Yan Wang and Vineet Pruthi, Trust Enhanced Security for Mobile Agents, 2005 IEEE International Conference on E-commerce Technology (IEEE CEC'05), Germany, 2005, pp. 231-238.

Toward Exploiting Location-Based and Video Information in Negotiated Access Control Policies

Ernesto Damiani, Marco Anisetti, and Valerio Bellandi

Department of Information Technology, University of Milan,
via Bramante, 65 - 26013, Crema (CR), Italy
{anisetti, bellandi, damiani}@dti.unimi.it

Abstract. As the global information infrastructure is becoming more and more ubiquitous, digital business transactions are increasingly performed using a variety of mobile devices and across multiple communication channels. In this new paradigm of pervasive access, a much richer context representation regarding both users and the resources they access could be available to applications, potentially supporting highly expressive and intelligent policies regulating access and fruition. On the other hand, checking advanced context-related information when evaluating a policy involves several unsolved research issues, often due to underlying technology. Predicates representing users position and posture (e.g., as shown in a video feed), for instance, are semantically different from traditional ones inasmuch their outcome is both highly dynamic and uncertain. The aim of this work is twofold: (i) presenting some of our recent work in dynamic context representation, including data streams encoding users location and video images. (ii) discussing the integration of dynamic context representation within current approaches to negotiated access control in a mobile environment[1].

1 Introduction

As the global information infrastructure is becoming more and more pervasive, digital business transactions are increasingly performed in diverse situations, using a variety of mobile devices and across multiple communication channels. Rather than being forced to assume a fixed, pre-set position w.r.t. a machine, users can move freely around their work environment, starting and monitoring different transactions. Also, terminal devices are increasingly equipped with sensors, such as video cameras or audio/video equipment, capable of collecting information from the environment. In this new paradigm of distributed access to the communication and computing infrastructure, a much richer context representation regarding both users and the resources they access can be made available to applications. This is even more true in the perspective of *roomware*, i.e. systems

---

[1] This work was partly supported by the EU within the PRIME Project under contract IST-2002-507591 and by the Italian MIUR within the KIWI and MAPS projects.

S. Jajodia and C. Mazumdar (Eds.): ICISS 2005, LNCS 3803, pp. 21–35, 2005.

integrating information and communication elements into room elements such as wall and furniture [14]. In this pervasive computing scenario, the outcome of an interaction may well depend of where is the user when a certain application-related event takes place, where is she headed, or even whether is she sitting at her desk alone or walking accompanied by others. It is easy to see that this kind of fine-grained, customized context information potentially support highly expressive and intelligent policies regulating access and fruition to resources. On the other hand, exploiting this information poses a number of privacy-related problems. Traditionally, access control policies have included conditions based on *static context* information, e.g. a representation of the protocol used for carrying out a transaction. Checking out this new type of imprecise, time-variant context information when evaluating a policy involves several unsolved research issues, often due to underlying technology. Predicates representing users position and posture (e.g., as shown in a video feed), for instance, are semantically different from traditional ones inasmuch their outcome is both highly dynamic and uncertain. The aim of this work is twofold:

- presenting some of our recent work in dynamic context representation, including data streams encoding the users location and video images.
- discussing the integration of dynamic context representation within negotiated access control.

The paper is organized as follows: Section 2 describes the main features of some predicates of interest for pervasive computing, including the ones related to geolocation (Section 2.1), video identification (Section 2.2) and facial expressions (Section 2.3). Section 3 briefly discusses how these predicates could be used with in the framework of access control policy evaluation. Finally, Section 4 draws the conclusions.

2   Time-Variant Predicates

Predicates of interest for pervasive computing support an extended context of interaction for each user and resource in the environment, modeling their state and spatial-temporal relationships with other users/resources. Here, context is not the static situation of a predefined environment; rather, it is a dynamic part of the process of interacting with a changing environment, composed of mobile users and resources [23]. Some context-related predicates are commonly used in the framework of security policies based on human surveillance, e.g. `IsAlone(User))` and `IsNear(User,Resource))`; therefore, we will adopt the surveillance terminology and designate them as *time-variant* predicates. Generally speaking, these predicates are characterized by two main features:

- *Time-dependency.* The predicate value may vary in time, even during predicate evaluation itself.
- *Uncertainty.* At each given time, predicate values are only known with a degree of approximation, much like values in a probabilistic database.

In this Section, we shall describe in detail some of these predicates, outlining why traditional access control models do not provide enough guidance to account for the imprecise, time-variant properties of interaction context.

2.1 Location-Based Predicates

Location-based predicates provide all types of information regarding the spatial location of a user and/or a resource. Location-related information can be classified as follows:

- *Punctual location* absolute longitude-and-latitude geographical location provided by systems like GPS (*Global Positioning System*).
- *Logical* or *local* location, composed of location assertions with different levels of precision, for example specifying that the user in a specific country, city, building or room.

Obviously, given the necessary background information (in the form, say, of a map with coordinates) there may be a function that maps punctual locations to logical ones; indeed, assuming the existence of such a function is at the basis of the evaluation of access rules involving location predicates (e.g. rules requiring the user to be in a certain area to perform a given action). Recent research has proposed many location techniques producing logical location, punctual location or both depending on application requirements.

Location techniques have been proposed for local wireless networking: for instance, the Microsoft Research RADAR system requires an initial calibration in which 802.11 readings are made on a 1 meter (1m) grid. Then, this grid is used for positioning 802.11 access points (AP). If the APs are positioned correctly, knowing the readings of a device is sufficient for estimating its location.

Experience, however, has shown that estimating location based on readings from 802.11 base stations, besides requiring extensive calibration, can provide only 3m accuracy, not precise enough for indoor use. Place Lab is a research project that attempts to solve the ubiquity issues surrounding 802.11-based location estimate [19]. Place Lab does not rely on the availability of a grid of previous readings; rather, it predicts location via the positions of the APs, read from a database cached on each device.

The public database `wigle.net` contains the position of more than 2 million APs in the US and in Europe, providing quick-and-dirty location in some key urban areas. However, this approach was not designed to be very accurate.

In outdoor and rural environments GPS, when at least three satellite are visible, delivers position information with an acceptable accuracy. In dense urban areas or inside buildings, localization with GPS becomes critical because the satellites are not visible from the mobile terminal. Ground-based location service provides punctual location that can be mapped into local location with high confidence but with coarse granularity, at the level of a town quarter or a street. There are a number of variants of the basic GPS strategy that are used to improve its accuracy. Both ground-based and satellite-based versions of differential GPS improve accuracy from 8m to 5m for a non-enhanced unit. To-day, GPS chipsets are increasingly being integrated into mainstream cell phones and PDAs; nevertheless, the spread of GPS remains rather meager. More impor-tantly, like wireless, GPS-based techniques do not yet guarantee high accuracy in indoor environments[2].

Alternatively, location information can be determined with the help of the mobile network. In order to be equivalent to GPS from the privacy point of view (see Sect. 4), location based on the cell network must be entirely performed on the client device. In this case, the actual location of the terminal is communi-cated to applications only with the explicit consent of the user; on the other hand, computing power limitations of hand-held devices may affect location accuracy. This kind of approach can be used both indoors and outdoors and produces localization assertion that can be directly mapped into punctual or lo-cal location information. While in some applications it is sufficient to determine the cell where a given mobile terminal is located (i.e., the cell itself can be assim-ilated to a local location assertion), other services such as emergency rescue [1], urban traffic management and patients tracking require a very accurate terminal location.

To help meet the emergency rescue requirements, known in the US as E911/E112 [16], cell phone manufacturers are now producing handsets that use a mix of location technologies. When GPS is not available, the locations of nearby base stations are used to produce a coarse location estimate. Based on this quick-and-dirty location, the cell phone can download the expected position of the satellites, allowing the handset to lock on to GPS much faster (on the order of seconds instead of a minute or more) when GPS becomes available again. Other approaches monitor field power values [2], [3] as received from mobile terminals as well as propagation time [4] between terminals and based stations.

A major problem of these methods [5] is that, like GPS, they work better when LOS (*Line-Of-Sight*) between terminals and base stations is guaranteed. In urban environments, multi-path radiowave propagation leads to very com-plicated scenarios when there is no LOS between the mobile terminals and the base stations. In these kind of scenarios, localization techniques based on de-lay evaluations are not accurate enough. Path-loss methods that rely only on terminal side information or on database correlation techniques [6] do not sat-isfy our precision requirements for punctual location, even when urban-oriented propagation estimate methods like Walfisch-Ikegami [7] ray-tracing or intelligent ray-tracing [8] are applied.

The database correlation technique takes into account the field strength of the 6 best serving antennas and correlates the corresponding path losses to the entries of a look-up-table containing the prevision path loss for all antennas in the area, like the matrix shown on Fig. 1. Every row of the matrix in Fig. 1 represents one point of the coverage area (for instance expressed as (x, y) bitmap

---

[2] By 2008 the European Union will deploy Galileo, a next-generation GPS system that promises greater accuracy and operation covering both indoors and out, due to stronger radio signals that should penetrate most buildings.

Location		Cell			
x	y	1	2	i	n
x_1	y_1	$E_{1,1}$	$E_{2,1}$	$E_{i,1}$	$E_{n,1}$
x_2	y_2	$E_{1,2}$	$E_{2,2}$	$E_{i,2}$	$E_{n,2}$
⋮	⋮	⋮	⋮	⋮	⋮
x_m	y_m	$E_{1,m}$	$E_{2,m}$	$E_{i,m}$	$E_{n,m}$

Fig. 1. Look-up table structure

coordinates, or as a latitude and longitude pair for GPS representation). The path-loss prediction for n base stations to this given position are stored as entries in the line of the corresponding position. In other words, this matrix represents our look-up table for point location[3].

For locating a mobile terminal, the best matching entry in the look-up table is searched. During this process, the path loss measurement is compared to all entries of the matrix. This comparison can be done by several different criteria; we used a sum of squared errors between measured path loss M_j for every j antennas and the path loss defined by an entry i in the look-up table $E_{i,j}$ like the approach in [2]. We have:

$$E = \sum_{j=1}^{n}(M_i - E_{i,j})^2 \tag{1}$$

The location of the mobile terminal is then defined by the coordinate of the entry that produce the smallest error E. This technique produces an instant location value that includes an intrinsic error due to discrepancy between the real field strength and the predicted one.

In order to alleviate this problem, we improved conventional lookup-table location using a variable number n of position estimates. Our purpose is using all information that can be extracted from a map of the interested area in conjunction with prediction filtering to improve precision in location and tracking. For validating position estimates obtained with the look-up table described in the previous section, we developed a tracking method that uses a time-forwarding algorithm providing a first-level movement estimate.

Our algorithm uses m time position estimates to create an acyclic graph whose nodes represent possible positions, while arcs represent motion between positions. Every arc of the graph has a position-related weight. By searching the best path through the graph (the smallest total weight path from time t to time $t + m$) we obtain a filtered position (see Fig. 2). In our approach, the number m of parameters becomes critical. In fact, using long term prediction

---

[3] Note that look-up table filling can be done only once in a while, whenever changes affect interesting areas.

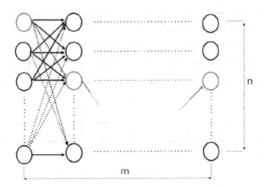

Fig. 2. Graph trough example for time-forwards tracking. In red the selected position node and the selected path, in black the possible position nodes.

(i.e., high m) we obtain a strong trend prediction that filters every out-of-trend movements. On the other hand, using small m we would get low quality results in high trend-correlation area like high speed motorways or one-way streets. Thus, we vary the m parameter to take into account information about the location available from GIS maps. In this way we obtain a map correlation of first-level movements estimates [20].

Using this approach, we significantly improved the tracking quality of the look-up table techniques[4].

Thanks to this information, we obtain *trusted location points* that satisfy map-specified constraints. These points define a movement trend having a high confidence and low error with respect to the real path of the mobile terminal. This trend is then filtered with a Kalman filter [9], obtaining a robust prediction tracking[5]. Fig. 3 shows an example of the difference between precise tracking in an indoor environment and vanilla lookup-table location. Looking at Fig. 3 and considering a time variant predicate like "X is in the red square", we see that our tracking method performs far better than a lookup table; however, the time-dependency problem still remains in border line areas and during time forwarding process[6].

---

[4] In many case the additional information provided by the map is poor or absent; when this happens, our technique dynamically builds an information data-base estimating all relevant knowledge.

[5] Note that using this filter-based location techniques we reduce the time-dependency of this location predicate (also considering that we could use local location assertion to reduce punctual location error), but we introduce a time delay that has a significant impact on the predicates uncertainty.

[6] In order to reduce uncertainty, we first build a sensibility map of the area, in order to identify the region in which tracking error probability is higher. This precaution hints to some preliminary action to reduce or limit uncertainty, e.g. fusing multiple sources of location [26].

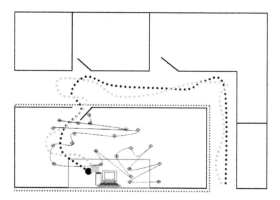

Fig. 3. Example of location in indoor environment. In black we show the real path of a device, in green (grey) our estimated path, while the other lines show the location computed with the vanilla look-up technique. The big square and circle show the static position held by the user for a long period of time.

2.2 Identification Predicates

Identification predicates provide information regarding the identity of the subject. In the past few years, video-identification techniques relying on face recognition have received significant attention as one of the most important applications in ambient security and environmental control. Other reliable methods of biometric personal identification such as fingerprint analysis and retinal or iris scans lend themselves to generating context data [25]; however, these methods - unlike video-identification - rely on full, active cooperation of the participants.

A personal identification system based on analysis of frontal or lateral face images can be effective without the participants cooperation or even knowledge. Also, other biometric methods may require special-purpose hardware, while cameras are nowadays available in inexpensive bundle with many electronic devices like cell phones. Also, facial recognition can be used for general surveillance, usually in combination with public video cameras. A well-known experiment was carried out in the US at 2001 and 2002 Super Bowl Finals, where pictures were taken of every attendee as they entered the stadium and compared against a database of known offenders. In England, where public surveillance cameras are widespread, the town of Newham has also experimented with the technology.

Although current face recognition systems have reached a certain level of maturity (for a complete overview, see [10]), their success has been thwarted by the constraints imposed by many real applications. For example, recognition of face images acquired in an outdoor environment with changes in illumination and/or pose remains a largely unsolved problem, as well as face recognition through expression changes. In other words, current systems are still far away from the capability of the human perception system. Not surprisingly, early approaches to face-recognition have shown high rates of both "false positives"

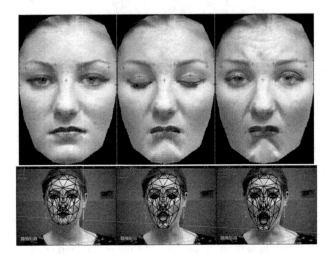

Fig. 4. Identification process: Example of posture and morphing estimate and frontal view normalization on Cohn-Kanade database

(wrongly matching innocent people with photos in the database) and "false negatives" (not catching people even when their photo is in the database).

Unfortunately, unlike other biometrics, faces do not stay the same over time, and early systems were easily deceived by changes in facial hair, body weight or by simple disguises. Recently, variations in pose and illumination, seen by many as the main challenges for face recognition, have been widely investigated [11][12][13]. Our identification service is based on a video stream acquired from a camera (e.g. a cellular camera, a web-cam or a set of surveillance cameras). Illumination conditions, posture and expression of the subject may be very different and *a priori* unknown. Our approach is based on face tracking as described by a 3D expression model, without requiring any frequency image intensity or neural network analysis.

Our 3D expression model also tackles the problem of face expression changes. Expression-deformable tracking promises to be an important first step toward developing a face representation protocol (e.g., one capable of providing evidence that someone is about to fall asleep), dramatically enlarging the scope of the entire identification process. Using a template tracking process, we compute expression and posture parameters estimates allowing to reconstruct normalized frontal views of faces (Fig. 4). Then, we use dissimilarity analysis to provide an acceptable degree of identification quality. Our identification process can be summarized as follows:

1. The user provides an image of herself (e.g., using a micro-camera on top of the badge scanner).
2. The system recovers the corresponding 3D template.
3. Face detection if performed on the cameras video streaming, with initial posture estimate.

4. Tracking is started with posture estimate from the previous step.
5. If tracking dose not converge, identity matching is rejected.
6. If tracking occurs in convergence, the system produce a normalized face representation using estimated posture and expression parameter.
7. A dissimilarity measure on normalization face is computed to assess the quality of identification.

When identifications is successful, the subject template is updated to prevent aging[7]. An interesting application of the tracking capability of our algorithm is certifying sequences of facial movements (Fig. 5).

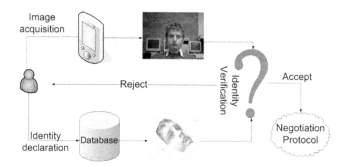

Fig. 5. Identity certification process overview

2.3   Facial Expression Predicates

Facial expression predicates provide information regarding emotional or fatigue states that can be inferred from the subjects facial expression. These predicates can be summarized as follows:

– *Low level features*: predicate like "left eyes closed", "mouth open" or any other movement of the head.
– *High level features*: predicates like "User is bored", "User is in pain" or "User is happy" and so forth.

Our work in this context is again based on the well-tested *morphable tracking algorithm* described in Section 2.2 for face identification. Using this algorithm, we are able to produce a FACS [15] classification for expression recognition purposes [17]. Our approach relies on the direct mapping of FACS Action Unit to the morphable model, in a single tracking step. The result is a real-time expression recognition system for surveillance purposes (Fig. 6 shows a sample expression tracking in the Cohn-Kanade database).

---

[7] Our experience shows that when two subject have a similar face 3D shape, tracking alone cannot provide a reliable identification.

For this reason, we improved the identification method with dissimilarity analysis to measure the quality of identification.

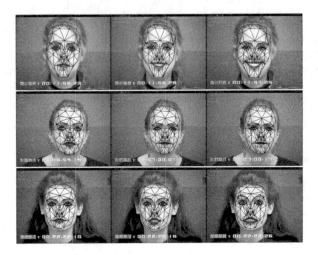

Fig. 6. Example of posture and morphing estimate on Cohn-Kanade DataBase

Table 1. Upper face features extracted, method used and correlated AU

Feature	Methods	AU
Iriss position	Canny and binarization techniques	61 - 62 63 - 64
Eyelids state	Multi-algorithm fusion: Feature Tracking and Canny and skin map	7 - 5 - 41 42 - 43 - 44 45 - 46
Forehead furrows (horizontal)	Gradients	1 - 2
Vertical furrows between the brows (*corrugator muscle*)	Gradients	4
Furrows under the eyes	Gradients	6 - 7
Crows-feet wrinkle	Gradients	6 - 7

Our technique assumes the initial availability of a sample frontal face produced by a tracking process, without expression normalization. Local low-level feature analysis is based on the idea that the contractions of the face muscles, produce some transient changes: wrinkles, brows, eyelids, mouth movements, and others.

We measure these changes on a retrieved normalized face. Outcomes (each associated with a reliability value) are directly correlated with the AU defined by Ekman (Table 1)[8].

When taking pictures of a subject, a particularly interesting feature is the state of the eyes (e.g., for estimating attention or direction of gaze). Our algorithm is based on the analysis of lids and iris position on a normalized face. In particular, lids are fundamental for determining the state of the eyes. In other security-

---

[8] In the following table we consider only the upper face features.

relevant applications like gesture recognition, a state-based model has also been used [18].

In our algorithm, the transition between "open eyes" and "closed eyes" states is defined by tracking the lids in conjunction with the possibility of finding the iris between them. For eyelid tracking we used a 1D (vertical) Lucas-Kanade feature tracker, in inverse compositional implementation and with linear-appearance variation (LAV) technique for illumination changes.

The main idea behind our lids tracking strategy is that the lids position is well defined by the no-skin region of the eye area. Our experience has shown that this idea works better for lower lids because of better general illumination condition. For upper lids, skin-map techniques may fail; therefore, we combine the skin results with Canny operator on the region of iris. Therefore, we need an estimate of the iris center to evaluate the reliability of the extracted values. When lids tracking fails, we proceed directly to estimating the iris center on the default area of the eyes.

Our algorithm for computing the size and position of the iris is composed of the following steps:

- Firstly the eyes area (i.e., the default area when tracking fails or the lids-delimited area when tracking works well) is equalized and a threshold is applied. Then, the contour of the binary thresholded images is computed. Finally the spot due to light reflection is erased for a better iris center location.

  By using a circle mask that is limited by two radiuses according to iris size[9], we determine the iris candidates that will be validated in the following step.
- We extract the edge maps of the eyes region limited by lids tracking and we compute the number of pixel belonging to edges P in the area of the circular masks of the previous step.
- We find the correct iris by searching the candidate with largest edge pixel number P. Each candidate position reliability is proportional to the number of the edge points found on the circular mask.

Now, we have all information about irises with their confidence measure. These information is used by our Skin-map/Canny lids tracker for defining the search area for the Canny edge operator. This approach permits to obtain several interesting assertions on the state of the eyes of the subject of interest. Other interesting features, however, are linked to muscle movements. For detecting them, we consider that muscle motion produces transient, darker skin-color lines called furrows or wrinkles. By checking the presence and the intensity of this furrows we extract some useful information about muscle movement. Furrows generally have one principal direction (perpendicular to the direction of contraction of the underlying muscle).

By segmenting the face region and defining the furrows principal direction in that region, we can determinate the presence and intensity of temporary,

---

[9] If a is the iris dimension, the two radius is $a - \delta_i$ and $a + \delta_e$ with $\delta_e < \delta_i$.

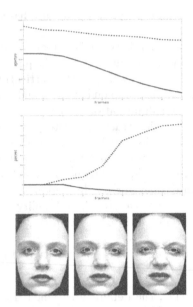

Fig. 7. Example of some crucial feature trend during AU4 and AU7 analysis of an example extracted from Cohn-Kanade

expression-related furrows[10]. Robustness w.r.t. illumination changes and occlusions is guaranteed by the robust tracking system used for retrieving the normalized image. Fig. 7 shows an example of features trend. Regarding eye tracking our algorithm exhibits a high precision, failing only on 2% of the cases. Expression predicates simply cannot reach, even with the best expression classification system, a full certainty level. Even for low level analysis, uncertainty often remains. Confidence attached to assertions like "User has left eyes closed" is however much greater that the attainable confidence of a high level assertion like "User is tired".

3   Evaluating Time-Variant Predicates Within Negotiated Access Control

As a complement to our current activity in designing and implementing support for diverse time-variant predicates relevant to security, research is being conducted to investigate if and how such predicates should be used within access control policy languages.

In this Section, we shall briefly comment on logic-based access control, as the most general and powerful modeling framework. In the logical approach to access control policy evaluation [27], evaluating a policy is interpreted as computing an

---

[10] We use a high gradient component detection in the temporal domain to avoid considering permanent wrinkles, which are mostly unrelated to the subjects status.

inference. In other words, for each access request r to a resource R, the policy evaluation system need to evaluate whether the access policy P_R implies the request r logically, taking into account all available predicates representing the context in which the access takes place. If this evaluation terminates correctly, access is granted/denied depending on its outcome. Otherwise, a *negotiation phase* takes place to extract additional information from the use and/or the environment, so that the evaluation can be concluded. At first sight, due to the intrinsic imprecision and time-dependency of time-variant predicates like the ones introduced in this paper, it may seem reasonable to keep the logic-based framework, introducing a logic that allows for uncertainty reasoning[11].

Combining time-variant, uncertain predicates with ordinary ones would enable writing access policies containing conditions like the following:

$$start(Vehicle) \vdash holdsLicence(User) \lor isInside(User, Vehicle) \lor \neg LooksTired(User))$$

In the above sample rule, a Boolean predicate is combined with two time-variant, uncertain ones. A request would consist in the *start* command plus all context representation available for the user issuing it, including the values for time-variant predicates.

However, while some temporal aspects of policy evaluation have been taken care since long [30], the choice of an appropriate probabilistic approach for evaluating conditions like the example above is still an open problem. Past research has shown that a combination of a (temporal) rule-based approach with probability theory can only be done at the price of inconsistencies[29] especially if event independence and disjointness cannot be assumed safely.

An alternative to managing inconsistency in policy evaluation could be giving a different status to time-variant predicates, using different *evaluation pipelines*.

In other words, time-variant predicates do not appear in rules; rather, they can be appended to conventional access control rules as *mark-up*. In our example, while ordinary negotiation is carried out in order to evaluate the condition $start(Vehicle) \vdash holdsLicence(User)$, a high (individual or combined) degree of uncertainty of the two time-variant predicates $isInside(User, Vehicle)$ and $LooksTired(User)$ may trigger further acquisition of data. While uncertainty reduction is taking place, only a crippled version of the requested transaction is activated (for instance, the engine is started but rounds-per-minutes are kept below 1000 rpm). Our current research is aimed at defining a general framework for employing time-variant predicates in policy languages.

4   Conclusion

In this paper we have seen how, in a pervasive computing scenario, diverse time-variant predicates express different context-related aspects like position in the environment, non-intrusive identification and posture recognition of the subject

---

[11] This kind of approach has indeed been adopted by other research communities; for instance, it set the framework for probabilistic Information Retrieval methods [28] as a development of ordinary database querying.

of interest. Also, we have briefly discussed how these uncertain predicated may affect negotiated policy evaluation strategy.

All the predicates introduced in this paper look promising for context representation in the framework of access control and security policies; nevertheless, they are characterized by high uncertainty and time-dependence, which pose some important open problems for their practical applicability. As a final remark, we note that unrestricted use of these predicates within software systems might raise privacy concerns. The European Union *Information Society Technology Program* (IST) produced design guidelines aimed at implementing privacy within the core of pervasive computing systems[24]. While these guidelines represent an important first step, much research is needed before privacy concerns posed by ubiquitous sensor and computing devices are fully addressed.

References

1. US FCC Enhanced 911 Fac Sheet 2001, "http://www.fcc.gov/ 911/enhanced/ release/factsheet_requirements_012001.pdf", (14 Jan 2004).
2. G. Wlfle, R. Hoppe, D. Zimmermann and F. M. Landstorfer, " Enhanced Localization Technique within Urban and Indoor Environments based on Acurate and Fast Propagation Models", European Wireless 2002, Firenze (Italy), February 2002.
3. P. Wertz, R. Hoppe, D. Zimmermann, G. Wlfle, F. M. Landstorfer, " Enhanced Localization Technique within Urban and Indoor Environments", 3rd COST 237 MCM-Meeting in Guildford, UK, January 2002.
4. J. Vidal, M. Njar, R. Jtiva, "High resolution time-of-arrival detection for wireless positioning systems", Proceedings of IEEE Vehicular Technology Conference (VTC), 2002.
5. James J. Caffery, Jr. and Gordon L. Stber : "Overview of Radiolocation in CDMA Cellular Systems". IEEE Communications Magazine, April 1998.
6. D. Zimmermmann, J. Baumann, M. Layh, F. Landstorfer, R. Hoppe and G. Wlfle : "Database Correlection for Positioning of Mobile Terminals in Cellular Networks using Wave Propagation Models". Proceedings of IEEE Vehicular Technology Conference (VTC) 2004.
7. E. Damosso et al. : "COST 231:Digital mobile radio towards future generation systems". Final report to European Commission, Bruxelles, 1999.
8. R. Hoppe, G. Wlfle, and F. Landstorfer : "Fast 3-D Ray Tracing for the Planning of Microcells by Intelligent Preprocessing of the Data Base". Proceedings of 3rd European Personal and Mobile Communication Conference (EPMCC), Paris, March 1999.
9. R. E. Kalman : "A New Approach to Linear Filtering and Prediction Problems ". Transactions of the ASME-Journal of Basic Engineering, 82 (Series D): 35-45, 1960.
10. W. Zhao, R. Chellappa, P. J. Phillips and A. Rosenfeld : "Face Recognition: A Literature Survey". ACM Computing Surveys, vol 35(4), pp. 399458, December 2003
11. A.S. Georghiades, P.N. Belhumeur and D.J. Kriegman : "From Few to Many: Illumination Cone Models for Face Recognition Under Variable Lighting and Pose". IEEE Transactions on Pattern Analysis and Machine Intelligence,Vol. 23(6), pp. 643-660, 2001.

12. P.W. Hallinan : "A Deformable Model for the Recognition of Human Faces under Arbitrary Illumination". Harvard Univ. Cambridge, 1995.

13. T. Sim and T. Kanade : "Combining Models and Exemplar for Face Recognition: An Illuminating Example". In Proc. of Workshop on Models versus Exemplar in Computer Vision, CVPR, 2001.

14. T. Prante, N. Streitz and P.Tandler :"Roomware: Computers Disappear and Interaction Evolves". IEEE Computer 37 (12), 2004.

15. P. Ekman and W. Friesen : "Facial Action Coding System: A Technique for the Measurement of Facial Movement". Consulting Psychologists Press, 1978.

16. D. Geer : "The E911 dilemma". Wireless Business and Technology, Nov./Dec. 2001

17. V. Bellandi, M. Anisetti, e F. Beverina " Upper-Face Expression Features Extraction System for Video Sequences", Proceeding of the Fifth IASTED Visualization Imaging, and Image Processing (VIIP05), pp. 83-88, Benidorm, Spagna, 2005.

18. Ying-Li Tian and T. Kanade and J. Cohn : "Dual-state Parametric Eye Tracking", Proceedings of the 4th IEEE International Conference on Automatic Face and Gesture Recognition (FG00), pp. 110 - 115, March 2000.

19. B. Schlit : "Ubiquitous location-aware computing and the Place Lab Initiative" In Proc. of the First ACM Intl. Workshop on Wireless Mobile Applications and Services on WLAN Hotspots (San Diego, CA, Sept. 2003)

20. M. Anisetti, V.Bellandi, E. Damiani and S. Reale , "Localization and tracking of mobile antenna in urban environment", Proceeding of the IST 2005 - International Symposium on Telecommunications ,Shiraz, Iran, 2005.

21. E. Damiani, M. Anisetti, V.Bellandi and F. Beverina, "Facial identification problem: A tracking based approach", IEEE International Symposium on Signal-Image Technology and InternetBased Systems (IEEE SITIS'05), Yaoundé, Cameroon, 2005.

22. J. Hightower and G. Borriello : "Location systems for ubiquitous computing". IEEE Computer 34, 8, August 2001

23. J. Coutaz, J.L. Crowley, S. Dobson and D. Garlan : "Context is Key". Comm. of the ACM 48 (3), March 2005

24. S. Lahlou and F. Jegou : "European Disappearing Computer Privacy Design Guidelines V1.0". Ambient Agoras Report D15.4, Disappearing Computer Initiative, October 2003

25. A. Azzini, P. Ceravolo, E. Damiani : "Generating Context Metadata Based On Biometric Systems". Proc. of KES 2005, Melbourne (Australia), September 2005

26. J. Hightower and G. Borriello : "Particle filters for location estimation in ubiquitous computing: A case study". Proc. of the VI Int. Conference on Ubiquitous Computing (Nottingham, U.K., Sept. 2004)

27. P. A. Bonatti and P. Samarati : "Logics for Authorization and Security". Logics for Emerging Applications of Databases 2003: pp. 277-323

28. C. J. van Rijsbergen : "A Non-Classical Logic for Information Retrieval". The Computer Journal 29(6), pages 481-485, 1986.

29. J. Pearl (1988) : "Probabilistic Reasoning in Intelligent Systems: Networks of Plausible Inference". Morgan Kaufman, 1988

30. J. Glasgow, G. Macewen and P. Panangaden : "A logic for reasoning about security". ACM Transactions on Computer Systems (TOCS) 10 (3), August 1992

Understanding Mutable Internet Pathogens, or How I Learned to Stop Worrying and Love Parasitic Behavior

Kevin R.B. Butler and Patrick D. McDaniel

Systems and Internet Infrastructure Security Laboratory,
Pennsylvania State University,
University Park PA 16802, USA

Abstract. Worms are becoming increasingly hostile. The exponential growth of infection rates allows small outbreaks to have worldwide consequences within minutes. Moreover, the collateral damage caused by infections can cripple the entire Internet. While harmful, such behaviors have historically been short-lived. We assert the future holds much more caustic malware. Attacks based on mutation and covert propagation are likely to be ultimately more damaging and long lasting. This assertion is supported by observations of natural systems, where similarly behaving *parasites* represent by far the most successful class of living creatures. This talk considers a parasite for the Internet, providing biological metaphors for its behavior and demonstrating the structure of pathogens. Through simulation, we show that even with low infection rates, a mutating pathogen will eventually infect an entire community. We posit the inevitability of such parasites and consider ways that they can be mitigated.

1 Introduction

Internet worms are possibly the most intimidating of all the malicious entities that can attack systems and users. They are representative of the most volatile attacks currently available. From as early as 1988, security researchers have been cognizant of the ease at which worms can rapidly propagate across a network [1]; the rates of propagation have only increased in the period of time since then. Consider the Slammer worm, which was able to strike 90% of its intended targets within ten minutes of being released [2]. Accordingly, so-called *flash worms* have been considered the most dangerous of all the worm variants, and attempting to contain them is a very active area of research.

In this work, however, we posit that as troubling as these fast-moving worms might be, with their ability to infect large portions of the population in a short amount of time (i.e., individual hosts potentially infected in under one second [3]), they still do not represent the worst possible scenario. We consider a new form of malevolent digital organism, the Internet parasite. The parasite exhibits worst-case behavior as follows:

S. Jajodia and C. Mazumdar (Eds.): ICISS 2005, LNCS 3803, pp. 36–48, 2005.

1. It operates silently within the host, which remains unaware as to its presence.
2. It transmits itself to other hosts with the same frequency and behavior as other traffic, making it non-anomalous and undetectable to intrusion detection systems.
3. It acts autonomously and evolves new methods of learning behavior and attack patterns against new systems.

We simulate how such a parasite would propagate in a network, using parameters for infection and recovery determined from historical epidemiological research. We find that small changes in the rates of infection, mutation, and inoculation can have dramatic changes on whether a parasite will die out or eventually fully propagate to every host in the network. For a sufficiently high rate of mutation within a parasite, even a well-defended network will eventually succumb. The effectiveness of a parasite's infection vector and its resistance to host inoculation also play major roles in determining whether the network will fall.

In order to understand these new digital organisms, we begin by examining biological species that provide the metaphor for parasitic behavior.

2   Physical Parasites

Unbeknownst to many, parasites are the most abundant lifeform on the planet, with as many as three parasite species existing for every one "free-living" species [4]. Their success has been predicated on many factors. Parasites can foist degrees of unwanted behavior on their hosts, spawning across multiple generations before reaching their intended target. This can be manifested through children not necessarily resembling their parents, a characteristic rarely found in other species. The reasons for these differences in resemblance are purely functional, in order to continue the multi-generational life cycle that some of these parasites exhibit. A vitally important trait is that the methods a parasite uses to attack a host can change depending on the species of the intermediate or final victim.

Toxoplamsa gondii is a parasite that lives in cats as their ultimate hosts. While many species can be infected by the parasite, cats are the only mammalian species that *T. gondii* will sexually reproduce within. The parasite multiplies within a cat's gut, and is shed in its feces [5]. Rats will eat cat feces that carry the parasite, which propagates back to the cat in an ingenious manner. Rats are naturally afraid of cats as a predator species. However, when *T. gondii* is ingested by the rat, it works through several organs to the rat's brain, creating cysts that alter the rat's behavior. Infected rats lose many of their environmental fears, making them act "bolder" and therefore more susceptible to being eaten by cats, returning the parasite back to its preferred host [6]. This is an example of exploiting vulnerabilities in a straightforward way—the parasite is able to control the rat's behavior by affecting its brain. In a similar manner, computer pathogens can take over a compromised system, making it work in a manner not in its best interest.

In humans, the blood fluke (*Schistosoma mansoni*) has existed for hundreds of years and causes schistosomiasis, a malady affecting over 200 million people worldwide [7]. The parasite exists as larva in freshwater snails. When the larvae are mature, they burst out of the snail into water in a free-swimming form, where they can penetrate into the skin of humans venturing into the contaminated water. They enter the bloodstream, and although they grow to between 9 and 12 mm in length, they evade detection from the body's immune system by sloughing off their own proteins and covering themselves with proteins from the host (i.e., human antigens) until they are ready to reproduce [8]. The parasites seek out the human liver as a spawning ground, and eggs enter the large intestine or the bladder, where they are passed through urine or feces into fresh water, to hatch into larvae and attack the snails that serve as their intermediate hosts [9].

In this example, we see the multiple attack vectors a parasite can employ in order to target different hosts, and how it transforms its shape and behavior in quest of a goal state that can be several stages away. *S. mansoni* exploits particular vulnerabilities specific to the host in question and transfers itself in an innocuous manner. It also makes itself indistinguishable in the human host, acting like part of the host and obfuscating its signature. Combined with its ability to change shape and behavior, the parasite presents a compelling analogy to a particularly malicious computer virus that possesses the ability to morph into multiple forms.

The final key to a fully-realized parasite is the specialized manner in which it manages to attack and flourish within its host. As we have seen, these behaviors are complex enough to appear as if they had been thought out in advance. However, they are the result of countless generations of evolutionary behavior. As Darwin wrote about the human eye,

> Although the belief that an organ so perfect as the eye could have been formed by natural selection, is more than enough to stagger any one; yet in the case of any organ, if we know of a long series of gradations in complexity, each good for its possessor, then, under changing conditions of life, there is no logical impossibility in the acquirement of any conceivable degree of perfection through natural selection [10].

This provides a powerful metaphor for artificial organisms, in that the most successful digital organisms should be able to morph and mutate to dynamically propagate.

3   A Model for a Computer Parasite

Let us consider a piece of malcode that exhibits parasitic properties. We propose that such an entity would have the ability to lie undetected in its host and transmit in a manner undifferentiated from other traffic. To that end, we suggest a parasite that exhibits the following behavior:

- It listens to incoming and outgoing traffic on its host and determines which ports are open based on this information.

- It infers the protocol in use by constructing a finite state machine based on the traffic flows observed.
- Using automated methods, it dynamically discovers new vulnerabilities, saving successful exploits as part of its attack arsenal.
- It exploits the found vulnerabilities and propagates to the victim host in an undetectable manner.

While these elements have been studied individually, it is their combination in this manner that makes them particularly dangerous. We examine the different elements of this behavior in greater detail below.

3.1 Traffic Observation and Protocol Inference

The first stage of the parasite's life cycle is to eavesdrop on the series of messages and infer flow relationships based on this information. Such a task is not onerous, as TCP sequence numbers and other methods can be used to determine this information. The parasite will listen over all of a host's interfaces to determine potential relationships. In the taxonomy of worms presented by [11], *passive worms* exhibit this form of behavior, waiting for host machines to contact or be contacted by other machines.

The parasite will then attempt to infer the protocol represented by a given flow through construction of a finite state machine. For example, it may be able to infer the existence of the FTP protocol in use by noting that an outgoing connection is made to port 21 of a remote server, with a USER message sent, and the subsequent message containing a PASS message followed by a string, followed by file transfer activity. Observing the USER and PASS messages at the beginning of every transaction to a given port can provide the basis for reconstructing the protocol.

Inferring a protocol from network flows has been studied at the network level. Such inference engines already exist for measuring TCP connection characteristics by observing traffic [12] and as model checking tools for probabilistic systems [13] and communication protocols [14].

3.2 Generating Attack Vectors

Based on the information inferred, the parasite constructs messages to send to peers it has already communicated with over previously used protocols. It can try fault-injection methods [15] to craft messages that exploit potential weaknesses in the protocol; for example, if the largest message seen is 250 bytes, it can try sending a 500-byte message to a peer and seeing if the connection terminates, or what the failure mode is.

One important quality of the parasite is that it can be capable of learning methods of exploitation and employing what works against future potential hosts. It can also continue probing and attempting random attacks against other hosts, making it usable against any potential platform and network protocol. The AGENT architecture [16] is a key piece allowing the generation of new attacks.

AGENT will systematically generate real attacks based on the information afforded it. Using rule-sets, it will exhaustively generate all possible attacks from a known attack instance, and can prove, based on a sequence of packets, that a sequence comprises an attack. Evolutionary and genetic algorithms are the foundation for this approach [17], and other systems such as THOR [18] add injection attacks to determine intrusion detection. Additionally, tools such as GARD [19] will generate a signature for complex attacks; hence, it is possible for a permuted set of functions to be compared against the signature for determination of whether an attack will be successful and potentially increasing the effectiveness of mutated instances. The generation of new attacks is indicative of the polymorphic behavior we seek to exploit.

3.3   Covert Transmission

If an exploit is discovered that the parasite can take advantage of, it transfers itself to the host using the communication channel discovered in a "low and slow" manner. That is, it divides itself into small blocks that will fit into a packet of typical size for the protocol it is exploiting, and reassembles itself through when it has finished transferring. Current protocols such as BitTorrent [20] are capable of subdividing files into small blocks to be transferred; the parasite would employ similar behavior.

The host should be unable to distinguish parasitic traffic because of the strict use of already-established relationships. Additionally, the only clues to its existence would be the occasional dropping of connections or potential system crashes, depending on the nature of the potential exploit attempted by the parasite. However, given the varied reasons for connection failure and the computational cycles consumed by spyware and adware on many users' machines, attempting to diagnose such random activity could prove extremely difficult. Worms that behave in this manner (i.e., only propagating across currently existing communication channels) are defined as *contagion* worms [21], capable of stealthily spreading across networks but limited by the reliance on pre-programmed vulnerabilities to exploit in the client and server hosts. While these worms infect only hosts that are connected to legitimately, they derive much of their power from the *small-world* nature of the network topology [22], where an infection of highly connected machines allows the potential for many more hosts to be infected. In addition, peer-to-peer communication is another manner in which these worms can spread between hosts.

4   Simulating Parasitic Propagation

We have considered the methods by which propagation of parasites can occur. In this section, we provide empirical results based on simulation of a system that models real propagation. Our simple model is instructive for showing how parasitic behavior differs in important ways from regular worm propagation.

Our *parasim* simulator models a network of 500 nodes. For simplicity, we assume that all nodes have the ability to directly connect with each other. We model the probability of infection P_i by the pathogen from an infected host to a victim, the probability of inoculation P_n that cures the host of the infecting pathogen, and the probability of mutation P_m, which considers the likelihood of a particular pathogen changing into a new attack strain.

We examined literature in epidemiology and parasitology to determine a numerical basis for the values of P_i, P_n, and P_m. Previous work on the introduction of the parasite *Plagiorchis muris* in mice—itself based on the pioneering epidemiological studies of Greenwood et al. [23]—found that within the colony of mice, there was a transmission coefficient of 0.0056 per day, with a corresponding recovery coefficient of 0.04 per day [24, 25]. We assume that the probabilities of infection, mutation and inoculuation are exponentially distributed. Recall that an exponential distribution has the form

$$f(x) = \lambda e^{-\lambda x} \tag{1}$$

with mean $E(X) = \frac{1}{\lambda}$. Accordingly, we select $P_i = \frac{1}{0.0056}$ and $P_n = \frac{1}{0.04}$, equivalent to the transmission and recovery coefficients discovered from the forementioned experiments. Newly generated parasites receive values randomly selected from the distributions.

Figure 1 shows the results of 100 trials for a range of mutation probabilities. For each trial, we assume an initial infection of 25 hosts, representing 5% of the total population. We simulated 5000 rounds in each trial, and found that in the vast majority of cases, either the number of infected hosts converged on zero or the network became fully saturated. We observe that with the chosen parameters, the percentage of fully infected hosts increases almost linearly from a mutation probability of 0.002 until an equilibrium point is reached at $P_m = 0.03$. Variations in the graph and the lack of full saturation are attributable to randomness within the distribution.

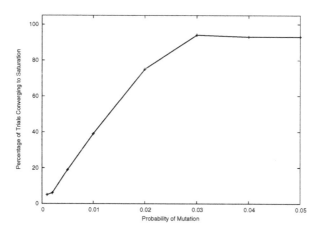

Fig. 1. Percentage of trials (out of 100) where entire network was infected

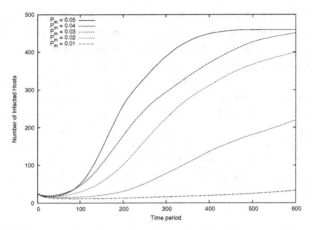

(a) Average number of attempted infections per time period

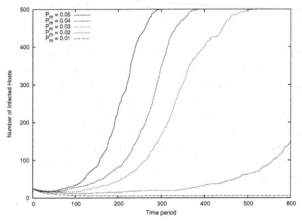

(b) Median number of attempted infections per time period

Fig. 2. Average and median attempted infections for varying values of mutation rates

As the probability of mutations rises, the rate at which hosts are infected increases dramatically. Figure 2(a) shows the average number of infected hosts per time period for mutation probabilities between 0.01 and 0.05, with the number of time periods limited to 600 rounds for clarity. Some interesting trends emerge in this graph: note that for each data series, the average number of infected hosts decreases slightly in the first few rounds of the infection, because of the inoculation rate being higher than the attack rate. For $P_m = 0.01$, the average number of infected hosts does not increase appreciably in this time period. For $P_m = 0.03$ and above, however, note that there are points in the curve where the rate of infection increases dramatically. These *points of criticality* are dependent

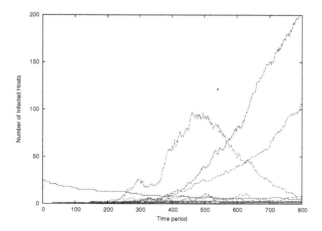

Fig. 3. Distributions of infected hosts from the first 100 virus mutations of a parasite trial with 5% mutation rate. Note that the majority of mutations fail, but a very small number infect large numbers of hosts.

on the parameters, but it is clear that past this point, infections that previously had been contained to a small number of hosts suddenly become epidemic in nature. Figure 2(b), which shows the median number of infected hosts at each time period, illustrates these points of criticality even more starkly, as they approximately appear at times $t = 280$, 210 and 120 for $P_m = 0.03$, 0.04 and 0.05, respectively. As these graphs show, the rate at which the parasite mutates can have dramatic implications on whether it will saturate the network and how quickly this will occur.

To see the effect that individual mutation strains have on the infection rate, we consider the distribution from a single trial with $P_m = 0.05$, shown in Figure 3. The first 100 mutant strains are shown in the graph. Notice that in this trial, the initial strain that begins the infection does not go on to infect many hosts; the number of infected hosts steadily declines to zero as hosts inoculate themselves. The majority of the mutated variants, in fact, infect no more than a handful of hosts before dying out. However, a strain begins spreading at $t = 200$ and begins to infect hosts, rapidly increasing the rate of infection at approximately $t = 350$ and eventually infecting over 100 hosts before hosts are inoculated. This curve, which displays a peak after rapid growth, followed by dwindling to zero, is commonly seen in epidemiological studies of pathogens dating back to some of the first quantitative studies [26]. The graph also shows that while the vast majority of mutations are failures, some mutations will result in spectacularly successful growth, a key observation in the evolutionary process of any organism.

We now consider the effect of the other variables considered on rates of infection. Unless stated otherwise, the tests keep the same parameters for P_i and P_n as previously described (0.0056 and 0.04, respectively), with 25 hosts initially infected. For clarity in the graphs, we assume a mutation rate P_m of 0.01. The first variable considered is the number of initial hosts. Figure 4 shows how the number

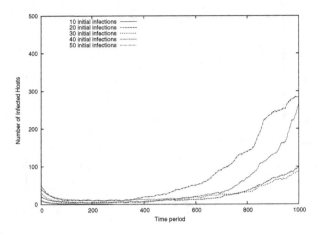

Fig. 4. Number of infected hosts for differing values of the initially infected set

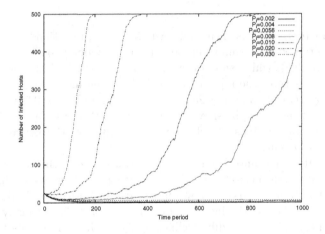

Fig. 5. Number of infected hosts for differing rates of infection

of infections varies depending on the initial number of infected hosts. As shown, increasing the number of hosts does not dramatically change the characteristics of the infection, although with a sufficiently small number of initial infections, the infection will end (note that for an initial set of 10 infected hosts, the total number of infected hosts quickly diminishes to zero). By contrast, Figure 5 displays that saturation will occur for $P_i \geq 0.008$. This graph bears similarities with the median infections found by varying the mutation rate in Figure 2(b). Past the saturation parameters, increasing the infection rate merely causes saturation to occur more quickly. This is another case where a small increase in the effectiveness of an infection vector can cause a network to quickly be overcome.

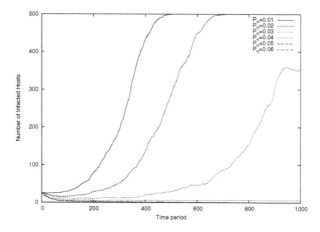

Fig. 6. Number of infected hosts for differing rates of inoculation

In a similar fashion, varying the rates of infection, as displayed in Figure 6, shows a saturating point at 0.03 (the number of hosts saturates over a long time period at 0.03). As P_n decreases, the amount of time required for network saturation decreases.

While changing the parameters will change the slopes of these lines, the lessons are clear: for a sufficiently high rate of mutation within the parasite, tantamount to it learning new avenues for infection, even a well-defended network will eventually succumb. The effectiveness of a parasite's infection vector and its resistance to host inoculation also play major roles in determining whether the network will fall. We defer more detailed analysis and simulation, and consideration of network topologies that mimic real-world operation, for future work. In particular, research in modern parasitology has considered the virulence of parasites and its effect on host mortality [27, 28, 29, 30, 31] and coevolution between parasites and their hosts [32, 33], including the possibility of hosts losing immunity to infection after being inoculated. We will revisit these issues in detail in future work.

5   Resisting Countermeasures

Detection and containment systems to resist attackers have been extensively examined. In this section, we consider how parasites act in the face of these systems.

Traditional intrusion detection systems (IDS) attempt to detect attackers based on their signature. Because parasites hide themselves as normal files and conceal themselves by transmission through innocuous protocols, they will not trigger alerts from an IDS. Similarly, transmitted parasites will not trigger traditional filtering mechanisms unless they are set to be aggressive enough that they attempt to quarantine or contain every incoming file. Additionally, the random protocol failures that would likely precede a successful exploit andcorresponding parasite transmission could leave the defending IDS in a more vigilant state. As with a biological parasite, transmission can be detected in some cases, but methods of transmission and attack vectors can be difficult and non-intuitive to determine.

From the host's perspective, the parasite would be similarly lacking in a signature, as we assume it maintains the ability to employ polymorphic code and behavior. The less polymorphism displayed by the parasite, and the less it changes, the easier it is to defend against. Optimally, it carries no demonstrable signature. Because it acts autonomously and learns new behaviors as it evolves and traverses the network, a parasite on one system may well appear considerably different from one on another system, making static detection very difficult. Additionally, if the parasite can exploit a system, it can be forced to act in ways that prevent the parasite from being discovered. Like the rat, whose brain processes are altered by the influence of *T. gondii*, the host system can be subverted so that the parasite's existence remains undetected through mechanisms such as buffer overflows.

Countermeasures against polymorphic worms have been suggested [34], and the AGENT architecture itself (which forms the basis of the protocol inference engine for our parasite) can be calibrated to work in either white-hat or black-hat mode, making it a potentially valuable defender against parasitic behavior. The parasite's potential for random behavior, however, could stymie efforts to ensure a full 100% success rate against any attacks it could generate. As an analog to biological parasites, although the methods of transmission and the full life cycles of many parasites are known, effectively immunizing and defending against them can still be very difficult.

Methods of detecting behavioral patterns in worms could potentially discover parasites that repeatedly employ the same methods of exploiting hosts [35], however, by searching and randomly testing for new vulnerabilities, the parasite's behavior itself can be seen as polymorphic. Similarly, methods of generating a content-based signature usable by intrusion detection systems exist, and are based on analyzing network flows without understanding the protocol behavior above TCP [36]. These methods could similarly detect parasites using similar behavioral models.

6   Conclusions

In this work, we have put forth the idea of employing parasitic behavior to create a new form of Internet pathogen, merging disparate threads of research to create a new understanding and classification. Because of the undetectable nature of network parasites and their ability to learn and evolve as they move through successive hosts, they have the potential to mimic their biological counterparts and spreading throughout the virtual world. They will form an unwelcome relationship with machines and their users.

References

1. Spafford, E.H.: The Internet worm program: An analysis. ACM Computer Communication Review **19** (1989) 17–57
2. Moore, D., Paxson, V., Savage, S., Shannon, C., Staniford, S., Weaver, N.: Inside the Slammer worm. IEEE Security and Privacy Magazine (2003) 33 – 39
3. Staniford, S., Moore, D., Paxson, V., Weaver, N.: The top speed of flash worms. In: Proceedings of the 2nd Workshop on Rapid Malcode (WORM 2004), Fairfax, VA, USA (2004)
4. Zimmer, C.: Parasite Rex: Inside the Bizarre World of Nature's Most Dangerous Creatures. Free Press (2001)
5. Denkers, E.Y., Gazzinelli, R.T.: Regulation and function of T-cell-mediated immunity during *Toxoplasma gondii* infection. Clinical Microbiology Reviews **11** (1998) 569–588
6. Berdoy, M., Webster, J., Macdonald, D.W.: Fatal attraction in rats infected with *Toxoplasma gondii*. In: Proceedings of the Royal Society of London: Biological Sciences, London, UK (2000) 1591–1594
7. Centers for Disease Control: Parasitic disease information: Schistosomiasis fact sheet (2005) http://www.cdc.gov/ncidod/dpd/parasites/schistosomiasis/factsht_schistosomiasis.htm.
8. McKerrow, J.H.: Cytokine induction and exploitation in schistosome infections. Parisitology **115** (1997) S107–S112
9. Anderson, R., Mercer, J., Wilson, R., Carter, N.: Transmission of *Schistosoma mansoni* from man to snail: experimental studies of miracidial survival and infectivity in relation to larval age, water temperature, host size and host age. Parasitology **85** (1982) 339–360
10. Darwin, C.: The Origin of Species. 6th edn. John Murray (1872)
11. Weaver, N., Paxson, V., Staniford, S., Cunningham, R.: A taxonomy of computer worms. In: Proceedings of the 1st Workshop on Rapid Malcode (WORM 2003), Washington, DC, USA (2003)
12. Jaiswal, S., Iannaccone, G., Diot, C., Kurose, J., Towsley, D.: Inferring TCP connection characteristics through passive measurements. In: Proceedings of IEEE INFOCOM 2004, Hong Kong (2004)
13. de Alfaro, L., Kwiatkowska, M., Norman, G., Parker, D., Segala, R.: Symbolic model checking of probabilistic processes using MTBDDs and the Kroenecker representation. In: Proceedings of the 6th International Conference on Tools and Algorithms for the Construction and Analysis of Systems (TACAS'2000), Berlin, Germany (2000)
14. Edelkamp, S., Leue, S., Lluch-Lafuente, A.: Directed explicit-state model checking in the validation of communication protocols. International Journal on Software Tools for Technology Transfer (STTT) **5** (2004) 247 – 267
15. Voas, J., McGraw, G., Kassab, L., Voas, L.: A "crystal ball" for software liability. IEEE Computer **30** (1997) 29–36
16. Rubin, S., Jha, S., Miller, B.P.: Automatic generation and analysis of NIDS attacks. In: Proceedings of the 20th Annual Computer Security Applications Conference (ACSAC 2004), Tuscon, AZ, USA (2004)
17. Spears, W., DeJong, K., Baeck, T., Fogel, D., de Garis, H.: An overview of evolutionary computation. In: Proceedings of the 4th European Conference on Machine Learning (ECML'93), Vienna, Austria (2003)

18. Marty, R.: THOR: A tool to test intrusion detection systems by variations of attacks. Master's thesis, Swiss Federal Institute of Technology, Zurich, Switzerland (2002)
19. Rubin, S., Jha, S., Miller, B.P.: Language-based generation and evaluation of NIDS signatures. In: Proceedings of the 2005 IEEE Symposium on Security and Privacy, Oakland, CA, USA (2005)
20. Qiu, D., Srikant, R.: Modeling and performance analysis of Bit Torrent-like peer-to-peer networks. In: Proceedings of ACM SIGCOMM 2004, Portland, OR, USA (2004)
21. Staniford, S., , Paxson, V., Weaver, N.: How to 0wn the Internet in your spare time. In: Proceedings of the 11th USENIX Security Symposium, San Francisco, CA, USA (2002)
22. Bu, T., Towsley, D.: On distinguishing between Internet power law topology generators. In: Proceedings of IEEE INFOCOM 2002, New York, NY, USA (2002)
23. Greenwood, M., Bradford Hill, A., Topley, W.W.C., Wilson, J.: Experimental Epidemiology. His Majety's Stationary Office, London, UK (1936) Privy Council, Medical Research Council.
24. Anderson, R., May, R.: Population biology of infectious diseases, part 1. Nature 280 (1979) 361–367
25. May, R., Anderson, R.: Population biology of infectious diseases, part 2. Nature 280 (1979) 455–461
26. MacDonald, G.: The Epidemiology and Control of Malaria. Oxford University Press, New York, NY (1957)
27. Davies, C., Webster, J., Woolhouse, M.: Trade-offs in the evolution of virulence in an indirectly transmitted macroparasite. In: Proceedings of the Royal Society of London: Biological Sciences, London, UK (20001) 251–257
28. Levin, B., Svanborg-Eden, C.: Selection and evolution of virulence in bacteria: an ecumenical and modest suggestion. Parasitology 100 (1990) S103–S115
29. Dwyer, G., Levin, S., Buttel, L.: A simulation model of the population dynamics and evolution of myxomatosis. Ecological Monographs 60 (1990) 423–447
30. Anderson, R.: Parasite pathogenicity and the depression of host population equilibria. Nature 279 (1979) 150–152
31. Lewontin, R.: The units of selection. Annual Review of Ecology and Systematics 1 (1970) 1–18
32. May, R., Anderson, R.: Parasite-host coevolution. Parasitology 100 (1990) S89–S101
33. Levin, S., Pimentel, D.: Selection of intermediate rates of increase in parasite-host systems. The American Naturalist 117 (1981) 308–315
34. Chistodorescu, M., Jha, S.: Static analysis of executables to detect malicious patterns. In: Proceedings of the 13th USENIX Security Symposium, Washington, DC, USA (2003)
35. Ellis, D.R., Aiken, J.G., Attwood, K.S., Tenaglia, S.D.: A behavioral approach to worm detection. In: Proceedings of the 2nd Workshop on Rapid Malcode (WORM 2004), Fairfax, VA, USA (2004)
36. Kim, H.A., Karp, B.: Autograph: Toward automated, distributed worm signature detection. In: Proceedings of the 14th USENIX Security Symposium, San Diego, CA, USA (2004)

Building India as the Destination for Secure Software Development – Next Wave of Opportunities for the ICT Industry

Prem Chand

Mahindra British Telecom Limited, Sharda Centre,
Off Karve Road, Pune 411004, India
prem@mahindrabt.com

Abstract. Information and Communications Technology is becoming synonymous with the survival and sustenance of human race in social, economic, political and military terms. As a result of this the security of ICT is becoming a serious global concern. USA alone looses about $38B in security lapses and tracking of virus incidents alone runs into the range of $80B per year worldwide. These losses are incurred despite an estimated security market size of $36B expected by the year 2007-08. There are no foolproof solutions in sight.

Software is the lynchpin of information systems. However software is prone to suffer disability, damage, denial, disruption or destruction in information systems. Thus insecure software is the single most serious security concern being faced by the society. The new focus across the global ICT community is therefore to eliminate threats and vulnerabilities to software by removing the root causes of its weaknesses by revisiting the life cycle approach to software engineering, whereby security is built into each stage rather than bolting it down as an after thought. The secure software is a demand of every customer. Efforts are underway in many countries to answer the call for this demand.

In this talk I will present how ICT security is emerging a 21 century global nightmare, the new global vision of ICT security, where the world is moving to in the context of cyber security, why and how software is the weakest building block in ICT security journey, how the development of secure or trustworthy software can address majority of the cyber security concerns, what are the challenges of developing secure or trustworthy software, why a global initiative and collaboration is necessary, why should India position itself to be the secure or trustworthy software power house, what will it take India to create secure software development capability, what is India's value proposition in terms of education, emerging R&D base, quality, manpower etc. to succeed in secure software initiative, how to mobilize India to develop secure software development capability. The analysis presented to build a case for India will cover protection of Information Age Infrastructures as immediate national necessity, standards driven security framework for National Information Infrastructures, life cycle approach to secure software development and outlines of a blue print for India to develop into a secure software development destination.

S. Jajodia and C. Mazumdar (Eds.): ICISS 2005, LNCS 3803, pp. 49–65, 2005.

1   Introduction

Information and Communications Technology (ICT) is becoming synonymous with the survival and sustenance of the human race in social, economic, political and military terms. As a result, ICT Security is of critical importance for the 21st century. Software is the lynchpin of information systems. However software is prone to suffer disability, damage, denial, disruption or destruction in information systems. Thus, insecure software is the single most serious security concern being faced by society. The new focus across the global ICT community is therefore to eliminate threats and vulnerabilities to software by removing the root causes of its weaknesses by revisiting the life cycle approach to software engineering, whereby security is built into each stage rather than bolting it down as an after thought. Secure software is a demand of every customer. Efforts are underway in many countries to answer the call for this demand.

This paper examines how ICT security is emerging as a 21 century global nightmare, the new global vision of ICT security, where the world is moving in the context of cyber security, why and how software is the weakest building block in the ICT security journey and how the development of secure or trustworthy software can address a majority of the cyber security concerns. It also examines the challenges of developing secure or trustworthy software and the need for a global initiative and collaboration. The paper examines what will it take of India to create a secure software development capability, what is India's value proposition in terms of education, emerging R&D base, quality, manpower etc. to succeed in secure software initiatives and how to mobilise India to develop secure software development capability. The analysis presented to build a case for India covers protection of Information Age Infrastructures as an immediate national necessity, standards driven security framework for National Information Infrastructures, life cycle approach to secure software development and outlines of a blue print for India to develop into a secure software development destination. The paper signifies that India should position itself as a secure and trustworthy software power house for the emerging global market.

2   ICT Security: A 21 Century Global Nightmare

The Information and Communication Technology (ICT) systems are becoming synonymous with the survival and sustenance of the human race in social, economic, political and military terms. The persistence security, safety and all time availability of these systems is taking center stage and engaging the attention of governments, academia and the ICT industry world over. Although extensive efforts and expenses have been incurred in evolving comprehensive security overlays for these systems; no fool proof security solutions are foreseen. For example USA is spending billions on its Home Land Security (HLS) initiative, but with no 100% security guarantee. The Task Force to Improve Software Life Cycle security, constituted by the HLS, in its report has revealed that USA looses about $38b in security lapses and that the tracking of virus incidents alone runs into the range of $80b per year worldwide in terms of damage incurred and clean up costs. These losses occur despite an estimated global security market size of $36b by 2007-08. Security has been described as the, "Nightmare of the 21st century" [1, 2, 3,4].

3 The New Global Vision of ICT Security

The global software community recognises that fool proof security would require revisiting, "The Life Cycle Approach to Software Engineering", whereby security is built into each stage rather than bolting it down as an after thought [1]. The life cycle approach to secure software development would require that security forms a part of the solution architecture. This will require risk assessment, formulating the security objectives, defining the security policy, capturing the security requirements viz. audit, testing, cryptographic support, user data protection, identity, authentication, privacy, security management, protection of security functions, resource utilisation, trusted paths, system access etc. It will also include design for security, implementation and testing aspects.

A part of the software community has gone a step further stating that, "Capability to Develop Trustworthy Software" is the answer. This would involve building security, safety, availability, performance and survivability features into software as a part of the life cycle approach [3].

4 Where Is the World Moving in the Context of Cyber Security?

Countries with highest ICT penetration have recognized cyber security as the gravest concern. This is evident from a large number of initiatives in the form of directives, committees and reports involving governments, academia, institutions and industry alliances. USA has already invested considerable efforts in this direction. Some of them are listed below:

- National Cyber Security Partnership, USA. The Cyber Security Industry Alliance Report on Security Across the Software Development Life Cycle, Apr 04 [4].
- Findings and Recommendations by the Cyber Security Industry Alliance on the Funding for Security R&D, July 2005.
- The National Strategy to Secure Cyberspace. "Software 2015: A National Software Strategy to Ensure U.S. Security and Competitiveness", Sep 04 [3].
- "Cyber Security: A Crisis of Prioritization". A report by the President's Information Technology Advisory Committee, February 2005 [5].
- "Security and Dependability R&D for Europe", ICT Taskforce Initiatives, 2005 [6].
- "Security and Application Development Process", Report of Frances Group, 2005 [7].

- "The Trustworthy Computing Security Development Lifecycle", Steve Lipner & Michael Howard, Microsoft, Mar 05 [8].
- "Microsoft Security Development Lifecycle", Microsoft Corporation, May 05 [9]
- "Russia Security Software Forecast & Analysis", 2002-07, Dec 03 [10].
- "China-Shape of Software Industry & Information Security Services", 2005 [11].

A comprehensive multi-prong strategy is being adopted by USA to address cyber security. The Industry Alliance has recommended building security into the Software Life Cycle through education, R&D and improved practices. The Center for National Software Studies Report recognizes, "Software: The Critical Infrastructure within the Critical Infrastructures" and has recommended a national strategy to ensure US security and competitiveness through improvements in software work force, trustworthy software systems, re-energizing R&D and renewed emphasis on innovation. There are Sustainable Software and Trusted Computing initiatives underway through partnership. Microsoft is perusing a massive security initiative on its own. Similar initiatives are being planned in Europe signifying seriousness, volume and complexity of the problem. Large number of regulatory steps in the forms of legislations, acts, directives, frameworks and industry best practices have emerged viz. COBIT, Sarbanes Oxley Act, HIPAA, European Data Protection Act, OECD Guidelines etc. There are no specific and focused initiatives evident in Russia, China etc. yet reported in open literature.

5   Why Is Software the Weakest Building Block in ICT?

During the past 50 years, software innovations have benefited the society through efficiency enhancement across all sectors of economy. Software has become the lynchpin of information society from a survival and sustenance perspective. However software has the potential to suffer disability, damage, denial, disruption or destruction through natural or manmade attacks. This makes software embedded systems under-pinning the Critical National Infrastructures (CNI) the single most serious security target of such attacks. The efforts to fully secure software systems have not been very successful. Thus software has come to stay as the weakest building block in modern ICT.

The focus of all stake holders owning and operating the ICT infrastructures is therefore to eliminate threats and vulnerabilities to software by removing the root causes of its weaknesses. Historically security had not been the guiding factor for software. The emphasis of the software engineering community has always been to address the functional, technical and performance aspects of the software. There are some mission and safety critical applications in defence, space, healthcare, banking and manufacturing industries where some security aspects have been addressed. Consequently security seldom formed a part of the software life cycle activity viz. requirements, design, coding, testing, integration and post deployment support. Therefore a new beginning is needed to build intrinsic security upfront into the software viz. Development of, "Secure Software" or

"Trustworthy Software". Some efforts in this direction have been examined. The report refers to the guidelines articulated in the ISO 15408, Common Criteria and ISO 21827, SSE-CMM and other initiatives underway.

6 Will Development of "Secure" or "Trustworthy Software" Alone Address the Cyber Security Concerns? What Else Will Be Required?

Building secure or trustworthy software would be a logical transition from the present state to address known and perceived risks. However this would be applicable to only future systems and the meaningful results would be evident only in 3 to 5 years or more when such systems enter service. On the other hand the existing systems and those under development also need to be secured. These systems will have to co-exist with the future systems and can only be phased out gradually. Thus the challenge for India and the rest of the world is to continue the efforts to develop "end-to-end" security solutions to minimize, mitigate or transfer risks for environments where all possible generations of ICT infrastructures can co-exist. A large number of initiatives are underway across the globe in terms of development of security technologies, secure processes, hardening of systems, authentication architectures, persistent security through application of Digital Rights Management and improvements in business continuity to evolve "end-to-end" security solutions. This effort would have to be dovetailed with Secure Software Development [12,13]. This would require very large and dedicated efforts for India in creating expertise, solutions and support infrastructure. USA is a forerunner and very large programs are underway as a part of Home Land Security and other initiatives. The size of this segment of security market is expected to grow to US $32 billion by 2007-08.

It therefore emerges that while there should be no looking back to develop Secure and/or Trustworthy software, an equal emphasis has to be laid on development of expertise and infrastructures to address security of existing systems and those already under development. At the same time it would be necessary to telescope this effort to future generation of systems for evolving a seamless cyber security environment.

7 Why Focus Only on "Secure" or "Trustworthy Software" as a Placeholder for ICT Security Initiatives?

Security in its totality manifests itself in 3 domains viz. Physical, Personnel and Information, which intersect as overlapping circles. All 3 domains rely heavily on ICT. Physical security often relies on ICT sensors and devices, such as physical access control relying on a card reader or biometric devices which in turn are partially dependent on software, or natural events such as hurricanes or Tsunami relying on ICT dependent sensors. In a similar manner, Personnel Security also relies on ICT for background checks or Identification, Authentication and Access Control. Information Security is more obvious in its dependence on ICT and thus software and is visible through computers, networking components, communication links, database systems etc.

From the practical security practitioner's or even security industry's point of view, the dependence on ICT and more particularly software is less obvious. This is because we deal more often with practical issues whose dependence upon software is less obvious and visible.

The intent and prime focus of this paper is not to portray or project software as, "Be All or End All" of security. Physical and Information aspects are equally crucial to address security in its totality. The intent of this paper is to telescope and project secure and trustworthy software as an answer to most of the cyber security concerns which the software community has not been able to address hitherto by bolting down piece meal security as an after thought.

8   What Are the Challenges of Developing "Secure Software"?

The development of secure software poses an unprecedented challenge for the global software community in terms of domain expertise, life cycle mapping of the security into business functions, work flow processes and the technology. This kind of work has not yet been done by the software community and requires high end research, education, training and know how in the security domain. These are complex and challenging issues and require very large collective efforts on the part of government, academia and industry.

In order to put these issues in the correct perspective, there is a need to develop an understanding of the complex information infrastructures, their security concerns and articulate how software in these infrastructures turns out to be the weakest risk prone building block. Development of secure software requires a well thought out standards–driven security framework to foster a life cycle approach. The Home Land Security Task Force for secure software life cycle has suggested a 6 to 8 years road map to develop this capability [1,4].

9   What Are the Challenges of Developing "Trustworthy Software"?

Trustworthy software involves attributes of security, safety, reliability, performance and survivability. As brought out by the Center for National Software Studies, USA in its Report, "Software 2015: A National Software Strategy to ensure U.S. Security and Competitiveness", Apr 2005, the development of Trustworthy Software will require us to identify and examine trustworthiness properties, develop metrics, technology, and ways and means to evolve next generation software engineering life cycle processes to imbibe these attributes. Thus development of Trustworthy Software is a very challenging task for the software community and will require unprecedented efforts in R&D, innovation, education and training collaboratively by governments, academia and industry across the globe. The report has suggested a 10 year road map for USA to develop this capability [3].

10   What Will It Take to Create Critical Mass in Secure Software Development Capability by India?

Development of secure software would require India to develop expertise in software, security and application domains. This would also require the expertise in frameworks and secure software development practices to be pooled together and cross fertilised as industry accepted norms. The state of the art in these areas would need to be enhanced beyond the current level of practice to Ph.D. level effort. All this would require 5 to 7 years of focused and sustained effort as is being mooted by USA under its Home Land Security partnership initiative and Software Engineering Institute's (SEI) Team Software Process and Sustainable Computing Consortium programs underway at SEI, USA [1,14].

The practice framework for software engineering, security engineering, and business domains would need to be aligned, blended and married in terms of life cycle approach and relevance to technical, financial, privacy, safety, quality and other regulatory compliance needs. The expertise and facilities required for security testing, verification, validation, assurance and certification in consonance with ISO 17799, ISO 15408, ISO 21827 etc. would need to be created and impregnated across the industry. This would require unprecedented efforts and synergy between industry, academia and the government agencies. Once the critical mass of competence is created and transitioned to key industry players, the market forces will take over for further scale up and penetration.

11   Why Should India Position Itself to Be the "Secure" or "Trustworthy Software" Power House?

Today it is universally conceded that, as it evolves, Secure and Trustworthy software would become a multibillion dollar industry. Secure and trustworthy software is the demand of every customer. Somebody has to answer the call for this demand. Could it be USA, Russia, China, Europe or India? Who ever takes the lead will have a clear first mover advantage of 4 to 6 years. This is a typical catch up time for major life cycle improvement in software. The size and scale of India's software industry is such that this differential will create steep outsourcing demand and price premium of 12 to 18%. Going by the literature survey, the next improvement cycle in software engineering will emerge from "Secure Software" and India should take this as step 1. "Trustworthy Software"/"Sustainable Computing" as of now has too many unknowns to be addressed and India should only attempt it as a step 2 initiative [3]. India has the critical mass to attempt step 1. By the time India attains the Secure Software capability, the research in Trustworthy Computing would have achieved a much higher level of maturity. It would then be easy for India to combine its expertise in secure and high quality software and cross fertilise with safety, performance and survivability expertise available from the market to develop trustworthy software capability.

What will it take India to create "Secure Software" development capability

It would take unprecedented collaborative efforts on the part of government, academia and industry to build a sustainable national capability in secure software development. The principal constituents are as follows.

1. Public-private effort to build academic education to combine advancement of security knowledge and expertise. University education in information protection up to graduation, post gradation and doctoral levels as well as research to enhance state of the art for high end secure solutions need to be developed. This will also require creation of Centres of Excellence (CoE) in security, security certification and accreditation programs, software security metrics etc.

2. Develop, adopt and perfect framework, methodologies and practices which can measurably reduce software specification, design and implementation defects. Bench mark available practices for their effectiveness to reduce software vulnerabilities, establish security validation and verification programs to measure the effectiveness of secure software practices, place these practices under a certification program and introduce measures to transition them to the industry through training and certification. This framework will enable the software community to understand problems involved in producing secure software, articulate requirements for processes and practices to produce secure software, key practices for producing secure software, organisational changes needed for introduction, use and improvement in processes and practices, build expertise in validation, verification and approval of processes, practices, people and products, adapt already prevailing practices such as Software Engineering Institute's Team Software Process to make a beginning.

3. Promote information security services industry in the country through professional training in security products, solutions, protocols, standards, regulatory framework etc. Create Centres of Excellence in emerging areas such as Digital Rights Management, Identity Management, Voice over Internet Protocol (VoIP) Security, Managed Security Services, Functional Security Testing, Next Generation Network Security, Vulnerability Assessment, Incidence Analysis, Business Continuity, Disaster Recovery and Management, Computer Forensics, Cyber Fraud, Security Audits etc.

4. Collaborate in large national and global information infrastructure initiatives. Promote India's security services overseas. Bring legislations for security compliance across all sectors of economy, health care, banking, governance etc.

12   Options for India: "Secure Software" or "Trustworthy Software" Route?

India has the unique proposition and critical mass to development into a "Secure Software" development destination for the global ICT industry over a period of

5 to 7 years. India should collaborate and synergize its efforts for development of "Secure Software" expertise with USA, Europe and other countries. This will not only cut down efforts, expenses, risks and time to reach a minimum maturity level, but will create the requisite brand image and ready to exploit market. India should take advantage of the presence of over 100 MNCs who already have R&D facilities in the country and collaborate with them in this initiative. Microsoft in particular has a very large security initiative which can help both sides immensely.

The development of "Trustworthy Software" would require considerable scientific research & engineering effort and building of competencies in software security, safety, performance, reliability and survivability. The understanding of safety, reliability, performance and survivability as applicable to software is still at a very early or nascent stage amongst academia and industry. India does not have the critical mass to address these issues yet. The "Software 2015: National Software Strategy to ensure U.S. Security and Competitiveness" initiative is being planned under the aegis of Center for National Software Studies, USA and is likely to get US federal funding to develop competencies in the development of Trustworthy Software. Similarly some work is already underway at SEI CMU under the "Sustainable Computing" initiative and "Security and Dependability R&D for Europe" initiative. India should collaborate in these programs to gain insight and create critical mass of competencies before making any large scale investments in this area. These competencies when combined with expertise in Secure Software will enable India to take the next logical step to develop expertise in Trustworthy Software. Thus the route to directly attempt development of Trustworthy Software is not recommended for India.

13 What Is India's Value Proposition to Succeed in "Secure Software" Initiative?

India possesses a critical mass to launch the Secure Software initiative at national scale in most areas. However in some areas it is still to be reached. Following steps are clear value propositions which are unique to India.

1. Well established ICT education and training system, matured over the past 30 years, capable of producing software engineering, computer science, IT management and related competencies. Given the right visibility, focus and career options, a large segment of this community can be educated and trained in security. Few other countries as of now have this advantage.
2. India has over 80 SEI SW CMM level 5 software companies. This number is larger than that of USA, Europe and rest of the world put together. The other quality initiatives coupled with this makes India one of the most quality conscious software industries in the world. This capability makes it easier to blend and align security life cycle processes in consonance with ISO 21827 for security engineering, ISO 17799 for security management, ISO 15408 for security testing and assurance.

3. The training and certification facilities for Certified Information Systems Security Professionals (CIISP), Certified Information Systems Auditors (CISA), BS 7799 Auditors, Certified Business Continuity Professionals (CBCP), Certified Fraud Examiners (CFE), Health Insurance (HIPAA), COBIT, SEE-CMM etc. are available in the country.

4. The facilities for product training and certifications for Identity Management, Fire Walls, Intrusion Detection, Anti-Virus, Anti-Spam, Authentication, Cryptology, Public Key Infrastructure (PKI) etc. are available in the country. Graduate and Post Graduate level security education through universities are under active consideration of concerned agencies. Some collaborative security programs with overseas universities are already underway. The Ph. D. level security education and research has not yet taken roots and requires dedicated efforts.

5. There are ICT companies engaged in overseas projects involving New Generation Network (NGN) security and Security Framework for large enterprises. Many Indian companies are engaged in co-developments with overseas partners in the Authentication, Digital Rights Management, Cryptology, Public Key Infrastructure etc. The Government of India is in the process of setting up a Common Criteria Laboratory. Many other government initiatives are at planning stage. NASSCOM is engaged in many national level security related awareness and confidence building programs.

6. India is already home to many R&D initiatives in ICT. Over 100 MNCs including IBM, Microsoft, Intel, Texas Instrument, Oracle, SAP, CA, SUN, GE, LG, SAMSUNG, NOKIA, MOTOROLA, Philips etc. have setup their R&D facilities in India. This uniqueness is not exclusively driven by low cost. It has more to do with quality of manpower and the support infrastructure now available in the country. This positions India in the most unique position to collaborate and share the security related developments with world's most advanced ICT majors. This would also make India a more trusted development partner in secure systems development alongside these companies. The case of Microsoft R&D facility is of particular significance.

7. India created its regulatory framework for the cyber environment through promulgation of its IT Act 2000, which has been revised as late as 2005. It has the national PKI infrastructure, Computer Emergency Response Team-India (CERT- I), and a government and industry-wide commitment to recognize cyber security a pervasive and critical national necessity. There are many government initiatives including secure citizen services underway to secure national critical infrastructures.

It therefore emerges that India is indeed in a unique position to collaborate with rest of the world, particularly the USA in development of Secure Software and support initiatives for "end-to-end" security in terms of technology, people and processes. However it is conceded that there is a need to undertake considerable preparatory and coordination work to reach that stage. The recent developments at political level between India and USA can make government, industry and academia level collaborations with USA easy.

14   How to Mobilise India to Develop "Secure Software" Development Capability?

A national initiative of this dimension and complexity will require fusion of core academic excellence, proactive role and participation of industry and committed sponsorship from government. In the past SEI, CMU and US industry's secure software forums have made similar attempts. Their results are not yet visible. Many mission mode national level initiatives in the past have seen mixed results. The starting level in this direction in security specific areas is very low. Therefore a well thought out and researched model need to be evolved and implemented. Following approach is suggested.

1. Evolve a consortium approach, through a limited no of participants to peruse a budgeted program under a, "Secure Software Foundation of India (SSFI)". The consortium should develop strategy, a blue print and road map, tie it up to time bound fully funded and ownership driven program. For example the entire capability development can be divided and structured into 10 work programs of 5 years each, with clearly defined 6 monthly milestones. These 10 programs can be assigned to clearly defined consortium teams, each constituted from institutions, industry and government with specific roles, responsibilities and deliverables. A very high level empowered review and evaluation team should be constituted with equally well defined roles responsibilities and deliverables. The management, control and monitoring be assigned to full time employed professionals with responsibility for deliverables. The whole program should work as a well funded OUT SOURCED work package to the consortium, which would function as an enterprise on the lines of a software services company. The professionals should be drawn from across the globe and quality, not cost, should be the driving vector for the entire initiative. The creation of expertise should to be driven by industry and academia. Therefore the initiative should be driven through public-private sector participation.
2. A well thought out mechanism be evolved to transition the developments to end user community across the industry, academia and the government through a robust business model.

15   Analysis Needed to Build a Case for India

Building secure software development capability is a multi-billion dollar opportunity for India. However this challenge is extremely complex, unprecedented and requires fusion of core academic, industry and government efforts. However understanding of these issues requires understanding the complexities of this initiative. These have been researched and presented in this paper in the form of a set of the following 4 separate areas.

15.1   Protection of Information Age Infrastructures - An Immediate National Necessity

This area should examine the societal promise of NII. As we are aware the NII of any nation would be aimed to provide universal online connectivity to every citizen; be it a student, soldier, businessman, scientist, engineer, or doctor, without regard to geography, distance, resources, or disability. The NII would be a single thread traversing through, and, underpinning every national infrastructure in energy, transport, finance, banking, healthcare, defense, business, industry, education and the government. Therefore NII would signify more than the physical facilities used to collect, collate, transmit, store, process and display voice, data, text, and images. It would encompass ever-expanding range of equipment including cameras, scanners, keyboards, telephones, fax machines, computers, switches, compact discs, video and audio tapes, cable, wire, satellites, fiber optics transmission lines, microwave links, switches, televisions, printers, monitors etc.

The NII would interconnect and integrate these physical components in a technologically neutral manner. The NII would encompass content in the form of video programming, scientific or business databases, images, sound recordings in laboratories, studios, publishing houses, government etc. The NII applications software would allow end users to access, manipulate, organize and digest the mass of information. The NII by itself will be under pinned by a framework of standards and specifications to facilitate connectivity, interoperability, security, reliability and availability. The people would form the most significant component of NII who will create information, develop applications and services, construct facilities and train others to tap its potential. The people would exist as owners, vendors, operators, service providers etc.

The most critical issue would be to embed safety, security, confidentiality, integrity and availability of the National Information Infrastructures. This will ensure protection at all levels, for all times, against the impending internal or external threats. Many dramatic changes expected from development of NII will grow out of advances in wireless technologies. Therefore access to NII resources by anyone, at anytime from anywhere will have direct bearing on the control and management of Radio Frequency (RF) spectrum and its security issues. NII security would also need to be examined with respect to internal and cross border, natural or man made threats, arising out of economic competition, political and social mismatch and military dominance. The security would also have to be examined in terms of intrinsic or built up vulnerabilities during design, operations and support of NII, arising out of technology, processes and environmental limitations. The threats and vulnerabilities to the NII would be mapped as risks, which would have to be mitigated or minimized through a set of cost-benefit trade-offs.

Threats and vulnerabilities to NII at individual, agency, state and national level would have to be identified in terms of gaps or weakness in protection policy, processes, and regulatory framework. These would have to be further amplified in terms of safety, security, confidentiality, availability, integrity, non-repudiation and time sensitivity. A scalable security framework in terms of architecture, policy, people and technology need to be outlined. A security model addressing information, databases, computing resources, networking components, communications, personnel and physical environment has to be examined. A preparatory framework to support this initiative in terms of technology, people and processes would have to be articulated. However this articulation will serve the needs of NII for existing systems and technologies only. For the future software systems, there will be a need to build security as a part of development process, which should be based on a framework of standards.

15.2   Building Standards Driven Security Framework for National Information Infrastructures

Today, security awareness and expectations of customers and stakeholders are growing. Customers are no more inclined to consider these assumptions as sufficient in order to claim a secure system. Some recent requirements from customers wishing to establish large components of NII in banking, finance, defense etc. have clearly requested security assurance and compliance to IT security standards to be included from vendors' solutions. Customers have even demanded an appraisal or audit of the vendors' security maturity and level of compliance.

There is a need to examine security related work undertaken by many agencies engaged in development of NII in different countries, identify gaps, recommend focus areas and priorities. There is a need to survey security assurance frameworks prevalent in industry, academic institutions and research community and their applicability to NII and present a way ahead for a security program. The purpose should be to enable all stakeholders help develop a consistent, cost-effective framework, within which security for the NII and its components can be engineered. The proposed framework should also allow the stakeholders to evaluate the security of any component or combination of components of NII, either in operation or in development, based upon an agreed assurance level.

Some prevailing assumptions about NII security are dated and need to be revisited. We should also examine how NII security is an issue that can be addressed by adapting and applying the IT security frameworks standards, such as Common Criteria (ISO/IEC 15408), SSE-CMM (ISO/IEC 21827), GMITS (ISO/TR 13335), ISMS (ISO 17799), FRITSA (ISO/TR 15443) and IATF 3.1 (Information Assurance Technology Framework of NSA). We should come out with a clear understanding as to how these standards can be used effectively to provide the framework for a secure and assured NII.

15.3   Life Cycle Approach to Secure Software Development

There is a need to examine the issues leading to the threats and vulnerabilities to software and identifies the root causes of software weaknesses. It emerges that historically security had not been the guiding factor for software. The emphasis of the software engineering community has always been to address the functional, technical and performance aspects, except in certain mission and safety critical applications in defence, space, healthcare, banking and manufacturing industry.

Consequently security seldom formed a part of the software life cycle activity viz requirements, design, coding, testing, integration and post deployment support.

Fool proof security would require revisiting the life cycle approach to software engineering, whereby security is built into each stage rather than bolting it down as an after thought, which is precisely being done currently. There is also a need to understand the secure software development life cycle, risk assessment, forming the security objectives, defining the security policy, capturing the security requirements viz. audit, testing, cryptographic support, user data protection, identity, authentication, privacy, security management, protection of security functions, resource utilisation, trusted paths, system access, architecture and design for security, implementation and testing aspects.

Development of secure software poses an unprecedented challenge for the software community in terms of domain expertise, life cycle mapping of the security into business functions, work flow processes and the technology. These are complex issues and require collective efforts on the part of government, academia and industry.

15.4   Developing India into a Secure Software Development Destination

There is a need to examine the expectations of global ICT industry from India as a secure software destination in terms of global collaborative secure work environment, secure outsourcing destination, secure ODC operations, a provider of security services and how will the country meet them. It is also necessary to address how secure software can be developed through collaborative efforts and what role each constituent viz. government, academia and industry should play.

16   India Cannot Succeed in the Development of Secure or Trustworthy Software by Going Alone. India Must Join Global Collaborative Effort

Efforts to build security in software through a life cycle approach and graduate to development of trusted software has unprecedented complexity. More over the solutions for secure software need to be blended with rest of security aspects of existing ICT systems and made technically acceptable to the end user software community across the globe. The most crucial would be to blend these efforts of software community in the USA, which controls 90% of the $ 200 billion strong software industry sales in the world. On the other hand from a total current security market size of $ 23 B, USA accounts for 50%, Europe 40% and the rest of the world 10%. Therefore efforts on the part of India would gain credibility only if they were positioned more strongly within the context of similar international efforts that are currently underway – particularly those in the USA and Europe as brought out above.

Given the global nature of security threats and the global nature of the Internet and the IT industry, any purely national initiative realistically can not hope to accomplish much. Following is recommended.

– India's goal should be to collaborate with and complement global initiatives.
– India should aim to select areas to establish best-in-class global stature, take on an international leadership role in certain areas, while consciously leaving other nations to focus in other areas.

17 Funding and Control Options

Following funding and control options are proposed.

Option 1: A Public-Private consortium lead program, proportionately funded by the stakeholders should be evolved and implemented. Exclusive funding by the government is not recommended. However backing of such programs by the government would lead to easy adoption, visibility and scaling up to national level. Moreover security of cyber space is directly linked to national security, and therefore government can and should play a pivotal role.

Option 2: The program should be conceptualized, developed and funded by a consortium of software industry as a Venture Funding model. The initiative should be developed on a clearly defined business model, with winning strategy, well articulated goals, deliverables, time lines, stakeholders etc.

The government and institutional participation at home or those from overseas, guidance and assistance should be sought with clear commitments at both ends. Both, the government and the institutions would be open to such suggestions if approached with convincing business cases. The IPR and Innovation cell with in the consortium can coordinate inter-agency participation from government and academia. The NASSCOM should be involved in appropriate role.

18 Conclusions

The ICT is becoming synonymous with the survival and sustenance of human race in social, economic, political and military terms. Therefore ICT security has become very crucial and is recognized as a nightmare for the 21 century.

Software constitutes a very vital component of ICT but it is vulnerable to security attacks. Fool proof security would require revisiting the life cycle approach to develop secure and trustworthy software.

The secure software is emerging a demand of every customer. The size and scale of India's software industry is such that secure software capability can create steep outsourcing demand and price premium of 12 to 18% for India. India's differentiators are as follows:

1. Trustworthy Software development, as of now there are too many unknowns in terms of attributes viz. security, safety, reliability, performance and survivability to build. India is not geared to develop Trustworthy software capabilities.

2. India has well established ICT education and training system, matured over the past 30 years. It has over 80 SEI SW CMM level software companies. This capability makes it easier to blend and align security life cycle processes in consonance with ISO 21827 for security engineering, ISO 17799 for security management, ISO 15408 for security testing and assurance.
3. The training and certification facilities for Certified Information Systems Security Professionals (CIISP), Certified Information Systems Auditors (CISA), BS 7799 Auditors, Certified Business Continuity Professionals (CBCP), Certified Fraud Examiners (CFE), Health Insurance (HIPAA), CO-BIT, SEE-CMM etc. are available in the country.
4. Facilities for product training and certifications for Identity Management, Fire Walls, Intrusion Detection, Anti Virus, Anti Spam, Authentication, Cryptology, Public Key Infrastructure (PKI) etc. are available in the country.
5. Indian ICT companies are engaged in overseas projects involving New Generation Network (NGN) security and Security Framework for large enterprises.
6. India is becoming home to many R&D initiatives in ICT. Over 100 MNCs including IBM, Microsoft, Intel, Texas Instrument, Oracle, SAP, CA, SUN, GE, LG, SAMSUNG, NOKIA, MOTOROLA, Philips etc. have created their R&D facilities in India.
7. India created its regulatory framework for the cyber environment through promulgation of its IT Act 2000, which has been revised as late as 2005. It has established the national PKI infrastructure and Computer Emergency Response Team-India (CERT- I).

It therefore emerges that India is indeed in a unique position to collaborate with rest of the world, particularly the USA and Europe in development of Secure Software and support initiatives for "End to end" security in terms of technology, people and processes.

The development of "Trustworthy Software" would require considerable scientific research & engineering effort and building of competencies in software security, safety, performance, reliability and survivability. The understanding of safety, reliability, performance and survivability as applicable to software is still at a very early or nascent stage amongst academia and industry. India does not have critical mass to address these issues yet. These competencies when combined with expertise in Secure Software will only enable India to take the next logical step to develop expertise in Trustworthy Software. Thus the route to directly attempt development of Trustworthy Software is not suited for India.

19   Recommendations

Foster and facilitate a national initiative through fusion of core academic excellence, proactive role and participation of industry and committed sponsorship from government to build national capability in secure software development As the starting level in security specific areas is very low, evolve a thought out and researched strategy and roadmap.

Evolve a consortium approach with a limited participation to peruse a budgeted program under a, "Secure Software Foundation of India" (SSFI). The consortium should develop strategy, a blue print and road map, tie it up to time bound fully funded and ownership driven program.

Two funding options have been proposed.

Option 1: A Public-Private consortium lead program, proportionately funded by the stakeholders. No exclusive funding by the government is proposed. However backing by the government is necessary and would lead to easy adoption, visibility and scaling up to national level.

Option 2: The program be conceptualized, developed and funded by a consortium of software industry as a Venture Funding model. The initiative should be developed on a clearly defined business model, with defined strategy, goals, deliverables, time lines, stakeholders etc. NASSCOM should be drawn in with appropriate role. The proactive participation of government should be sought.

References

1. Report, "Processes to Produce Secure Software, Volume I", Home Land Security, USA, Task Force on Security Across the Software Development lifecycle, March 04.
2. Report, "Cyber Security for Home Land" US House of Representatives Select Committee on Home Land Security, Dec 2004.
3. Software 2015: A National Software Strategy to Ensure U.S. Security and Competitiveness www.cnsoftware.org/nss2report/NSS2FinalReport04-29-05PDF.pdf
4. Full Report: Security Across the Software Development Life Cycle. http://www.cyberpartnership.org/init-soft.html
5. Cyber Security: A Crisis of Prioritization, A report by the President's Information Technology Advisory Committee, February 2005. http://www.nitrd.gov/pitac/reports/20050301_cybersecurity/cybersecurity.pdf
6. Security and Dependability R&D for Europe, Overview of Security Task Force Initiatives, 2005.
7. Report, "Security and Application Development Process", Robert Frances Group.
8. Report, "The Trustworthy Computing Security Development Lifecycle", Steve Lipner & Michael Howard, Microsoft, Mar 05.
9. Report, "Microsoft's Security Development Lifecycle", May 05.
10. Report, "Russia Security Software Forecast and Analysis - 2002-07", Dec 03.
11. Report, "China - Shape of he Software Industry and Information Security Services (2005)".
12. IT Security and Operational Management Must Converge (G00124711) Nov 2004 - Nicolett, Girard.pdf
13. How to Develop an Effective Vulnerability Management Process (G00124126) Mar 2005 - Nicolett.pdf
14. Report, "Security and Survivability Resourcing Frameworks and Architectural Design Tactics", CMU / SEI - 2004 - TN022.

Auditable Anonymous Delegation

Bruce Christianson, Partha Das Chowdhury, and James Malcolm

Computer Science Department,
University of Hertfordshire, England
{P.Das-Chowdhury, B.Christianson, J.A.Malcolm}@herts.ac.uk

Abstract. The contribution of this paper is an alternative mechanism for delegation, whereby users can share their credentials in such a way that it is difficult for the delegatee to re-use credentials of the delegator. An auditor in our protocol can link actions to individuals from the audit records but cannot forge audit records. We do not greatly restrict the choice of the delegation model semantics which can be adopted. Although the primary aim of our protocol is to provide support for anonymous delegation, it is still useful even if anonymity is not required at all, because of the ability to weaken trust assumptions.

1 Introduction

There are several commercial web-sites where users can log in and watch movies by paying a monthly or yearly membership fee. Such a web-site will require a user to register with their credit/debit card number to become a member. The aim of registration is to produce an identification token that binds one of the user's conventional identities (credit card) to a bit pattern (login name) which uniquely identifies the user in the computer system [1]. So long as a member wishes to continue his/her subscription, his/her login name remains the same. Every time a member wishes to watch a movie they authenticate using the fixed login name and password.

However it is a legitimate real world requirement that adult members allow their children (below 18) to watch a movie using the credentials of their parents. We refer to the principal that delegates as the delegator, and the principal that acts using the credentials of the delegator is referred to as the delegatee. The problem in this scenario is that once a child has learnt the fixed login name and password of their parents he can re-use them at a later date without the explicit knowledge or consent of their parents. The risk is more when parents have anonymous credentials instead of conventional credentials; to share anonymous credentials such as those proposed in [2], [3], [4], [5] the owner also has to share their secret key. This is a major problem in such situations where delegation is a legitimate requirement.

The contribution of this paper is an alternative mechanism where users can share their credentials in such a way that it is difficult for the delegatee to re-use credentials of the delegator. Users in our protocol use different transient identities or surrogates for each different transaction in order to preserve their

S. Jajodia and C. Mazumdar (Eds.): ICISS 2005, LNCS 3803, pp. 66–76, 2005.

privacy, but a locally trusted auditor can uniquely and irrefutably link actions to individuals. In our protocol it is difficult for an adversary to masquerade as a legitimate user; in particular although the auditor can link actions to individuals, it cannot forge audit records. Our protocol also makes it difficult for a delegatee to further delegate the credentials of the delegator without the explicit knowledge and consent of the delegator.

Our protocol does not greatly restrict the choice of the semantics which can be adopted, although for exposition we adhere to Crispo's delegation model [6] in this paper. This delegation model considers threats posed by the delegator, thus addressing attacks involving repudiability of actions. The trust assumptions between the delegator and the delegatee are explicitly spelt out in the specification of the delegation mechanism. It is hard for the delegator to frame the delegatee or for the delegatee to frame the delegator. The principle of consent is also explicitly implemented; thus the delegator can delegate only with the explicit knowledge and consent of the delegatee.

The mechanism we propose in this paper is useful even if anonymity is not required at all, because of the ability which it gives us to systematically weaken trust assumptions [7], [8]. For example the merchant (from whom customers request services) does not need to trust the authentication mechanism of a third party such as the customer's bank. From the point of individual privacy users are no longer required to trust merchant web-sites with credentials linked to long term fixed identity using which an adversary can identify the user. The auditor in our protocol can link actions to individuals from the audit records but cannot forge audit records, so users do not need to have trust in the honesty (or competence) of the auditor. Thus our system shows a way which allows clients to control the risks to which they are exposed, by bearing the cost of relevant countermeasures themselves, rather than forcing clients to trust the system infrastructure (and bear an equal share of the cost of all countermeasures which may or may not be effective for them).

Although the example used to motivate and illustrate the protocol involves payment, what we present here is a delegation protocol, not a payment protocol. However our protocol can be integrated with a payment mechanism as shown in [9]. We start with a mechanism to generate keys and transient identities called surrogates in section 2 which is followed in section 3 by our design goals and assumptions. The protocol is presented in section 4 which is followed by an analysis of its properties in section 5. We briefly discuss related previous work in section 6 which is followed by our conclusions in section 7.

2   Generation of Keys and Surrogates

A detailed description of Diffie-Hellman (DH) key systems can be found in [10], here we give a brief description of generation of DH keys which is as follows: the user, Carol selects a generator $g \bmod P$ (*i.e.* calculating consecutive powers of g generates all the elements in the multiplicative group modulo P) and selects a secret $s_c \in Z_P^*$ (*i.e.* s_c is an element between 1 and $(P-1)$), where Z_P^* is a multiplicative group [11] modulo a large prime P. Carol constructs her public key X_c from the secret s_c as

$$X_c = g^{s_c} \bmod P \tag{1}$$

It is hard for an adversary to calculate s_c from X_c and P as this is the discrete logarithm problem [11], which is considered to be intractable. The user proves ownership of X_c by proving knowledge of s_c without revealing s_c. A surrogate K_i^+ and its corresponding private value K_i^- are generated from a seed $\tau_i \in 1\dots(P-1)$ by the following equations:

$$K_i^- = \tau_i * s_c \bmod (P-1) \tag{2}$$
$$K_i^+ = X_c^{\tau_i} \bmod P \tag{3}$$

The important point to note is that, because

$$g^{P-1} \bmod P = 1 \tag{4}$$

we have

$$g^{\tau_i * s_c} = g^{K_i^-} \bmod P \tag{5}$$

and hence

$$K_i^+ = X_c^{\tau_i} = (g^{s_c})^{\tau_i} = g^{K_i^-} \bmod P \tag{6}$$

The initial value τ_0 of the seed and the long term values A and L are supplied by a (partially) trusted third party [12] such as the user's bank, and are secrets shared between the user and the partially trusted third party. The subsequent values (τ_i) of the seed, used to generate the surrogates and their corresponding private values, are generated using the linear congruence equation,

$$\tau_i = (A * \tau_{i-1} + L) \bmod P - 1 \tag{7}$$

Then, using τ_i, surrogate K_i^+ and the corresponding private value K_i^- for the ith transaction are generated from equations 3 and 2 respectively.

To use a surrogate K_i^+ for transaction i, Carol proves knowledge of the corresponding K_i^-. A potential signing mechanism that can be used to prove knowledge of K_i^- is explained in [7]. Only the legitimate owner of X_c and s_c can generate and use surrogates corresponding to X_c. Neither an adversary nor the partially trusted third party can masquerade as the legitimate owner of X_c, as the corresponding s_c is secret to the owner. But a partially trusted third party which knows the seed τ_i can resolve disputes, and can correlate transactions conducted with surrogates generated from X_c using equations 7 and 3, thus facilitating auditing. However various transactions conducted by the same user cannot be correlated with each other by an adversary at the point of use of the surrogates. Learning one set of K_i^+, K_i^- values does not help the attacker in any way, neither can the attacker generate the current K_i^+, K_i^- values, nor can the attacker generate future surrogates or their corresponding private values. With τ_i, A and L values, the adversary might be able to correlate various surrogates belonging to a particular user but cannot masquerade as the user.

3   Design Goals and Assumptions

Carol registers her public key with a bank and the bank sends Carol the information she uses to generate her surrogates. The bank acts as the partially trusted third party here in this protocol. The bank sends to the merchant web-site the surrogates Carol will be using to watch movies. Surrogates of various different customers are sent together in a batch. Carol does not need to go back to the bank before every different transaction. The merchant web-site performs eligibility authentication *i.e.* whether or not Carol is allowed to watch particular movies, but not authentication of the user's identity. Only the bank can link a surrogate back to the owner of the surrogate. In the real world the bank must apply appropriate technical and organisational security measures, and divulge the link only in circumstances specified under legal authority, such as contract, legislation, search warrant or court order. For each different transaction Carol uses a different surrogate. She can also lend her son Bob a surrogate to watch a movie but only lends a surrogate to Bob and not the secret corresponding to the surrogate. The delegation protocol which we describe ensures that Bob cannot re-use the surrogate nor can he lend the surrogate to somebody else.

3.1   Design Goals

The requirements can be summarised as:

1. Auditability and Accountability in Delegation – An unbiased auditor should be able to link actions to individuals with the explicit knowledge and consent of the legitimate owner of the surrogate. It should be difficult for Carol to frame Bob or for Bob to frame Carol. Although auditors can link actions to individuals, they should not be able to forge audit records.
2. Protection from (partially) Trusted Third Party – No adversary should be able to pretend to be a legitimate owner of a surrogate. Although a third party (the bank here) generates and issues the information users need to generate and use their surrogates, the third party should not be able to masquerade as the legitimate owner of a surrogate belonging to a different user.
3. Theft/Re-use of Surrogates – Even if Bob is malicious and retains the surrogate he receives from Carol, it should still be hard for him to generate and use future surrogates. It should also be difficult for Bob to further delegate a surrogate without the explicit knowledge and consent of Carol.
4. Un-correlatability – It should be hard for an adversary to link actions to individuals retrospectively even if the adversary manages to obtain the surrogate used for the transaction along with the transaction details. Someone observing the network should not be able to gain any additional information about the nature of communication and the communicating parties more than its *a priori* belief.

3.2   Assumptions

For our protocol we assume that principals have a public key generated from a secret key using the conventional Diffie-Hellman mechanism as described in section 2. The association between a principal and its public key is known by a partially trusted third party (*e.g.* the bank) and can be implemented using some offline certification authority. Entities can verify the association between principals and their keys by fetching certificates and this verification is done with the explicit knowledge and consent of the principal. Ownership of surrogates are verified and established by proving knowledge of the corresponding private value using the signing mechanism discussed in [7].

Our protocol depend on certain properties about the underlying communication channels above which they operate. Since we use our protocols for secure web access, and for remote access to distributed objects and as our protocols also can potentially be used for commercial purposes, we choose to use Mixminion [13], a secure anonymous communication channel. Mixminion uses TLS over TCP for link encryption between remailers and uses ephemeral keys to ensure forward anonymity for each message. Mixminion also supports replies which cannot be correlated with the initial message, enabling two way communication between the communicating partners.

We also assume the existence of a secure authenticated communication channel such as SSL/TLS. SSL/TLS allows for two-way authentication, preserves data integrity and confidentiality and is widely used. SSL/TLS can also be used for the scenarios we describe here in this dissertation for *e.g.* remote web access, secure submission of personal information *etc.*

To counter various attacks based on the poor choice of the prime number P as discussed in [11] for our protocols we choose a cyclic group for which computing the order is thought to be very difficult. If $(P - 1)$ has small prime factors then computing discrete logarithm is easy [14]. For our protocols P is chosen such that $(P - 1)$ has one large prime factor. This can be done by choosing a large prime Q and selecting P as the smallest prime congruent to 1 mod Q or by choosing P of the form $2Q + 1$ where P and Q are both prime [15].

4   The Protocol

4.1   Summary of Notations

- P denotes as a large prime with the properties mentioned in section 3.2. g is a generator modulo P. P is public and so is g.
- X_c represents the Diffie-Hellman public key of Carol. s_c represents the corresponding secret key of Carol. X_b represents the Diffie-Hellman public key of Bob. s_b represents the corresponding secret key of Bob.
- K_i^+ represents the surrogate used for the ith transaction. K_i^- represents the private value corresponding to the surrogate K_i^+.
- τ_i denotes the seed used to generate surrogates and is calculated using the linear congruence equation 7.

- A and L are the parameters used in the linear congruence equation (see equation 7) and are global and fixed.
- $\longrightarrow_s$ stands for a secure authenticated communication channel with properties similar to SSL/TLS throughout this dissertation. $\longrightarrow_m$ stands for an anonymous communication channel with properties similar to Mixminion throughout this dissertation.
- Items within $\prec, \succ$ separated by commas denote individual elements of a shuffled message being transmitted and the braces denote the beginning and end of message respectively. The elements of a shuffled message are actually sent in a random order not in the order in which they appear in the braces.

4.2   Message Exchanges

Carol generates her public key X_c using equation 1 from her secret s_c and similarly Bob generates his public key X_b as:

$$X_b = g^{s_b} \bmod P \tag{8}$$

where Bob's secret key is s_b.

Carol registers with the bank using her public key and the bank sends her the information she needs to generate her surrogates.

1. $Carol \longrightarrow_s bank : X_c$

2. $bank \longrightarrow_s Carol : \prec \tau_0, L, A \succ$

On receipt of Carol's public key the bank selects $\tau_0, L \in Z_P^*$ as described in section 2. So that Carol does not need to contact the bank before every single transaction, the bank sends Carol the information she will need to prepare m surrogate pairs using the equations 7, 2 and 3.

Carol uses her surrogates serially from $1...m$.

For each member, the bank sends the merchant m surrogates by repeating equations 7 and 3 for each of the next m values of i. Surrogates of various different customers are sent together in a batch as,

3. $bank \longrightarrow_s merchant : \prec K^+_{c(i...m)}...K^+_{f(i...m)} \succ$

where $K^+_{c(i...m)}$ denotes surrogates belonging to Carol and $K^+_{f(i...m)}$ denotes surrogates belonging to some other customer. In the rest of the paper we refer to Carol's i^{th} surrogate as K^+_i and the corresponding secret as K^-_i.

For the ith transaction Carol generates the exponent τ_i, the secret corresponding to the ith surrogate K^-_i and her i^{th} surrogate K^+_i using equations 7, 2 and 3 respectively. Carol selects a random value $r \in Z_P$ and blinds Bob's public key as

$$(X_b)^r = (g^{s_b})^r \bmod P \tag{9}$$

Carol signs $M = (X_b)^r$ using K_i^- using El Gamal signature scheme and produces the signature (a, b) of M as:

$$a = g^k \bmod P \tag{10}$$

$$b = (M - K_i^- * a) * (k)^{-1} \bmod (P - 1) \tag{11}$$

where $k \in Z_{(P-1)}$ is secret and known only to Carol. Carol sends to Bob via a secure anonymous channel the following:

4. *Carol* $\longrightarrow_m$ *Bob* : r, K_i^+, a, b

Bob generates M by repeating equation 9 with the r he receives from Carol and verifies that M is being signed by someone who knows the secret corresponding to K_i^+ by verifying the following equation:

$$g^M = (K_i^+)^a * a^b \bmod P \tag{12}$$

and thus Bob can also be sure that Carol has signed his blinded public key and not something else.

Bob generates his secret corresponding to his blinded public key as:

$$s_b' = s_b * r \bmod (P - 1) \tag{13}$$

and generates the El Gamal signature a', b' of transaction description T using s_b' as:

$$a' = g^{k'} \bmod P \tag{14}$$

$$b' = (T - s_b' * a') * (k')^{-1} \bmod (P - 1) \tag{15}$$

where $k' \in Z_{(P-1)}$ is a secret only known to Bob. Bob sends the merchant via a secure anonymous communication channel

5. *Bob* $\longrightarrow_m$ *Merchant*: $M, a, b, K_i^+, T, a', b'$

where M is Bob's blinded public key.

The merchant has access to the list of surrogates the bank had sent in step 3. This can be thought of as similar to a revocation list proposed in public key infrastructures. Thus it is difficult for an someone who is not a customer of the bank to forge a transaction with random Diffie-Hellman public keys. The merchant verifies that M is being signed someone who knows the secret corresponding to K_i^+ by repeating equation 12 and Bob knows the secret corresponding to M which is the blinded public key of Bob by doing the following.

$$g^T = (M)^{a'} * a'^{b'} \bmod P \tag{16}$$

Only when Bob proves knowledge of the secret s_b corresponding to M does the merchant accept the fact that Bob has been authorised to use K_i^+ by the legitimate owner of K_i^+.

5 Analysis

1. Auditability and Accountability in Delegation – The bank can generate the surrogates using equations 7 and 3 and in cases of dispute involving a surrogate the bank can determine the owner of a surrogate; thus an auditor with appropriate authority can uniquely and irrefutably link actions to principals. Although Carol can decide who can use the surrogate, she herself cannot use the surrogate she has delegated and pretend that it was actually used by the delegatee, as s_b is secret.

   If K_i^+ is not delegated then Carol will use it by signing T with K_i^-. It is in Carol's interest to delegate by signing the blinded public key of Bob else Bob can frame Carol or further delegate Carol's surrogate. If a signed blinded public key can be verified using K_i^+ by using equation 12 then an auditor can be sure that Carol signed it as K_i^- is only known to Carol. Carol cannot masquerade as Bob since s_b is secret and known only to Bob. Bob also cannot masquerade as Carol as K_i^- is secret and known only to Carol. Thus it is difficult for Carol to frame Bob or for Bob to frame Carol. Although an auditor can link actions to principals still it cannot forge audit records as it cannot generate Carol's or Bob's signature in steps 4 or 5 respectively. In the protocol described in this paper, identity resolution is local; neither the bank nor the merchant need to know Bob's identity. There can also be two different auditors, one who links the surrogate back to Carol while the other can prove that it was Bob who used it. This is significant because all trust is now local and Bob does not need to trust the bank or the merchant with personal information in order to use the service of the merchant. This has implications in the design of role based authorisation systems: using mechanisms like ours users can activate roles across domains without revealing personal information and auditors can still link actions back to the original user. An external auditor can link actions back to originating domain but linking the individual user requires the co-operation of an auditor trusted locally. Thus users have control over their personal information without compromising the goals of audit and authorisation.

2. Protection from (partially) Trusted Third Party – The (partially) trusted third party cannot masquerade as the legitimate owner of X_c as the corresponding s_c is secret. Calculating s_c requires an adversary to solve the equation

$$\log_g X_c = s_c \bmod P \qquad (17)$$

   which is thought to be hard. Moreover even if the value of some exponent τ_i is known, still without the knowledge of s_c it is hard to generate the secret K_i^- corresponding to a surrogate K_i^+ using equation 2. Thus the bank cannot masquerade as Carol to Bob.

3. Theft/Re-use of Surrogates – An adversary stealing the numbers in step 4 cannot masquerade as Bob as he/she cannot generate a', b' without s_b' which is secret. Moreover Carol can specify who can use the surrogate, because to

further delegate Bob would have to share his secret s_b. Thus Bob cannot share Carol's surrogate with his friend without Carol's consent nor can an adversary masquerade as Bob. Even if Bob could steal the values the bank sends to Carol in step 2, still he cannot generate or use future surrogates from K_i^+ as s_c is secret and known only to Carol.

4. Un-correlatability – Different transactions initiated by a particular principal cannot be linked to each other or back to the initiator of the transaction without the explicit consent of the legitimate owner of the surrogate. Linking K_i^+ to K_{i+1}^+ and back to X_c would require an adversary to solve the equation

$$\log_{X_c} K_i^+ = \tau_i \bmod P \tag{18}$$

and calculate τ_{i+1} from τ_i using the values A and L, as shown in equation 7. The values A and L are shared between Carol and the bank. It is difficult for someone other than the bank to calculate τ_i by solving equation 18 is thought to be an intractable problem. If an adversary cannot calculate τ_i then it cannot calculate τ_{i+1} using equation 7 and the surrogate using equation 3. Thus it is difficult for an adversary to link surrogates to each other or to the parent public key. An auditor can only link surrogates back to the parent public key with the explicit knowledge and consent of the legitimate owner of the surrogates.

6   Relation to Other Work

Idemix is an anonymous credential management system and a detailed description of idemix can be found in [4]. In idemix a user first registers his/her own pseudonym with a global pseudonym authority (PA) which issues a credential stating that the pseudonym is valid. The user then can use the pseudonym to get a reference for a credit card payment from a different organisation. The organisation issuing payment tokens trusts the PA. A user can then use the payment tokens with other organisations. The user, PA and other organisations have to be part of the idemix system: idemix issues IP addresses as well as SSL certificates to each of them. It is difficult in idemix for users to auditably transfer their credentials and idemix relies upon the existence of a global pseudonym authority which everyone needs to trust.

Another scheme for tying attributes to pseudonyms was proposed in [16]. A user contacts a registrar with a proof of his/her identity. The registrar is not a single entity but a group of principals and the user must contact a threshold number of them. The registrar then contacts an issuer who issues a globally unique pseudonym to the user and binds the pseudonym with the public key for signature and encryption using a credential which is called a GUP certificate. Issuers like registrars are threshold entities. Only the owners of pseudonyms can use their pseudonyms and delegation of pseudonyms requires users to share their secret keys.

Traditionally correlation of transaction records and identity theft has been the primary concern for the designers of anonymity systems [4], [5], [16]. Such systems do not allow principals to share their credentials, which has the effect of preventing principals from delegating their credentials. However it is often a legitimate real world requirement that users are able to delegate their credentials in an auditable manner. We believe our system satisfies the requirements of auditable delegation along with anonymity.

Trust relationships in our system are local; users only reveal their permanent credentials to local entities (unlike Global Pseudonym authorities) *e.g.* their own bank. Moreover all identity resolution in our system is also local. An external auditor can only link surrogates to users with the help of a locally trusted authority *e.g.* the bank, and the local authority would divulge the link only in circumstances specified under legal authority. Thus in our system entities are not compelled to transitively trust the external entities which form part of a system in order to preserve their privacy or for auditing purposes.

Moreover building a global pseudonym authority is as difficult [17] as building a global public key authority and both in any case are developments yet to come to fruition. The problem with the more usual global trust relationship is that users have no control of the risks they are exposed to and entities are compelled to transitively trust [12] external entities (Certificate Authorities, Pseudonym Authorities, Registration Authorities) to preserve their privacy as well as for auditing purposes.

7   Conclusions

The ability to delegate is a significant improvement over previous approaches because delegation is useful [6]. Because the designers of anonymity systems [4], [16] have mostly been concerned to prevent correlation of transaction records and identity theft, such systems do not allow principals to share their credentials. Using the approach we describe in this paper, a user can delegate a surrogate without the delegatee being able to figure out the secret used to generate the surrogate or re-use the surrogates of the delegator.

The approach we present here allows users to control the risks to which they are exposed to rather than forcing users to enter into an unnecessary trust relationship with the system infrastructure. Merchants do not have to trust the authentication mechanism of a third party, and users do not need to trust merchants with personal sensitive information. Although they can link actions to principals it is difficult for auditors to forge audit records. It is difficult for the delegatee to frame the delegator or for the delegator to frame the delegatee.

References

1. Bruce Christianson and J. A. Malcolm. Binding Bit Patterns To Real World Entities. *Proceedings of the* 5th *International Workshop on Security Protocols Lecture Notes in Computer Science Series*, 1361:105–113, 1998.
2. David Chaum. Security Without Identification: Transaction Systems To Make Big Brother Obsolete. *Communications of the ACM*, 28(10):1030–1044, 1985.

3. Anna Lysyanskaya, Ronald Rivest, Amit Sahai, and Stefan Wolf. Pseudonym Systems. *Proceedings of the* 6th *Annual International Workshop on Selected Areas in Cryptography: Lecture Notes in Computer Science*, 1758:184–199, 1999.

4. Jan Camenisch and Els Van Herreweghen. Design And Implementation Of The *idemix* Anonymous Credential System. *Proceedings of the* 9th *ACM conference on Computer and Communications Security*, pages 21–30, 2002.

5. Paul Syverson and David Goldshlag. Unlinkable Serial Transactions: Protocols And Applications. *ACM Transactions on Information and Systems Security*, 2(4):354–389, 2000.

6. B. Crispo. *Delegation of Responsibility*. PhD thesis, University of Cambridge, 1999.

7. Partha Das Chowdhury, Bruce Christianson, and J.A. Malcolm. Anonymous Authentication. *To Appear in the Proceedings of the* 12th *International Workshop on Security Protocols Lecture Notes in Computer Science Series*, 2004.

8. Partha Das Chowdhury, Bruce Christianson, and J.A. Malcolm. Anonymous Context Based Role Activation Mechanism. *To appear in the Proceedings of the* 13th *International Workshop on Security Protocols: Lecture Notes in Computer Science*, 2005.

9. Partha Das Chowdhury. *Anonymity and Trust In The Electronic World*. PhD thesis, University of Hertfordshire, 2005.

10. W. Diffie and M. Hellman. New Directions In Cryptography. *IEEE Transactions on Information Theory*, 22:472–492, 1976.

11. Carl Pomerance. *Cryptology And Computational Number Theory: Proceedings of the Symposia on Applied Mathematics*, volume 42. American Mathematical Society, 1989.

12. Bruce Christianson and William Harbison. Why Isn't Trust Transitive. *Proceedings of the* 3rd *International Workshop on Security Protocols: Lecture Notes in Computer Science Series*, 1189:171–176, 1996.

13. George Danezis, Roger Dingledine, and Nick Mathewson. Mixminion: Design Of A type III Anonymous Remailer. *Proceedings of the* 24th *IEEE Symposium on Security and Privacy*, pages 2–15, 2003.

14. S. Pohlig and M. Hellman. An Improved Algorithm For Computing Logarithms And Its Cryptographic Significance. *IEEE Transactions on Information Theory*, 24:106–110, 1978.

15. Bruce Christianson, Michael Roe, and David Wheeler. Secure Sessions From Weak Secrets. *Proceedings of the* 11th *International Workshop on Security Protocols Lecture Notes in Computer Science Series*, 3364:190–212, 2003.

16. Paul F. Syverson and Stuart Stubblebine. Authentic Attributes With Fine Grained Anonymity Protection. *Proceedings of the* 4th *Annual Conference on Financial Cryptography: Lecture Notes in Computer Science*, 1962:276–294, 2000.

17. Carl Ellison and Bruce Schneier. Ten Risks of PKI: What You Are Not Being Told About Public Key Infrastructure. *Computer Security Journal*, 16(1):1–7, 2000.

A Robust Double Auction Protocol Based on a Hybrid Trust Model

JungHoon Ha[1], Jianying Zhou[2], and SangJae Moon[1]

[1] School of Electrical Eng. & Computer Science,
Kyungpook National University, Daegu, Korea
short98@ee.knu.ac.kr, sjmoon@knu.ac.kr
[2] Institute for Infocomm Research (I2R),
21 Heng Mui Keng Terrace, Singapore 119613
jyzhou@i2r.a-star.edu.sg

Abstract. Recently, Wang and Leung proposed a set of double auction protocols with full privacy protection based on distributed ElGamal encryption. Unfortunately, their protocols are expensive in computation and are not robust in dealing with system malfunction or user misbehavior. In this paper, we propose a secure and practical double auction protocol based on a hybrid trust model, where computation load is distributed to buyers and sellers while a semi-trusted manager handles the registration phase. A prominent feature of the proposed protocol is its high robustness, achieved by using a publicly verifiable secret sharing scheme with threshold access structure.

1 Introduction

Currently, many auction services exist on the Internet that satisfies a variety of requirements. Auction protocols can be classified into two types, namely *one-sided auction protocols* in which a single seller (or buyer) accepts bids from multiple buyers (or seller), and two-sided or *double auction protocols* in which multiple buyers and sellers are permitted to bid/ask [1] for designated goods [7]. For one-sided auctions, such as English auction, Vickrey auction and sealed-bid auction, there have been many papers in the literature considering various security properties [11, 14]. However, not much research has been done regarding the security issues in double auctions.

Recently, Wang and Leung proposed a set of double auction protocols with full privacy protection [15], in which trust and computation are distributed among sellers and buyers themselves. Although their protocols possess good security properties, they are expensive in computation and weak in robustness. Specifically, to identify the winning buyers and sellers in an auction after the determination of the trading price, all participating buyers and sellers are required to perform a distributed ElGamal decryption. The auction process fails even if

---

[1] We use the term *bid* for a buyer's declaration of value, and *ask* for a seller's declaration of value.

S. Jajodia and C. Mazumdar (Eds.): ICISS 2005, LNCS 3803, pp. 77–90, 2005.

only one seller or buyer does not contribute to the distributed decryption. This requirement is apparently too strong and therefore impractical - lost or failed buyers and sellers may refuse to corporate or drop out from the auction session early; even if all buyers and sellers are willing to perform the distributed decryption, they may be cut off from the auction session due to system or network malfunctions.

In this paper, we propose a secure, efficient and highly robust double auction protocol. The high robustness of the protocol is realized by using a publicly verifiable secret sharing scheme with threshold access structure. In our protocol, computation related to the determination of winning traders is distributed to all the buyers and sellers; however, participation of a subset of buyers and sellers is sufficient for an auction session to be successfully completed. In addition, to meet most of the properties for a secure double auction, we employ a *semi-trusted* manager which is only trusted not to disclose the pseudonyms of participants until the winner announcement stage.

The rest of this paper is structured as follows. Section 2 specifies the requirements for secure double auctions and introduces our assumptions. Section 3 reviews the necessary cryptographic primitives, and Section 4 presents our secure and practical double auction protocol. We analyze security and efficiency of our protocol in Section 5. Finally, Section 6 contains our conclusions.

2   Requirements and Assumptions

2.1   Requirements for Secure Double Auction

Security requirements for secure double auctions are similar to these for one-sided auctions. The following properties that are desirable in secure electronic auction systems have been identified in the literature [2].

- **Anonymity.** During the auction process, identities of participants remain confidential except winners identification or user misbehavior.
- **Impossibility of Impersonation.** No one can impersonate any other traders.
- **Robustness and Correctness.** Malicious behavior of any party should not collapse the system or lead to an incorrect result. That is, if some party acts honestly, the correct trading price and winners will be identified according to auction rules.
- **Non-repudiation.** All participants including the winning and lost buyers/sellers cannot deny that they have submitted bids/asks.
- **Public Verifiability.** Everybody can verify the validity of asks/bids and can confirm whether asks/bids are submitted from valid participants or not.

2.2   Assumptions and Model

In most of the previous secure auction protocols, trust models can be classified into three types. In the *threshold trust model*, there are m auctioneers, out of which a fraction are assumed to be trustworthy [8]. The *third-party trust model* assumes a third party who is not fully trusted but does not collude with other parties including auctioneers [3]. The *buyer/seller self-resolving model* distributes trust to all the buyers/sellers [1]. These models might be selected based on the security requirements and the application environments. However, any of these trust models alone cannot achieve most of the properties for secure double auction.

In our proposed double auction protocol, we employ a hybrid model with the relevant assumptions. First, we distribute both trust and computation for the determination of winners and trading price to buyers and sellers themselves. With a publicly verifiable secret sharing scheme based on a threshold access structure, the proposed auction protocol works well even if some buyers or sellers do not fully corporate in an auction process due to an unstable network or malicious behaviors, so that it can achieve flexibility and robustness. Second, we make use of a semi-trusted manager, in which the manager is assumed not to release the pseudonyms of participants except at the winner announcement stage or because of user misbehavior. The manager may impersonate a valid trader and illegally attend an auction using an auction ticket of other participants. However, the manager's action can be monitored by buyers and sellers, thus his misbehavior can be detected.

3   Cryptographic Primitives

3.1   Signature of Knowledge

We use the signature of knowledge introduced by B. Lee *et al.* [9] as anonymous signature, in which they extended the signature of knowledge discrete logarithm introduced by Camenisch and Stadler [5].

That is, it can be used as an anonymous signature if (y^r, g^r) are challenged for a secret random number $r \in \mathbb{Z}_q$ instead of (y, g) of Camenisch and Stadler' scheme. The signer computes (c, s) satisfying $c \stackrel{?}{=} h(m\|y^r\|g^r\|(g^r)^s(y^r)^c)$ for challenged (y^r, g^r). We denote this signature as

$$V = SK[x : y^r = (g^r)^x](m),$$

where SK represents both the proof of knowledge of the private key x and a signature on message m. Readers are refereed to [9] for the technical details.

3.2   PVSS Scheme

The proposed protocol requires a publicly verifiable secret sharing (PVSS) scheme rather than a verifiable secret sharing (VSS) scheme [4]. In a VSS scheme, the objective is to resist malicious players such as

- a dealer sending incorrect shares to some or all of the participants, and
- participants submitting incorrect shares during the reconstruction phase.

In a PVSS scheme, however, it is an explicit goal that not just the participants can verify their own shares, but that anybody can verify that the participants received correct shares [13]. To allow for public verifiability in double auction, we employ Schoenmakers' PVSS [12] which is much simpler than other schemes [6, 13]. Readers are refereed to [12] for technical details.

3.3 McAfee's Protocol

Our proposed double auction protocol is based on McAfee's PMD protocol [10]. Let declared buyers' evaluations (*bids*) be $b_1, \ldots, b_m$ and declared sellers' evaluations (*asks*) be $s_1, \ldots, s_n$, where

$$b_{(1)} \geq b_{(2)} \geq \ldots \geq b_{(m)} \quad \text{and} \quad s_{(1)} \leq s_{(2)} < \ldots \leq s_{(n)}$$

Please note the different orderings for buyers' and sellers' evaluations. We use the notation (i) for the i-th highest evaluation value of buyers and the i-th lowest evaluation value of sellers. Choose k so that $b_{(k)} \geq s_{(k)}$ and $b_{(k+1)} < s_{(k+1)}$ hold. Since for (1) to (k), the evaluation value of the buyers is larger than that of the sellers, at most k trades are possible. The candidate of a trading price p_t is defined as

$$p_t = \frac{1}{2}(b_{(k+1)} + s_{(k+1)})$$

The PMD protocol works as follows,

1. If $s_{(k)} \leq p_t \leq b_{(k)}$ holds : the buyers/sellers from (1) to (k) trade at price p_t.
2. If $p_t > b_{(k)}$ or $p_t < s_{(k)}$ holds : the buyers/sellers from (1) to $(k-1)$ trade. Each buyer pays $b_{(k)}$, and each seller gets $s_{(k)}$.

If the second condition holds, since the price for buyers $b_{(k)}$ is larger than the price for sellers $s_{(k)}$, the amount $(k-1) \cdot (b_{(k)} - s_{(k)})$ is left over. It is usually assumed that the auctioneer receives this amount. In our protocol, the manager receives this amount.

This protocol is proven to be dominant-strategy incentive compatible if there exists no false-name bid. Since our double auction protocol prevents malicious buyers/sellers from submitting false bids/asks by non-repudiation and removes them before the determination of the trading price and winners, our protocol is obviously dominant-strategy incentive compatible.

4   Proposed Double Auction Protocol

The double auction process, to be presented below, consists of the following four phases: *system set-up, registration, bid/ask submission,* and *bid/ask opening*.

4.1   Notation

B_i	:	identity of i-th buyer ($i = 0, 1, .., m-1$)
S_j	:	identity of j-th seller ($j = 0, 1, .., n-1$)
T_{B_i}, T_{S_j}	:	an auction ticket for B_i and S_j, respectively
$Cert_A$	:	certificate of A issued by CA (Certification Authority)
$Sig_A(m)$	:	digital signature of message m generated by entity A
$(m_1 \| \cdots \| m_n)$	:	concatenation of n (binary) strings
$H(m_1 \| \cdots \| m_n)$	:	one-way hash function with input strings $m_1, ..., m_n$

4.2   System Set-Up

The entities involved in the proposed double auction protocol include a manager M, m buyers B_i for $i \in \mathbb{Z}_m$ and n sellers S_j for $j \in \mathbb{Z}_n$. The role of each entity is as follows:

Manager M

- is in charge of the registration of buyers/sellers and provides each participant with an auction ticket as pseudonym.
- publishes the signature scheme, the public key for verification of signature and the certificates.
- announces the offer valuation range.
    - let $L = \{l_1, \ldots, l_w\}$ be a set of w possible discrete bidding/asking prices.
- releases G_q which has a group of prime order q.
    - let g denote the selected generator of G_q.
- on behalf of participants, verifies the proofs of buyers and sellers in reconstruction step of bids/asks, and then determines the trading price and winners according to the auction rules.
- publishes the original identity of participants at the winner announcement step or because of user misbehavior.

Buyer B_i

- registers with the manager and receives an auction ticket T_{B_i}.
- submits a bid in the submission phase and, in the ask opening phase, decrypts the encrypted shares that a seller S_j has submitted.

Seller S_j

- registers with the manager and receives an auction ticket T_{S_j}.
- submits an ask in the submission phase and, in the bid opening phase, decrypts the encrypted shares that a buyer B_i has submitted.

In the proposed protocol, 4 bulletin boards are used, i.e., a registration bulletin board, a submission bulletin board, an opening bulletin board, and a winner announcement bulletin board. A bulletin board is a public communication channel which can be read by anybody but only be written by the legitimate party in an authentic way [9].

4.3   Registration Phase

All buyers B_i and sellers S_j register with the manager M as follows:

1. Suppose that every buyer B_i has private key x_i and the corresponding public key $y_i = g^{x_i}$ certified by CA, where $x \in_R \mathbb{Z}_q$, $i = 0, 1, .., m-1$ and B_i is the identity information of the buyer(e.g., ID card number).
2. B_i chooses a random number r_i and $k_i \in \mathbb{Z}_q$ and keeps them confidential.
3. B_i computes $c_i = H(m_i\|y_i^{r_i}\|g^{r_i}\|g^{k_i})$ and $s_i = r_i^{-1} \cdot k_i - c_i \cdot x_i$, where $m_i = (B_i\|Cert_{B_i}\|Buyer)$ and $Buyer$ indicates that he wants to buy goods.
4. B_i sends $(m_i, c_i, s_i, y_i^{r_i}, g^{r_i})$ to M secretely.
5. The manager checks $c_i \overset{?}{=} H(m_i\|y_i^{r_i}\|g^{r_i}\|(g^{r_i})^{s_i} \cdot (y_i^{r_i})^{c_i})$.
6. After verifying the correctness of (c_i, s_i) and authenticating the buyer, the manager computes $h_i = H(y_i^{r_i})$ and $v_i = Sig_M(y_i^{r_i}\|h_i)$, generates an auction ticket $T_{B_i} = (y_i^{r_i}\|h_i\|v_i)$ and shuffles it on the registration bulletin board.

After the above registration, each buyer B_i can easily confirm whether his auction ticket is on that bulletin board or not. Because the auction ticket T_{B_i} can be recognized only by the buyer who knows the relevant y_i and r_i for T_{B_i}, it could be used as a pseudonym for anonymity.

Similarly, seller S_j registers with the manager M and obtains her auction ticket $T_{S_j} = (\tilde{y}_j^{\tilde{r}_j}\|\tilde{h}_j\|\tilde{v}_j)$ [2] from the registration bulletin board.

4.4   Bid/Ask-Submission Phase

Every buyer and seller first determines their own evaluation for an item traded by auction. Note that the proposed double auction protocol assumes w possible discrete bidding/asking price steps. First consider the submission from a buyer B_i. Each buyer B_i chooses an evaluation $l_e \in L$, $e = 1, \ldots, w$ and selects a random polynomial $p_i(x)$ such that

$$p_i(x) = \prod_{k=0}^{t-1} \alpha_k x^k = \alpha_{t-1}x^{t-1} + \ldots + \alpha_0,$$

where $\alpha_0 = l_e$ and $t \leq n$, n is the total number of sellers participating in the auction. The buyer B_i keeps this polynomial secret. Each buyer then computes shares $p_i(k+1)$ for $0 \leq k \leq n-1$ and encrypts them using the auction ticket of the seller, i.e., using the anonymous public key $\tilde{y}_j^{\tilde{r}_j}$ included in the auction ticket T_{S_j} on the registration bulletin board. Then, the buyer B_i signs the encrypted shares including the pseudonym of sellers as follows:

---

[2] To avoid the notation confusion between buyers and sellers, we just use the tilde symbol on some parameters related to sellers.

$$V_{B_i} = SK[x_i : y_i^{r_i} = (g^{r_i})^{x_i}](m_i),$$

$$m_i = ((T_{S_0}, (\tilde{y}_0^{\tilde{r}_0})^{p_i(1)}) \| \cdots \| (T_{S_{n-1}}, (\tilde{y}_{n-1}^{\tilde{r}_{n-1}})^{p_i(n)})),$$

and sends the signed message [3] to the submission bulletin board.

In a similar way, each seller S_j chooses the polynomial, computes shares and signs the message including both the encrypted shares and the auction tickets of buyers. Table 1 indicates the information published on the submission bulletin board after the bid/ask submission phase is finished [4].

Table 1. Submission bulletin board

Buyers		Sellers	
T_{B_1}	V_{B_1}	T_{S_1}	V_{S_1}
$\vdots$	$\vdots$	$\vdots$	$\vdots$
$T_{B_{m-1}}$	$V_{B_{m-1}}$	T_{S_n}	V_{S_n}
T_{B_m}	V_{B_m}	$-$	$-$

4.5 Bid/Ask-Opening Phase

The bid/ask opening phase consists of the following four steps: decryption of encrypted shares, reconstruction of bid/ask, determination of the trading price, and winner announcement.

Decryption of Encrypted Shares. Each participant first verifies the correctness of auction tickets related to the entities who have sent the messages. To have a clear understanding, we consider a simple example. Assume some buyers B_0, B_1 and B_2 encrypted their shares $p_0(1), p_1(1)$ and $p_2(1)$ using an auction ticket T_{S_0} in the bid submission phase, and then they submitted the encrypted shares to the submission bulletin board. For decryption of encrypted shares, the seller S_0 first confirms whether her auction ticket exists in the messages that the buyers submitted to the submission bulletin board. After checking the integrity of her own auction ticket, she verifies the correctness of the auction tickets T_{B_0}, T_{B_1} and T_{B_2} corresponding to the buyers B_0, B_1 and B_2, respectively. If the verification is correct, she decrypts the encrypted shares $(\tilde{y}_0^{\tilde{r}_0})^{p_0(1)}, (\tilde{y}_0^{\tilde{r}_0})^{p_1(1)}$ and $(\tilde{y}_0^{\tilde{r}_0})^{p_2(1)}$ using her secret keys $\tilde{x}_0$ and $\tilde{r}_0$ as follows:

$$((\tilde{y}_0^{\tilde{r}_0})^{p_0(1)})^{1/\tilde{x}_0 \cdot \tilde{r}_0} = ((g^{\tilde{x}_0 \cdot \tilde{r}_0})^{p_0(1)})^{1/\tilde{x}_0 \cdot \tilde{r}_0} = g^{p_0(1)}$$

$$((\tilde{y}_0^{\tilde{r}_0})^{p_1(1)})^{1/\tilde{x}_0 \cdot \tilde{r}_0} = ((g^{\tilde{x}_0 \cdot \tilde{r}_0})^{p_1(1)})^{1/\tilde{x}_0 \cdot \tilde{r}_0} = g^{p_1(1)}$$

$$((\tilde{y}_0^{\tilde{r}_0})^{p_2(1)})^{1/\tilde{x}_0 \cdot \tilde{r}_0} = ((g^{\tilde{x}_0 \cdot \tilde{r}_0})^{p_2(1)})^{1/\tilde{x}_0 \cdot \tilde{r}_0} = g^{p_2(1)}$$

---

[3] The buyer B_i should prove the correctness of the encrypted shares using the methods such as Chaum's proof of equality of discrete logarithm [4] or $DLEQ$ protocol [12].

[4] We assume that the total number of buyers m are larger than the total number of sellers n.

After decrypting the encrypted shares, the seller S_0 signs the decrypted shares and releases the signed messages [5] to the opening bulletin board as follows:

$$V_{S_0} = SK[\tilde{x}_0 : \tilde{y}_0^{\tilde{r}_0} = (g^{\tilde{r}_0})^{\tilde{x}_0}](\tilde{m}_0),$$

$$\tilde{m}_0 = ((T_{B_0}, g^{p_0(1)}) \| (T_{B_1}, g^{p_1(1)}) \| (T_{B_2}, g^{p_2(1)}))$$

Now, consider the decryption for the encrypted shares of sellers in a generalized case. Like the seller in the previous example, each buyer B_i verifies the messages and auction tickets of sellers and decrypts the shares encrypted by them. Then he signs the message $m_i = ((T_{S_0}, g^{\tilde{p}_0(i+1)}) \| \dots \| (T_{S_{n-1}}, g^{\tilde{p}_{n-1}(i+1)}))$, where $i \in \mathbb{Z}_m$, and publishes it on the opening bulletin board.

Reconstruction of Bid/Ask. To recover an evaluation of each participant, at least t correctly decrypted shares are needed. After verifying the messages and proofs of sellers submitted in the previous step, on behalf of participants, the manager M recovers the evaluation l_e of buyer B_i using Lagrange interpolation (Suppose that t sellers produce correct values for $g^{p_i(k)}$, for $k = 1, \dots, t$) :

$$\prod_{k=1}^{t} (g^{p_i(k)})^{\lambda_k} = g^{\sum_{k=1}^{t} p_i(k)\lambda_k} = g^{p_i(0)},$$

where $\lambda_k = \prod_{j \neq k} \frac{j}{j-k}$ is a Lagrange coefficient and $p_i(0) = l_e$. Because the manager holds w discrete bidding/asking prices in the system set-up phase, he can pre-compute g^{l_e} for $e = 1, \dots, w$ so that he gets the evaluation l_e of the buyer from the above value $g^{p_i(0)}$.

In the same way, the manager recovers the evaluation of each seller S_j.

Determination of the Trading Price. In this step, the trading price is determined according to McAfee's protocol. Note that the anonymity of participants is still satisfied in this step. Let SB_f be the set of auction tickets corresponding to buyers who have bidden at the price l_f, $f = 1, \dots, w$. Also, SS_f indicates the set of auction tickets related to sellers who have asked at the price l_f. For the reverse ordering of McAfee's protocol, let $s_{(i)}$ denote the representing ask of the set SS_f and $b_{(i)}$ denote the representing bid of the set SB_f, $i = 1, \dots, w$. We use the notation (i) for the i-th highest evaluation value of SB_f and the i-th lowest evaluation value of SS_f. At this time, the order statistics are as follows.

$$
\begin{array}{cccccc}
l_1 & l_2 & \cdots & l_k & \cdots & l_w \\
\overbrace{SS_1, s_{(1)}} < & \overbrace{SS_2, s_{(2)}} < & \cdots & < \overbrace{SS_k, s_{(k)}} < & \cdots & < \overbrace{SS_w, s_{(w)}} \\
SB_w, b_{(1)} > & \cdots & > \underbrace{SB_k, b_{(w+1-k)}} > & \cdots & > \underbrace{SB_2, b_{(w-1)}} & > \underbrace{SB_1, b_{(w)}} \\
l_w & \cdots & l_k & \cdots & l_2 & l_1
\end{array}
$$

---

[5] The signed message must include the proof that the decrypted shares are correctly computed, which is possible by a zero-knowledge such as $DLEQ$ protocol [12] or Chaum's proof of equality of discrete logarithm [4].

Note that $\Sigma_{f=1}^{w}|SB_f| = m$ (total number of buyers) and $\Sigma_{f=1}^{w}|SS_f| = n$ (total number of sellers), where $|SB_f|$ and $|SS_f|$ are size of sets SB_f and SS_f, respectively.

Now the manager determines the trading price. That is, he first chooses a k such that $s_{(k)} \leq b_{(k)}$ and $s_{(k+1)} > b_{(k+1)}$, then defines the candidate of a trading price $p_t = \frac{1}{2}(b_{(k+1)} + s_{(k+1)})$. The protocol is defined as follows.

1. If $s_{(k)} \leq p_t \leq b_{(k)}$ holds, SB_f and SS_f for $f = 1, \ldots, k$ trade at price p_t. In other words, those buyers whose bids are equal to or higher than $b_{(k)}$ trade with those sellers whose asks are equal to or lower than $s_{(k)}$.
2. If $p_t > b_{(k)}$ or $p_t < s_{(k)}$ holds, SB_f and SS_f for $f = 1, \ldots, k-1$ trade, which means those buyers whose bids are equal to or higher than $b_{(k-1)}$ trade with those sellers whose asks are equal to or lower than $s_{(k-1)}$. Each buyer pays $b_{(k)}$ and each seller gets $s_{(k)}$.

If the second condition holds, since the price for buyers $b_{(k)}$ is larger than the price for sellers $s_{(k)}$, the amount $(k-1) \cdot (b_{(k)} - s_{(k)})$ is left over. The manager receives this amount.

Winner Announcement. After determining the winning sets, the manager releases the original identities of the winners on the winning announcement bulletin board. For public verification, he publishes the registration information $(c_i, s_i, m_i = (B_i\|Cert_{B_i}\|Buyer), y_i^{r_i}, g^{r_i}, T_{B_i})$ related to winning buyers. Note that (c_i, s_i, m_i) are values used to authenticate an identity. Therefore, all entities including the lost participants or observers can identify the winning buyers. In the same way, the manager releases the registration information corresponding to the winning sellers, so that any entities can identify the winners.

5   Analysis

In this section, we perform an informal analysis of our protocol with respect to security and efficiency.

5.1   Security

Anonymity. We have assumed the semi-trusted manager who doesn't open the real identity during the auction process except at the winner announcement step or because of user misbehavior, while he may try to illegally attend an auction by impersonating other participants. Thus, as long as the manager does not open the real identity, the anonymity is guaranteed by the following Lemma 1.

Lemma 1. *Nobody, except the manager, can associate an auction ticket T_{B_i} or T_{S_j} with the real identity B_i or S_j of buyer or seller, respectively.*

Proof: An auction ticket is in the form of $T = (y^r\|h\|v)$, where $h = H(y^r)$, $v = Sig_M(y^r\|h)$ and $y = g^x$, and it doesn't include the identity information. That is, to recover the original ID, one has to be able to at least find the parameter y from anonymous public key y^r. Since the manager doesn't release the public key y, the only way to break anonymity is to find the private key x from $g^{x \cdot r}$ and compute $y = g^x$, then finally compare it with some certificate lists [6]. However, this is to solve discrete logarithm problem and it is also too difficult to determine a correct x because another random secret number r is used.

Impossibility of Impersonation. Since an anonymity service is provided in the proposed double auction protocol, an entity may try to illegally submit a faked bid or ask and impersonate a legal entity using the auction ticket of other participants. However, impersonation is technically impossible in our scheme, as shown in the following Theorem 1.

To induce Theorem 1, we first prove the following lemmas.

Lemma 2. *If solving the discrete logarithm problem is hard under a group for the given quintuplet* (m, y^r, g^r, c, s), *where* x *is the secret key and* $y(= g^x)$ *is the public key, finding random element* k *of the group satisfying both* $c = H(m\|y^r\|g^r\|g^k)$ *and* $s = r^{-1} \cdot k - c \cdot x$ *is equivalent to the difficulty of the discrete logarithm problem.*

Proof: It is straightforward to show the proof. Since we don't know the value of x and r from $(g^x)^r$ by the intractability of DLP under a group that solving DLP is hard in the polynomial time and k is also random elements, the only way to get k is to find the discrete logarithm of $((g^r)^s \cdot ((g^x)^r)^c)$ such that $g^k = ((g^r)^s \cdot ((g^x)^r)^c)$. It leads to solve DLP again.

Lemma 3. *An attacker who intercepts the valid signature information,* (y^r, g^r), *of another entity and then injects the faked bid or ask cannot generate a valid signature.*

Proof: Suppose an attacker can generate a valid signature (c', s') to inject a faked bid or ask message m' using the intercepted valid value (y^r, g^r). The attacker then releases (m', c', s', y^r, g^r), *i.e.*, $V = SK[x : y^r = (g^r)^x](m')$, on the submission bulletin board, so that he can impersonate an entity corresponding to the parameter y^r. To pass a successful signature verification, the following equation should be satisfied:

$$c' \stackrel{?}{=} H(m'\|y^r\|g^r\|(g^r)^{s'} \cdot (y^r)^{c'}) \tag{1}$$

That is, the attacker generates c' as follows:

$$c' = H(m'\|y^r\|g^r\|g^{k'}) \tag{2}$$

From equations (1) and (2), the following equations are induced:

$$g^{k'} = (g^r)^{s'} \cdot (y^r)^{c'} \tag{3}$$

$$= g^{r \cdot s' + c' \cdot x \cdot r} \tag{4}$$

---

[6] We also consider the case that y and the corresponding certificate have been released in another auction, so that people have some lists related to them.

From equations (3) and (4), we know that the attacker needs to generate k' such that $k' = r \cdot s' + c' \cdot x \cdot r$. However, the only way to get both r and x is to find the discrete logarithm of g^r and then to solve another discrete logarithm problem of $y^r = (g^x)^r = (g^r)^x$, respectively. Since this is contradictory to the intractability of DLP under a group, our assumption that an attacker can generate a valid signature using the parameters (y^r, g^r) of another entity is not valid.

Lemma 4. *The manager also cannot impersonate a valid trader.*

Proof: This can be proved straightforwardly by means of Lemmas 2 and 3, so we will omit the detailed proof.

From Lemmas 2, 3 and 4, we can induce the following security theorem.

Theorem 1. *In our proposed double auction protocol, nobody, not even manager, can forge the valid signature to submit a faked bid or ask, so that he cannot impersonate other entities.*

Non-repudiation. Every trader, who has his unique key pair *i.e.*, private key x and the corresponding public key y, certified by CA, signs all messages related to bid or ask information. Thus, we can also induce the following theorem by the foregoing sentence and Theorem 1.

Theorem 2. *In the proposed scheme, every entity participating in auction process cannot deny that he has submitted ask or bid.*

Robustness and Correctness. Even though some buyers and sellers cannot participate in or are dropped from an auction process due to an unstable network environment or their misbehavior, the proposed auction protocol still works well as long as at least t sellers and buyers among n sellers and m buyers are able to honestly attend an auction process. This robustness and correctness, *which is a major property being emphasized in our protocol*, is satisfied by the threshold access structure, and the evaluation of participants is obtained by using Lagrange interpolation as follows:

$$\prod_{k=1}^{t} (g^{p(k)})^{\lambda_k} = g^{\Sigma_{k=1}^{t} p(k)\lambda_k} = g^{p(0)},$$

where $\lambda_k = \prod_{i \neq k} \frac{i}{i-k}$ is a Lagrange coefficient and $p(0) = l_e$.

Public Verifiability. In the proposed protocol, any one can check the validity of submitted signatures and offers from traders. This is achieved by the publicly verifiable secret sharing scheme, the signature of knowledge, and some zero-knowledge proofs.

5.2   Efficiency

Communication. Our protocol has very low communication overheads: one round for registration, one round for bid/ask submission, one round for bid/ask opening, one round for determining the trading price and winners.

Computation. In terms of computation overheads, we compare the proposed protocol with Wang and Leung's protocol [15], because both schemes are based on McAfee's protocol. Excluding the computational cost of registration, we only consider the cost from the bid/ask submission phase to the bid/ask opening phase. The computational cost is considered in terms of modular arithmetic, including modular exponentiation and modular multiplication, and zero-knowledge for proving the correctness of private key, encrypted shares and decrypted shares. We assume that both protocols use the same zero-knowledge.

In Wang and Leung's protocol, the computational overheads are as follows, where m and n are the number of buyers and sellers, respectively, and w indicates the possible offering prices.

1. computation of bids and asks

   $-$ buyers $\begin{cases} \text{Multiplication} : M = m * w \\ \text{Exponentiation} : E = m * 2w \\ \text{Zero-knowledge} : ZK = w \end{cases}$

   $-$ sellers $\begin{cases} \text{Multiplication} : M = n * w \\ \text{Exponentiation} : E = n * 2w \\ \text{Zero-knowledge} : ZK = w \end{cases}$

2. product computation of all bids and asks
   $-$ manager : Multiplication : $M = 2((m-1)^w + (n-1)^w)$

3. computation for the total demand and supply

   $-$ buyers $\begin{cases} \text{Multiplication} : M = m * w \\ \text{Zero-knowledge} : ZK = m * w \end{cases}$

   $-$ sellers $\begin{cases} \text{Multiplication} : M = n * w \\ \text{Zero-knowledge} : ZK = n * w \end{cases}$

   $-$ manager : Multiplication : $M = 2w * (m + n + 1)$

4. determination of the winning buyers and sellers

   $-$ buyers $\begin{cases} \text{Multiplication} : M = m * w \\ \text{Zero-knowledge} : ZK = m * w \end{cases}$

   $-$ sellers $\begin{cases} \text{Multiplication} : M = n * w \\ \text{Zero-knowledge} : ZK = n * w \end{cases}$

Note that the manager does not exist in their protocol but in fact the auctioneer serves as the manager.

The computational overheads of our protocol are as follows, where t is threshold value of (t, m) and (t, n) threshold access structure.

1. bid/ask submission phase

   $-$ buyers $\begin{cases} \text{Exponentiation} : E = m * n \\ \text{Multiplication} : M = m \\ \text{Zero-knowledge} : ZK = m * n \end{cases}$

   $-$ sellers $\begin{cases} \text{Exponentiation} : E = n * m \\ \text{Multiplication} : M = n \\ \text{Zero-knowledge} : ZK = m * n \end{cases}$

2. decryption of encrypted shares

- buyers $\begin{cases} \text{Exponentiation}: E = m * 2n \\ \text{Multiplication}: M = m \\ \text{Zero-knowledge}: ZK = m * n \end{cases}$

- sellers $\begin{cases} \text{Exponentiation}: E = n * 2m \\ \text{Multiplication}: M = n \\ \text{Zero-knowledge}: ZK = m * n \end{cases}$

3. reconstruction of bid/ask
   - manager : Exponentiation : $E = 2 * t$

Table 2 represents the total computational overheads, from which we can see the price range w has no effect on the computational overheads in our protocol. As a result, our protocol is more efficient than Wang and Leung's protocol, especially when w becomes large.

Table 2. Total computation comparison

Computational cost		Wang and Leung	Proposed Protocols
Buyers	E	$2mw$	$3mn$
	M	$3mw$	$2m$
	ZK	$w(2m+1)$	$2mn$
Sellers	E	$2nw$	$3mn$
	M	$3nw$	$2n$
	ZK	$w(2n+1)$	$2mn$
Manager	E	$-$	$2t$
	M	$2\{(m-1)^w + (m-1)^w + w(m+n+1)\}$	$-$

6   Conclusion

We presented a secure and practical double auction protocol with hybrid trust model under realistic assumptions, which is based on McAfee's protocol. As a threshold access structure is used, even if some participants dropped out of the auction process early due to an unstable network or misbehavior, the proposed protocol is still able to be successfully completed. Our proposal satisfies most properties for secure double auction, and is relatively efficient in terms of computation and communication.

Acknowledgment

This research was supported by University IT Research Center Project.

References

1. F. Brandt. Fully Private Auctions in a Constant Number of Rounds. *Financial Cryptography'03*, LNCS 2742, pp. 223-228, Springer Verlag, 2003.
2. C. Boyd and W. Mao. Security Issues for Electronic Auctions. *HPL-2000-90*, Hewlett Packard, 2000.
3. O. Baudron and J. Stern. Non-interactive Private Auctions. *Financial Cryptography'01*, LNCS 2339, pp. 364-378, Springer Verlag, 2001.
4. D. Chaum and T.P. Pedersen. Wallet Databases with Observers. *CRYPTO'92*, LNCS 740, pp. 89-105, Springer Verlag, 1992.
5. J. Camenisch and M. Stadler. Efficient Group Signature Scheme for Large Groups. *CRYPTO'97*, LNCS 1294, Springer Verlag, 1997.
6. E. Fujisaki and T. Okamoto. A Practical and Provably Secure Scheme for Publicly Verifialbe Secret Sharing and its Applications. *EUROCRYPT'98*, LNCS 1403, pp. 32-46, Springer Verlag, 1998.
7. D. Friedman and J. Rust. The Double Auction Market. Addison-Wesley Publishing Company, 1993.
8. H. Kikuchi. $(M+1)$st-Price Auction Protocol. *Financial Cryptography'01*, LNCS 2339, Springer Verlag, 2001.
9. B. Lee, K. Kim, and J. Ma. Efficient Public Auction with One-Time Registration and Public Verifiability. *Indocrypt'01*, LNCS 2247, Springer Verlag, 2001.
10. M. Preston. A Dominant Strategy Double Auction. *Journal of Economic Theory*, (56), pp 434-450, 1992.
11. K. Omote and A. Miyaji. A Practical English Auctin with One-Time Registration. *ACISP'01*, LNCS 2119, pp. 221-234, Springer Verlag, 2001.
12. B. Schoenmakers. A Simple Publicly Verifiable Secret Sharing Scheme and its Application to Electronic Voting. *CRYPTO'99*, LNCS 1666, pp. 148-164, Springer Verlag, 1999.
13. M. Stadler. Publicly Verifiable Secret Sharing. *EUROCRYPT'96*, LNCS 1070, pp. 190-199, Springer Verlag, 1996.
14. W. Vickrey. Counterspeculation, Auction, and Competitive Sealed Tenders. *Journal of Finance*, 16(1): 8-37, 1961.
15. C. Wang and F. Leung. Secure Double Auction Protocols with Full Privacy Protection. *ICISC'03*, LNCS 2971, pp. 215-229, Springer Verlag, 2003.

VTrust: A Trust Management System Based on a Vector Model of Trust

Indrajit Ray, Sudip Chakraborty, and Indrakshi Ray

Colorado State University,
Computer Science Department,
Fort Collins, CO 80523, USA
{indrajit, sudip, iray}@cs.colostate.edu

Abstract. Trust can be used to measure our confidence that a secure system behaves as expected. We had previously proposed a vector model of trust [1]. In this work we address the problem of trust management using the vector model. We develop a new trust management engine which we call VTrust (from Vector Trust). The trust management engine stores and manages current as well as historical information about different parameters that define a trust relation between a truster and a trustee. We propose an SQL like language called TrustQL to interact with the trust management engine. TrustQL consists of a Trust Definition Language (TDL) that is used to define a trust relationship and a Trust Manipulation Language (TML) that is used to query and update information about trust relationships.

1 Introduction

Traditionally, security challenges in computing have been addressed through the use of techniques such as passwords, access control, program verification, intrusion detection, cryptographic protocols and so on. However, with the growing use of distributed open systems such as the Internet and pervasive computing environments, traditional approaches to security are often found lacking. For example, open systems applications such as e-commerce or e-government presents interesting problems to security. In such systems, human users and computational agents and services often interact with each other without having sufficient assurances about the behavior of the other party. There is often insufficient information for deciding how much access to authorize and how much information to share in a multi-user environment. These problems have led researchers to explore the potential of security mechanisms that are based on some aspects of social control.

The notion of *trust* has often played a crucial role for the proper formulation of security policies and in reasoning about expectations from agents and systems to work with confidentiality, integrity and availability. Thus, using trust to enable secure interaction among computational agents seems appropriate. Unfortunately there is no well accepted model for the specification of and reasoning about trust. For the most part, trust is considered to be a binary entity; confidence is measured in terms of either total trust or no trust. This had motivated us earlier to propose a new vector model of trust [1]. In this model trust is a quantitatively measurable entity which can have different degrees. We define methods and algorithms to measure trust and to compare two trust relationships.

S. Jajodia and C. Mazumdar (Eds.): ICISS 2005, LNCS 3803, pp. 91–105, 2005.

To use this trust model however, we need a corresponding trust management system. The current work presents a step in that direction.

A trust management system is a comprehensive framework designed to facilitate the specification, analysis and management of trust relationships. It focuses on specifying and interpreting security policies, credentials, and relationships [2]. The trust management system also provides trust establishment, trust evaluation, trust monitoring and trust analysis service. Traditionally, trust managment has always focused on how one can make authorization and access control more efficiently [3]. Blaze, et al. first introduced the trust management problem as a distinct and important component of security in network services [4]. The *PolicyMaker* trust management system [4, 5] is a framework for expressing in a common language authorization policies, certificates and trust relationships. The *PolicyMaker* service appears to applications very much like a database query engine [4]. *KeyNote* [2] derives from PolicyMaker and was designed to improve some of its weaknesses. *KeyNote* provides a simple language for describing and implementing security policies, trust relationships, and digitally-signed credentials. KeyNote has a built-in credential verification system and a simple notation to express authorization predicates. Grandison [3] proposes *SULTAN* (Simple Universal Logic-oriented Trust Analysis Notation), an abstract, logic-oriented framework designed to facilitate the specification, analysis and management of trust relationships. The IBM Trust Management System [6] implements trust management on top of the Role Based Access Control model. The underlying trust model is binary. The XML based Trust Policy Language that is used to interact with the system is flexible and can be easily expanded. However, it often requires defining custom XML tags for complex situations.

In this paper, we present the VTrust (from Vector Trust model) trust management framework. Major components of the trust management system include a database engine to store and manage trust data, a trust specification engine for defining and managing trust relationships, a trust analysis engine to process results of a trust query, a trust evaluation engine for evaluating trust expressions and a trust monitor for updating trust relationship information in the database engine. We have also developed an SQL like language to interact with the trust management system. We call it TrustQL.

The rest of the paper is organized as follows. In section 2 we describe the main components of the vector trust model. We discuss the extensions to the model that are needed to implement it in the VTrust framework. In section 3 we describe the VTrust system architecture. Section 4 presents the conceptual entity-relationship model for the VTrust system. The section begins with a description of relational entities involved. We discuss inter-relationship of these entities. We then showcase the idea with a running example. Section 5 identifies components of a query based language, called TrustQL, to interact with the trust management system. In this section we also discuss the rationality for choosing such a language. We conclude the paper in Section 6 with some discussion on extensions that we are currently working on.

2   Overview of Vector Trust Model

For the purpose of implementing the model in the trust management system we needed to introduce several modifications to the original model. In this discussion we include the extensions we have made. The interested reader is refered to [1] for the original model. We bgin by defining trust along the lines of Grandison and Sloman [7].

Definition 1. *Trust is defined to be the firm belief in the competence of an entity to act dependably and securely within a specific context.*

Definition 2. *Distrust is defined as the firm belief in the incompetence of an entity to act dependably and securely within a specified context.*

Although we define trust and distrust separately in our model, we allow the possibility of a neutral position where there is neither trust nor distrust.

We specify trust in the form of a trust relationship between two entities – the truster – an entity that trusts the target entity – and the trustee – the target entity that is trusted. This trust is always related to a particular context. An entity A needs not trust another entity B completely. A only needs to calculate the trust associated with B in some context pertinent to a situation. The specific context will depend on the nature of application and can be defined accordingly. Based on our current model, trust is evaluated under one context c only. The simple trust relationship $(A \xrightarrow{c} B)_t$ is a vector with three components – *experience*, *knowledge*, and *recommendation*. It is represented by $(A \xrightarrow{c} B)_t = [_AE_B^c, _AK_B^c, _\psi R_B^c]$, where $_AE_B^c$ represents the magnitude of A's experience about B in context c, $_AK_B^c$ represents A's knowledge and $_\psi R_B^c$ represents the cumulative effect of all B's recommendations to A from different sources.

To compute a trust relationship we assume that each of these three factors is expressed in terms of a numeric value in the range $[-1,1] \cup \{\perp\}$. A negative value for the component is used to indicate the *trust-negative* type for the component, whereas a positive value for the component is used to indicate the *trust-positive* type of the component. A 0 (zero) value for the component indicates *trust-neutral*. To indicate a lack of value due to insufficient information for any component we use the special symbol $\perp$.

2.1 Computing the Experience Component

We model experience in terms of the number of events encountered by a truster A regarding a trustee B in the context c within a specified period of time $[t_0, t_n]$. An event can be trust-positive, trust-negative or, trust-neutral depending on whether it contributes towards a trust-positive experience, a trust-negative experience or, a trust-neutral experience. Intuitively, events far back in time does not count as strongly as very recent events for computing trust values. Hence we introduce the concept of *experience policy* which specifies a length of time interval subdivided into non-overlapping intervals. It is defined as follows.

Definition 3. *An* experience policy *specifies a totally ordered set of non-overlapping time intervals together with a set of non-negative weights corresponding to each element in the set of time intervals.*

Recent intervals in the experience policy are given more weight than those far back. The whole time period $[t_0, t_n]$ is divided in such intervals and the truster A keeps a log of events occurring in these intervals.

If e_k^i denote the kth event in the ith interval, then $v_k^i = +1$, if $e_k^i \in P$, $v_k^i = -1$, if $e_k^i \in Q$ or $v_k^i = 0$, if $e_k^i \in N$, where, P = set of all trust-positive events, Q = set of all trust-negative events and N = set of all trust-neutral events.

The *incidents* I_j, corresponding to the jth time interval is the sum of the values of all the events, trust-positive, trust-negative, or neutral for the time interval. If n_j is the number of events that occured in the jth time interval, then $I_j = \perp$, if there is no event in $[t_{j-1}, t_j]$, and $I_j = \sum_{k=1}^{n_j} v_k^j$, otherwise.

The *experience* of A with regards to B for a particular context c is given by $_AE_B^c = \frac{\sum_{i=1}^n w_i I_i}{\sum_{i=1}^n n_i}$. where, w_i is a non-negative weight assigned to i^{th} interval.

2.2   Computing the Knowledge Component

The knowledge component has two parts - *direct knowledge* and *indirect knowledge (or, reputation)*. The truster A assigns two values to these two parts. Her *knowledge policy* regarding B in context c determines the weights to express relative importance between these two. Sum of the product of values and weights for the parts gives us a value for knowledge.

The *knowledge* of A with regards to B for a particular context c is given by

$$_AK_B^c = \begin{cases} d, \text{if } r = \perp \\ r, \text{if } d = \perp \\ w_d \cdot d + w_r \cdot r, \text{if } d \neq \perp, r \neq \perp \\ \perp, \text{if } d = r = \perp \end{cases}$$

where $d, r \in [-1, 1] \cup \{\perp\}$ and $w_d + w_r = 1$. d and r are the values to direct and indirect knowledge respectively and w_d and w_r are the corresponding non-negative weights.

2.3   Computing the Recommendation Component

Recommendation is evaluated on the basis of a *recommendation value* returned by a recommender to A about B. Truster A uses the "level of trust" he has on the recommender in the context "to provide a recommendation" as a weight to the value returned. This weight multiplied by the former value gives the actual *recommendation score* for trustee B in context c.

The *recommendation* of A with regards to B for a particular context c is given by

$_\Psi R_B^c = \frac{\sum_{j=1}^n (v(A \xrightarrow{rec} j)_t^N) \cdot V_j}{\sum_{j=1}^n (v(A \xrightarrow{rec} j)_t^N)}$ where Ψ is a group of n recommenders, $v(A \xrightarrow{rec} j)_t^N) =$ trust-value of jth recommender and $V_j = j^{th}$ recommender's recommendation value about the trustee B.

2.4   Trust Vector

We next observe that given the same set of values for the factors that influence trust, two trusters may come up with two different trust values for the same trustee. We believe that there are two main reasons for this. First, during evaluation of a trust value, a truster may assign different weights to the different factors that influence trust. The weights will depend on the trust evaluation policy of the truster. So if two different trusters assign two different sets of weights, then the resulting trust value will be different. The second reason is applicable only when the truster is a human being and is completely subjective in nature – one person may be more trusting than another. We believe that this latter concept is extremely difficult to model. At this stage we choose to disregard this feature in our model and assume that all trusters are trusting to the same extent. We capture the first factor using the concept of a *normalization policy*. The normalization policy is a vector of same dimension as of $(A \xrightarrow{c} B)_t$; the components are weights that are determined by the corresponding trust evaluation policy of the truster and assigned to experience, knowledge, and recommendation components of $(A \xrightarrow{c} B)_t$. The normalization policy together with the experince policy and the knowledge policy form the truster's *trust evaluation policy*.

We use the notation $(A \xrightarrow{c} B)_t^N$, called *normalized* trust relationship to specify a trust relationship. It specifies A's *normalized* trust on B at a given time t for a particular context c. This relationship is obtained from the simple trust relationship – $(A \xrightarrow{c} B)_t$ – after combining the former with the normalizing policy. It is given by $(A \xrightarrow{c} B)_t^N = \mathbf{W} \odot (A \xrightarrow{c} B)_t$. The $\odot$ operator represents the normalization operator. Let $(A \xrightarrow{c} B)_t = [_AE_B^c, _AK_B^c, _\psi R_B^c]$ be a trust vector such that $_AE_B^c, _AK_B^c, _\psi R_B^c \in [-1,1] \cup \{\bot\}$. Let also $\mathbf{W} = [W_e, W_k, W_r]$ be the corresponding trust policy vector such that $W_e + W_k + W_r = 1$ and $W_e, W_k, W_r \in [0,1]$. The $\odot$ operator generates the normalized trust relationship as

$$
\begin{aligned}
(A \xrightarrow{c} B)_t^N &= \mathbf{W} \odot (A \xrightarrow{c} B)_t \\
&= [W_e, \ W_k, \ W_r] \odot [_AE_B^c, \ _AK_B^c, \ _\psi R_B^c] \\
&= [W_e \cdot _AE_B^c, \ W_k \cdot _AE_B^c, \ W_r \cdot _\psi R_B^c] \\
&= [_A\hat{E}_B^c, \ _A\hat{K}_B^c, \ _\psi\hat{R}_B^c]
\end{aligned}
$$

We next introduce a concept called the *value* of a trust relationship. This is denoted by the expression $\mathbf{v}(A \xrightarrow{c} B)_t^N$ and is a number in $[-1,1] \cup \{\bot\}$ that is associated with the normalized trust relationship. The special symbol $\bot$ is used to denote the value when there is not enough information to decide about trust, distrust, or neutrality. This value together with the vector now represents a trust of certain degree.

Finally, we investigate the dynamic nature of trust – how trust (or distrust) changes over time. We make a couple of observations. First, trust depends on trust itself; that is a trust relationship established at some point of time in the past influences the computation of trust at the current time. If an agent is positively trusted to begin with then negative factors are often overlooked (that is given less weightage) when trust is re-evaluated in the agent. Second, trust decays with time. This is owing to the effect of forgetfulness of the human mind. The second idea is captured by the equation – $\mathbf{v}(T_{t_n}) = \mathbf{v}(T_{t_i})e^{-(\mathbf{v}(T_{t_i})\Delta t)^{2k}}$ where, $\mathbf{v}(T_{t_i})$, be the value of a trust relationship, T_{t_i}, at time t_i and $\mathbf{v}(T_{t_n})$ be the decayed value of the same at time t_n. We have developed a method to obtain a vector of same dimension as of $(A \xrightarrow{c} B)_t^N$ from this value $\mathbf{v}(T_{t_n})$. The effect of time is captured by the parameter k which is determined by the truster A's *dynamic policy* regarding the trustee B in context c. The current normalized vector together with this time-affected vector are combined according to their relative importance. Relative importance is determined by truster's *history_weight policy* which specifies two values α and β in $[0,1]$ (where, $\alpha + \beta = 1$) as weights to current vector and the vector obtained from previous trust value. The new vector thus obtained gives the actual normalized trust vector at time t for the trust relationship between truster A and trustee B in context c. This is represented by the following equation

$$(A \xrightarrow{c} B)_{t_n}^N = \begin{cases} [_A\hat{E}_B^c, _A\hat{K}_B^c, _\psi\hat{R}_B^c] & \text{if } t_n = 0 \\ [\frac{\mathbf{v}(\hat{T})}{3}, \frac{\mathbf{v}(\hat{T})}{3}, \frac{\mathbf{v}(\hat{T})}{3}] & \text{if } t_n \neq 0 \text{ and } _A\hat{E}_B^c = _A\hat{K}_B^c = _\psi\hat{R}_B^c = \perp \\ \alpha \cdot [_A\hat{E}_B^c, _A\hat{K}_B^c, _\psi\hat{R}_B^c] + \beta \cdot [\frac{\mathbf{v}(\hat{T})}{3}, \frac{\mathbf{v}(\hat{T})}{3}, \frac{\mathbf{v}(\hat{T})}{3}] \\ \qquad \text{if } t_n \neq 0 \text{ and at least one of } _A\hat{E}_B^c, _A\hat{K}_B^c, _\psi\hat{R}_B^c \neq \perp \end{cases}$$

where $[\frac{\mathbf{v}(\hat{T})}{3}, \frac{\mathbf{v}(\hat{T})}{3}, \frac{\mathbf{v}(\hat{T})}{3}]$ is the time-effected vector and $\mathbf{v}(\hat{T}) = \mathbf{v}(T_{t_n})$.

3 The VTrust System Architecture

The high level system architecture consists of the components as shown in the following figure 1. Values of the different parameters needed for the computation of trust relationships are maintained in the VTrust database. The truster interacts with the trust management system through the external interface. The communication is done using the language TrustQL that we have developed. The TrustQL language parser in the interface parses the command and sends it to the appropriate component in the next layer. This layer has the following major components. A *specification server* is managing and updating the trust database schema. The *analysis engine* processes all trust related queries. It interacts with specification server and an *evaluation engine*. The latter is responsible for computing trust related information according to the underlying model. The evaluation engine takes a parsed trust query string, finds the associated information and policy, and returns the final trust vector and value to the analysis engine. The *trust monitor* is responsible for acquiring relevant trust formulation parameters. It maintains the VTrust database, updates the trust data while truster and trustee interacts with each other and also updates periodically trust component values like experience and knowledge.

All these information (trusters, trustees, recommenders, policies and trust parameter information) are stored in the VTrust database. The database is implemented as described in section 4. Since TrustQL can not interact with the database directly, an SQL translator beneath the component layer does this job. The specification server, analysis engine and evaluation engine takes a trust operation specified in TrustQL and maps the command to an equivalent SQL command to interact with the underlying database. After receiving an answer from the database, each of those components again does a reverse mapping to output the answer in terms of TrustQL.

The following algorithm is used by a truster to compute the trust relationship with a trustee for a given context at any given time.

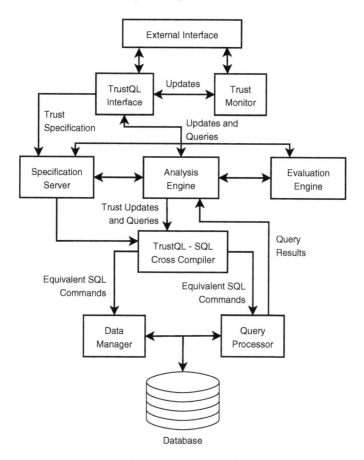

Fig. 1. Trust Management System Architecture

Algorithm 1. *1. If not already available, initialize the truster's trust evaluation policy corresponding to the trustee and the specific context. If needed update the same to reflect current circumstances.*

2. Initialize dynamic policy and history_weight policy if not already available. Update as needed.

3. Compute truster's experience with trustee.

   (a) Determine last point in time when trust was evaluated for current trustee in the given context. If such a time exists call it t_{last}.

   (b) Read off experience values from database starting from most recent first till either t_{last} or start of experience table.

   (c) Apply experience policy to evaluate current experience value.

4. Compute truster's knowledge with trustee by applying knowledge policy to current direct knowledge and reputation values.

5. Compute recommendation value for trustee.

6. *Compute truster's simple trust on trustee using values obtained in steps 3 - 5. Apply normalization policy as appropriate to the simple trust.*
7. *Let trust value at t_{last} be termed T_{last} (assuming available); compute decayed value for T_{last} by applying dynamic policy to it.*
8. *Combine trust values obtained in steps 6 and 7 using the history_weight policy to get the truster's current trust relationship with the trustee in the given context.*
9. *Record current time of trust evaluation as t_{last} corresponding to this truster, trustee and context.*

4   Conceptual Trust Model

We model the underlying trust components using Entity-Relationship techniques (see Figure 2). Both the entity sets and the relationship sets are then converted to tables in a relational database with columns representing the "attributes" of the entity and relationship sets. ACTOR is a generalization of three specific types – TRUSTER, TRUSTEE, and RECOMMENDER as *Role*. A TRUSTER has the the following relationships with a TRUSTEE: EVENTS, EXPPOL, KNOWLEDGE, KNOWLPOL, NORMPOL, DYNPOL, and HWTPOL. The relationship RECOMMENDATION involves all three types of ACTOR (i.e Truster, Trustee and Recommender). The TRUSTER calculates his 'experience' with a TRUSTEE on the basis of EVENTS and EXPPOL. The entity EVENTS is a log of events happened between the truster and the trustee in the context at certain time. Experience is calculated by summing up the net effect of events within some consecutive intervals of time. The EXPPOL specifies the length of that time interval. KNOWLEDGE returns a value which is evaluated based on KNOWLPOL which determines weights for direct knowledge (*DKnolWt*) and reputation (*RepuWt*). The truster assigns values for direct knowledge (*DirectKnol*) and repuation (*Repuation*). RECOMMENDATION (*RecommendationScore*) is evaluated based on the value returned by the recommender (*RecoValue*) and the recommender's weight (*RecommenderWt*) according to the truster. These three values (i.e., experience score, knowledge score and recommendation score) are normalized according to a normalization policy (NORMPOL). They are multiplied with their corresponding weights – *ExpWt, KnolWt,* and *RecoWt*. The DYNPOL determines the parameter k to get the current value of the last available trust value. A vector from this trust history is derived and HWTPOL specifies weights to be assigned to this vector and the current normalized vector. Composition of these two vectors results in actual trust vector with components Experience score, Knowledge score and Recommendation score and they, in turn, return trust value between the truster and the trustee in a context on a particular date.

We now use a hypothetical trust relationship example to descibe how the VTrust database works. Let Alice be developing a software that has several modules with diffrent functionality. She wants to get every module tested by an expert software engineer before she merges two modules. Assume that she assigns this testing responsibility to Bob. Thus, Alice wants to evaluate her 'trust' on Bob in the context of 'efficiency to test a software' (say, EST; acronym for the context) to decide her further course of action with Bob in the context EST. Alice sets up a trust-relationship with Bob in the context EST. She thinks of consulting Charlie, her friend who happens to know Bob,

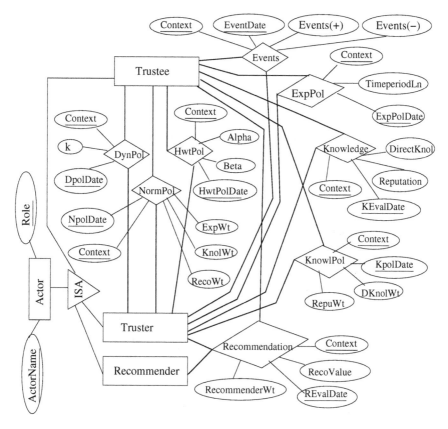

Fig. 2. ER-diagram of the VTrust system

Table 1. Initial ACTOR table

ACTORNAME	ROLE
Alice	Truster
Bob	Trustee
Charlie	Recommender

Table 2. Alice's experience policy

ACTOR.ACTOR-NAME1	ACTOR.ROLE1	ACTOR.ACTOR-NAME2	ACTOR.ROLE2	CONTEXT	EXOPOLDATE	TimeperiodLn
Alice	Truster	Bob	Trustee	EST	01/01/2004	1 month

to get his view about Bob's efficiency in this context. To store the information Alice creates the table called ACTOR as shown in Table 1.

Alice starts interacting with Bob from 1st January, 2004. She decides to keep track of events that occured between her and Bob on a monthly basis. Alice forms her EXP-

Table 3. Alice's knowledge policy

ACTOR.ACTOR-NAME1	ACTOR.ROLE1	ACTOR.ACTOR-NAME2	ACTOR.ROLE2	CON-TEXT	KPOLDATE	Dknol Wt	Repu-Wt
Alice	Truster	Bob	Trustee	EST	06/30/2004	0.7	0.3

Table 4. Alice's normalization policy

ACTOR.ACTOR-NAME1	ACTOR.ROLE1	ACTOR.ACTOR-NAME2	Actor.Role2	CONTEXT	NPOL DATE	Exp Wt	Knol Wt	Reco Wt
Alice	Truster	Bob	Trustee	EST	10/31/2004	0.5	0.3	0.2

Table 5. Alice's EVENTS table on 31st December, 2004

ACTOR.ACTOR-NAME1	ACTOR.ROLE1	ACTOR.ACTOR-NAME2	Actor.Role2	CONTEXT	EVENT DATE	Eve nts(+)	Eve nts(-)
Alice	Truster	Bob	Trustee	EST	01/06/2004	1	0
Alice	Truster	Bob	Trustee	EST	01/19/2004	1	1
...	...	...	...	...	...	...	...
Alice	Truster	Bob	Trustee	EST	07/27/2004	0	1
Alice	Truster	Bob	Trustee	EST	10/10/2004	0	1
Alice	Truster	Bob	Trustee	EST	11/07/2004	2	0

Table 6. Alice's knowledge value on 31st December, 2004

ACTOR. ACTOR NAME1	ACTOR.ROLE1	ACTOR. ACTOR NAME2	Actor.Role2	CONTEXT	KEVAL DATE	Direct Knol	Reput ation
Alice	Truster	Bob	Trustee	EST	12/31/2004	0.8	0.2

Table 7. Alice's recommendation score on 31st December, 2004

ACTOR. ACTOR NAME1	ACTOR. ROLE1	ACTOR. ACTOR NAME2	ACTOR. ROLE2	CONTEXT	REVAL DATE	ACTOR. ACTOR NAME3	ACTOR. ROLE3	Reco value	Recomm enderwt
Alice	Truster	Bob	Trustee	EST	12/31/2004	Charlie	Recom mender	0.55	0.8

POL as shown in Table 2. Alice also sets up her knowledge policy regarding Bob. She decides to assign 70% weight on direct knowledge and 30% to indirect knowledge she gets about Bob regarding EST. Thus, her KNOWLPOL table looks like that in Table 3. Alice can set her knowledge policy anytime before the first time she evaluates trust for Bob in EST. She can also set the normalization policy anytime prior to first evaluation of trust for Bob in EST. Let she have the NORMPOL as shown in Table 4. Now let

Table 8. Alice's trust on Bob in the context EST on 31st December, 2004

ACTOR. ACTOR NAME1	ACTOR. ROLE1	ACTOR. ACTOR NAME2	ACTOR. ROLE2	CONTEXT	EVALUAT ION DATE	Exper- ience Score	Know- ledge Score	Recom mendati on Score	Trust value
Alice	Truster	Bob	Trustee	EST	12/31/2004	0.077	0.186	0.088	0.351

us assume that Alice evaluates Bob's trust in EST for the first time on 31st December, 2004. On that day her EVENTS table looks like Table 5. Alice calculates the 'experience value' from the above log with the help of her 'experience policy'. The policy defines the time-period length as 1 month. Let us assume that Alice specify the start-date for calculation as 01/02/2004. Then the above log is devided in 30-day periods and net effect of positive and negative events are calculated within those periods. Thus Alice got her experience value as 0.1543. Alice next builds the KNOWLEDGE, and RECOM-MENDATION databases. She assigns two values for direct knowledge and reputation for Bob in EST. During the year Alice possibly makes several visits to Bob's office to get idea about Bob's infrastructure; she checks tools and techniques used by Bob for testing. She hears about Bob's efficiencey in the job. Based on these information Alice assigns those two values according to her own policy. The knowledge value, which comes as 0.62, is calculated based on the two values she provides and their correspond-ing weights specified in Table 3. Finally, before evaluating trust in Bob Alice consults Charlie to get his view on Bob in the context of EST. Charlie returns his judgment about Bob as a recommendation value to Alice. Alice evaluates Charlie's recommendation on the basis of the trust she has on Charlie. Alice calculates recommendation score of Bob with these information as 0.44 and the RECOMMENDATION table is of the form of Ta-ble 7. Now Alice evaluates the actual trust vector as well as the trust value based on these information. All these component values are normalized before calculating the trust value with the values available from Table 4. These calculations are automatically computed by the system. The final trust vector and the trust value of Alice for Bob in the context EST as obtained on 31st December, 2004 shown in the Table 8.

Let us next assume that Alice again wants to evaluate Bob after 4 months. Therefore, on 30th April, 2005 she wants to have a trust for Bob in the same context EST. We assume that after evaluating trust on 31st December, she purges all events prior to that date and start keeping log afresh. Rationale is that at any later time, her decision would be influenced by the previous trust value. She does not need the whole set of events to derive current trust value. Only the events after the previous evaluation are considered to evaluate current experience. We also assume that she has not changed any policy and nothing happened between her and Bob during these 4 months. Thus there will not be any change in Alice's EVENTS table on 30th April, 2005. Let us assume that Alice changes the values assigned to direct knowledge and repuation on the basis of her current judgment. So she adds a new entry to the KNOWLEDGE table and calcu-lates the new knowledge value as 0.66 (say). Maybe also the trust relationship of Alice with Charlie on the context of "providing a recommendation" changes from 0.8 to 0.7 and this time Charlie returns a lower value 0.4 for Bob in the context EST. Hence the

Table 9. Alice's dynamic policy

ACTOR. NAME1	ACTOR ROLE1	ACTOR. ROLE1	ACTOR. NAME2	ACTOR ROLE2	ACTOR. ROLE2	CONTEXT	DPOLDATE	k
Alice		Truster	Bob		Trustee	EST	03/31/2005	1

Table 10. Alice's policy on assigning weights to previous trust value at current time

ACTOR. NAME1	ACTOR ROLE1	ACTOR. ROLE1	ACTOR. NAME2	ACTOR ROLE2	ACTOR. ROLE2	CONTEXT	HWTPOL DATE	Alpha	Beta
Alice		Truster	Bob		Trustee	EST	04/01/2005	0.6	0.4

Table 11. Alice's trust on Bob in the context EST on 30th April, 2005

ACTOR. ACTOR NAME1	ACTOR. ROLE1	ACTOR. ACTOR NAME2	ACTOR. ROLE2	CONTEXT	EVALUAT ION DATE	Exper ience Score	Know ledge Score	Recom mendati on Score	Trust value
Alice	Truster	Bob	Trustee	EST	12/31/2004	0.077	0.186	0.088	0.351
Alice	Truster	Bob	Trustee	EST	04/30/2005	0.0064	0.4024	0.1744	0.5832

RECOMMENDATION table changes and (possibly) the new recommendation score for Bob is evaluated as 0.28. Now the trust value evaluated earlier (i.e., on 31st December, 2004) will have some effect on Alice's present decision. For that Alice has to form the dynamic policy which gives the current 'level' of the previous value. Alice can form this table DYNPOL anytime before 30th April, 2005. Let us assume that Alice set k in DYNPOL as 1 on 31st March, 2005. This is presented in Table 9.

To combine the vector having current value of the parameters with the vector derived from the time-affected value of trust, Alice needs to form HWTPOL on or before 30th April, 2005 to put relative weight on these two vectors. Let us assume that Alice put 60% weight to the vector with currently evaluated values and rest 40% to the vector derived from the time-affected value. It is shown in Table 10. The final trust vector and value on 30th April, 2005 is presented in the Table 11. Alice keeps on adding a new entry in the tables everytime she evaluates Bob's trust vector in EST.

5   TrustQL: The Trust Query Language

Users of the trust management system need a language to interact with the system. The language should be able to interact with the database implementation of the model. Therefore, we introduce a trust language similar to Structured Query Language (SQL). We call this language as Trust Query Language or TrustQL.TrustQL consists of Trust Definition Language (TDL) and Trust Manipulation Language (TML). TDL is used to create, alter and drop entities, policies, parameters and context. TML is used to add, modify and delete trust records as well as query the trust engine to get trust values. Trust

```
CREATE POLICY
     {policy_name}
WEIGHT
{(experience_weight, knowledge_weight, recommendation_weight)}
EXPERIENCE POLICY {experience_policy_name}
KNOWLEDGE POLICY {knowledge_policy_name}
RECOMMENDATION POLICY {recommendation_policy_name}
DYNAMICS POLICY {dynamics_policy_name}
HISTORY POLICY {history_policy_name}
```

Fig. 3. Defining trust evaluation policies using TrustQL

```
INSERT TRUST
BETWEEN {<truster>} AND {<trustee>}
CONTEXT {context_name}
[WHEN {some_date}]
[EXPERIENCE VALUES {(<experience_values>)}]
[KNOWLEDGE VALUES {(<knowledge_values>)}]
[RECOMMENDATION VALUES {(<recommendation_values>)}]

<truster> ::= {entity_name}
<trustee> ::= {entity_name}
<experience_values> ::= {time_interval, experience_value} [,...n]
<knowledge_values> ::= {direct_knowledge_value,
                        indirect_knowledge_value }
<recommendation_values> ::= {<recommender>, recommendation_value}[,...n]
<recommender> ::= {entity_name | group_name}
```

Fig. 4. Populating trust relationships using TrustQL

Definition Language (TDL) consists of TrustQL keywords, Identifiers, Statements, and TrustQL convention. Trust Manipulation Language (TML) consists of commands like INSERT, UPDATE, DELETE, SELECT, and commands to query trust value after the trust management system has been set up using Trust Definition Language. TrustQL differs from general purpose procedural language such as C and Java in that users specify what they want instead of how to get the result. It is up to the VTrust engine to manipulate the data and present the final trust value to end users. From the user's point of view, this approach makes it easy to interact with the trust management system.

Some examples of TrustQL statements are shown in figures 3 and 4.

6   Conclusion and Future Work

The vector model of trust gives a technique to measure trust quantitatively on the basis of some parameters. The model has methods to specify policies to evaluate those parameters. Using this model we can define "multilevel" trust and distrust. In this paper we present a trust management framework, named as VTrust, based on vector-based trust model. In this framework, information regarding trust relationships are kept in a trust database. The trust relationship, the entities involved in it (e.g., truster, trustee, context etc.), the parameters to evaluate trust, and the policies to determine values are represented as relational entities. All these are translated to tables of the database and the attributes of these entities are expressed as columns in the tables. The working principle of the database system is explained with an example. The system architecture of VTrust, which contains a user interface, trust management components in the middle layer and the trust database as the lower layer is also introduced. We also introduce a query language, called TrustQL, to interact with the components of trust management system. We present some of the features of TrustQL with examples. The detail syntax and semantics of TrustQL are left out.

A lot of work remains to be done. We are currently extending the underlying trust model to define more operations on trust relationships. Presently we have single entity as truster or trustee. We want to incorporate the idea of a group of truster or a group of trustee. In our current representation, the user (i.e., the truster) needs to enter a lot of values. We are trying to minimize the number of user input by giving more power to the analysis engine. An efficient design of the underlying database and a good user interface are need to be developed. We believe that achieving above goals would result in a complete trust management framework based on the vector-based trust model.

Acknowledgment

This work was partially supported by the U.S. Air Force Research Laboratory (AFRL) and the Federal Aviation Administration (FAA) under contract F30602-03-1-0101. The views presented here are solely that of the authors and do not necessarily represent those of the AFRL or the FAA. The authors would like to thank Mr. Pete Robinson of the AFRL and Mr. Ernest Lucier of the FAA for their valuable comments and their support for this work.

References

[1] Ray, I., Chakraborty, S.: A vector model of trust for developing trustworthy systems. In: Proceedings of the 9th European Symposium on Research in Computer Security (ESORICS'04). Volume 3193 of Lecture Notes In Computer Science., Sophia Antipolis, Frech Riviera, France, Springer-Verlag (2004) 260–275

[2] Blaze, M., Feigenbaum, J., Ioannidis, J., Keromytis, A.: The keynote trust management system (version 2). http://www.crypto.com/papers/rfc2704.txt (1999)

[3] Grandison, T.: Trust Specification and Analysis for Internet Applications. PhD thesis, Imperial College of Science Technology and Medicine, Department of Computing, London, UK (2001)

[4] Blaze, M., Feigenbaum, J., Lacy, J.: Decentralized trust management. In: Proceedings of 17th IEEE Symposium on Security and Privacy, Oakland, California, USA, IEEE Computer Society Press (1996) 164–173

[5] Blaze, M., Feigenbaum, J., , Strauss, M.: Compliance checking in the policymaker trust management system. In: Proceedings of the 2nd Financial Crypto Conference. Volume 1465 of Lecture Notes in Computer Science., Anguilla, Springer-Verlag (1998) 254–274

[6] Herzberg, A., Mass, Y., Mihaeli, J., Naor, O., Ravid, Y.: Access control meets public key infrastructure, or: Assigning roles to strangers. In: Proceedings of IEEE Symposium on Security and Privacy, Washington, DC, USA, IEEE Computer Society Press (2000) 2–15
[7] Grandison, T., Sloman, M.: A survey of trust in internet applications. IEEE Communications Surveys and Tutorials **3** (2000) 2–16

Analysis and Modelling of Trust in Distributed Information Systems

Weiliang Zhao[1], Vijay Varadharajan[1,2], and George Bryan[1]

[1] School of Computing and Information Technology,
University of Western Sydney
{wzhao, g.bryan}@cit.uws.edu.au
[2] Department of Computing,
Macquarie University
vijay@ics.mq.edu.au

Abstract. In this paper, we consider the analysis and modelling of trust in distributed information systems. We review the relations of trust relationships in our previous work. We discuss trust layers and hierarchy based on formal definition of trust relationship. We provide a set of definitions to describe the properties of trust direction and trust symmetry under our taxonomy framework. In order to analyze and model the scope and diversity of trust relationship, we define trust scope label under our taxonomy framework. We provide some example scenarios to illustrate the proposed definitions about properties of trust relationship. The proposed definitions are new elements of the taxonomy framework for enabling the analysis and modelling of trust. We provide some discussions about the life cycle of trust relationships. The proposed trust structure and properties are currently being used in the development of the overall methodology of life cycle of trust relationships in distributed information systems.

1 Introduction

Trust has been studied in multiple dimensions in the computing world. As a concept of security, trust was firstly introduced in trusted systems [1] and trusted computing [2]. Marsh has tried to formalize trust as a computational concept [3]. Several community-based reputation systems [4,5], trust negotiation systems [6,7,8] and trust management systems [9,10,11]have been proposed.

Trust plays an important role in distributed information systems. The properties of trust and how to define/model trust relationships are important concerns in the analysis and design of distributed information systems. Our main objective of this research is to develop a sound understanding of trust and to create a powerful set of tools to analyze and model trust relationships in distributed information systems. In our earlier work [12], we have outlined a formal definition of trust relationship. The target of the formal definition of trust relationships is not only to reflect many of the commonly used notions of trust but also to provide a taxonomy framework where a range of useful trust relationships can be

S. Jajodia and C. Mazumdar (Eds.): ICISS 2005, LNCS 3803, pp. 106–119, 2005.

expressed and compared. The research in [12] only provides a starting point for the analysis and design of trust relationships. We provide a set of definitions for the properties of trust direction and trust symmetry between involved entities in distributed environments. We provide trust scope label and rules to compare trust scope labels. The operations, definitions and rules are enabling tools in the analysis and design of trust relationships in distributed information systems. We provide examples of scenarios to show users how to understand and use the proposed definitions about trust relationships in the real world. The research provided in this paper is an important part of the overall methodology of life cycle of trust relationships in distributed information systems.

The remainder of the paper is organized as follows. In section 2, we provide the definition of trust relationship. In section 3, we describe a set of operations and definitions for relations of trust relationships in distributed environments. In section 4, we discuss the trust layers and hierarchy. In section 5, we provide a set of definitions for trust direction and trust symmetry. We employee the Microsoft's domain trust as a regressive scenario example to illustrate the definitions in this section. In section 6, we discuss the scope and diversity of trust relationships. In section 7, we provide some discussions about our overall methodology of the life cycle of trust relationships in distributed environments. Finally section 8 provides some concluding remarks.

2   Definition of Trust Relationship

We have given a formal definition of trust relationship with a strict mathematical structure in our previous work [12]. This definition of trust relationship has a broad expressive power and it is the cornerstone of our trust taxonomy framework. All trust notions proposed in this paper is based on this definition. The definition of trust relationship is expressed as:

Definition 1. *A trust relationship is a four-tuple $T =< R, E, C, P >$ where:*

- *R is the set of trusters. It contains all the involved trusters. It is a non empty set.*
- *E is the set of trustees. It contains all the involved trustees. It is a non-empty set.*
- *C is the set of conditions. It contains all conditions (requirements) for the current trust relationship. Normally, a trust relationship has some specified conditions. If there is no condition, the condition set is empty.*
- *P is the set of properties. The property set describes the actions or attributes of the trustees. It is a non-empty set. The property set can be divided into two sub sets:*
  - *Action set: the set of actions that the trusters trust that trustees will and can perform.*
  - *Attribute set: the set of attributes that trusters trust that trustees have.*

The formal definition of trust relationship can reflect the commonly used notions of trust and provides a taxonomy framework. When trust relationships are used, the full syntax (four-tuple $< R,\ E,\ C,\ P >$ must be followed. Trust relationship T means that under the condition set C, truster set R trust that trustee set E have the properties in set P. The definition of trust relationship provides a starting point for capturing different forms of commonly understood notions of trust. The above strict definition of the trust relationship is the basis for the discussions of all properties of trust in this paper.

3   Relations of Trust Relationships

In the this section, we provide some operations and definitions about the relations of trust relationships. The relations of trust relationships play an important role in the analysis and design of trust relationships in distributed information systems. From the nature of trust relationship and its mathematical structure, some new trust relationships can be derived based on the existing trust relationships. The operations of using two existing trust relationships to generate a new trust relationship under specific constraints and operations of decomposing one existing trust relationship into two new trust relationships under specific constraints are defined as follows:

OPERATION 1. Let $T_1 = (R_1,\ E_1,\ C_1,\ P_1)$ and $T_2 = (R_2,\ E_2,\ C_2,\ P_2)$. There is a set $T = (R_1 \cap R_2,\ E_1 \cap E_2,\ C_1 \cup C_2,\ P_1 \cup P_2)$. If $R_1 \cap R_2 = \emptyset$ or $E_1 \cap E_2 = \emptyset$, $T = \emptyset$.

If $R_1 = R_2$ and $E_1 = E_2$, the operation becomes:

OPERATION 1A. Let $T_1 = (R,\ E,\ C_1,\ P_1)$ and $T_2 = (R,\ E,\ C_2,\ P_2)$. There is a set $T = (R,\ E,\ C_1 \cup C_2,\ P_1 \cup P_2)$.

If $R_1 = R_2$, $E_1 = E_2$ and $C_1 = C_2$, the operation becomes:

OPERATION 1B. Let $T_1 = (R,\ E,\ C,\ P_1)$ and $T_2 = (R,\ E,\ C,\ P_2)$. Then there is a set $T = (R,\ E,\ C,\ P_1 \cup P_2)$.

OPERATION 2. Let $T_1 = (R_1,\ E_1,\ C,\ P)$ and $T_2 = (R_2,\ E_2,\ C,\ P)$. There is a set $T = (R_1 \cup R_2,\ E_1 \cap E_2,\ C,\ P)$.

If $E_1 = E_2$, the operation becomes:

OPERATION 2A. Let $T_1 = (R_1,\ E,\ C,\ P)$ and $T_2 = (R_2,\ E,\ C,\ P)$. There is a set $T = (R_1 \cup R_2,\ E,\ C,\ P)$.

OPERATION 3. Let $T_1 = (R_1,\ E_1,\ C,\ P)$ and $T_2 = (R_2,\ E_2,\ C,\ P)$. There is a set $T = (R_1 \cap R_2,\ E_1 \cup E_2,\ C,\ P)$.

If $R_1 = R_2$, the operation becomes:

OPERATION 3A. Let $T_1 = (R,\ E_1,\ C,\ P)$ and $T_2 = (R,\ E_2,\ C,\ P)$. There is a set $T = (R,\ E_1 \cup E_2,\ C,\ P)$.

OPERATION 4. *Let* $T =< R,\ E,\ C,\ P >$. *If there are* $R_1,\ R_2$ *and* $R = R_1 \cup R_2$, *then there are trust relationships* $T_1 =< R_1,\ E,\ C,\ P >$ *and* $T_2 = < R_2,\ E,\ C,\ P >$.

OPERATION 5. *Let* $T =< R,\ E,\ C,\ P >$. *If there are* $E_1,\ E_2$ *and* $E = E_1 \cup E_2$, *then there are trust relationships* $T_1 =< R,\ E_1,\ C,\ P >$ *and* $T_2 = < R,\ E_2,\ C,\ P >$.

OPERATION 6. *Let* $T =< R,\ E,\ C,\ P >$. *If there are* $P_1,\ P_2$ *and* $P = P_1 \cup P_2$, *then there are trust relationships* $T_1 =< R,\ E,\ C,\ P_1 >$ *and* $T_2 = < R,\ E,\ C,\ P_2 >$.

This operation has the following special case:

OPERATION 6A. *Let* $T =< R,\ E,\ C,\ P >$ *and there are* $P_1,\ P_2,\ C_1,\ C_2$ *and* $P = P_1 \cup P_2,\ C = C_1 \cup C_2$. *If* C_1 *is the condition set for* P_1 *and* C_2 *is the condition set for* P_2, *then there are trust relationships* $T_1 =< R,\ E,\ C_1,\ P_1 >$ *and* $T_2 =< R,\ E,\ C_2,\ P_2 >$.

All operations can be used to generate new trust relationships from the existing trust relationships under some specific constraints. The **Operation 1** deals with any two trust relationships and a new trust relationship is generated, if the result is not $\emptyset$. The **Operation 1A, 1B, 2A, 3A** deal with how to use two trust relationships to generate new trust relationship under some specific constraints. The **Operation 4, 5, 6 and 6A** deal with how to decompose one trust relationship into two trust relationships under some specific constraints. **Operation 1A** and **Operation 6A** are inverse operations. **Operation 1B** and **Operation 6** are inverse operations. **Operation 2A** and **Operation 4** are inverse operations. **Operation 3A** and **Operation 5** are inverse operations.

In the discussion of trust relationships, we have defined the equivalent, primitive, derived, direct redundant and alternate trust relationships and have classified the direct redundant trust relationships into different types. They are as follows:

Definition 2. *Let* $T_1 =< R_1,\ E_1,\ C_1,\ P_1 >$ *and* $T_2 =< R_2,\ E_2,\ C_2,\ P_2 >$. *If and only if* $R_1 = R_2$ *and* $E_1 = E_2$ *and* $C_1 = C_2$ *and* $P_1 = P_2$, *then* T_1 *and* T_2 *are equivalent, in symbols:*

$$T_1 = T_2 \iff R_1 = R_2 \text{ and } E_1 = E_2 \text{ and } C_1 = C_2 \text{ and } P_1 = P_2$$

Definition 3. *If a trust relationship cannot be derived from other existing trust relationships, the trust relationship is a primitive trust relationship.*

Definition 4. *If a trust relationship can be derived from other existing trust relationships, the trust relationship is a derived trust relationship.*

Note: Trust relationships are predefined in information systems. A derived trust relationship is always related to one or more other trust relationships. For an independent trust relationship, it is meaningless to judge it as a derived trust relationship or not.

Definition 5. *Let* $T = < R, E, C, P >$. *If there is trust relationship* $T' = < R', E', C', P' >$ *and* $T \neq T'$, $R \subseteq R'$, $E \subseteq E'$, $C \supseteq C'$, $P \subseteq P'$. T *is a direct redundant trust relationship.*

We now discuss several special cases of direct redundant trust relationships based on the single tuple of trust relationship. We believe that these special cases play important roles in the analysis and design of trust relationships.

TYPE 1 : DRLR (Direct Redundant of Less Trusters)
Let $T = < R, E, C, P >$. *If and only if there is a trust relationship* $T' = < R', E, C, P >$ *and* $R' \supset R$, T *is a DRLR trust relationship.*

T is DRLR trust relationship means that there is another trust relationship with super set of trusters and all other tuples are same as peers in T.

TYPE 2 : DRLE (Direct Redundant of Less Trustees)
Let $T = < R, E, C, P >$. *If and only if there is a trust relationship* $T' = < R, E', C, P >$ *and* $E' \supset E$, T *is a DRLE trust relationship.*

T is DRLE trust relationship means that there is another trust relationship with super set of trustees and all other tuples are same as peers in T.

TYPE 3 : DRMC (Direct Redundant of More Conditions)
Let $T = < R, E, C, P >$. *If and only if there is an alternate trust relationship* $T' = < R, E, C', P >$ *and* $C' \subset C$, T *is a DRMC trust relationship.*

T is DRMC trust relationship means that there is another trust relationship with a subset of conditions and all other tuples are same as peers in T.

TYPE 4 : DRLP (Direct Redundant of Less Properties)
Let $T = < R, E, C, P >$. *If and only if there is a trust relationship* $T' = < R, E, C, P' >$ *and* $P' \supset P$, T *is a DRLP trust relationship.*

T is DRLP trust relationship means that there is another trust relationship with super set of properties and all other tuples are same as peers in T.

Definition 6. *Let* $T = < R, E, C, P >$, $T' = < R, E, C', P >$ *and* $C \neq C'$. T *and* T' *are alternate trust relationships of each other.*

An alternate trust relationship means that there is an alternate condition set for the same truster set, trustee set and property set. Perhaps, there are multiple alternate trust relationships. In distributed computing, multiple mechanisms and multiple choices are necessary in many situations and it is the main reason why we define and discuss alternate trust relationships here.

Scenario Example: Consider an online e-commerce service called FlightServ, which can provide flight booking and travel deals. FlightServ is designed using web services. FlightServ connects with customers, airlines, hotels and credit card services (some of these may also be web services). The whole system could be very complicated, but in this example, we only consider some basic trust relationships in the system. In the system, customers are classified into normal flyers and frequent flyers. Originally, some trust relationships are modelled as follows:

TS2- 1. *Airlines trust normal flyers can make their airline bookings, if they have address details & confirmed credit card information.*

TS2- 2. *Airlines trust frequent flyers with no condition that frequent flyers can make their airline bookings.*

TS2- 3. *Hotels trust normal flyers can make their hotels booking, if they have address details & confirmed credit card information.*

TS2- 4. *Hotels trust frequent flyers can make their hotels booking, if they have address details & confirmed credit card information.*

TS2- 5. *Credit card services are trusted by all possible entities without any condition that the credit card services will give the correct evaluation of credit card information.*

TS2- 6. *Credit card services are trusted by all possible entities without any condition that the credit card services will keep the privacy of credit card information.*

For the above trust relationships in the system, based on definitions and operations in section 3, we have the following analysis:

- All above trust relationships are primitive.
- Using the **Operation 3A**, trust relationships **TS2-3** and **TS2-4** can be merged to a new trust relationship **TS2-(3)(4)**: "Hotels trust customers if they have address details & confirmed credit card information that customers can make their hotels booking". If **TS2-(3)(4)** has been defined in the system, **TS2-3** and **TS2-4** becomes DRLE trust relationships and will be removed out of the system.
- Using the **Operation 1B**, trust relationships **TS2-5** and **TS2-6** can be merged to a new trust relationship **TS2-(5)(6)**: "Credit card services are trusted by all possible entities without any condition that the credit card services will give the correct evaluation of credit card information & the credit card services will keep the privacy of credit card information". If **TS2-(5)(6)** has been defined in the system, **TS2-5** and **TS2-6** becomes DRLP trust relationships and will be removed out of the system.

We hope that the above scenario example can provide a general picture of modelling trust relationships in distributed environments. We believe that these operations and definitions are useful but they are not sufficient for the overall methodology of modelling trust relationships in distributed environments. In following sections, we will expand the taxonomy framework and discuss the classification of trust, trust layers, direction and symmetry of trust and the life cycle of trust relationships in distributed environments.

4   Trust Layers and Hierarchy

Some researchers have tried to identify different forms of trust relationships [13]. Grandison et al [13] have given a bottom-up classification and used the terms as

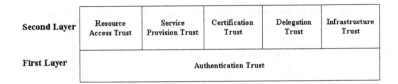

Second Layer	Resource Access Trust	Service Provision Trust	Certification Trust	Delegation Trust	Infrastructure Trust
First Layer	Authentication Trust				

Fig. 1. Trust Layers

resources access trust, service provision trust, certification trust, delegation trust
and infrastructure trust. From the view point of establishment or evaluation of
trust relationships, all the above trust types must build on a more basic trust
relationship which is the authentication trust or identity trust. We will categorize
the trust relationships into two layers. Authentication is on layer one and other
types are on layer two. We will give a hierarchy of trust based on the nature of
the four tuples of trust relationship.

Authentication has continuously been an important topic in information security community. There are many popular authentication schemes such as X.509
and PGP. Authentication trust belongs to a separate layer and all other trust
types belong to another layer above the authentication trust. This is illustrated
in Figure 1. Note that trust types of layer two may not be necessarily specified
in terms of an identity. Anonymous authorization belongs to access trust and
it is an example that there is no specified identity. Anonymous authorization
can be implemented using certificates with capabilities. The real identity of the
involved trustee will not be revealed. For example, a customer has a certificate
for accessing some resources on the Internet. The customer's behaviors of accessing the resources can be recorded. If it is desirable that the customer cannot be
identified, the related access trust is a kind of anonymous access trust. Particularly for the resource access trust and service provision trust, the anonymous
authentication is desirable in some cases. In such a situation, the layer of authentication still needs to provide a mechanism to deal with the same entity as the
trustee in the whole scope of the trust process. Normally, there is a temporary
and dynamic identification which will be uniquely connected with the involved
trustee in the scope of the trust process.

Authentication trust is the only type of trust at layer one. At layer two, trust
relationships can be classified in different ways. In the following, we will give another kind of classification which is different from the bottom-up classification
of Grandison et al. Based on strict definition of trust relationship, trust relationships at layer two can be classified according to the nature of the trustees in trust
relationship $< R, E, C, P >$. If E is an infrastructure, the trust relationship
belongs to infrastructure trust. If E is not an infrastructure, the trust relationship belongs to non-infrastructure trust. Non-infrastructure trust relationships
can be classified based on the ownership of the property set. If the trusters have
the ownership of the property set, the trust relationship belongs to access trust.
If the trustees have the ownership of the property set, the trust relationship belongs to provision trust. If some properties are owned by trustees and some other

Fig. 2. Trust Hierarchy

properties are owned by trusters, then the trust relationship belongs to mixture (A&P) trust. The hierarchy of trust relationships at layer two is illustrated in Figure 2. In such a classification, delegation trust and certification trust are not independent types. As we have discussed, the delegation trust is a special form of provision trust, trustees are the providers of delegated decisions on behalves of trusters. A certification trust can be any subtype of non-infrastructure trust based on the nature of its property set.

5   Direction and Symmetry of Trust

In this section, we will provide a set of definitions for the properties of trust direction and trust symmetry. The properties of trust direction and trust symmetry play an important role in the analysis and modelling of trust in distributed information systems. These definitions provide general descriptions about the properties of trust direction and trust symmetry. A scenario example is provided to illustrate these definitions and their usage. We hope that these definitions can cover most situations in the real world and can be used as standard scenarios for analyzing and modelling trust about properties of direction and symmetry. In real systems, one or multiple kinds of trust direction and trust symmetry can be chosen based on the specified requirements of the information systems.

The properties of trust direction and symmetry are related to each other and they should be cooperatively used to analyze and model the properties of direction and symmetry of trust in distributed environments. For the properties of trust direction, one-way trust relationship, two-way trust relationship and reflexive trust relationship are defined. For the properties of trust symmetry, symmetric trust relationships, symmetric two-way trust relationship, and the whole set of trust relationships are defined. The details of the definitions are described as follows.

Definition 7. *One-way trust relationship is the trust relationship with a unique trust direction from the trusters to trustees.*

One-way is the default feature of a trust relationship if there is no further description.

Two-way trust relationship can be defined and used in information systems such as Microsoft's domain trust. Actually, two-way trust relationship is the result of binding two one-way trust relationships together. We define two-way trust relationship as follows:

Definition 8. *Two-way trust relationship TT' is the binding of two one-way trust relationships $T =< R, E, C, P >$ and $T' =< R', E', C', P' >$ with $R' = E$ and $E' = R$. T and T' are the reflective trust relationships with each other in the two-way trust relationship.*

In the above definition, "binding" is the key word. If there are two one-way trust relationships between R and E but they are not bound with each other, then they are only two one-way trust relationships and there is no two-way trust relationship. When two one-way trust relationships are bound together, there is a two-way trust relationship and these two one-way trust relationships can be called reflective trust relationships with each other.

If the trusters and the trustees are the same, the trust relationship is reflexive. The reflexive trust relationship is defined as follows:

Definition 9. *Trust relationships $T =< R, E, C, P >$ is an reflexive trust relationship when $R = E$.*

The symmetry of two trust relationships could be an important concern in the analysis or modelling of trust relationships in distributed information systems. The symmetry of two trust relationships is defined as the follows:

Definition 10. *If there is trust relationship $T' =< R', E', C', P' >$ which is the result of swapping trusters and trustees in another trust relationship $T =< R, E, C, P >$ (the swapping includes all possible ownerships in condition set and property set), there is symmetry between T and T', T and T' are symmetric trust relationships with each other.*

In the above definition, the swapping of trusters and trustees includes all possible ownerships in condition set and property set. The two trust relationships have the same condition set and property set except the possible ownerships in them. The symmetric/asymmetric two-way trust relationship is defined as follows:

Definition 11. *A two-way trust relationship TT' is symmetric two-way trust relationship if there is symmetry between T and T'; otherwise TT' is an asymmetric two-way trust relationship.*

Sometimes it is necessary to discuss the symmetry of all trust relationships between a truster set and a trustee set, we have the following definition:

Definition 12. *WTR(R,E) is the whole set of trust relationships with same truster set R and trustee set E.*

Definition 13. *If every trust relationship in WTR(R,E) has a symmetric trust relationship in WTR(E,R) and every trust relationship in WTR(E,R) has a symmetric trust relationship in WTR(R,E), the trust between R and E are symmetric.*

Scenario Example: Here we use Microsoft's domain trust as a regressive scenario example to discuss the properties of trust direction and trust symmetry defined in this section. Domain trust allows users to authenticate to resources in another domain. Also, an administrator is able to administer user rights for users in the other domain. Our general definitions for the properties of direction and symmetry of trust relationships have general expressive power and can cover broad range of commonly used notations. The related concepts in domain trust can be viewed as specific cases of these general definitions. In the following, we will use our terms defined in this paper to review some concepts in domain trust.

- Based on **definition 1** in section 2, the domain trust can be expressed as "entities in domain A trust entities in domain B without any condition that entities in domain B have the right to get access of the set of resources in domain A".
- Microsoft's domain trust includes both one-way trust and two-way trust. In Microsoft's domain trust, one-way trust is defined as a unidirectional authentication path created between two domains. This means that in a one-way trust between domain A and domain B, users in domain A can access resources in domain B. However, users in domain B cannot access resources in domain A. Microsoft's one-way trust is an example of one-way trust relationship in **definition 7**. In a two-way domain trust, authentication requests can be passed between the two domains in both directions. Two-way trust is an example of two-way trust relationship in **definition 8**.
- The entities in same domain trust each other without any condition that entities have the right to get access of the set of resources in the same domain. This is an example of reflexive trust relationship in **definition 9**.
- There is symmetry in the two-way domain trust. The two one-way trust relationships bound in the two-way trust relationship are "entities in domain A trust entities in domain B without any condition that entities in domain B have the right to get access of the set of resources in domain A" and "entities in domain B trust entities in domain A without any condition that entities in domain A have the right to get access of the set of resources in domain B". These two one-way trust relationships are symmetric trust relationships with each other in **definition 10**. Microsoft's two-way trust is symmetric two-way trust relationship in **definition 11**.
- In domain trust, the $WTR(A,B)$ based on **definition 12** has only one trust relationship from truster domain A to trustee domain B. For two-way domain trust, the trust between domain A and domain B is symmetric based on **definition 13**.

The above definitions about the properties of trust direction and trust symmetry are new elements of the taxonomy framework about trust. We believe that they can cover most situations related with direction and symmetry of trust relationship in the real world. These definitions can provide suitable terms and can be used as scenario examples in the analysis and modelling of trust in distributed information systems.

6 Scope and Diversity of Trust Relationship

In this section, we will discuss the scope and diversity of trust relationship in distributed information systems. The diversity of trust has been discussed by Jøsang [14] who expresses trust in three diversity dimensions. The first dimension represents trusters or trust originators, the second represents the trust purpose, and the third represents trustees. Jøsang uses the term trust purpose based on the observation that trust is relative to a domain of actions. In our formal definition of trust relationship, trusters and trustees are two tuples and they are similar to the terms of Jøsang. The origin diversity about trusters and target diversity about trustees are straightforward and have been described clearly by Jøsang [14]. Jøsang's term of trust purpose is related to a domain of actions. Under our taxonomy framework, we will define trust scope label to take the place of the trust purpose. There are multiple benefits of trust scope label other than the trust purpose and they will be discussed later in this section. The trust scope label is the binding of the condition set and property set based on the formal definition of trust relationship. The trust scope label is a new element of our taxonomy framework. The definition of trust scope label is expressed as follows:

Definition 14. *A trust scope label is a two-tuple $TSL =< C,\ P >$ where C is a set of conditions and P is a set of properties.*

The details of condition set C and property set P can be found in the formal definition of trust relationship in section 2. Actually, trust scope label provides a new layer of abstraction under the trust relationship and it defines the properties of the trust and its associated conditions. To compare two trust scope labels $TSL_1 =< C_1,\ P_1 >$ and $TSL_2 =< C_2,\ P_2 >$, we have the following rules:

1. $C_1 \subseteq C_2$ and $P_1 \supseteq P_2$ $\iff$ $TSL_1 \geq TSL_2$;
2. $C_1 = C_2$ and $P_1 = P_2$ $\iff$ $TSL_1 = TSL_2$;
3. $C_1 \supseteq C_2$ and $P_1 \subseteq P_2$ $\iff$ $TSL_1 \leq TSL_2$.
4. In other cases, TSL_1 and TSL_2 can not be compared with each other.

The trust scope label is beyond the trust purpose in several aspects. Trust scope label composes of a subspace of trust relationships (two tuples out of four tuples) and describes the characteristics of the combination of condition set C and property set P. Trust scope labels could be treated as an independent subspace of trust relationships in the analysis and design of overall information systems. The property set in trust scope label covers not only actions but also attributes of trustees. Two trust scope labels could be compared with each other based on the rules given above.

Scenario Example: Consider an online software shop. We assume that anybody who wants to enter the online shop must register as a member of the online shop first. For describing the condition set and property set in possible trust relationships between the shop and possible customers, we use the following notations:

- $p1$ stands for that customers can read the documentation of the software.
- $p2$ stands for that customers can download the software.
- $c1$ stands for certificate of membership.
- $c2$ stands for the commitment of the payment for the software.
- $c3$ stands for the payment for the software.

We have the following trust scope labels:

1. $TSL1 =< \{c1\}, \{p1\} >$
2. $TSL2 =< \{c1, c2\}, \{p1, p2\} >$
3. $TSL3 =< \{c1, c2, c3\}, \{p1, p2\} >$

Based on the rules to compare two trust scope labels, we have

- $TSL1$ cannot be compared with $TSL2$ (or $TSL3$). There is no obvious relationship between $TSL1$ and $TSL2$ (or $TSL3$).
- $TSL2 > TSL3$. It means that the trust scope of $TSL2$ is less strict than that of $TSL3$.

The scope and diversity of trust is another aspect to be considered in the analysis and modelling of trust in distributed information systems. The trust scope label may be quite complicated and the above comparison rules provide helpful tools in making judgements. The scope and diversity of trust may be coupled with other trust properties such as trust direction and trust symmetry.

7   Life Cycle of Trust Relationships

We are currently working on a methodology for life cycle of trust relationships using the definition of trust relationship, operations of trust relationships and the properties of trust relationship. Trust relationships between possible entities play crucial roles in the collaborative interactions in distributed environments. The analysis and design of trust relationship must be integrated with other requirements of the whole distributed information system. The modelling, implementing and maintaining of trust relationships is an incremental, iterative process. The whole life cycle of trust relationships includes several stages such as extracting trust requirements in system, identifying possible trust relationships from trust requirements, choosing and refining the whole set of trust relationships from possible trust relationships, implementing trust relationships in systems and maintaining trust relationships in systems. The initial trust relationships will be refined in multiple life cycles. There are two ways to accommodate new business requirements. One way is to introduce new trust relationships and another way is to modify existing trust relationships. When new trust relationships are introduced, several things need to be considered such as the scope and diversity of these trust relationships, the properties of direction and symmetry of these trust relationships and the relations between them and existing trust relationships. In section 3, 4,5 and 6, we have proposed a set of operations and definitions to enable the analysis of the above. We have also given some example scenarios.

We believe that they are helpful in the analysis and design of trust relationships for collaborative interactions in the distributed environments and they are part of our overall methodology of life cycle of trust relationships. When trust relationships are modified, the change management of trust relationships must be considered. We are in the process of developing change management schemes for trust relationships, which will become part of our overall methodology as well.

8   Concluding Remarks

In this paper, we have focused on the analysis and modelling of trust in distributed information systems. We have reviewed the definition of trust relationship and operations and definitions about relations of trust relationships. We have discussed the classification of trust under our taxonomy framework. We have discussed different forms of trust and put authentication at layer one of trust and other trust types on layer two. Authentication plays a foundation role for other trust types on layer two. We have proposed a hierarchy of layer two trust relationships based on the nature of four tuples of a trust relationship. This hierarchy is helpful to understand the purposes of trust relationships in the real world. We provide multiple definitions about the properties of trust direction and trust symmetry. We have defined trust scope label to model the properties of scope and diversity of trust. All the definitions proposed in this paper are new elements of our taxonomy framework and they can be used as enabling tools in the analysis and modelling of trust in distributed information systems.

In real implementations, properties of trust discussed in this paper will be customized and configured based on the specific requirements. We are currently working on an overall methodology of life cycle of trust relationships in distributed information systems. This research focuses on the properties of trust relationships and taxonomy framework. The definition of trust relationship provides a starting point and it is the cornerstone of this research. The relations of relationships can provide useful tools for enabling the analysis, design and implementation of trust in distributed information systems. The classification of trust are helpful for better understanding of trust and is helpful in the analysis of trust. The definitions about trust direction, trust symmetry and trust scope can provide suitable terms for the related properties and they can be used as tools for enabling the analysis and modelling of trust in distributed information systems. In the web services paradigm, we hope that the proposed properties of trust and tools for analysis and modelling trust can provide solid foundation for trust related issues in WS-Trust, WS-Security, WS-Policy and WS-Federation.

References

1. TCSEC. Trusted computer system evaluation criteria. Technical report, U.S.A National Computer Security Council, 1985. DOD standard 5200.28-STD.
2. J. Landauer, T. Redmond, and T. Benzel. Formal policies for trusted processes. In *Proceedings of the Computer Security Foundations Workshop II, 1989*, pages 31–40. 1989.

3. S. Marsh. *Formalising trust as a computational concept.* Phd thesis, University of Sterling, 1994.

4. Y. Wang and J. Vassileva. Trust and reputation model in peer-to-peer networks. In *Proceedings of Third International Conference on Peer-to-Peer Computing*, pages 150–157, 2003.

5. L. Xiong and L. Liu. A reputation-based trust model for peer-to-peer e commerce communities. In *IEEE International Conference on E-Commerce*, pages 275–284, 2003.

6. M. N. Huhns and D. A. Buell. Trusted autonomy. *Internet Computing, IEEE*, 6(3):92–95, 2002.

7. W. H. Winsborough, K. E. Seamons, and et al. Automated trust negotiation. In *Proceedings of DARPA Information Survivability Conference and Exposition*, 2000.

8. M. Winslett, T. Yu, and et al. Negotiating trust in the web. *IEEE Internet Computing*, 6(6):30–37, 2002.

9. M. Blaze, J. Feigenbaum, and J. Lacy. Decentralized trust management. In *Proceedings of IEEE Symposium on Security and Privacy*, pages 164–173. 1996.

10. M. Blaze, J. Feigenbaum, and A.D. Keromytis. KeyNote: Trust management for public-key infrastructures (position paper). *Lecture Notes in Computer Science*, 1550:59–63, 1999.

11. Y. H. Chu, J. Feigenbaum, B. LaMacchia, P. Resnick, and M. Strauss. REFEREE: Trust management for Web applications. *Computer Networks and ISDN Systems*, 29(8–13):953–964, 1997.

12. W. Zhao, V. Varadharajan, and G. Bryan. Modelling trust relationships in distributed environments. In *Lecture Notes in Computer Science*, volume 3184, pages 40–49. Springer-Verlag, 2004.

13. T. Grandison and M. Sloman. A survey of trust in internet application. *IEEE Communications Surveys*, pages 2–16, Fourth Quarter, 2000.

14. A. Jøsang. The right type of trust for distributed systems. In *Proceedings of the 1996 New Security Paradigms Workshop*, pages 119–131. ACM, 1996.

EPAL Based Privacy Enforcement Using ECA Rules

Jaijit Bhattacharya and S.K. Gupta

Department of Computer Science and Engineering, Indian Institute of Technology, Delhi
New Delhi – 110016, India
{Jaijit, skg}@cse.iitd.ernet.in
http://www.cse.iitd.ernet.in

Abstract. This paper uses an ECA based policy implementation engine to enforce simple EPAL based enterprise-wide privacy policies. This architecture supports simplified EPAL policies and enforcement requirements of a system that can autonomically manage data-privacy based on pre-specified EPAL policies. The policies are defined through a Graphical User Interface (GUI) and this paper discusses the main features of our proposed GUI. The objective of such an approach is to facilitate privacy administrators, with low IT skills, by setting privacy policies for managing the system.

1 Introduction

In order to prevent data privacy violations, nations across the world are coming out with privacy protecting legislations. However, such legislations now expose organizations to the issue of unintentionally violating privacy of data. The first attempt to provide tools to enterprises to protect themselves from unintentionally privacy violation was the P3P standards [14]. However, P3P only provided a mechanism to publish the privacy policy of an enterprise in a machine-readable form. It did not help in enforcing the privacy policy.

Detailed work has been done by Bhattacharya and Gupta [14] to develop middleware that uses modified P3P to enforce privacy policies within an enterprise.

In order to provide tools to organizations to protect themselves from privacy violation committed on data under their possession, a standard privacy language called the Enterprise Privacy Authorization Language (EPAL) has been devised [15].

EPAL is a formal language for writing enterprise privacy policies to govern data handling practices in IT systems according to fine-grained positive and negative authorization rights. It concentrates on the core privacy authorization while abstracting data models and user-authentication from all deployment details such as data model or user-authentication.

However, even with tools like the IBM Policy editor, it is very complex to write and manage EPAL based privacy policies. Most users who need to define privacy policies are not highly skilled in IT and it would not be appropriate to expect them to write the complex EPAL policies.

Thus there is a need to create a solution architecture that is able to capture the privacy policies in a user-friendly manner and that enforces the privacy policies. Similar work has been done by Batra et al for generic policies [16].

S. Jajodia and C. Mazumdar (Eds.): ICISS 2005, LNCS 3803, pp. 120–133, 2005.

In this paper we discuss the architecture for a ECA based privacy policy enforcer that is based on EPAL semantics. ECA (Event-Condition-Action) rules [10] are composed of event definitions, conditions and actions to be taken once the event has occurred and the corresponding condition has been satisfied. In the proposed architecture, the policies are defined by the decision makers/ policy administrator using a friendly graphical user interface and then these policies are modeled as ECA (Event-Condition-Action) like rules [1]. The events triggering the policy execution could be from within the database, i.e. internal events, or they could be from outside the database, i.e. external events. These policies are then executed by a policy engine, based on the specified event and on satisfaction of the corresponding condition.

This paper maps the EPAL based policies to a ECA rule and uses the ECA based policy engine [16] to enforce privacy policies.

Many active database systems have been developed using ECA rules [2], [3] and [4]. Also, implementations of flexible execution models for active databases have been attempted earlier [5]. However, these work do not provide a solution for data privacy administration based on policies.

This paper details the work done on the prototype for managing data based on pre-specified privacy policies using EPAL and implemented using ECA. The paper is organized as follows. It begins with a short overview of related work in this area, followed by the architecture for ECA based privacy administration for a centralized database scenario. Section 4 describes the semantics used for representing policies. Section 5 describes the mechanism adopted for defining and storing policies. Section 6 details the mechanism for execution of the policy model. Finally, the paper concludes with the benefits of such a system and future work that needs to be done.

2   Related Work

The issue of privacy in database has been addressed primarily in two directions (a) defining privacy specification and enforcement language, and (b) ensuring that the database itself ensures privacy [17].

The second approach attempts to make database systems responsible for managing private information under its control. Attempts at such solutions are largely based on Statistical databases [18] and Secure databases [19]. A third approach is that of Hippocratic databases [17] that uses components of secure database and introduces privacy control within the database itself. However, such an approach makes the solution wedded to the database and hence requires fundamental changes in the Kernel of the database. This makes it difficult to be deployed on existing databases. Moreover, it does not allow individuals to authorize specific individuals to access their data (for eg. Individuals might need to give access to their hospital health records to their family physician or employer).

It appears that the privacy middleware concept introduced by Bhattacharya and Gupta in [14], addresses the shortcomings of the above approaches. However, this middleware is based on a non-standard modification of P3P. Therefore there is a need to use a standard language like EPAL to develop a similar middleware.

Since EPAL can be mapped to a set of events, conditions and actions, as is shown in the next section, hence it is worthwhile to study related work in ECA implementations. The two key issues with policy based data privacy administration are (a) how to represent policies and (b) how to execute the policies automatically. These two issues fall under the research areas of rule representation and rule execution respectively. The rule executions have been thoroughly investigated in research work related to active databases [11][12].

Numerous works has been done in these two areas. In the area of rule representation, work has been done in formulating semantics for ECA rules [8]. There has been alternative rule representations experimented, among others by T. Coupaye et al [5] and S. Gatziu [4]. In this paper, we have adopted SNOOP like representation of ECA rules, proposed in the Sentinel [9] and later used to develop EPPE [16]. In the area of active databases, the primary focus has been event detection and application of rules like ECA. A number of powerful research prototypes have been built eg. SAMOS [6] and Sentinel [7] as representative of the field. Limited production rule capabilities have already been included in many commercial databases such as DB2, INGRES, InterBase, Oracle, Rdb and Sybase.

3   EPAL Based Privacy Policy Representation Mapping to ECA

An EPAL policy is essentially a list of privacy rules that are ordered with descending precedence (i.e., if a rule applies, subsequent rules are ignored). A rule is a statement that includes a ruling, a user category, an action, a data category, and a purpose. A rule may also contain conditions and obligations. For example, an enterprise may have the following rule in its privacy policy (ref. Table 1).

Table 1. EPAL Privacy Policy specification for a given rule

Privacy Policy (informal)	Allow a sales agent or a sales supervisor to collect a customer's data for order entry if the customer is older than 13 years of age and the customer has been notified of the privacy policy. Delete the data 3 years from now
EPAL Privacy Rule	
Ruling	Allow
user category	sales department
Action	Store
data category	customer-record
Purpose	order-processing
condition	customer is older than 13 years of age
Obligation	delete the data 3 years from now

Rules are used to determine if a request is allowed or denied. A request contains a user category, an action, a data category, and a purpose. Continuing with the same enterprise as above, consider the following request (ref. Table 2).

Table 2. EPAL based request for Privacy constrained data

Request (informal)	A person acting as a sales agent and an employee requests to collect a customer's email for order entry
user category	sales department
Action	Store
data category	customer-record
Purpose	order-processing

The above rule allows the request, so the sales agent would be permitted to store the customer's contact information. Additional rules can then govern how this stored data may be used. EPAL policy must be capable of executing all obligations given the unique name of the obligation [15].

Each privacy rule is encoded as a <rule> element in EPAL. Rules have two types: An 'allow'-rule allows an action while 'deny-rules define that the action must not be allowed.

3.1 Mapping Simple Requests to ECA

A simple authorization request contains (a) a single user-category U that is defined in the vocabulary, (b) a single data-category T that is defined in the vocabulary, (c) a single purpose P that is defined in the vocabulary, (d) a single action A that is defined in the vocabulary, and (e) the container data required by this policy that must be valid against the container definition.

The tuple (U, T, P, A) is called the authorization-quadruple. The intuition behind a request is "Is the given user-category (and all its children) allowed to perform the given action on the given data-category (and all its children) for the given purpose (and all its children). If yes, what obligations apply?". A consequence of this intuition is that a request to access, e.g., an action on a data-category 'customer record' is only allowed if it is allowed on all its parts.

The algorithm must output (1) A ruling that is either "allow", "deny", or "not-applicable", (2) A single rule "id" that mandated this ruling (or the empty string if the ruling was the default ruling) and (3) the set of obligations specified in the rule.

The algorithm determines the ruling by processing each rule with descending precedence. Before starting, it checks that the global-condition is satisfied. If not, the default-ruling is returned. For each rule, the algorithm checks (1) are the elements of the authorization request in the scope of this rule? And (2) is the condition satisfied?

If these conditions are satisfied, the algorithm acts on the rule. If all rules have been processed (but no 'allow' or 'deny' satisfied these two conditions), the algorithm returns the default-ruling.

Once we have reduced EPAL to the above representation, it is easy to see that the tuple (U,T,P) forms the condition C for the action A to be performed. The condition is checked when an event E occurs. The event E can be a temporal event like completion of 30 days from the day the privacy-constrained data was recorded or can be non-temporal like request to provide data from a user for a certain purpose. Therefore simple EPAL can be mapped to a *event-condition-action (ECA) rule* [2].

3.2 Mapping Compound Requests to ECA

The intuitive question that corresponds to this request is "I belong to multiple user categories. Is there any of my user categories that allows me to perform all actions for all purposes on all data categories?". For a given user-category that is allowed or denied to perform the action, the resulting obligations are collected from all applicable rules and then returned.

This problem is solved in EPAL in two parts: First, it is resolved for one user-category. Then, the procedure is repeated for all user-categories [15].

A compound authorization request contains (a) a non-empty set of user-categories U, (b) a non-empty set of data-categories T, (c) a non-empty set of purposes P, (d) a non-empty set of actions A, and (e) a container provider as defined above.

The algorithm must output (1) a ruling that is either "allow", "deny", or "not-applicable", (2) a set of rule "id"s that mandated this ruling (or the empty set if the ruling was the default ruling).and (2) a set of pairs (obligation, rule-id-set) with disjoint obligations (obligations with different parameters are considered to be disjoint) and a list of rule-"id"s that mandated this particular obligation.

The compound query for a particular user-category is decomposed into simple requests [15]. After processing the simple requests for all combinations of elements in the compound request, one can determine the ruling for this user category as follows:

- If all rulings are 'not-applicable', the ruling is 'not-applicable' with an empty rule-id-set.
- Else, if at least one ruling is 'allow' and no ruling is 'deny', the algorithm returns "allow", the allowRules rule-id-set, and the allowObligations set.
- Else, (if there is one or more 'deny' rulings), the algorithm returns 'deny', the denyRules rule-id-set, and the denyObligations.

Multiple user categories are processed in the order that they are defined inside the vocabulary of the policy: The detailed processing syntax for multiple categories and design features of EPAL are given by M. Schunter et al [15].

Hence again we see that the above representation is essentially a *event-condition-action (ECA) rule* [2] with composite events and composite conditions (ref. section 3.3). So again the tuple (U,T,P) forms the composite condition whereas A becomes the action.

Therefore the next challenge is to represent the privacy policies in a rule language and then to model them for fast access and execution. For the privacy engine defined in this paper, the policy representation needs to be powerful enough to capture all the possible privacy policies required to manage data, and it should be simple enough to allow a GUI design for policy specification, which can be handled by a non-IT expert. This language is based on the interpretation of ECA (Event-Condition-Action) rule [10]8. In this paper we describe a user interface language to specify policies that defines policies more self-explanatory and provides easy to follow steps for modifying them (see Section 5). In the proposed graphical language, the definitions of Event, Condition and Action are defined through user interface. In next section, we outline the different types of events that have been considered in our initial prototype.

3.3 Types of Events

An *event* is defined to be an atomic (happens completely or not at all) occurrence. The event can be a primitive event or a combination of primitive events, called *composite events*. A *primitive event* is an event that cannot be broken down into further independent events. The primitive events considered in our initial prototype are (a) *Database events*, (b) *Temporal events* and (c) *External notifications*. *Database events* include attempts to *Insert, Delete, Access* and *Update* operations. *Temporal events* are of the type *absolute, relative* and *periodic*. *External Notifications* are application-defined events. The external notifications are in the form of "interrupts" from the external environment wherein the external environment consists of the domain excluding the native database. In our graphical language (for policy definition), we also consider limited composite events which are formed by applying various operators such as OR, AND, ANY, SEQUENCE on primitive and/or temporal events. For more detailed information about these operators, we refer the reader to see the event specification language, called SNOOP, for Sentinel system.

4 Architecture for a Policy Driven Data Administration

In this section we describe the architecture of the proposed system that can be loosely coupled with the underlying database systems. The conceptual architecture of a loosely coupled enterprise privacy policy enforcer (EPPE) in a centralized environment is shown in Fig. 1. EPPE component is built on top of underlying database systems. The main function of EPPE is to enforce privacy on the records based on the policies defined in the privacy policy database.

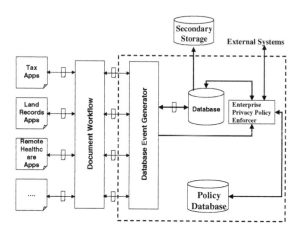

Fig. 1. Conceptual architecture of a loosely coupled EPPE based system

Fig. 2 shows the layer architecture of the *Enterprise Privacy Policy Enforcer* that includes *Privacy Policy definition Interface, Authentication and Authorization Manager, Policy Validator, Privacy Policy Translator* and a *Privacy Policy Execution Engine*. The user with low IT-skills can define the policy through the *Privacy Policy definition Interface*, which is a user-friendly GUI. The policies are defined like ECA (Event-Condition-Action) rules where the events are stored in a event table and policy definitions are stored in a rule table. *Privacy Policy Translator* converts the policy specified by the user through the *Privacy Policy definition Interface* to a format that can be stored directly in the database and can be executed by the *Privacy Policy Execution Engine*. The functioning of the *Privacy Policy Execution Engine* is detailed out in section 6.

The Transaction Notification Layer in the layered architecture of EPPE (ref. Fig. 2) captures the events (ambiguous sentence) and sends them to the Privacy Policy Execution Engine. The Privacy Policy Execution Engine is responsible for detecting the situations and then reacting against the situations that have occurred.

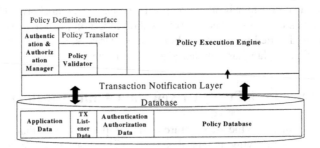

Fig. 2. Layered architecture of EPPE

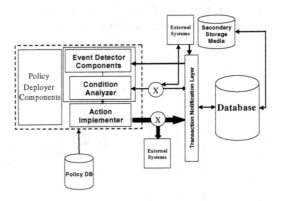

Fig. 3. Privacy policy execution engine

The Authentication and Authorization Manager manages the access control of the EPPE framework. The Policy Validator in EPPE ensures that all a-priori conflicts in policy definition are flagged out for the user to resolve. This layer is a critical first level filter for controlling policy conflicts and is missing in the other rule-based systems like Sentinel [9], SAMOS [8] etc.

The block level description of the *Privacy Policy Execution Engine* is shown in Fig. 3. The Engine consists of *Event Detector, Condition Analyzer* and *Action Implementer*. Its prime responsibility is to detect the events, check the conditions and then execute the actions defined in the policies. As defined earlier, the event can come from the database, or it can be from an external source, or it can be temporal event. The *temporal events* are generated and detected by the *Event Detector* itself while the *external events* and the *database events* are fed to the *event detector*. Similarly, conditions for the policy can be database condition or external conditions. For checking database (state variable) conditions, the *condition analyzer* queries the database to verify the condition. For external conditions, the *condition analyzer* sends out a query to the external system and gets a reply from the system, confirming or denying the satisfaction of the condition.

5   Mechanism for Defining and Storing Privacy Policies

The GUI for policy specification has three main screens, corresponding to the event specification, the condition specification and the action specification. Each of the screens is functionally complete in specifying the respective part of the rule. Thus each component of the policy is treated as an *atomic* entity having no direct impact on the specification of any other component of the policy. In the next three sections, an overview of each screen of the GUI is given along with the manner in which they store their respective components.

5.1   Event Specification Screen

For defining a new event, a unique *Event Name* needs to be entered in to the event specification screen. If the event name already exists in the database, then the GUI should prompt the user to check the event name and definition. The event defined can be a primitive or a composite event.

The type of event is to be specified in the 'Event Type' drop down box. There are three types of primitive events; (1) database event, (2) temporal event and (3) external event. In the prototype implemented, only two types of events have been allowed which are database events and temporal events. Users can either create a new event from scratch or can use an already existing (primitive or composite) event and may create a new event. A drop down list of the databases, tables and fields, according to the access privileges, along with allowed operations are shown to the policy creator in order to specify the location of occurrence of the event.

Once the user has filled the required parameters and presses the submit button, the event definition is temporarily cached and the condition screen gets displayed.

5.2   Condition Specification

In the condition screen, the user can specify the database site (i.e. where the condition needs to be checked), department (owner of the database), table (the name of the table on which the condition is to be tested), the field whose value needs to be checked and the specific binary operator and comparison value.

Using the operators, a composite condition can be formed. Upon the submit button, the condition is stored in a temporary session variable while the server provides the user with the action specification.

5.3 Action Specification

In order to manage data, four types of actions are required, namely *notification, purge, archive* or *database action* (insert, delete or update). *Notification* action sends a notification to an external system. This notification can be used to trigger action on an external system. *Purge* action purges the records from the database while *archive* action removes the records from the main memory and backs it up in a secondary storage. Database actions include insertion, deletion or modification of records. Each action takes a fixed set of parameters and is appended to the action string. Once the action string is submitted, the complete definition of the policy is displayed before the user presses the final submit button. If the user wants to change the definition of any component (i.e. event, condition or action), he/she is allowed to make the changes.

5.4 Policy Storage Mechanism

Once the events are defined, they are stored in the database tables. Each type of event (i.e. primitive, composite or temporal) is stored in different event table.

The *Primitive Event Table* schema is defined as {Event ID (*Integer*), Creation Time (*Var Char*), Event Name (*Var Char*), Event Type (*Var Char*), Event Owner (*Var Char*), Database Name (*Var Char*) and Table Name (*Var Char*)}.

Event ID is the system generated event identification number, which in combination with *Event Name* makes the primary key. *Creation Time* is the event creation time. *Event Type* indicates the type of operation the event is about to perform, namely Insert, Update or Delete. *Event Owner* stores the name of the creator who has created the policies.

The *Composite Event Table* schema is defined as {Event ID (*Integer*), Creation Time (*Var Char*), Event Name (*Var Char*), Event Owner (*Var Char*), Primitive Event Name (*Var Char*), Operator (*Var Char*), Next ID (*Integer*)}. In composite event table schema, *Primitive Event Name* denotes the name of the primitive events, which form a part of the composite event tree. *Operator* denotes the name of the operator by which the corresponding primitive event is connected by the event shown by Next ID.

The *Temporal Event Table* schema is defined as {Creation Time (*Var Char*), Event Name (*Var Char*), Event Type (*Var Char*), Event Owner (*Var Char*), Starting Time (*Var Char*), Event Occurance Time (*Var Char*), Ending Time (*Integer*)}.

In a temporal event table schema, *Creation Time* is stored as a string in the sec/min/hour/day/date/month/year format. *Event Type* indicates whether it is an absolute event or a periodic event. *Starting Time* is the time when the detection of a relative or a periodic event starts; this entry is null if the event is an absolute event. *Event Occurrence time* denotes the period/interval, in case of periodic events, after which the event will recur. *Stop Time* is the time whence the periodic event will stop occurring. The *Rule Table* schema is defined as {Rule Name (*Var Char*), Rule Creation Time (*Var Char*), Event Name (*Var Char*), Condition String (*Var Char*), Action String (*Var Char*), Class Name (*Var Char*)}.

Table 3. Example of an entry in the Rule Table

Rule Name	Rule Creation Time	Event Name	Condition String	Action String	Class Name
Rule1	10/07/10/Thrs/22/11/2005	Primitive e1	Cond_str1	Act_str1	ActionDbClass 1
Rule2	10/50/15/Fri/25/12/2005	Primitive e2	Cond_str2	Act_str2	ActionDbClass 2

Once the rule has been specified the condition and action part need to be stored in the rule table as shown in Table 3 to completely specify the rule definition.

Once the rule is detected, the rule execution engine hands over the action string to the class responsible for the action. The class is a generic one and it parses the action string and performs the required action.

6 Implementation Architecture and Policy Execution Model

The policy implementation architecture follows a layered model, consisting of *Transaction Notification Layer, Event Detection Layer, Condition Analyzer, Action Implementer* and *Authentication & Authorization Service*.

6.1 Transaction Notification Layer

Transaction notification layer provides single point access to database services. The application components interface with *Transaction Notification Layer* for viewing, updating, deleting and inserting records. No application component is expected to interface directly with the database so that the data consistency is maintained. The layer assists in event detection by 'informing' Event Detection Layer about transaction details and data changes (if any).

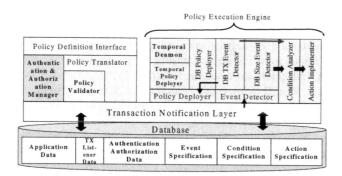

Fig. 4. Implementation Architecture

6.2 Event Detection Layer

Event Detection Layer is responsible for detecting and broadcasting events specified in *Event table*. For each event occurrence, the layer *broadcasts* events to their respective event listeners that are registered with the system. The *Transaction Notification Layer* notifies the *Event Detection Layer* about the database transactions and data changes in the system and the application databases. For performance reasons, *Event Detection Layer* then processes the information in its own thread and decouples processing from client, which in this case is the *Transaction Notification Layer*.

Event detection is a simple process of checking user-defined events in *Event table*. This is achieved by comparing transaction type, target database name and the data value in transaction (data value, if any, is specified in Policy Event definition). One or more event may be detected for a given transaction. The layer thus identifies all the events and performs event broadcasting to the individual *Event Listener Components* (i.e. Policy Deployer Layer and Condition Analyzer Layer) that have been registered for the specific event. The *Event Detection Layer* efficiently broadcasts events using parallel processing. For example, a default system event is specified for Policy database transactions. These details are stored with *Event Listener Table*.

6.3 Condition Analyzer Layer

Condition Analyzer Layer checks for satisfactory conditions once an event is detected. *Event Detection Layer* notifies the *Condition Analyzer Layer* for any event occurrence as per policy event definition. Event data associated with event is also passed to the *Condition Analyzer Layer*. Condition Analyzer evaluates the condition specified in the policy. If there are multiple conditions associated for a specific event, *Condition Analyzer Layer* may choose to evaluate conditions concurrently. On positive condition evaluation, the layer finally notifies *Action Implementer Layer* for action execution. There can be multiple action components, in the *Action Implementer Layer,* for a specific policy. Action components may also define a workflow and are thus invoked serially as per action definition.

6.4 Action Implementer Layer

Action Implementer Layer defines core action execution logic for any specified policy. *Action Implementation Layer* consists of action components. On successful event detection and condition evaluation, *Action Implementation Layer* executes a predefined action. Workflow may also be defined by specifying more than one action component for a policy, in the appropriate execution sequence. The system defines a set of action components specified frequently in Policy Action requirements. These components can be the *Mail Notification Component* (the component which sends out a mail notification), *Database transaction component* (the component which sends notification when a transaction is performed), *Data archive and backup component* (the component which performs data archiving and backup) etc. Custom action implementers can be developed by sub-classing pre-defined interface. They can be deployed in the system through a configuration XML file.

6.5 Authentication and Authorization Service

Authentication and Authorization Service (AAS) provides single point access to user privileges and rights to access/ modify application data. Database transaction notification layer allows database transactions only after AAS has verified the authenticity and the authorization of the user. AAS maintains a separate set of pre-defined user access and privileges table. These database tables are again accessed and modified using Database transaction notification layer.

6.6 Policy Deployment and Execution Model Workflow

This section describes a high level workflow across the functionality layers for policy deployment and execution.

The process starts when a user logs onto the system and is authenticated to use the system. User business action privileges are loaded through AAS and are cached in User Session for further User Business Requests.

User Is of Type: Policy Writer

1. Privacy Policy definition Interface responds with ECA pages to create/ modify/ view policies. Privacy Policy Translator translates policy definition from 'machine language' to 'user view' and vice-versa. Policy Validator validates policies against format schema and conflicts with existing Policies. On validation, Policy Builder requests Database Transaction Notification (DTN) layer to persist Policy Specification (ECA Definition) in Policy database. DTN provides database transaction service and on successful transaction, notifies Event Detector for the executed transaction.
2. Event Detector checks for event in event specification table for the executed database transaction. Policy database modification event is default system defined event. Event Listener components are specified in separate Event Listener Component table. Policy Deployer is notified for the updates in Policy Database.
3. Policy Deployer pulls in Policy details from Policy Database and categorizes Policy Event for Temporal type and Database Transaction type. Policy Deployer then 'handover' policy details to appropriate policy deployer (Temporal Policy Deployer, DB Tx Policy Deployer).
4. Temporal policy deployer validates the new/updated policy against the existing deployed ('in execution') temporal policies. If any exists on the same, Temporal Policy deployer removes its entry from active temporal policy database. A new temporal policy is inserted in the temporal policy database and temporal event generator daemon is notified. Temporal Event Daemon passively checks for temporal events and triggers the same to Event Detector on event occurrence.
5. Database policy deployer updates "Event Listener Component table" for the specified database transaction over specified database. The component first checks for any pre-existing records over the same policy event. No duplicate entries are persisted in "Event Listener Component table".

User Is of Type - Application Business Executor

1. Application business execution interface allows user to update/ view/ modify application data. Application AAS component validates user privileges before allowing user to undertake business request. Application data is transacted using "Database Transaction Notification Service".
2. DTN undertakes database transaction and 'notifies' Event Detector for the same.
3. Event Detector component 'consults' "Event - Event Listener Component table" for registered policy events. A database transaction becomes a Policy Event if the same is specified in the above table. Event Listeners are then broadcasted for the event occurrence with event data. A default event listener for application database transaction is "Condition Analyzer". Temporal Policy Manager can be other commonly used event listener to update "in-execution" temporal policies.
4. Condition Analyzer is notified for event occurrence with event details (transacted data). Condition Analyzer evaluates event condition with Policy Condition definition. On positive evaluation, Condition Analyzer notifies Action Implementer to undertake policy action. If multiple Action Implementers are registered for the given policy, Condition Analyzer invokes them in sequence of specification. Temporal Event generation daemon may also notify Condition Analyzer for event occurrence.
5. Action Implementer gets Event and Condition Notification from Condition Analyzer. "Action Implementer" components are pre-defined policy action execution components. These components pull in their execution parameters from Policy Action database.

7   Conclusions and Future Work

In this paper we have presented a architecture for using simple ECA, using active database components available in commercial databases, to implement an EPAL based privacy policy. This architecture supports *privacy policy specification* and *privacy policy execution* requirements of a system that can autonomously manage data based on pre-specified policies. We have designed a GUI for specifying privacy policies by considering the fact that these policies would be defined by non-IT expert and have discussed the model for storing and executing these policies in the database.

The solution is independent of the database and sits as a layer on top of the database. Thus it can be implemented on any existing legacy database. Hence it acts as a user-friendly privacy middleware.

Future work required would be to have a more rigorous semantic proof of equivalence of EPAL and ECA. We also plan to capture and pass on event parameters [10] in beta version of our prototype. We also plan to include role based access control mechanism defined on the different components of the policies and to investigate algorithms for identifying conflicts between policies.

References

1. U. Dayal et al., 'The HiPAC Project: Combining Active Databases and Timing Constraints', ACM Sigmod Record, 17:1, March 1988.
2. S. Chakravarthy (ed.)., 'Active Databases', Special Issue of the Bulletin of the IEEE TC on Data Engineering 15:1-4, 1992.
3. S. Chakravarthy, J. Widom, Proc. of the 4th Intl. Workshop on Research Issues in Data Engineering: Active Database Systems, Houston, February 1994.
4. Stella Gatziu, Klaus R. Dittrich, 'SAMOS', Active Rules in Database Systems 1999: 233-247
5. Thierry Coupaye, Christine Collet, 'Semantics Based Implementation of Flexible Execution Models for Active Database Systems', Proc. 14ème Journées Bases de Données Avancées, BDA 1998: 0-
6. S. Gatziu, A. Geppert, and K.R. Dittrich, 'Integrating active concepts into an object-oriented database system', 3rd Int'l.Workshop on Database Programming Languages, Naflion, August 1991.
7. S. Chakravarthy, E. Anwar, and L. Maugis, 'Design and implementation of active capability for an object-oriented database', Technical Report UF-CIS-TR-93-001, University of Florida, January 1993.
8. S. Chakravarthy, R. Le, R. Desai, 'ECA Rule processing in Distributed and Heterogeneous Environments', Proceedings of the International Symposium on Distributed Objects and Applications
9. S. Chakravarthy, V. Krishnaprasad, Z. Tamizuddin, R.H. Badani, 'ECA Rule Integration into an OODBMS: Architecture and Implementation', Proc. Of the 11th Intl. Conf. On Data Engineering. Taipei, Taiwan, March 1995.
10. S. Chakravarthy and D. Mishra, 'Snoop: An expressive event specification language for active databases', Knowledge and Data Engineering Journal, 14:1--26, 1994
11. Elisa Bertino, Giovanna Guerrini, Isabella Merlo, 'Triggers in Java-based Databases', L'OBJET 6 (3): (2000)
12. Elisa Bertino, Giovanna Guerrini, Isabella Merlo, 'Trigger Inheritance and Overriding in an Active Object Database System', TKDE 12(4): 588-608 (2000)
13. Emil Lupu, Morris Sloman, 'Conflicts in Policy-Based Distributed Systems Management', IEEE Transactions on Software Engineering (TSE) 25(6): 852-869 (1999)
14. J. Bhattacharya and S.K. Gupta, 'Privacy Broker for Enforcing Privacy Policies in Databases', KBCS-2004. Fifth international conference on knowledge based computer systems. Hyderabad, India, December 19-22, 2004.
15. M. Schunter et al, Enterprise Privacy Authorization Language (EPAL 1.1), IBM Research Report, http://www.zurich.ibm.com/security/enterprise-privacy/epal
16. V. Batra et al. 'Policy Driven Data Administration'. POLICY 2002, IEEE 3rd International Workshop on Policies for Distributed Systems and Networks, 2002
17. R. Agrawal, J. Kiernan, R. Srikant, Y. Xiu. Hippocratic Databases (Vision Paper). IBM Almaden Research Center. 2002
18. Nabil R. Adam and John C. Wortman. Security-control methods for statistical databases. ACM Computing Surveys, 21(4):515-556, Dec. 1989.
19. S. Castano, M. Fugini, G. Martella, and P. Samarati. Database Security. Addison Wesley, 1995

An Attribute Graph Based Approach to Map Local Access Control Policies to Credential Based Access Control Policies*

Janice Warner[1], Vijayalakshmi Atluri[1], and Ravi Mukkamala[2]

[1] Rutgers University, Newark NJ 07012, USA
{janice, atluri}@cimic.rutgers.edu
[2] Old Dominion University, Norfolk, VA 23529, USA
mukka@cs.odu.edu

Abstract. Due to the proliferation of the Internet and web based technologies, today's collaborations among organizations are increasingly short-lived, dynamic, and therefore formed in an ad-hoc manner to serve a specific purpose. Such example environments include web-services, dynamic coalitions, grid computing and ubiquitous computing. These environments necessitate the need for dynamic, efficient and secure sharing of resources among disparate organizations. Although such secure sharing of resources can be achieved by means of traditional access control and authentication mechanisms, they are administratively difficult when the partnerships and interactions are short-lived and constantly changing. When allowing sharing of resources, the organization must ensure that its own security policies are adhered to. Our proposal is to allow users, external to the organization, access to internal resources of the organization, if they possess certain attributes *similar* to those possessed by the internal users. We begin by first examining the internal security policies within an organization and attempt to *map* them to credential based policies. In essence, we identify the attributes possessed by internal users relevant to a security policy, and map them to credential attributes that are understood across organizations. Access can then be granted to users once they submit these required credentials with the identified attributes. We present an attribute graph based methodology to accomplish such a mapping. In this paper, we assume that the local access control policies are limited to Role Based Access Control (RBAC) policies.

1 Introduction

With the connectivity available to companies and organizations today, collaboration supported by sharing of electronic resources (e.g., sharing information, working in common business process such as a supply chain or joint marketing) has become commonplace. However, techniques to ensure secure and automatic sharing of resources to entertain collaboration do not exist. Although traditional access control and authentication mechanisms can be adopted, they are administratively difficult to be implemented in a

* The work of Warner and Atluri is supported in part by the National Science Foundation under grant IIS-0306838.

S. Jajodia and C. Mazumdar (Eds.): ICISS 2005, LNCS 3803, pp. 134–147, 2005.

collaborative environment where the entities involved are not long standing partners or when the interactions are short-term. Even when the entities involved have long-term agreements, there are dynamic requirements that come into play. The members of the entity may change over time, resources may be added, updated or deleted, reasons for collaboration may change, or the policies of sharing themselves may change. Given the administrative difficulties, ad-hoc sharing of resources has become the norm.

Ad-hoc sharing of resources is currently being practiced in one of the following ways: Authentication identifiers are given to a small set of individuals, who in turn may give access to others, typically in an uncontrolled fashion. This results in individuals having access or authority over a larger set of resources than they should have. Alternatively, information is e-mailed as attachments via a secure channel, making updates difficult and again resulting in uncontrolled sharing. In the best situation, a collaboration repository is created and all shared resources are stored there. However, if the same resources need to be shared in different collaborations, duplicate copies are needed, which again may lead to lack of control.

Similar problems exist in a *web services* environment where resources and services are offered by and shared among registered collaborating entities. A typical way to accomplish this is to create a user identity specific to the service in question. Not only is this an administrative burden for the resource provider, it is also a burden to the user who needs to maintain separate identities for each resource to which access is needed. Moreover, if the services are to be components of a larger transaction, as envisioned for semantic web services, this approach will be impractical since the same identity may not be usable across the multiple domains providing the component services.

Access control research in the area of collaboration is relatively new. Philips et al. [13, 12] have described the dynamic coalition problem by providing several motivating scenarios in defense and disaster recovery settings. Cohen et al. [4] have proposed a model that captures the entities involved in coalition resource sharing and identifies the interrelationships among them. In [3, 7], the researchers have addressed the issue of automating the negotiation of policy between coalition members in a dynamic coalition. In [16], Yu et al. propose automated mechanisms for trust building between entities using digital credentials. Altenschmidt et al.[1] propose a mediated approach to querying for data between untrusted entities. Our previous work [2, 15] addresses the issue of automatic translation of coalition level policies to the implementation level policies, and vice versa.

In addition, access control based on user attributes rather than identity has been proposed as a solution to the dynamic granting of access rights to unknown users in several of the models cited above [16, 1, 2, 15] as well as in [14]. Using attributes simplifies administration because specific users do not have to be given specific identities. Instead, access rights are determined purely on the basis of attributes and these attributes can apply to many different users, who would present their attributes through the use of credentials.

While a part of the solution, attribute based access control (ABAC) and credential discovery is not sufficient. It is a mechanism, but the problem remains of determining what attributes will be used and what attribute values are acceptable by an organization to allow access by external users. If the attributes used are identity-based (e.g., name, e-mail address, etc.), the problem has not been solved. Likewise, there is the issue of determining semantic equivalence between attributes since disparities are likely to exist in the distributed environments for which ABAC would be of use. Finally, the shared resources will likely be protected internally using established access control mechanisms such as Discretionary Access Control (DAC), Lattice Based Access Control (LBAC) or Role Based Access Control (RBAC). An automated process for transforming the local access rules into attribute based rules would greatly facilitate the ability of an organization to dynamically share resources with external entities. Such a process applies the same rules externally as are applied internally by requiring the same attributes from external users to perform a specific operation on a specific resource that characterize internal users who have the same permission set.

This paper examines the issue of automatically transforming the local access policies into credential based policies. In particular, it automates the selection of credential attributes and attribute values required by external users (belonging to external organizations) to obtain access to resources of an organization. The methodology involves transforming the access control policies applicable to internal user access so that they can be applied to external users. In this paper, we describe a methodology for transforming Role Based Access Control (RBAC) policies into attribute requirements that must be presented by external users via credentials.

Koch et al. [8] have shown, using graph transformations, how DAC and LBAC can be specified in a uniform framework so that an accurate analysis of the interaction between policies could be performed. Likewise, it has been shown that RBAC can be generalized to enforce DAC and LBAC[11, 6]. To our knowledge, transformation of DAC, LBAC, or RBAC into policies based on attributes has not yet been adequately addressed. Li et al. [10, 9] address the problem with a set of policy languages and algorithms, Role-Based Trust Management (RT), that addresses the issues of semantic differences between RBAC policy instances as well as credential discovery. The algorithms are similar to what we propose here in that they attempt to answer the question of what credentials are needed in order to map to a role. However, their algorithms do not address strategies for selecting the subset of credentials (and values) required to allow external entities to obtain rights to resources. As will be shown, our algorithms also consider what to do with attribute requirements that cannot be satisfied by external credentials. Finally, although we use RBAC as the basis of the discussion in this paper, the algorithms can be generalized to any access control policy. It can be used with our overall architecture or the secure mediation architecture proposed in [1].

This paper is organized as follows. The remainder of this section presents a motivating example. Section 2 provides preliminary formalisms of the basic constructs needed in our proposed methodology. Section 3 presents our methodology for transforming RBAC policies to attribute requirements. Section 4 presents conclusions and future research.

1.1 Motivating RBAC Example

Let HapSys be a software development company that controls access to its resources using five basic roles - Requirements Analyst, Software Developer, Tester, Project Manager and Client Manager. The basic role hierarchy is illustrated in Figure 1, in which

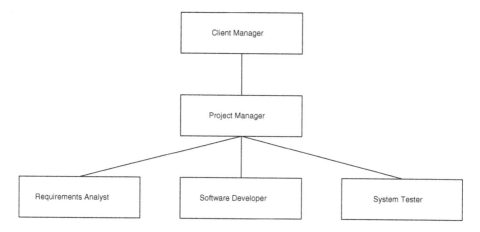

Fig. 1. An Example of Basic Role Hierarchy of HapSys

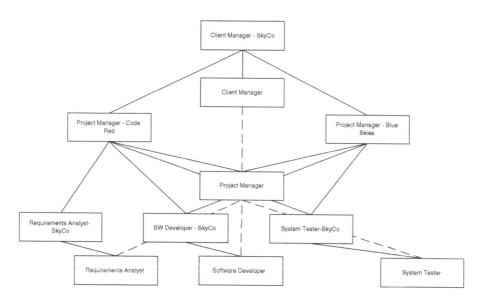

Fig. 2. An Example of a Complex Role Hierarchy of HapSys

the project manager inherits permissions from Requirements Analyst, Software Developer and Tester, and the Client Manager in turn inherits permissions from the Project Manager.

Since HapSys works on projects for many different clients, due to the need-to-know requirements and to prevent leakage of intellectual property between clients, access to resources associated with any one project should not be shared among employees working for other clients. Therefore, specialized roles for each client, are needed. Assuming

SkyCo is one of the clients of HapSys, the specialized roles for employees who work on projects for SkyCo have been added. The same also applies to different projects, in this case, 'Code Red' and 'Blue Skies' for the same client. We arbitrarily assume the project managers for the two projects are different and will have different rights to project resources, but requirements analysts, software developers, and system testers may work on components of both projects to ensure commonality and consistency in analysis, coding and testing. Figure 2 shows the resultant role hierarchy. The relationships among the newly created roles are represented by solid lines, whereas the original ones are shown by dashed lines. As can be seen, System Tester-SkyCo has permissions to all resources for which the role System-Tester has permissions. In addition, it also has permissions to system testing resources specific to SkyCo. Clearly, this is just a small portion of an overall role hierarchy that can be shown for HapSys, which would include specific roles for all clients and all projects as necessary.

Now suppose SkyCo would like to allow members from a third organization, Test-it-Sys, to review the test results for project "Blue Skies" and HapSys has agreed to permit this access. Each of these users of Test-it-Sys could be issued a user id to the HapSys system where the material is housed and these user ids could be added to the appropriate role. However, if the number of users is large or if there are many projects that require external access by clients or their associates, the process would be administratively difficult for HapSys. Instead, we propose a methodology based on mapping attributes of HapSys roles that have permissions to the requested resource to credential attributes that are known among the three organizations. Now, to gain access to resources at HapSys, a Test-it-Sys user simply needs to submit his/her credentials.

2   The Preliminaries

We briefly present the necessary formalism required to describe our approach.

2.1   Resources

Each organizational entity maintains a set of resources that can be shared with other organizational entities. Resources may include data objects as well as services offered by the coalition entity. Each resource belongs to a resource-type, organized via a resource-type hierarchy. Let RT and RES be the set of resource types and resources, respectively.

Definition 1. [Resource-type] A resource-type rt is a pair (rt_id, RA), where $rt\_id \in RT$ is a unique resource-type identifier; and RA is the set of attributes associated with rt_id. Each $ra_i \in RA$ is denoted by an attribute name.

Definition 2. [Resource] A resource res is a triple $(rt\_id, res\_id, res\_attr\_values)$, where $rt\_id \in RT$, $res\_id \in RES$, $res\_attr\_values = (ra : v_1, \ldots, ra : v_n)$, where $\{ra_1, \ldots, ra_n\} \subseteq RA(rt)$. $RA(rt)$ denotes the set of attributes associated with rt.

We use $res(res\_id)$, $res(rt\_id)$ and $res(res\_attr\_values)$ to denote the resource id, the resource-type id, and the set of attribute values of the resource res, respectively. The set of resource attributes describe the resource such as keywords or concepts.

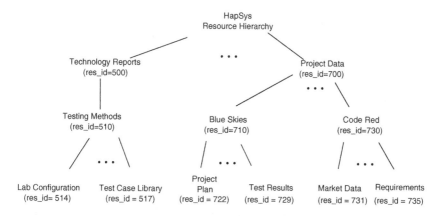

Fig. 3. An example of a Resource Type Hierarchy

Example 1. HapSys has a resource type hierarchy, part of which is represented by Figure 3. Each of the resources depicted is identified by a resource identifier "res-id".

2.2   The RBAC Model

We adopt the NIST standard of the Role Based Access Control (RBAC) model [5]. For the sake of simplicity, we do not consider sessions or separation of duties constraints. In addition, we include other derived terms of this model.

Definition 3. [RBAC]

- $U, ROLES, OPS$, and RES are the set of users, roles, operations, and resources.
- $UA \subseteq U \times ROLES$, a many-to-many mapping user-to-role assignment relation.
- PRMS (the set of permission) $\subseteq \{(op, res)|op \in OPS \bigwedge res \in RES\}$
- $PA \subseteq PRMS \times ROLES$, a many-to-many mapping of permission-to-role assignments.
- $assigned\_users(r) = \{u \in U|(u,r) \in UA\}$, the mapping of role r onto a set of users.
- $assigned\_permissions(r) = \{p \in PRMS|(p,r) \in PA\}$, the mapping of role r onto a set of permissions.
- $required\_roles(p) = \{r \in ROLES|(p,r) \in PA\}$, the mapping of permissions to roles.

Example 2. For HapSys, required_roles(read, res_id = 729) = {SystemTester-SkyCo, Software Developer-SkyCo}.

2.3   Credentials

We assume that each user is associated with one or more *credentials*. Credentials are assigned when a subject is created and are updated according to the profile of the subject. Let CT be the set of credential types.

Definition 4. [Credential-type] A credential-type ct is a pair (ct_id, CA), where $ct\_id \in CT$ is a unique identifier and CA is the set of attributes belonging to ct_id. Each $ca_i \in CA$ has an attribute name and $CA(ct)$ is the set of attributes belonging to ct.

Definition 5. [Credential] A credential c, an instance of a credential-type ct, is a 4-tuple
$(ct\_id, c\_id, user\_profile)$, where $ct\_id \in CT$, c_id is a unique credential identifier, and $user\_profile = (a_1 : v_1, \ldots, a_n : v_n)$, where $\{a_1, \ldots a_n\} \subseteq CA(ct)$.

Example 3. An example of a credential for credential type "project manager" is as follows:
(project manager, (certification: PMI, experience level: high, project: Blue Skies)).

3   Transformation of RBAC Policies to Credential Based Policies

In this section, we demonstrate how RBAC policies specified on roles can be mapped to credential based policies. Specifically, we first extract the attributes of the subjects relevant to a policy and map them to the credential attributes. In particular, our transformation method depends on associating permissions (to access the resource in question) with the attributes of roles, specifically, the attributes of the users who are members of a role, and then generating the required set of attributes.

We use A to denote the set of attributes, and $A(u)$ to denote the attributes associated with a specific user u. Furthermore, given an attribute $a_i \in A(u_j)$, we use $(a_i : v_{ij})$ to denote the value associated with an attribute a_i for a specific user u_j. Let O represent an organization. We assume that users in U may belong to any organization.

However, not all attributes are relevant in the transformation process, and moreover, some attributes cannot be easily dealt with. Specifically, the attributes that are specific to a single user or a single organization are difficult to be transformed into the attributes of the universally agreeable credentials. On the other hand, certain attributes that are common to users of different organizations are easier to deal with. As such, we categorize the attributes into three types: *identifier, local* and *general*, and use IA, LA and GA, to denote these sets respectively. Essentially, $A = IA \cup LA \cup GA$. Formally,

Definition 6. [Attribute Types] There are three attribute types (at):
Identifier Attributes: $IA = \{a \in A | \forall (u_i, u_j) \in U, a : v_i \neq a : v_j\}$
General Attribute: $GA = \{a \in A | \exists (u_i, u_j) \in U \text{ such that } a : v_i = a : v_j\}$
Local Attribute: $LA = \{a \in A | \forall (O_i, O_j), \text{ if } (a \in O_i \wedge a \in O_j), \text{ then } (a : v_i) \not\equiv (a : v_j)$, where v_i and v_j are values of a in O_i and O_j, respectively.$\}$

Essentially, an identifier attribute is one for which there is a one-to-one correspondence between the attribute value and a user. Examples of such attributes include user name and e-mail address. A general attribute is one for which there is a one-to-many correspondence between the attribute value and a set of users. A specific certification, academic degree, etc., are examples of general attributes. A local attribute is any general attribute for which values are valid only within one organization. For example, a department name is a local attribute. It may exist in other organizations but cannot be assumed to assume the same value. Likewise, even if the value is the same, it may be irrelevant (e.g.,, "room number").

Our RBAC to credential transformation essentially identifies the attributes required by users who play the specific role, and attempts to map them to the credential attributes. This is accomplished in the following three steps. Given an RBAC policy, we first identify the potential required attribute to access the resources stated in the policy. Second, a subset of attributes are selected from the above set, using certain *selection strategies*. Third, general, local and identifier attributes (if they are selected) are transformed to comparable credential attributes. The following three subsections describe these steps in detail.

3.1   Identifying Potential Attribute Requirements

We begin with assuming that each user is associated with a set of attributes say $A(u_i)$ where $A(u_i) \subseteq A$. We use $U(a_i)$ to denote the set of users that possess a_i. We assume that there exist a specific order among the different types of attributes. We denote the order of an attribute as $o(a)$. Specifically, the order of general attributes is higher than that of local or identifier attributes, and the order of local attributes is higher than that of identifier attributes. Formally,

Definition 7. Given two attributes a_i and a_j, $o(a_i) > o(a_j)$ if

(i) $a_i \in GA \wedge a_i \in LA$, or
(ii) $a_i \in GA \wedge a_i \in IA$, or
(iii) $a_i \in LA \wedge a_i \in IA$.

Our goal is to select attributes that are most common to users among the role associated with a permission. To accomplish this, we build an *attribute graph* (AG) that has the following properties.

Definition 8. [Attribute Graph] Given a permission p, let $U_p = \cup$ assigned_users(r_i) where $r_i \in$ required_roles(p). Let $A(U_p) = \cup A(u_i)$ where $u_i \in U_p$. We define an attribute graph, $AG(p)$, as follows:

- Every node $a_i \in AG(p)$ should be such that $a_i \in A(U_p)$.
- Every node a_i is associated with a weight w_i and a value range, $vr_i)$
- Every edge $a_i \rightarrow a_j$ is a directed edge such that $o(a_i) \geq o(a_j)$ and $|U(a_i)| \geq |U(a_j)|$.

The above graph may not necessarily be fully connected, but may as well be a forest. Each path from the root to a leaf in an attribute graph represents the set of attributes associated with a group of one or more users.

The steps for creating the attribute graph for a specific permission, p, (which is formalized in Algorithm 1) is as follows:

1. Sort in descending order the set of users with the permission p, U_p, based on the number of attributes associated with them ($|A(u_i)|$). Let this be Q_u.
2. Sort the attributes in $A(U_p)$ in descending order, based on their order as well as based on the number of users associated with the attribute ($U(a_i)$). Let the position of the attribute a_i in the sorted list be $so(a_i)$.

3. Let u_0 be the first user in Q_u. The initial tree is nothing but the sorted attributes of $A(u_i)$. In other words, attributes in $A(u_0)$ are the nodes, and there exist a directed edge $a_i \rightarrow a_j$ if $so(a_i) > so(a_j)$. Each node is assigned a weight of 1, and a value range which is equal to the value (say v_0) of a_i for user u_0. The root of the tree is added to the set $roots$.

4. Pick the next user $u_i \in Q_u$. Select the attribute $a_j \in A(u_i)$ such that for every $a_k \in A(u_i)$, $so(a_j) > so(a_k)$.

   (a) If a_j is not in the set of $roots$ construct the tree as in step 3. This will be a new attribute tree is added to the forest. Add a_j to the set $roots$.

   (b) Otherwise, retrieve the tree with a_j as the root, Increment the weight of a_j by 1, and if the value range does not include the value of the attribute for this user, then include it the value range.

   (c) Select the attribute $a_k \in A(u_i)$ with the next higher value of so. If it is the same as one of the descendants of a_j, then increment the weight of a_k by 1, and if the value range does not include the value of the attribute for this user, then include it in the value range. Repeat this step until all attributes are exhausted or the above condition is not true.

   (d) If it is not same as the descendent a_j, then add a directed edge from a_i to a_k. Assign a weight of 1, and a value range which is equal to the value (say v_i) of a_i for user u_i. Include all remaining attributes of nodes in the descending order by connecting them with directed edges, add the weight of 1 and value range as the value of the attribute for this user u_i.

5. Repeat step 4 until all users in Q_u are exhausted.

To perform the transformation, the attributes of the users who are members of the role which has the requisite rights for the requested resource must be examined. The attribute graph (which could be a forest), as created above, is used to make decisions as to whether to include the attributes (and associated values) as attribute requirements. If the resource is accessible by more than one role, then if the roles are in the same tree, only the lowest level role must be considered. Otherwise, if the roles are not in the same tree, each role's users' attributes must be considered unless a predetermined precedence rule applies between the roles in question.

3.2   Attribute Selection Strategies

There are many strategies that can be considered in selecting attributes to be required of external users to access a resource. A logical, but not an exhaustive list of strategies is described below:

Conservative Strategy: Without using the attribute graph, the most stringent credential requirement would be the full collection of attributes held by all users assigned to a role r involved in permission p (This has been adopted in [2]). However, this would clearly be a greater requirement than any single internal user and would likely result in no external user gaining access.

Largest Attribute Group Strategy: The attribute graph aids in determining all potential subsets of the attributes that apply to members of the roles with the requisite rights.

Algorithm 1. Attribute Graph Creation

1: $Q_u \leftarrow$ Descending-sort(U_p) by $|A(u_i)|$ {Step 1}
2: $SA \leftarrow$ Descending-sort(A(U_p)) by $|U(a_i)|$ {Step 2}
3: Let $so(a_i) =$ position of a_i in SA
4: Let $roots = \emptyset$ {roots contains the root nodes of each tree}
5: Let $tree - num = 1$
6: **for all** $u_i \in Q_u$ **do**
7:     $a = A(u_i)$ in SA order
8:     **if** $a_1 \in roots$ **then**
9:         extract $T[root - num]$ {If the user's first attribute is the root of a tree, expand the root of that tree - Step 4b}
10:        $w(a_1) = w(a_1) + 1$
11:        **if** $v_1 \cap vr(a_1) = \emptyset$ **then**
12:            expand $vr(a_1)$
13:        **end if**
14:    **else**
15:        $roots = roots \cup \{a_1\}$ {Create a new tree - Steps 3 and 4a}
16:        create-tree $T[tree - num]$
17:        $tree - num = tree - num + 1$
18:        $w(a_1) = 1$
19:        $vr(a_1) = \{v_1\}$
20:    **end if**
21:    Let $a_i = a_1$ {Examine all other attributes of the user}
22:    **for all** $a_j \in a - \{a_1\}$ **do**
23:        **if** $a_j \equiv descendent[a_i]$ **then**
24:            $w(a_j) = w(a_j) + 1$ {Update attribute node - Step 4c}
25:            expand $vr(a_i)$
26:        **else**
27:            $create - node(a_j)$ {Add new attribute node to tree - Step 4d}
28:            $create - edge(a_i, a_j)$
29:            $w(a_j) = 1$
30:            $vr(a_j) = v$
31:        **end if**
32:        Let $a_i = a_j$
33:    **end for**
34: **end for**

Since each path from root to leaf in any tree $T \in AG$ represents the full set of attributes of one or more users in U, the longest path would have the next most conservative attribute requirements. The set of attributes on the longest path is thus the next most restrictive attribute requirement. However, if the set of attributes are not held by many of the users (i.e., the weights on the nodes along this path, $w \ll |U_p|$), it may not be the best choice.

Typical Profile Strategy: This strategy chooses attributes based on perceived importance of a user attribute. Using the attribute graph, a user attribute is considered to be

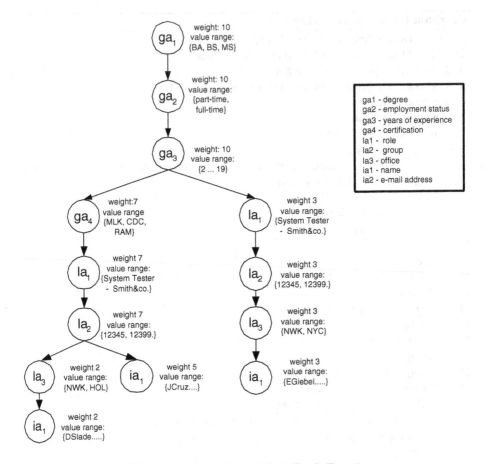

Fig. 4. An example of an Attribute Graph (Forest)

a critical attribute if it is held by at least ρ permissible users where ρ is a settable parameter and the number of users of an attribute is the weight of the node representing the attribute. If more than one path in T has nodes with weights greater or equal to ρ, the sets of attributes in each path can be considered as a set of alternative attribute requirements, where any one of the sets can be used to allow a particular access request.

Example 4. Suppose SkyCo asks Ellen Jones of Test-it-Sys to review the test results for project Blue Skies (res_id = 729 in Figure 3).

The relevant RBAC policy at HapSys is that System Tester-SkyCo and Software Developer-SkyCo have access to res_id = 729.

The attribute graph for the members of that role is shown in Figure 4.

Under the Largest Attribute Group *strategy, the leftmost path would be selected by HapSys as the attribute requirements on external users. That is, attributes ga_1, ga_2, ga_3, ga_4, la_1, la_2, la_3 and ia_1. In other words, the required attributes would include: degree, employment status, years of experience, certification, role, group, office and name.*

Fig. 5. Local Attribute Ontology Concept

However, since other internal users who have rights to the resources have a different set of attributes, a decision could be made to use a smaller set of attribute requirements. Let us say, under the Typical Profile Strategy, *that HapSys has set $\rho = 0.5 \times |U_p|$. Since, in this example there are 10 users with the required permission, $\rho = 5$ and the attributes selected would be ga_1, ga_2, ga_3, ga_4, la_1, la_2, and ia_1. In other words, the required attributes would include: degree, employment status, years of experience, certification, role, group and name.*

$\triangle$

3.3   Transformation of Required Attributes to Credential Requirements

In this section, we explain how attribute requirements can be selected based on attributes associated with those users who have the requisite rights. However, as explained earlier, not all attributes are appropriate for external users. This section examines the transformation of general, identity and local attributes into external attributes that can be presented in credentials.

Since general attribute values could be held by any individual (inside or outside of the organization in question), they may not require any transformation. If a credential contains the attribute and the attribute value falls within the range requirement, the resource may be accessed externally. However, if the attribute name and range of values are not globally uniform, the semantics of attributes received may need to be translated, possibly through the aid of an ontology. As can be seen in Figure 5, it can be used to map different attribute names in the credential attribute base with those in the local attribute base. This ontology would be a terminological ontology whose categories are distinguished by typical instances. For our purposes, we assume that general attributes are standard attributes that are globally understood.

Three options exist for transforming identity attributes and local attributes into general attributes:

1. Require Attribute - External users can be required to present an identification or group attribute of the correct form, but no particular values would be required. Any value in a valid credential could be presented. However, the value presented would be stored so that a record of access is made. In the case of local attributes, the presented attribute could be used to build up an ontology of local attribute equivalents.
2. Modify Attribute - Rather than present an identity attribute for themselves or a local attribute, they could be required to present an identity attribute for someone or

something else, such as the person who delegated rights to them or the organization to which they belong.

3. Ignore Attribute Requirement - The attribute can be ignored and rights be based solely on the other required attributes presented with appropriate credentials.

4 Conclusions

In this paper, we have proposed an attribute graph based approach to enable secure sharing of information among disparate organizations. Our approach ensures that internal security policies are adhered to when providing access to users of external organizations. Our approach is based on the premise that it allows subjects, external to the organization, access to internal resources of the organization, if they possess attributes that are in some sense *similar* to those possessed by the internal subjects. It essentially maps internal security policies within an organization to credential based policies. In this paper, we have assumed that the local access control policies are limited to Role Based Access Control (RBAC) policies. Our future work includes addressing this problem when local access control is based on DAC. While RBAC policies have some sense of grouping of users, the mapping of internal attributes to the credential attributes is relatively easier. To come up with groups of users that have, in some sense, similar behavior, one may need to resort to mining techniques. We will also explore the use of ontology to map heterogeneous attribute names.

References

1. Christian Altenschmidt, Joachim Biskup, Ulrich Flegel, and Yücel Karabulut. Secure mediation: Requirements, design, and architecture. *Journal of Computer Security*, 11(3):365–398, 2003.
2. V. Atluri and J. Warner. Automatic enforcement of access control policies among dynamic coalitions. In *International Conference on Distributed Computing and Internet Technology (ICDCIT 2004*, December 2004.
3. V. Bharadwaj and J. Baras. A framework for automated negotiation of access control policies. *Proceedings of DISCEX III*, 2003.
4. E. Cohen, W. Winsborough, R. Thomas, and D. Shands. Models for coalition-based access control (cbac). *SACMAT*, 2002.
5. D. Ferraiolo, R. Sandhu, S. Gavrila, D. Kuhn, and R. Chandramouli. Proposed nist standard for role-based access control. *TISSEC*, 2001.
6. S. Jajodia, P. Samarati, L. Maria, and V. S. Subrahmanian. Flexible support for multiple access control policies. *ACM TODS*, June 2001.
7. H. Khurana, S. Gavrila, R. Bobba, R. Koleva, A. Sonalker, E. Dinu, V. Gligor, and J. Baras. Integrated security services for dynamic coalitions. *Proc. of the DISCEX III*, 2003.
8. M. Koch, L. Mancini, and F. Parisi-Presicce. On the specification and evolution of access control policies. *SACMAT*, May 2001.
9. Ninghui Li, John C. Mitchell, and William H. Winsborough. Design of a role-based trust-management framework. In *IEEE Symposium on Security and Privacy*, pages 114–130, 2002.
10. Ninghui Li, William H. Winsborough, and John C. Mitchell. Distributed credential chain discovery in trust management. *Journal of Computer Security*, 11(1):35–86, 2003.

11. S. Osborn, R. Sandhu, and Q. Munawer. Configuring rbac to enforce mandatory and dac policies. *ACM TISSEC*, May 2000.
12. C. Philips, E. Charles, T. Ting, and S. Demurjian. Towards information assurance in dynamic coalitions. *IEEE IAW, USMA*, February 2002.
13. C. Philips, T.C. Ting, , and S. Demurjian. Information sharing and security in dynamic coalitions. *SACMAT*, 2002.
14. Lingyu Wang, Duminda Wijesekera, and Sushil Jajodia. A logic-based framework for attribute based access control. In *FMSE'04*, October 2004.
15. J. Warner, V. Atluri, and R. Mukkamala. A credential-based approach for facilitating automatic resource sharing among ad-hoc dynamic coalitions. In *Proceedings of IFIP 11.3*, 2005.
16. T. Yu, M. Winslett, and K.E. Seamons. Supporting structured credentials and sensitive policies through interoperable strategies for automated trust negotiation. *ACM Transactions on Information and System Security*, 6(1):1–42, February 2003.

Protection of Relationships in XML Documents with the XML-BB Model

Frédéric Cuppens, Nora Cuppens-Boulahia, and Thierry Sans

GET/ENST Bretagne, 2 rue de la Châtaigneraie,
35576 Cesson-Sévigné Cedex, France
{frederic.cuppens, nora.cuppens, thierry.sans}@enst-bretagne.fr

Abstract. Since XML tends to become the main format to exchange data over the Internet, it is necessary to define a security model to control the access to the content of these documents. Several such models have already been suggested, but we claim that none of them is sufficiently expressive to properly express some basic security requirements, especially those related to entity relationships protection. To cope with these limitations, we suggest to structure the access control policy using the new concept of *block*. This is used to hide relationships between nodes selected in different blocks. It provides means to specify confidentiality restriction associated with some relationships. An access control model, called XML-BB (XML Block Based Access Control), that includes this concept of block is presented and a formal semantics for this model is defined.

1 Introduction

XML is more and more widely used to exchange information over the Internet. Compared with other formalisms such as the relational model, XML provides a more expressive and flexible model to represent semi-structured data.

Since XML documents may contain sensitive and confidential data, we also need a security model to express access control restrictions to XML documents. Such a model already exists for the relational model. It is based on the GRANT and REVOKE instructions. The GRANT instruction enables the administrator to assign a permission to have an access to a relational view. REVOKE is the opposite instruction used to remove a permission granted onto a view. In SQL/92, GRANT and REVOKE instructions only apply to database users. This is extended in SQL/99 by considering that these instructions also apply to roles as suggested in the RBAC model [1]. In this latter case, a user will be permitted to have an access to a view if this user is assigned to a given role and this role is granted the permission to have an access to the view. Actually, the GRANT and REVOKE instructions combined to the paradigm of view provides a well-founded and expressive language to control the access to relational databases. In the following we call it the RBAC-SQL model.

Several access models have also been defined for XML documents [2, 3, 4, 5, 6, 7]. We may expect that these models are at least as expressive as the RBAC-SQL

S. Jajodia and C. Mazumdar (Eds.): ICISS 2005, LNCS 3803, pp. 148–163, 2005.
© Springer-Verlag Berlin Heidelberg 2005

model. Unfortunately, this is not the case. Indeed, access restrictions to some SQL views have no counterpart in these XML access control models. This is typically the case when the restriction applies to relationships between entities. For instance, we may have two entities Hospital and Patient and a relationship H_P between these entities to represent that a given patient is healed in a given hospital. In a relational database, it is easy to specify that a given user is granted an access to the entities Patient and Hospital but not to relationship H_P. However, it is not possible to specify such a restriction in existing access control models for XML documents.

Intuitively, the cause of the problem is the following. Let us consider that an XML document is represented by a tree and let us assume that there are two nodes in this tree connected by an edge. Using existing XML access control models, it is impossible to grant an access to these two nodes without also granting an access to the edge that connects the nodes. For instance, the two nodes may respectively represent elements Hospital and Patient and the edge the relationship saying that the patient is healed in this hospital. Thus, it is impossible in these models to protect the relationship H_P between Hospital and Patient separately from the entities Hospital and Patient.

Our objective in this paper is to define an extension to existing XML access control models to cope with this problem. Our proposal is based on the new notion of block. Intuitively, relationships between nodes selected in the same block are preserved whereas relationships between nodes selected in two different blocks are broken. Thus, an access control policy is specified using several blocks. In some sense, this is similar to the Chinese Wall security model suggested by Brewer-Nash [8]. In a Chinese Wall policy, a user may be permitted to have an access to different entities, but due to some conflict of interest between these entities, this user is not permitted to aggregate these information. When we use two different blocks to specify an access control policy, we can in some sense consider that there is a wall between these two blocks.

Notice also that existing XML access control models consider that the structure of the authorized view of an XML document presented to a user must be as close as possible to this XML document. We do not follow this direction. In particular, such a principal does not apply to the RBAC-SQL model. In RBAC-SQL, the view of the database presented to a user is generally different from the schema of the underlying relational database. We claim that a similar approach must be used when defining an access control model for XML documents and is actually necessary if we want to protect some relationships between entities that exist in XML documents.

The remainder of this paper is organized as follows. In section 2, we further motivate our approach and more deeply investigate the problems addressed in this paper. In section 3, we present the model, called XML-BB (XML Block Based Access Control), to express access control policies for XML documents. Section 4 defines the semantics for this model. Finally, section 5 concludes the paper.

2   Motivation

2.1   Motivating Example

Let us consider the following entity-relationship example (see figure 1). There are three different entities called *Hospital*, *Department* and *Patient* and two relationships called *H_P* (between entities *Hospital* and *Department*) and *D_P* (between entities *Department* and *Patient*). We assume that cardinality of relationship *D_P* is 1 to many meaning that a department may be associated with several patients but a patient is associated with exactly one department. Similarly, relationship *H_P* is also 1 to many.

If we apply the relational model to this example, we shall obtain three different relations:

- *Hospital(Hosp_id, Hosp_name, Hosp_address)* where *Hosp_id* is the key of this relation.
- *Department(Dept_id, Speciality, Hosp_id)* where *Dept_id* is the key of this relation and *Hosp_id* is a foreign key referencing the *Hospital* relation.
- *Patient(Patient_id, Patient_name, Dept_id)* where *Patient_id* is the key of this relation and *Dept_id* is a foreign key referencing the *Department* relation.

Let us now assume that John and Mary are two users of this relational database. We consider that John and Mary are authorized to have an access to both relations *Hospital* and *Department*. Thus we have:

- GRANT SELECT ON Hospital TO John, Mary;
- GRANT SELECT ON Department TO John, Mary;

John is authorized to have an access to data stored in relation *Patient* except the relationship *D_P* between the entity *Department* and *Patient*. For this purpose, we have to create a view called *Patient_bis* as follows:

- CREATE VIEW Patient_bis AS
  SELECT Patient_id, Patient_name FROM Patient;
  Patient_bis is defined as a projection of relation *Patient* over the two first attributes *Patient_id, Patient_name*.
- GRANT SELECT ON Patient_bis TO John;
  Thus John cannot observe the attribute *Dept_id* so that the relationship *D_P* is hidden.

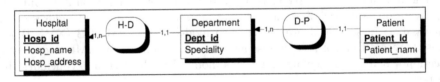

Fig. 1. Example of Entity-Relationship schema

Mary is also not authorized to have an access to relationship D_P but she is authorized to know in which hospital the patient is healed. For this purpose, we have to create a view called *Patient_ter* as follows:

- `CREATE VIEW Patient_ter AS`
  `SELECT P.Patient_id, P.Patient_name, H.Hosp_id`
  `FROM Patient P, Department D, Hospital H`
  `WHERE P.Dept_id = D.Dept_id AND D.Hosp_id = H.Hosp_id;`
- `GRANT SELECT ON Patient_ter TO Mary;`

Notice that we implicitly assume that there are several hospitals and departments. Else, John and Mary will trivially infer in which hospital and/or department a given patient is healed. Notice also that the order in which the patients are selected in *Patient_bis* and *Patient_ter* must not depend on the departments in which these patients are healed. Else, we would have an inference channel. A possible solution to avoid this inference channel is to use the GROUP BY instruction.

We investigate in the following sections how to model similar access controls using XML data structure. Before, we show why current XML access control models are not expressive enough to specify the security policy we have just introduced.

2.2   Limitations of Current XML Access Control Models

We claim that none of existing XML access control models is actually able to properly manage access restriction associated with John and Mary as presented in the previous section.

To illustrate the problem, we first need to fix an XML schema corresponding to the entity-relationship example presented in figure 1. There are actually many possible candidate schemas, a possible one being presented in figure 2.

An XML document instance of this XML schema may be represented by a tree. See figure 3 for a simplified instance of the XML schema presented in figure 2 in which only elements H (Hospital), D (Department), P (Patient) and

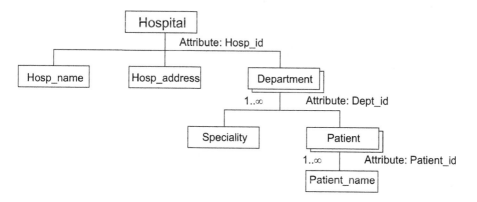

Fig. 2. Example of XML schema

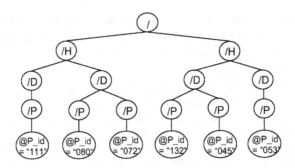

Fig. 3. Example of XML document

attribute @P_id (Patient_id) are presented. Notice that in XML, there is generally no explicit representation of the relationships, namely H_D and D_P in our example. In the XML schema of figure 2, the fact that there are 1 or more nodes *Department* below nodes *Hospital* implicitly represents the relationship 1 to many H_D in the entity-relationship schema and similarly for nodes *Department* and *Patient*.

Let us now analyze how to specify access restrictions associated with John. To specify these restrictions, we shall use the model suggested by Gabillon in [6] but we shall have similar problems with other access control models for XML documents such as [2, 4, 7]. All these models are based on XPath [9]. An XPath expression selects a set of nodes in the tree corresponding to an XML document. For instance the XPath expression "/Hospital/Department" selects all departments of every hospital.

John is actually permitted to have an access to every data stored in the XML document except the relationship that a given patient is healed in a given department. Using [6], this is expressed by the two following requirements:

- `GRANT read /P ON /Hospital TO John`
  This requirement means that John is permitted to read every Hospital node of the XML document. The /P means "propagate", that is the read privilege is extended to every sub-node of Hospital nodes.
- `REVOKE read /P ON /Hospital/Department/Patient TO John`
  The model defined in [6] assumes the last matching principle, that is when several rules apply to a selected node, the last defined rule is preferred. Thus, this second rule applies as an exception to the first rule for Patient nodes. It says that John is denied to read every Patient node and, due to the /P option, John is also denied to read every sub-node of Patient nodes.

Thus combining these two first rules, John is permitted to read every Hospital node and sub-node *except* the Patient nodes.

However, this is not exactly what we want because John is actually permitted to read Patient information *except* the relationship D_P. Using [6], this may be expressed by the following requirement:

- `GRANT read /P ON /Hospital/Department/Patient TO John`

However, using the last matching principle, this third requirement will actually remove the second and, combining the first and third requirement, John will be finally permitted to read every Hospital node and sub-node.

This is clearly not what we want and thus [6] fails in expressing access control requirement associated with John. A similar analysis shows that it is also not possible to express access control requirement associated with Mary. One can check that similar problems happen when applying other access control models such as [2, 4, 5, 7].

2.3 Our Proposal

Let us analyze what is going wrong in the previous section. Each XPath selects a set of nodes in the XML document. As in SQL, [6] assumes that the policy is closed, i.e. without an explicit GRANT to have an access to a given node, the access is denied. The rules are then parsed in the order they are written. If the rule is a GRANT, the corresponding nodes selected by the XPath expression are added to the permitted nodes. If the rule is a REVOKE, the corresponding nodes are removed from the permitted nodes.

Notice that [6] also implicitly applies two principals, we call them the *cumulative* and *connectivity* principles, to build the authorized view associated with an XML document:

Cumulative principle: The effect of two GRANT rules is cumulative, that is the resulting permissions actually correspond to the *union* of the nodes respectively selected by these rules.

Connectivity principle: If two selected nodes are connected by an edge in the XML document, then this edge will appear in the view presented to the user.

It is the combination of these two principles that does not provide means to express access control requirements associated with John and Mary in our example. As a matter of fact, if a node corresponding to a given Department is selected and another node corresponding to a patient healed in this department is also selected, it will not be possible to hide the edge that connects these two nodes and thus to hide the *D_P* relationship.

Our proposal is thus to change these principles. We suggest specifying an access control model for XML documents using the new concept of *Block*. Using this notion, the access control requirements associated with John and Mary are modelled using two different blocks as follows:

```
− BEGIN BLOCK HOSPITAL
      GRANT read /P ON /Hospital
      TO John, Mary
      REVOKE read /P ON
      /Hospital/Department/Patient
      TO John, Mary
   END BLOCK HOSPITAL
```

```
— BEGIN BLOCK PATIENT
      GRANT read ON /Hospital TO Mary
      GRANT read /P /S ON
      /Hospital/Department/Patient
      TO John, Mary
  END BLOCK PATIENT
```

Access control requirements associated with John are actually similar to the ones suggested in the previous section. The main difference is that they are separated into two different blocks called HOSPITAL and PATIENT[1].

Within a block, we apply both the cumulative and connectivity principles. Between two different blocks, we only apply the cumulative principle but not the connectivity principle. Thus, John will be permitted to read the Hospital and Department nodes (in block Hospital) and the Patient nodes (in block Patient), but since these nodes are selected into two different blocks, John cannot observe an edge between a department and a patient and so cannot observe the D_P relationship. Notice that the last GRANT rule uses the /S option. This option means "shuffle", that is the selected Patient nodes will be shuffled before being presented to John. This is to avoid a possible inference channel if the selected patients are presented in the same order as the departments.

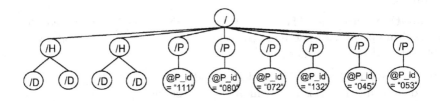

Fig. 4. John's authorized view

Access control requirements associated with Mary are similar to John except that Mary is permitted to read Hospital nodes in block PATIENT. This block specifies that Mary is both permitted to read Hospital node (without the /P option) and Patient nodes. There is no direct edge between nodes Hospital and Patient, but since there is an indirect path between a given hospital and a given patient through a node Department, this hospital will be connected to the patient in the resulting view. Thus, Mary is permitted to know in which hospital the patient is healed as in relation *Patient_ter* presented in section 2.1.

Figures 4 and 5 respectively show John and Mary's authorized views corresponding to the document presented in figure 3. Notice that the shuffling option applied to Mary's view must preserve the relationship between patients healed in the same hospital. We call that the "Children link preservation principle".

---

[1] Another difference is that we use the /S option in the last GRANT rule. This option is explained below.

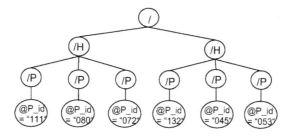

Fig. 5. Mary's authorized view

3   The XML-BB Model

As suggested in [6], the language of XML-BB is syntactically close to SQL. In [6], A. Gabillon considers the read access privilege and also three write privileges insert, update and delete. These write privileges are defined to be compatible with an XML database supporting XUpdate [10]. However, due to space limitation, we shall focus in this paper on the read privilege. Since role is a useful concept to structure the policy specification, we also consider that privileges apply to both users and roles.

The remainder of this section is organized as follows. We first present how to manage users and roles. We then present the access control policy language. The semantics of this language is defined in section 4.

3.1   User and Role

Like in SQL/99, this language includes basic constructors CREATE USER and CREATE ROLE.

Creation of users and roles is respectively done via the following commands:

- CREATE USER *login_name*
- CREATE ROLE *role_name*

In the following, we call subject a user or a role. Assignment of roles to users (or roles) is done via the following command:

- GRANT *roles* TO *set of subjects*

Assigning a role to another role is used to represent a role hierarchy. This role hierarchy is associated with inheritance of security rules.

3.2   Access Control Policy Language

Definition 1. An access control policy (ACP) is defined as a set of blocks:
- *ACP :: set of blocks*

Each block has a name and is defined as a set of security rules:

- *block* :: BEGIN BLOCK *block_name set of security_rules* END BLOCK *block_name*

A security rule is expressed using the GRANT or REVOKE instructions as follows:

- *security_rule* :: GRANT read [*set of options*] ON *set of nodes* TO *set of subjects*
- *security_rule* :: REVOKE read [/P] ON *set of nodes* TO *set of subjects*

Definition 2. *set of nodes* represents a set of nodes selected by an XPath expression. In the following, we say that this set of nodes is the *target* of the security rule.

Definition 3. If a subject is a member of *set of subjects*, then we say that this subject is a *recipient* of the security rule. As mentioned above, a subject is a user or a role identified by their name.

There are three possible options one can use when specifying a security rule:

- *option* :: /P (Propagate option: This option will select every sub-node of a selected node)
- *option* :: /S (Shuffle option: This option will randomly shuffle the selected nodes. If a shuffled node is the root of a sub-tree, then this node will be the root of the same sub-tree after the shuffling operation.
- *option* :: /M *val* (Masquerade option: This option will replace the value of a selected node by the new value *val* specified in the option. This is used to hide the value of a given node without hiding the existence of this node. For instance, *val* may be *restricted* or *dummy* as respectively suggested in [6] or [11]. Notice that the *position* privilege suggested in [6] is actually equivalent in our language to the read privilege with the option /M restricted.)

Notice that within a single GRANT security rule, we can combine the propagate, shuffle and masquerade options, but in a REVOKE security rule, we can obviously only use the propagate option.

4   Language Semantics

4.1   Modelling XML Documents

Tree Definition. An XML document is modelled as a finite valued tree. For this purpose, we first define a finite valued oriented graph (FVOG).

To define an FVOG, we consider a finite set $Node$ of nodes and a set Dom of domain values. $\mathbb{N}^*$ represents the set of non null integers and $\mathcal{L}(Node)$ denotes the set of ordered lists of nodes.

Definition 4. A FVOG G is defined by a triple $(Node_G, Value_G, Children_G)$ where:

- $Node_G \subseteq Node$. $Node_G$ is the set of nodes of the FVOG G.
- $Value_G$ is a total injective function from $Node_G$ into Dom. If o is a node, then $Value_G(o)$ represents the value of node o in FVOG G.
- $Children_G$ is a total function from $Node_G$ into $\mathcal{L}(Node_G)$. If o is a node, then $Children_G(o)$ represents the finite list of child nodes o in FVOG G.

In the following we shall use the following notations:

- $Root_G$ is a boolean function from $Node_G$ into $\{0,1\}$. If o is a node, then $Root_G(o)$ is true if an only there is no node o' such that o is a children of o': $Root_G(o) \leftrightarrow \forall o', o \notin Children(o')$.
- $Child_G$ is a function from $Node_G \times \mathbb{N}^*$ into $Node_G$. If o is a node and n is an integer, then $Child_G(o,n)$ represents the nth child of o. Thus, if $Children_G(o) = [o_1, ..., o_n]$ then for every $i \in [1,n]$, we have $Child_G(o,i) = o_i$. If $i > n$, $Child_G(o,i)$ is not defined.
- $Descendant_G$ is a function from $Node_G$ into the powerset of $Node_G$. $Descendant_G$ is defined as the transitive closure of $Children_G$.

We can now define a finite valued tree as follows.

Definition 5. A finite valued tree is a FVOG $T = (Node_T, Value_T, Children_T)$ that satisfies the following conditions:

- There is no cycle in the graph: For every $o \in Node_T, o \notin Descendant_T(o)$.
- Every node has at most one parent: For every node o and o' in $Node_T$ and every integer i and i', $Child_T(o,i) = Child_T(o',i') \rightarrow (o = o' \wedge i = i')$.
- There is a unique node $o \in Node_T$ such that o is the root of $Node_T$: For every node o and o' in $Node_T$, $(Root_T(o) \wedge Root_T(o')) \rightarrow o = o'$.
- If $Root_T(o)$ is true then $Value_T(o) =' /'$.

For instance, in the example of tree presented in figure 6, we have $Value_T(o5) = "/D"$ and $Children_T(o5) = [o9, o10]$.

4.2   Position of a Node in a Tree

Let $T = (Node_T, Value_T, Children_T)$ be a finite valued tree.

Definition 6. The position of a node $o \in Node_T$ in tree T, denoted $Pos_T(o)$, is recursively defined as follows:

- If $Root_T(o)$ is true then $Pos_T(o) = [\,]$ where $[\,]$ represents the empty list.
- If $Pos_T(o) = p$ and $Child_T(o,i) = o'$ then $Pos_T(o') = p.i$

Definition 7. We associate the set $Node_T$ with a total order relation denoted $\preceq_T$ and defined as follows. Let o and o' two nodes of $Node_T$ such that $Pos_T(o) = p$ and $Pos_T(o') = p'$. We have $o \preceq_T o'$ if one of the following conditions holds:

- $p' = p.p''$.
- $p = p_1.n.p_2$ and $p' = p_1.n'.p_2'$ with $n < n'$

For instance, in the example of tree presented in figure 6, we have $Pos_T(o9) = 1.2.1$ and $Pos_T(o10) = 1.2.2$ and thus $o9 \preceq_T o10$.

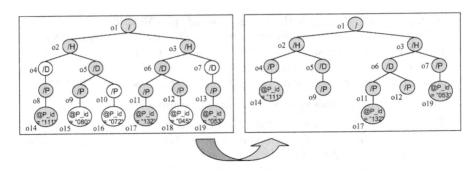

Fig. 6. Example of selection

4.3   Operations on Trees

Selection. Let $T = (Node_T, Value_T, Pos_T)$ be a tree and $Node_S$ be a selected set of nodes such that $Node_S \subseteq Node_T$. We always assume that the root of T belongs to $Node_S$, else the result of the selection may not correspond to a tree.

Definition 8. $select(T, Node_S)$ is a tree $S = (Node_S, Value_S, Children_S)$ where:

- $Value_S$ is the restriction of functions $Value_T$ to the selected nodes $Node_S$.
- $Children_S$ is defined as follows. Let o be a node of $Node_S$. We have:
  $o' \in Children_S(o)$ if and only if (1) $o' \in Node_S$ and $o' \in Descendant_T(o)$ and (2) there is no node $o'' \in Node_S$ such that $o' \in Descendant_T(o'')$ and $o'' \in Descendant_T(o)$.
  To obtain a list, nodes belonging to $Children_S(o)$ are then totally ordered according to the $\preceq_T$ relation defined above.

Figure 6 provides an example of selection.

Masquerade. Let $T = (Node_T, Value_T, Children_T)$ be a tree, $Node_M \subseteq Node_T$ a set of nodes and $v \in Value$.

Definition 9. $masquerade(T, Node_M, v)$ is a tree $M = (Node_T, Value_M, Children_T)$ where:

- $Value_M$ is identical to $Value_T$ except that for every node $o \in Node_M$, we have $Value_M(o) = v$.

Shuffling. Let $T = (Node_T, Value_T, Children_T)$ be a tree, $Node_S \subseteq Node_T$ a set of nodes. Then, let $permutation$ be a random permutation on $Node_S$, i.e. a bijection from $Node_S$ to $Node_S$.

Definition 10. $shuffling(T, Node_S)$ is a tree $S = (Node_T, Value_T, Children_S)$ where:

- $Children_S$ is identical to $Children_T$ except that if $o_1 \in Nodes_S$ and $permutation(o_1) = o_2$ and $o_1 \in Children_T(o)$ then o_2 takes the place of o_1 in $Children_T(o)$.

Definition 11. In the following, we assume that every permutation used in the shuffling operation satisfies the "Children Link Prevention Principle" defined as follows:

- If $permutation(o_1) = o_2$ and $o_1 \in Children_T(o)$ then $o_2 \in Children_T(o)$.

See Mary's authorized view presented in figure 5 for an application of the "Children Link Prevention Principle".

Fusion. The *fusion* function transforms two trees $S = (Nodes_S, Values_S, Pos_S)$ and $T = (Node_T, Value_T, Pos_T)$ into another tree $F = (Node_F, Value_F, Pos_F)$.

Definition 12. $F = fusion(S, T)$ is defined as follows:

- **Renaming**
  It may happen that some nodes belong to both trees S and T but with different values. For instance, this occurs when the value of a node has been masqueraded in a tree but not in the other. To avoid the conflict when merging the tree, we rename these nodes in tree T.
  For this purpose, let $NODES = \{node \in Nodes \cap Node_T \mid Value_S(node) \neq Value_T(node)\}$
  Then $rename(T, Nodes)$ is a tree $U = (Node_U, Value_U, Pos_U)$ defined as follows:
  - $Node_U$ is equal to $Node_T$ except that (1) each node n belonging to $NODES$ is replaced by a new node $copy_n$ and (2) every descendant n' of a node n belonging to $NODES$ is also replaced by a new node $copy_{n'}$.
  - $Value_U$ and $Children_U$ are identical to $Value_T$ and $Children_T$ except that each node belonging to $NODES$ is replaced by its copy.
- **Merging**
  F is a tree defined as follows:
  - $Node_F = Nodes_S \cup Node_U$
  - $Value_F$ is a function from $Node_F$ into Dom such that, if $n \in Nodes_S$ then $Value_F(n) = Value_S(n)$ and, if $n \in Node_U$ then $Value_F(n) = Value_U(n)$.
  - $Children_F$ is a function from $Node_F$ into $\mathcal{L}(Node_F)$ such that:
    * If $node \in (Nodes_S \backslash Node_U)$ then $Children_F(node) = Children_S(node)$
    * If $node \in (Node_U \backslash Nodes_S)$ then $Children_F(node) = Children_U(node)$
    * If $node \in (Nodes_S \cap Node_U)$, then
      let $L = Descendant_U(o) \backslash Children_U(o)$
      Let $L_1 = Children_S(node) \backslash L$

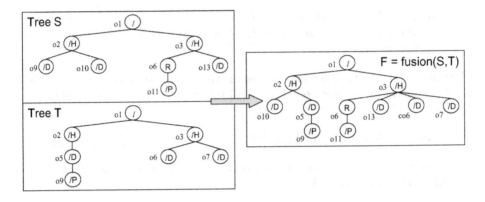

Fig. 7. Example of fusion

Let $L_2 = Children_U(node) \backslash Nodes_S$
Then we have:
$Children_F(node) = concat(L_1, L_2)$
where the result of function $concat(L_1, L_2)$ is a list corresponding to
the concatenation of lists L_1 and L_2

Figure 7 gives an example of fusion. Notice that node $o13$ is selected in tree S and node $o7$ in tree T. There is an edge between $o7$ and $o13$ in the initial tree presented in figure 6 but this link does no longer appear in tree F. Position of node $o9$ in tree S also changes in tree F. This is due to the computation of list L_1 above. Notice finally that the value of node $o6$ was masqueraded by value R in tree S. Since this object is also present in tree T, it is renamed in $co6$ in tree F.

The fusion operation will be used in section 4.4 to give the semantics to the block concept.

4.4   Access Control Semantics

We can now define the semantics of the access control language presented in section 3. For this purpose, let us consider an XML document modelled by a tree $T = (Node_T, Value_T, Pos_T)$ and let Pol be an access control policy that applies to T. Following section 3, Pol corresponds to a finite set of blocks $\{b_1, ..., b_n\}$, each block b_i being a set of security rules $\{r_{i_1}, ..., r_{i_k}\}$.

Our approach consists in defining, for each auhtorized user u, the authorized view of document T. To define this authorized view, we shall first define the authorized sub-view associated with a given block and then define how to merge these different authorized sub-views to obtain the global authorized view.

Authorized Sub-view Associated with a Block. Let b be a block of security rules that belongs to the access control policy Pol and let $\{r_1, ..., r_k\}$ be the sub-set of security rules of block b that applies to user u. A security rule r applies to

u if (1) u belongs to the recipient of the security rule[2] or, (2) a role r is assigned to u and r belongs to the recipient of the security rule or, (3) a role r is assigned to u and r inherits from another role r' and r' belongs to the recipient of the security rule.

We assume that every user has an access to the root node of the document. This means that we assume that observing the root of the document, whose value is always equal to "/" does not reveal any information. This assumption is a useful simplification because every authorized sub-view will be always equal to a tree. Else, it may happen that the result would be equal to a forest.

The authorized sub-view of u associated with a given block b corresponds to a sub-tree T' of T. Using operations defined in section 4.3, T' is computed by the following algorithm:

- **initialization**
  $Temp := T$ and $Res = \{root\}$ where $root$ represents the root node of T.
- **security rules application**
  For $i = 1$ to k do
  Let $Nodes$ be the set of nodes of T selected by the XPath expression that defines the target of security rule r_i.
      If the propagate /P option is used then if a node n belongs to $Nodes$ then every nodes that belongs to $Descendant_T(n)$ also belongs to $Nodes$.
      If the masquerade /M val option is used then $Temp :=$ $masquerade(Temp, Nodes, val)$.
  If rule r_i is a GRANT then $Res := Res \cup Nodes$.
  If rule r_i is a REVOKE then $Res := Res \backslash Nodes$.
- **selection**
  Let $Temp := select(Temp, Res)$
- **shuffling**
  For $i = 1$ to k do
  If the shuffle /S option is used in rule r_i then $Temp :=$ $shuffling(Temp, Nodes)$ where $Nodes$ be the set of nodes of T selected by the XPath expression that defines the target of security rule r_i.
- **authorized sub-view in block** b
  $T' := Temp$

Merging the Blocks. Let $\{b_1, ..., b_n\}$ be the finite set of blocks that belong to the access control security Pol and let T_i be the authorized sub-view associated with each block b_i.

Then, the global authorized view $View(u)$ associated with user u is recursively defined by merging every sub-view T_i:

- $View(u) := T_1$
- If $n > 1$ then
    For $i = 2$ to n do
    $View(u) := fusion(View(u), T_i)$

---

[2] See definition 3 of section 3.2.

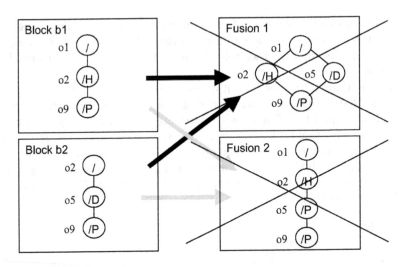

Fig. 8. Unsatisfactory block fusion

We already showed in figure 7, an example of tree fusion. Figure 8 presents another example. In the first *Block b1*, nodes *o2* and *o9* are selected, so that one can know that a given patient is healed in a given hospital. In the other *Block b2*, one can similarly know that this patient is healed in a given department. Applying our fusion algorithm to merge Blocks *b1* and *b2* is illustrated in *Fusion 1*. The result is not satisfactory since it does not correspond to a tree. The second possibility presented in *Fusion 2* is problematic since it discloses the fact that department in Block *b2* is part of the hospital selected in Block *b1*. Finally, one can attempt to rename the patient corresponding to node *o9* into a new node *co9*. In this case, we shall obtain a tree when merging blocks *b1* and *b2* but this is also not fully satisfactory since the authorized view contain a patient that actually does not exist.

Our conclusion with this example is that the best solution is to consider that it corresponds to a wrongly defined policy and reject it. This will be the case with our fusion algorithm since we do not obtain a tree and thus reject fusion cases that comply with this typical example.

5   Conclusion

In this paper, we have presented a new access control model for XML documents called XML-BB. This model introduces the concept of blocks and provides means to protect relationships in the XML documents. We also show that protecting these relationships were not possible in all previously suggested models.

There are several perspectives to this work. We need to extend the model to specify access control rules associated with update operations. As suggested in [6], this extension should be compatible with the XUpdate language.

We also have to consider that security policies are more and more dynamic. As suggested in [12], we need means to specify security requirements that depend on contexts, such as the date, or the location of the queries. Extending XML-BB to specify such contextual security requirements represents further work that remains to be done. As suggested in [7], modelling provisional authorization is another direction for future work.

Acknowledgement. This work was supported by funding from the French ministry for research under "ACI Sécurité Informatique: CASC Project".

References

1. R.Sandhu, E.J.Coyne, H.L.Feinstein, C.E.Youman: Role-based access control models. IEEE Computer (1996) 38–47
2. E.Bertino, S.Castano, E.Ferrari, M.Mesiti: Specifying and Enforcing Access Control Policies for XML Document Sources. World Wide Web Journal (2000)
3. E.Damiani, S.De Capitani di Vimercati, S.Paraboschi, P.Samarati: Securing XML Documents. In: International Conference on Extending Database Technology (EDBT2000), Konstanz, Germany (2000)
4. E.Damiani, S.De Capitani di Vimercati, S.Paraboschi, P.Samarati: A Fine-Grained Access Control System for XML Documents. ACM Transactions on Information and System Security (TISSEC) (2002)
5. A.Gabillon, E.Bruno: Regulating Access to XML documents. In: Fifteenth Annual IFIP WG 11.3 Working Conference on Database Security, Niagara on the Lake, Ontario, Canada (2001)
6. A.Gabillon: An Authorization Model for XML DataBases. In: ACM Workshop on Secure Web Services, Fairfax, VA (2004)
7. M.Kudo, S.Hada: XML Document Security Based on Provisional Authorisation. In: ACM Computer and Communications Security, Athens Greece (2000)
8. D.Brewer, M.Nash: The Chinese wall security policy. In: IEEE Symposium on Security and Privacy, Oakland (1989)
9. J.Clark, S.DeRose: XML Path Language (XPath) Version 1.0. Technical report, World Wide Web Consortium (W3C), http://www.w3c.org/TR/xpath (2000)
10. A.Laux, L.Martin: XML Update (XUpdate) language. Technical report, XML:DB working draft, http://www.xmldb.org/xupdate (1999)
11. W.Fan, C.Y.Chan, M.Garofalakis: Secure XML Querying with Security Views. In: SIGMOD. (2004)
12. F.Cuppens, A.Miège: Modelling contexts in the Or-BAC model. In: 19th Annual Computer Security Applications Conference, Las Vegas (2003)

EISA - An Enterprise Application Security Solution for Databases

V. Radha and N. Hemanth Kumar

IDRBT, Hyderabad
vradha@idrbt.ac.in, nhemanthkumar@mtech.idrbt.ac.in

Abstract. Recent paradigms like "database as a service" require an additional infrastructure to guarantee data security. Data protection laws such as HIPAA (Health Insurance Portability and Accountability Act), Gramm-Leach-Bliley Act of 1999, Data protection Act, Sarbanes Oxleys Act are demanding for the data security to an extent that the critical information should be seen only by the authorized users which means the integrity and confidentiality of the database must be properly accommodated. Hence we aim at building up a wrapper/interface in between encrypted database server and applications that ensures the data privacy and integrity. Specifically, we worked on querying over encrypted databases and our approach produces query results on encrypted data with no false hits and hence reduces the network consumption between applications and encrypted server.

1 Introduction

The Enterprises often depend solely on access controls to protect data where it is stored for 99% of time, believing that database systems within their own perimeter defenses were safe from attacks. But recent reports reveal that the threats coming from insiders are considerably higher than the ones posed by remote users [1]. A recent paradigm like "Database as a Service"[2] where the data is outsourced to Application Service Providers (ASP) requires protection of the data at the remote location. Hence data security has become a serious issue at the storage level too. Data security implies maintaining data integrity and guarding data privacy.

Database Encryption is obviously the solution for protection of the static data (data privacy) but with challenges [3,4]. There are trade-offs for the encryption techniques and the granularity of the data to be encrypted. It is found that hardware encryption is better than using software versions for computational reasons [6]. Similarly row level encryption is found preferable over column or file level encryption when tested over TPC-H benchmark [5]. Field level encryption increases the overhead over query evaluation.

The primary challenge of encrypting databases is deciding where the data is encrypted and decrypted or simply with whom the private keys are resided. The next challenge is performing the efficient execution of query over encrypted

S. Jajodia and C. Mazumdar (Eds.): ICISS 2005, LNCS 3803, pp. 164–176, 2005.
© Springer-Verlag Berlin Heidelberg 2005

databases. The data must be organized/indexed so that the query can be evaluated with fewer costs on server and client computation (processing cost), bandwidth consumption between server and client (communication cost).

Another challenge is maintaining data integrity while incurring minimal computational and bandwidth overhead. The applications must be empowered to accept/reject the data they pull from database based on integrity verification. In this paper we aimed at two things- ensuring data integrity and efficient query execution over encrypted databases by evaluating most of the query at application server and retrieving only the necessary records from the server.

Section 2 deals with the description of the motivation behind our work. Section 3 describes the proposed architecture for enterprises to maintain data security and Section 4 deals with the data organization for efficient query execution. Section 5 describes the mapping conditions. Section 6 deals with our experiment results. Section 7 gives a brief account on the research work in this area and Section 8 deals with the conclusion and future work that we want to implement.

2   Motivation

In present enterprise application development, the database and application are not being integrated tightly. The developers treat them separate and develop the final application in a much-disintegrated fashion. Main reason for this is due to lack of standards. Except SQL, ODBC and JDBC standards, which allow the data to be interchanged/queried across any kind of database, there is no standard for triggers, procedures, access controls etc. To make the application portable across any database, the developers tend to use only standard features of the database and ignore the special security features like access controls, encryption etc offered by a commercial RDBMS. So ultimately, the database has become just a data store and developers depend heavily on OS security controls even for database security.

Tampering and injecting or deleting or viewing certain sensitive information in the database by an administrator or a hacker with administrative privileges in spite of various security measures such as database access controls is a serious issue. In this communications world, where most of the transactions are done over the web/internet, there is a need for the applications to know whether the data they are retrieving from the database to act upon is authentic or not. The applications must also be ensured that the sensitive data cannot be viewed by the unauthorized. In addition, a number of legislative and commercial initiatives are requiring increased attention to the privacy, confidentiality and authenticity/integrity of electronic stored data to safeguard non-public personal information (NPI) and other sensitive enterprise data.

3   Proposed Architecture

The proposed architecture comprises three fundamental entities – Encrypted Database Server, Security Wrapper called EISA (Enterprise Information Security

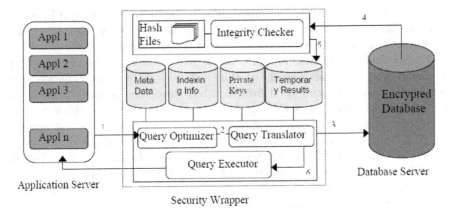

Fig. 1. Proposed Security Architecture for Enterprises

Adapter) and the Clients (Client Applications). The Encrypted Database Server consists of only the encrypted tuples. A user queries the client application that in turn connects to the EISA instead of directly connecting to the database. EISA maintains the metadata of the whole database, along with other indexing information for each table. It also contains the keys for encryption/decryption of the tuples. It also maintains the checksums of the records stored at the server.

EISA takes the query from the client and passes it to Query Engine part. The Query Engine optimizes the query and then separates it into Server query and wrapper query based on the index information it stores. The server query is pushed onto the encrypted database server where the query is evaluated and the results are send back to the EISA. The results from the Encrypted server are checked for integrity using checksums stored and decrypts the results and temporarily store them at the wrapper. The Query Executor part of the EISA executes the wrapper query on the temporarily stored decrypted data and the result is pushed onto the clients/client application.

The process of querying is as follows.

1. The Application queries the EISA wrapper instead of connecting to the Encrypted Database Server.
2. The Query is optimized and sent to the Query Translator part of Query Engine.
3. The Query Translator evaluates the query at the wrapper by means of indexing info stored and disintegrates the original query into Server query S_Q and Wrapper query C_Q.
4. S_Q is pushed onto the Encrypted Database Server and the results are retrieved.
5. The results are sent to the Integrity Checker of EISA where each record is checked for the integrity.
6. The Integrity Checker calculates hash on each record and compares it with the already stored hash from the hash files.

7. If the hash check doesn't match, the Integrity Checker returns a Tampered Message Alert.
8. If the hashes of all record matches, the results are decrypted and stored temporarily at the wrapper.
9. C_Q is evaluated over the temporarily stored records and the results are pushed onto the applications.

Hence, The Security Wrapper intercepts all the *ODBC* calls from the applications and categorizes them into one of the DDL/DML statements and processes them as done in the service for each category and redirect the query to the database through ODBC connection and get the results. and again necessary processing is done. The result is returned to the application only when the retrieved records are authentic else error messages are thrown onto the application.

4   Organization of the Data

At Server side:
For each relation R(A1,A2,..An), we store at the encrypted server R^s(id, etuple) where etuple is the encryption of all the attributes of the tuple i.e., encrypt{A1,A2,...An}. The first column 'id' represents an incremental variable maintained by the wrapper. The wrapper maintains separate id variables for each table. A plain text relation along with the corresponding relation to be stored on encrypted server is shown in Table 1. The tuple with ssn 123456789 is transformed into a tuple with id 1 and a string, which represents encrypt (Smith, 1234567789, 1982-01-09, Houston, 5). Any block cipher technique such as AES, DES, Blowfish, and RSA etc. can be used for encryption/decryption of the tuples.

At the Wrapper:
The wrapper maintains the indexing information in the form of Associated B-Trees. An Associated B-tree with fan-out n is a tree where every node can store information up to n-1 set of pairs and n pointers, and, except for the root and leaf nodes, has at least ?n/2? descendants. Each pair comprises a search key value and the associated information. All the leaves appear on the same level and the leaf level forms a complete, ordered index of the associated data file.

An internal node storing m pairs (m $<=$ n-1), {$(k_1, v_1), (k_2, v_2), \ldots (k_m, v_m)$}, each (k_i, v_i) is followed by a pointer p_i. (k_1, v_1) is preceded by p_0. Pointer p_0 addresses the subtree that contains key values less than k_1, p_m addresses the subtree that contains keys with values greater than or equal to k_m, and each p_i ($0<i<m$) addresses the subtree that contains keys with values included in the interval $[k_i, k_{i+1})$.

Figure 2 illustrates an example of B-Tree with associated information on attribute 'dno' of the emp relation in Figure 2. (a-b) in each node represents key dno and the associated information 'id' of encrypted tuple. To access the information associated with the key k, the following steps are to be followed. The root of the Associated B-Tree is searched for key k. If k is not found, then the

Table 1. Proposed Security Architecture for Enterprises

ename	ssn	bdate	addr	dno
Smith	123456789	1982-01-09	Houston	5
Wong	333445555	1979-12-08	Spring	4
Zelaya	999887777	1981-07-19	Houston	1
English	453453453	1980-07-31	Humble	4
Joyce	334555677	1976-08-09	Spring	6

id	etuple
1	100010101010000010..
2	111011100011100001..
3	010001111110101010..
4	000001010101110101..
5	111111100010101010..

node pointed by the pointer p is chosen for searching, where $p = p_0$ for $k<k_1$ or $p = p_m$ for $k>=k_m$ or $p = p_i$ for $k_i <k<k_{i+1}$. The traversal stops until the pair with key value k is found. If the traversal arrives at leaf node and the key is not found, then the desired tuple is not in the table. The Wrapper creates an Associated B-tree over the plain text values for each index attribute. Index attributes are those, which involve in search and join conditions. The Wrapper stores the attribute value as a search key and an id that uniquely identifies the tuple at the Encrypted server as the associated information. The conditional part of the query can be evaluated at the Wrapper by traversing the corresponding indexed B-trees and retrieving the entire id's that satisfies the condition over the search keys. These id's are used to retrieve the tuples from the Encrypted server.

For each table, the Wrapper creates another Associated B-tree. It contains the id and hash of each record that is inserted into the database. These B-trees are useful for checking the integrity of the records while retrieving from the encrypted server.

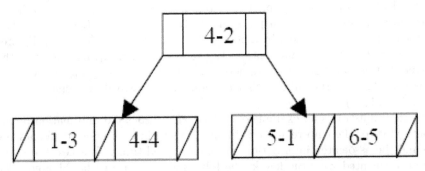

Fig. 2. Associated B-Treefor attribute 'dno' of relation 'emp'

5   Evaluation of Conditions

In this section, we show how to evaluate the conditions at the wrapper. Here the main idea is to get the id's by evaluating the conditions that are used for retrieving the tuples from the encrypted server. We categorize the conditions as follows.

1. cond ← Attribute op Constant
2. cond ← Attribute op Attribute
3. cond ← (cond AND cond) | (cond OR cond) | (!cond)

where op = { =, <, >, <=, >=}.

Some more notations are used here, in addition to that defined in previous sections.

A_i^B represents the B-Tree with Associated Information on Attribute A_i.

V represents a set of v_i values, i.e., set of Associated information

P represents a set of p_i values i.e., set of pointers to Nodes.

info(p_i) represents the set of all associated information or v_i's of the subtree pointed by p_i.

inorder(A_i^B) returns all the (k,v) pairs of the B-Tree A_i^B in sorted order wrt key k.

a) Attribute = Constant (A_i = c): -
   The B-tree associated with the attribute A_i is searched for the key value c as illustrated in the previous section.
   Cond(A_i = c) →V = { v_j / $A_i^B(k_j)$ = c}.
b) Attribute < Constant (A_i < c): -
   The operator < can be evaluated by the following algorithm.
   1. node n = Root Node of B-tree A_i^B, V = ϕ, P = ϕ.
   2. Traverse the node n until some k_j < c.
   3. V = V ∪ { v_0, v_1, v_2, ... v_{j-1} }.
   4. P = P ∪ { p_0, p_1, p_2,....p_{j-1} }.
   5. n = node pointed by p_j.
   6. Repeat steps 2,3,4 until c is found or leaf node is reached.
   7. for all p_i in P, V = V ∪ info(p_i).
c) Attribute > Constant (A_i > c): -
   The following algorithm can evaluate the operator >.
   1. node n = Root Node of B-tree A_i^B, V = ϕ, P = ϕ.
   2. Traverse the node n from the end until some k_j < c.
   3. V = V ∪ { v_{j+1}, v_{j+2}, ... v_m }.
   4. P = P ∪ { p_{j+1}, p_{j+2},....p_m }.
   5. n = node pointed by p_j.
   6. Repeat steps 2,3,4 until c is found or leaf node is reached.
   7. for all p_i in P, V = V ∪ info(p_i).
d) Attribute <= Constant (A_i <= c): -
   Attribute >= Constant (A_i >= c): -
   The evaluation of operators <=, >= (in this case) are similar to the above except v_i is also added to id if the key k_i = c is found.

e) Attribute = Attribute $(A_i = A_j)$: -

The condition may arise for join operation. The two attributes can be from two different tables or from instances of the same table. The condition can be evaluated as follows:

1. The in-order traversal of B-trees results in a sorted array of keys. Array $\text{Arr}^I = \text{inorder}(A_i^B)$, $\text{Arr}^J = \text{inorder}(A_j^B)$.
2. id-pair $= \phi$, where id-pair represents (v1, v2), v1ε { v/ (k,v) ε A_i^B}, v2ε { v/ (k,v) ε A_j^B}.
3. a=1,b=1.
4. Increment a until $\text{Arr}^I(a) < \text{Arr}^J(b)$ or End of Arr^I is reached.
5. If End of Arr^I is reached then exit.
6. If($\text{Arr}^I(a) = \text{Arr}^J(b)$) id-pair = id-pair $\cup$ (v_a, v_b).
7. Increment b until $\text{Arr}^I(a) > \text{Arr}^J(b)$ or End of Arr^J is reached.
8. If End of Arr^J is reached then exit.
9. If($\text{Arr}^I(a) = \text{Arr}^J(b)$) id-pair = id-pair $\cup$ (v_a, v_b).

f) Attribute < Attribute $(A_i < A_j)$: -

The condition can be evaluated by following these steps:

1. The in-order traversal of B-trees results in a sorted array of keys. Array $\text{Arr}^I = \text{inorder}(A_i^B)$, $\text{Arr}^J = \text{inorder}(A_j^B)$.
2. id-pair $= \phi$, where id-pair represents (v1, v2), v1ε { v/ (k,v) ε A_i^B}, v2ε { v/ (k,v) ε A_j^B}.
3. a=1, b=1, c=1.
4. while($\text{Arr}^I(a) < \text{Arr}^J(b)$ and End of Arr^I not reached)
   begin
   id-pair = id-pair $\cup$ (v_a, v_b);
   a =a+1:
   endwhile;
5. If End of Arr^I is reached then exit.
6. b = b+1;
7. if(End of Arr^J not reached)
   id-pair = id-pair $\cup$ (v_c, v_b), $\forall$ c = 1..a
   else exit;
8. goto step 4.

g) Attribute <= Attribute $(A_i <= A_j)$: -

The evaluation of this condition is similar to the above one except the change at step 4.

4. while($\text{Arr}^I(a) <= \text{Arr}^J(b)$ and End of Arr^I not reached)
begin
id-pair = id-pair $\cup$ (v_a, v_b);
a = a+1;
endwhile;

h) Attribute > Attribute $(A_i > A_j)$: -

The condition can be evaluated by simply transforming the operator > to <= and interchanging the operands.

i.e., Cond($A_i > A_j$) = Cond($A_j <= A_i$).

i) Attribute >= Attribute (A_i >= A_j): -
   This condition can be evaluated by simply changing the operator >= to <
   and interchanging the operands.
   i.e., Cond(A_i >= A_j) = Cond(A_j < A_i).

j) Condition1 OR Condition2, Condition1 AND Condition2 (cond1Vcond2,
   cond1 Λcond2): -
   The operations AND, OR are evaluated by evaluating the argument conditions independently and then applying the AND, OR operation on the id's
   returned by each condition.
   Cond(cond1 Λ cond2) → Cond(cond1) Λ Cond(cond2).
   Cond(cond1 V cond2) → Cond(cond1) V Cond(cond2).

Hence the arithmetic conditions over the constant returns set of id values. These
id values are used in the construction of the server query. The Arithmetic condition over the attributes returns a set of id pairs. Each element of the pair
corresponds to each table participated in the join operation.

5.1   Query Translation and Other SQL Operations

The query posed by the user must be disintegrated into Server query and Wrapper query. $Q = Q_s \cup Q_w$.

  In our architecture, all the mapping conditions of the selection operation can
be done at the wrapper itself, as explained in the above section. These conditions
after evaluation returns a set of id's that constitutes the selection operation of
Server query.

  The Server query returns the encrypted tuples to the wrapper. The wrapper
decrypts the tuples and stores them temporarily for execution of the Wrapper
query. The other operations like projection, Aggregation, Group by, Order by
and presentation operators like sort, duplication removal are evaluated at the
wrapper. As these conditions are evaluated on small number of tuples returned
by server, the computation overhead is less at the wrapper.

6   Experimental Evaluations

In this section, the experiment results are presented to show the effectiveness of
the proposed architecture. In addition to our approach, we have implemented
the mechanism of indexing by bucketing [9].

  We conducted the tests on TPC-H benchmark. Using dbgen tool of TPC-
H benchmark, the database is generated at a scale factor of 0.01 and 0.1 i.e.,
10MB and 100MB respectively. Two IBM Intel based Personal Computers with
Pentium 4 2.4GHz processors with 256MB RAM are used for conducting the
experiments. One of the computer acts as a server and the other as a Security
Wrapper and Application Server. Other relevant software components used are
Microsoft SQL Server, ZQL Parser (a SQL Parser) and Microsoft Windows 2000
as the Operating System.

6.1   Tables/Relations

Out of the multiple tables from TPC-H, we selected the following tables for our experimental purpose.

Lineitem : l_shipdate, l_discount, l_quantity, l_returnflag, l_linestatus, l_extendedprice.

Customer: c_custkey, c_mktsegment, c_name, c_acctbal, c_phone, c_addr, c_comment.

The attributes shown underlined are Index attributes.

We considered Q6 from TPC-H Benchmark to evaluate different aspects of the architecture. The query, as shown in figure 3, is a simple query on selection operation with unequi-predicates acting on a single table.

```
Q1 : select sum(l_eprice * l_discount) as revenue from lineitem
    where l_sdate >= ('1994-01-01')
    and l_sdate < ('1995-01-01')
    and l_discount between 0.06-0.01 and 0.06+0.01
    and l_quantity<24.
```

Fig. 3. Query used for the experiments

6.2   Analysis of Results

Figure 4 shows the various costs when Q1 is run over the benchmark database of different sizes 10MB to 50MB. The first set represents the costs in our approach and second set represents the costs on bucketing approach [9]. The graphs shows that the client and network cost of bucketing approach (2) is much higher than that of (1) due to more false hit tuples sent from the server to the wrapper in bucketing mechanism.

Figure 5b shows the network costs when Q1 is queried over databases of sizes 10MB to 50MB. The increase in network cost in our approach is gradual where as in bucketing approach there is much hike when database size is increasing. This is due to the more number of unwanted tuples returned to the client that must be decrypted and queried on.

The customer table is queried with the query "select * from customer" with a) no security wrapper i.e. directly querying the database and b) with security wrapper making Query engine off and Integrity Checker ON. Hence we evaluated the performances when data integrity check is present and without any data integrity check. The graph reveals the extra costs incurred by the data integrity checker when queried over various database sizes.

Hence our approach maintains data privacy and detects the unauthorized changes made to the database with lesser costs on network and client site.

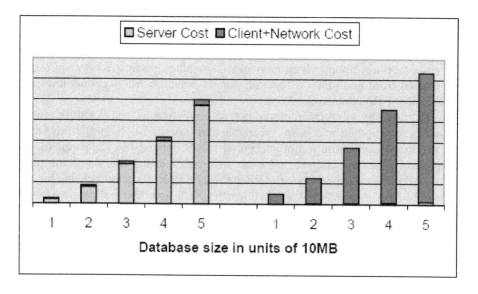

Fig. 4. Cost Factors for Query Execution Time for Query Q1

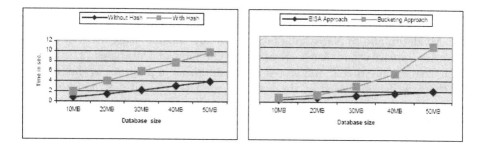

Fig. 5. (a) Evaluation of Integrity Checker (b) Comparison of network costs

7   Related Research Work

In [9], tuples are encrypted using conventional encryption algorithms and bucket id's are stored for every indexed attribute at the server. The domain of each indexed attribute is partitioned into buckets based on histogram construction techniques like equi-width, equi-depth etc. All the values in each bucket are represented by a single id. Hence the query on plain text can be transformed to the query on the bucket id's. This results in false hits and hence the query has to be processed again at the client side on the returned results from the server.

In [10], the authors proposed new indexing mechanisms – indexing by encryption and indexing by hashing in order to avoid inference and linking attacks. But these mechanisms face frequency based attacks and does not support interval-based queries. In another paper by the same authors [14], proposed using of auxiliary B+ Tree as indexing function. In this proposal, B+ Tree is constructed by trusted front end but stored on the server by encrypting each node. So, for processing of the query, all the required nodes are retrieved from the server and decrypted and act upon, which increases the traffic drastically between server and trusted front end. This is basically for the scenario where clients have less memory like PDA, Smart Cards etc.

In [16], heuristic encryption methods that preserve some relationships among the data are proposed which are reversible and based on polynomial functions. But the shape of distribution of encrypted values depends on the shape of distribution of plain text values that leads to reveal information about the plain text distribution. [17] proposes an Order Preserving Encryption Scheme for numeric data by flattening and transforming the plain text distribution onto target distribution. In [18], a tamper resistant hardware is used for running the encryption/decryption functions while hiding the execution from the server. This paper does not discuss the issue of indexing information and hence retrieves all the tuples from the server for processing the query.

R Graubart in his paper on "The Integrity-Lock Approach to Secure Database Management" [24] has proposed the concept of using checksums at record level and field level for integrity purpose. In this architecture, a trusted front end is introduced between the user/client and the untrusted DBMS for the verification of checksums. The paper also analyzed the advantages and disadvantages of this approach when checksums are used at record level and at field level.

E Mykletun and M Narasimha proposed a new scheme using Merkley's Hash Trees for Integrity and Authentication in Outsourced Databases [21]. Here a Hash Tree is constructed and stored at the database in addition to the records. All the records are placed at the leaves of the tree, the interior nodes are the hashes of the data at sons of that node, and the owner of data signs the root node. Whenever the client queries the database, all the relevant records and the necessary hashes unto the root are sent to the client. The client verifies the signature of the root and reconstructs the tree using the data sent to it and checks all the hashes of the Hash Tree. This approach solves the problem of *completeness of query replies* in addition to data integrity problem.

In a later paper by the same authors, they proposed two new schemes using Condensed RSA and BGLS signatures [23]. Another recent approach by C N Zhang, proposed an integrated approach for integrity of database and Fault Tolerance [25]. This approach utilizes the redundant residue number systems and Chinese remainder Theorem for checksum generation and verification. This approach also detects and corrects a single error in the data. However, this approach requires finding n number of big relative primes where n is the number of fields in the record and also the approach requires lot of security analysis to be done.

8   Conclusions

Data is the precious resource of an enterprise and its privacy is the need of the hour to protect the sensitive data from malicious attacks. Our solution encrypts the data and manages the query on the encrypted database. Query management is handled in a way that there will be no false hits from the server, hence reducing the communication overhead between the wrapper and database server. Our approach informs the applications whenever any breach occurs in the database. Also this architecture ensures the policy of separation of duties as database administrators have only access to the encrypted data but not to the indexed information at the wrapper. This architecture can be extended to ASP model by outsourcing the encrypted data. We have to extend our experiments on join queries. We have to extend the solution to subqueries and operators like 'in'.

The Outsourcing countries like US also stress the importance of data privacy. Hence, in near future acts like Data protection Act, HIPAA Act will be enforced in India. Once these acts are enforced, all the banking and financial applications can go for a product of this architecture.

References

1. Computer Science Institute, "CSI/FBI Computer Crime and Security Survey". www.gocsi.com/forms/fbi/pdf.html
2. The eCriteria DSP. www.ecriteria.net
3. J. He, M. Wang, "Cryptography and Relational Database Management Systems", Int. Database and Engineering and Application Symposium, 2001.
4. U.Mattsson, Secure Data Functional Overview, Protegity Technical Paper TWP-0011, 2000. http://www.protegity.com/White_Papers.html
5. TPC-H Benchmark Specification http://www.tpc.org
6. H. Hacigumus, B. Iyer, C. Li, and S. Mehrotra, "Providing database as a service", in Proc. Of the 18th International Conference on Data engineering, 2002.
7. L. Bouganium and P. Pucheral, "Chip-secured data access: Confidential data on untrusted servers", in Proc. Of the 28th International Conference on Very Large Data Bases, 2002.
8. D. Song, D. Wagner, and A. Perrig, "Practical techniques for searches on encrypted data", in Proc. Of the IEEE Symposium on Security and Privacy, 2000.
9. H. Hacigumus, B. Iyer, C. Li, and S. Mehrotra, "Executing SQL over encrypted data in the database-service-provider model", in Proc. of the ACM SIGMOD' 2002.
10. E. Damiani, S. D. C. di Vimercati, S. Jajodia, S. Paraboschi, and P. Samarati, "Balancing Confidentiality and efficiency in untrusted relational dbmss", in Proc of the 10th ACM Conference on Computer and Communications Society, 2003.
11. G. Davida, D. Wells, and J. Kam, "A database encryption system with subkeys" in ACM Transactions on Database Systems, 1981.
12. Advanced Encryption Standard, National Institute of Science and Technology, FIPS 197, 2001.
13. J. He and M. Wang, "Encryption in relational database management systems", in Proc. Of Fourteenth Annual IFIP WG11.3 Working Conference on Database Security, DBSec' 2000.
14. E. Damiani, S. D. C. di Vimercati, S. Jajodia, S. Paraboschi, and P. Samarati, "Implementation of a Storage Mechanism for Untrusted DBMSs", in Proc. of the 2nd IEEE International Security in Storage Workshop, 2004.
15. Neal R Wagner, Paul S Putter, "Encrypted Database Design: Specialized Approaches", 1986 IEEE.

16. Gultekin Ozsoyogulu, David A Singer, Sun S Chang, "Anti-Tamper databases: Querying Encrypted Databases".

17. Rakesh Agarwal, Jerry Kiernan, Ramakrishnan Srikant, Yirong Xu, "Order Preserving Encryption for Numeric Data", in ACM SIGMOD Conference on Management of Data, ACM Press, June 2004.

18. Murat Kantarciouglo, Chris Clifton, "Security Issues in Querying Encrypted Data", Purdue Computer Science Technical Report 04-013.

19. Arup Nanda, Donald K Burleson, Text Book on "Oracle Privacy Security Auditing".

20. Gramm-Leach Bliley Act, http://www.ftc.gob/privacy/glbact/glbsub1.html

21. E Mykletun, M Narasimha, and G Tsudik, "Providing Authentication and Integrity in Outsourced Databases using Merkley Hash Trees." UCI-SCONCE Technical Report, 2003. http://sconce.ics.uci.edu/das/MerkleODB.pdf

22. Hacigumis, B Iyer, and S Mehrotra, "Encrypted Database Integrity in Database Service Provider Model", in International Workshop on Certification and Security in E-Services (CSES'02 IFIP WCC), 2002.

23. E Mykletun, M Narasimha, and G Tsudik, "Authentication and Integrity in Outsourced Databases".

24. Richard Graubart "The Integrity-Lock Approach to Secure Database Management", The Mitre Corporation, Bedford, MA, 1984 IEEE.

25. Chang N Zhang, and Honglan Zhong, "An Integrated Approach for Database Security and Fault Tolerance", in Proceedings of the International Conference on Information technology: Coding and Computing (ITCC'04), 2004 IEEE.

26. White Papers form Application Security Inc. http://www.appsecinc.com/whitepapers

27. White Papers from nCipher http://active.ncipher.com/index.php

28. SHA http://www.itl.nist.gov/fipspubs/fip180-1.htm

29. Crypto Package http://www.acme.com/java/software/Package-Acme.Crypto.html

30. Tomcat Server http://www.apache.org/

Event Detection in Multilevel Secure Active Databases

Indrakshi Ray and Wei Huang

Department of Computer Science,
Colorado State University,
Fort Collins CO 80523-1873
{iray, hw3699}@cs.colostate.edu

Abstract. The event-condition-action paradigm (also known as *triggers* or *rules*) is a powerful technology. It gives a database "active" capabilities – the ability to react automatically to changes in the database or in the environment. One potential use of this technology is in the area of multilevel secure (MLS) data processing, such as, military, where the subjects and objects are classified into different security levels and mandatory access control rules govern who has access to what. Although a lot of research appears in MLS databases, not much work has been done in the area of MLS active databases. In this paper, we look at one very important aspect of an MLS active database – event detection.

An MLS rule, like any other object in an MLS database, is associated with a security level. Events in an MLS database are also associated with security levels. Since an MLS rule can be triggered by an event that is at a different security level than the rule, we cannot use the event detection techniques designed for non-MLS active databases. Using such techniques cause illegal information flow. Our goal is to propose new algorithms that prevent such illegal information flow. We first present an approach to detect primitive events – events that cannot be decomposed. Different types of primitive events can be combined using the event composition operators to form composite events. We also describe how to detect composite events using event graphs in an MLS database.

1 Introduction

Traditional database management systems are *passive*: the database systems execute commands when requested by the user or application program. However, there are many applications where this passive behavior is inadequate. Consider for example, a financial application: whenever the price of stock for a company falls below a given threshold, the user must sell his corresponding stocks. One solution is to add monitoring mechanisms in the application programs modifying the stock prices that will alert the user to such changes. Incorporating monitoring mechanisms in all the relevant application programs is non trivial. The alternate option is to poll periodically and check the stock prices. Polling too frequently incurs a performance penalty; polling too infrequently may result in not getting the desirable functionalities. A better solution is to use active databases.

Active databases move the reactive behavior from the application into the database. This reactive capability is provided by *triggers* also known as *event-condition-action*

S. Jajodia and C. Mazumdar (Eds.): ICISS 2005, LNCS 3803, pp. 177–190, 2005.

rules or simply *rules*. In other words, triggers give active databases the capability to monitor and react to specific circumstances that are relevant to an application. An active database system must provide trigger processing capabilities in addition to providing all the functionalities of a passive database system.

One potential use of this technology is in the area of secure data processing, such as, the military which uses an underlying multilevel secure (MLS) database. A multilevel secure database system is characterized by having a partially ordered set of security levels (the ordering relation is referred to as the dominance relation); all the database objects and the operations (transactions) on the database objects have security levels associated with them. Mandatory access control policies determine which transactions can access which objects. The idea is that information can flow from the dominated level to the dominating level but not in the other direction.

Providing reactive capabilities in an MLS database system requires event detection. We start by describing the different kinds of events in an MLS database and how to assign security levels to events. The rules in an MLS database are also associated with security levels. Since a rule can be triggered by events whose level is dominated by the level of the rule, the algorithms used for detecting events in an non-MLS database cannot be used. Using such algorithms causes illegal information flow. Our goal is to provide algorithms that do not cause such security breaches.

The first step in event detection is the detection of *primitive* events. Primitive events are atomic in nature – they cannot be decomposed into constituent events. Primitive event detection is complicated by the fact that a primitive event at the dominated level cannot automatically notify any rule at the dominating level. This requires us to have event detectors at each security level. Each level is responsible for detecting the events that are associated with the rules at that level.

The events in a rule may not be primitive events. Two or more primitive events can be combined using event composition operators to form a *composite* event. As expected, detection of composite events is non-trivial. We adapt the approach proposed by Chakravarty et al. [5] for detecting composite events. For each rule, we construct an *event tree* for detecting composite events associated with that rule. The level of this event tree is the same as the security level of the rule. Each node n_i corresponds to an event of this rule. Each directed edge (n_i, n_j) signifies that the event corresponding to node n_i is a constituent of the composite event corresponding to n_j. An event may be associated with more than one rule. Thus, an event can belong to multiple event trees. In such situations, as suggested by Chakravarty et al.[5], we can merge the event trees to form an event graph. There are two ways in which our composite event detection differs from Chakravarty's work. First, only event trees belonging to the same security level can be merged. Second, if a composite event is used by rules at different security levels, then multiple event trees need to be used – one for each security level. Finally, we provide algorithms for detecting composite events.

The rest of the paper is organized as follows. Section 2 briefly describes the underlying MLS model on which our work is based. Section 3 describes the structure of rules in an MLS active database system, how security levels are assigned to rules, and the relationship between the security levels of the different components of rules. Section 4 describes the possible architectures for an MLS active database. Section 5 focuses on event detection in an MLS active database. Section 6 describes the related work in this area. Section 7 concludes the paper with pointers to future directions.

2   Our Model of an MLS Database

A database system is composed of database objects. At any given time, the *database state* is determined by the values of the objects in the database. A change in the value of a database object changes the state. Users are responsible for submitting transactions and application programs that are to be executed on the database. A *transaction* is an operation on a database state. An *application program* may or may not perform an operation on the database state. Execution of a transaction or application program may cause the database to change state.

An MLS database is associated with a security structure that is a partial order, $(\mathbf{L}, <)$. $\mathbf{L}$ is a set of security levels, and $<$ is the dominance relation between levels. If $L_1 < L_2$, then L_2 is said to strictly dominate L_1 and L_1 is said to be strictly dominated by L_2. If $L_1 = L_2$, then the two levels are said to be equal. $L_1 < L_2$ or $L_1 = L_2$ is denoted by $L_1 \leq L_2$. If $L_1 \leq L_2$,then L_2 is said to dominate L_1 and L_1 is said to be dominated by L_2. Two levels L_1 and L_2 are said to be incomparable if neither $L_1 \leq L_2$ nor $L_2 \leq L_1$. We assume the existence of a level U, that corresponds to the level unclassified or public knowledge. The level U is the greatest lower bound of all the levels in $\mathbf{L}$. Each database object $x \in \mathbf{D}$ is associated with exactly one security level which we denote as $L(x)$ where $L(x) \in \mathbf{L}$. (The function L maps entities to security levels.) We assume that the security level of an object remains fixed for the entire lifetime of the object. The users of the system are cleared to the different security levels. We denote the security clearance of user U_i by $L(U_i)$. Consider a military setting consisting of four security levels: Top Secret (TS), Secret (S), Confidential (C) and Unclassified (U). The user Jane Doe has the security clearance of Top Secret. That is, $L(JaneDoe) = TS$. Each user has one or more principals associated with him. The number of principals associated with the user depends on his security clearance; it equals the number of levels dominated by the user's security clearance. In our example Jane Doe has four principals: *JaneDoe.TS*, *JaneDoe.S*, *JaneDoe.C* and *JaneDoe.U*. At each session, the user logs in as one of the principals. All processes that the user initiates in that session inherit security level of the corresponding principal. Each transaction T_i is associated with exactly one security level. The level of the transaction remains fixed for the entire duration of the transaction. The security level of the transaction is the level of the principal who has submitted the transaction. For example, if Jane Doe logs in as *JaneDoe.S*, all transactions initiated by Jane Doe will have the level Secret (S).

We require a transaction T_i to obey the *simple security property* and the *restricted ⋆-property*: may read a database object x only if $L(x) \leq C$ and (2) A transaction T_i with $L(T_i) = C$ may write a database object x only if $L(x) = C$. We give the formal definition of an MLS transaction and an MLS application below.

Definition 1. [MLS Transaction] *An MLS transaction T_i is a set of read and write operations on database objects which are preceded by the command* begin *and followed by the command* abort *or* commit. *The transaction T_i is associated with security level $L(T_i)$*

where $L(T_i) \in \mathbf{L}$; it accesses database objects in accordance with the simple security and the restricted $\star$-property.

Definition 2. [**MLS Application Program**] *An MLS application program A_i is a set of operations submitted by the user – the operations may or may not access the database objects. An application program A_i that accesses the database objects is associated with security level $L(A_i)$, where $L(A_i) \in \mathbf{L}$; it accesses database objects according to the rules specified by the simple security and the restricted $\star$-property.*

3   Rules in an MLS Active Database

In addition to transactions and application programs, an active database system also has *rules*. A rule is specified by three components: *event*, *condition* and *action*. An event causes a rule to be triggered. Active database systems have mechanisms that monitors the database to check whether an event has occurred. If an event associated with a rule occurs, the rule's condition is evaluated. If the rule's condition evaluates to true, then the rule's action is scheduled for execution. The details of rule execution are considerably more complex and have been omitted from this paper.

A rule is a database object on which we allow the following operations: (1) Create – this operation allows a new rule to be created. (2) Delete – this operation allows an existing rule to be deleted. (3) Update – this operation allows an existing rule to be modified. (4) Enable – this operation allows an existing rule to be enabled. Only enabled rules can be triggered. (5) Disable – this operation allows an existing rule to be disabled. A disabled rule cannot be triggered. (6) View – this operation allows an existing rule to be viewed. Like other database objects in an MLS database, rules are also associated with security levels. Each rule R_j is created by some principal, say P, and it inherits the security level of the principal that created it, that is, $L(R_j) = L(P)$. Creation, deletion, modification, disabling, enabling of the rule corresponds to writing of the rule object. Hence, by the restricted $\star$-property these operations can be performed only by transactions or applications whose security level is the same as that of the rule. Viewing the rule corresponds to a read operation of the rule object. Thus, the view operation can be performed by transactions or applications whose security levels dominate the level of the rule.

Definition 3. [**MLS Rule**] *An MLS rule R_j is defined as a triple $< e_j, c_j, a_j >$ where e_j is the event that causes the rule to be triggered, c_j is the condition that is checked when the rule is triggered and a_j is the action that is executed when the rule is triggered. The MLS rule R_j is associated with exactly one security level which we denote by $L(R_j)$ where $L(R_j) \in \mathbf{L}$. The operations allowed on rules obey the mandatory restrictions specified by the simple security and the restricted $\star$-property.*

3.1   Events in an MLS Active Database Systems

Event specifies what causes the rule to be triggered. Possible events that can be supported in an MLS active database system are as follows. (1) Data modification/retrieval event – the event is raised by an operation (insert, update, delete, access) on some database object. (2) Transaction event – the event is raised by some transaction command (e.g. begin, abort, commit etc.). (3) Application-defined event – the application program may signal the occurrence of an event. (4) Temporal events – events are raised at some point in time. Temporal events may be absolute (e.g., 25th December, 2002) or relative (e.g. 15 minutes after x occurs). (5) External events – the event is occurring outside the database (e.g. the sensor recording temperature goes above 100 degrees Celsius).

Events can further be classified into primitive and composite events. A *primitive event* cannot be divided into subparts. A *composite events* is raised by some combination of primitive events. For example, inserting a tuple in *Employee* relation is a primitive event. Two hours after a tuple has been inserted in *Employee* relation is a composite event. A composite event is constructed using two or more primitive events connected by an event operator. Any composite event e can be denoted as: $e = e_1 \ op_1 \ e_2 \ op_2 \dots \ e_n$ where $e_1, e_2, \dots, e_n$ are the primitive events making up the composite event E, and $op_1, op_2, \dots op_{n-1}$ are the event operators. Event operators can be logical event operators ($\vee, \wedge$, etc.), sequence operators (;), or temporal composition operators (*after*, *between*, etc.). In this paper, we consider only two most common event operators: $\vee$ – disjunction and ; – sequence. The composite event $e_1 \vee e_2$ is said to occur when either an instance of e_1 or e_2 occurs. The composite event $e_1; e_2$ is said to occur when an instance of e_2 occurs after an instance of e_1. We next describe how to assign security levels to events.

Security Level associated with Data Modification/Retrieval Event: The event e has the same security level as the operation O that caused it, that is, $L(e) = L(O)$. If this operation O is performed by some transaction T, then the level of O is the same as the level of T.

Security level associated with the Transaction Event: The event E has the same security level of the transaction T that caused it, that is, $L(e) = L(T)$.

Security Level associated with Application-Defined Event: The event e has the same security level as the level at which the application A that generated it is executing, that is, $L(e) = L(A)$.

Security Level associated with Temporal Event: An absolute temporal event e is observable by any body and so its security level is public, that is, $L(e) = U$. A relative temporal event is a composite event. The manner in which the level of composite event is calculated is given below.

Security Level associated with External Event: The level of the event e is the greatest lower bound of the security clearances of the users U_1, U_2, ..., U_n who can observe this external event e, that is, $L(e) = glb(L(U_1), L(U_2), \dots, L(U_n))$ (where $L(U_i)$ denotes the security clearance of user U_i).

An event like the outside air temperature is 110 degrees Fahrenheit, is observable by all users and so its level is public. Whereas, an event like the sensor reading from a military satellite that can be observed only by Top Secret personnel, will have a security level of Top Secret.

Security Levels associated with Composite Event: Consider the composite event E given by, $e = e_1 \ op_1 \ e_2 \ op_2 \dots \ e_n$, where e is composed of primitive events e_1,

$e_2, \ldots, e_n$. The security level of the composite event e is the least upper bound of the levels of the primitive events $e_1, e_2, \ldots, e_n$ composing it, that is, $L(e) = lub(L(e_1), L(e_2), \ldots, L(e_n))$.

3.2   Conditions in an MLS Active Database System

In an active database, when a rule has been triggered *condition* specifies the additional conditions that must be checked before the action can be executed. If the condition part of the rule evaluates to true, then the action is executed. Possible conditions are as follows. (1) Database predicates – the condition might be a predicate on the database state (average salary of employees greater than 50000). (2) Database queries – the condition might be a query on the database state. If the query returns some results, the condition is said to be satisfied. If the query fails to return any result, the condition is not satisfied. (3) Application procedures – the condition may be a specified as a call to an application procedure (example, *max_exceeded()*) which may or may not access the database.

We now describe how to assign security levels to conditions. The level of a condition c, denoted by $L(c)$, is the least upper bound of all the data that is accessed by the condition. That is, $L(c) = lub(L(D_1), L(D_2), L(D_3), \ldots, L(D_n))$ where $D_1, D_2, \ldots, D_n$ are the data objects accessed by condition c.

3.3   Actions in an MLS Active Database System

When the rule is triggered and its condition evaluates to true, the action of the rule must be executed. Possible actions in an MLS active database include the following. (1) Data modification/retrieval operation – the action of the rule causes a data operation (insert, update, delete, access). (2) Transaction operation – the action of the rule causes a transaction operation (e.g. abort). (3) Application-defined operation – the action causes some procedure in an application to be executed. (4) External operation – the action causes some external operations (e.g. informing the user).

Some active database languages allow a rule to specify multiple actions. Usually these actions are ordered which allows them to be executed sequentially. This is how we assign security levels for the actions.

Security Level associated with Data Modification/Retrieval Action: The action has the same level as the operation it causes, that is, $L(a) = L(O)$.

Security Level associated with Transaction Operation: The action a has the same level as the transaction T, that is, $L(a) = L(T)$.

Security Level associated with Application-defined operation: The action a has the same level as the application process A, that is $L(a) = L(A)$.

Security Level associated with External operation: The level of action a is the greatest lower bound of the security clearances of the users $U_1, U_2, \ldots, U_n$ who can observe this operation, that is, $L(a) = glb(L(U_1), L(U_2), \ldots, L(U_n))$ where $L(U_1)$, $L(U_2), \ldots, L(U_n)$ are the security clearances associated with users $U_1, U_2, \ldots, U_n$ respectively.

Security Level of Action Composed of Multiple Constituents: Consider a rule $R = < e, c, a >$ where the action a is composed of multiple actions, $a_1, a_2, \ldots, a_k$. The level of all the actions must be the same. That is, $L(a_1) = L(a_2) = \ldots = L(a_k)$.

3.4   Relationship of Security Levels Associated with a Rule

The following illustrates the relationship of the level of the rule R_j with the levels of the constituent event e_j, the condition c_j and the action a_j: (1) $L(e_j) \leq L(R_j)$, (2) $L(c_j) \leq L(R_j)$, and (3) $L(a_j) = L(R_j)$. Item (1) states that a rule may be triggered by an event whose level is dominated by the level of the rule. Item (2) states that a rule may require checking conditions at the dominated level before it can be fired. Item (3) states that a rule can take an action only at its own level.

In a secure environment it might be necessary for dominating levels to monitor suspicious events taking place at some dominated level and take some precautionary action; hence the need for $L(e_j) \leq L(R_j)$. Moreover, $L(e_j) \not> L(R_j)$ ensures that a dominating event does not trigger a dominated rule and create illegal information flow. The same reasoning applies for condition c_j; thus, the rule R_j might check conditions involving dominated level data (that is, $L(c_j) \leq L(R_j)$), but not data at the dominated levels ($L(c_j) \not> L(R_j)$). The level of the action is the same as the level of the rule, that is, $L(a_j) = L(R_j)$. Since $L(a_j) \not< L(R_j)$, a rule at the dominating level cannot result in an action at the dominated level and create illegal flow of information. Also, since $L(a_j) \not> L(R_j)$, a rule at the dominated level while executing its action cannot corrupt data at the dominating level.

4   Architecture of an MLS Active Database System

In this section we describe an architecture at a very abstract level of an MLS active database system (refer to figure 1). This will give an idea of the extra components that

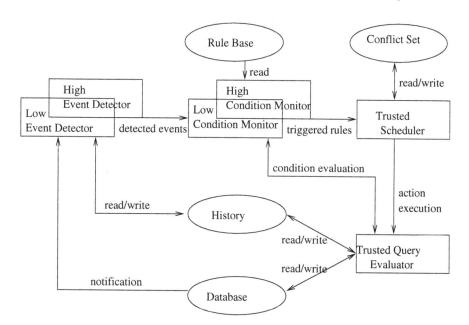

Fig. 1. A High-Level Architecture for Processing MLS Rules

must be supported for processing MLS rules. The principal components are depicted by rectangles and the data stores are depicted by ellipses. These are described next. **Event Detector at Level** l_i: This is responsible for detecting events at level l_i. Note that, event detector at level l_i can detect events at all levels that are dominated by l_i. Composite events are constructed using the knowledge about incoming primitive events and past events obtained from the history. **Condition monitor at Level** l_i: This is responsible for evaluating the conditions of rules that are triggered by the events detected by the event detector l_i. The condition monitor sends a request to the query evaluator to evaluate the condition. On the basis of the response from the query evaluator, the condition monitor decides which rules are triggered. These rules are then sent to the scheduler. **Trusted Scheduler**: This is responsible for scheduling which rule is to be executed. Since the scheduler accesses rules at different levels, it must be a trusted component. **Trusted Query Evaluator**: This is responsible for executing database actions and queries. We have shown the query evaluator to be a trusted component because it is responsible for executing database operations at all levels. In real world, the query evaluator will have several components, some of which are trusted and others which are not.

5   Event Detection

The process of event detection has been investigated by other researchers. In this section, we show how event detection can be adapted for MLS databases. One significant difference is that we have multiple event detectors that are responsible for detecting events that are of interest to the different security levels. The process in which the events get detected is different as well. Before describing these, we need to say a few words about event detection in non-MLS systems.

Chakravarthy et al. [5] describe event detection as the process of recognizing the occurrence of the event, collecting and recording its parameters. Examples of event parameters are the event type and time of occurrence. Event detection involves detecting primitive as well as composite events. Traditionally system clock and interrupts are used to detect primitive events. Detecting primitive events in non-MLS active database is achieved by using lower-level programmable interrupts or by embedding code in the system component that is responsible for reading and writing the data on the disk.

In an MLS environment, detecting primitive database events is non-trivial because an event at the dominated level may trigger a dominating rule. The dominated level in such a case should not be aware of the rule at the dominating level. Thus no actions can be taken at the dominated level when an event occurs. For instance, the dominated level cannot generate an interrupt to alert the dominating level about the occurrence of the event. Neither can code be embedded in the component that is responsible for reading and writing data on the disk.

In an MLS active database, if the level of the event is dominated by the level of the rule, the dominating level must monitor the dominated level to check for the occurrence of the event. For each type of primitive database event, we have a table which we call the *incident table* that records the occurrence of these events. The security level of the table is the same as the level of the event. The problem is that this solution is insecure – the dominated level can infer which events are of interest to the dominating level. To

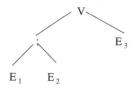

Fig. 2. An Event Tree for a Composite Event

overcome this problem, we can have incident tables for all events and for some non-events. The non-events appear to be like events but they are not part of any rule. In short, we introduce some noise in the inference channel. The dominated level no longer knows for certain whether an incident table belongs to an event or not.

Since an event may be associated with rules at one or more dominating levels, the issue is how long should we maintain information about event occurrence in the incident tables. For security reasons, a dominating level cannot inform the dominated level when it has completed event detection. We propose that the incident occurrences be recorded for a fixed duration of time in the incident tables. The duration is fixed for all incidents. Within this time frame, the event detector at the level of the rule associated with the event must read the incident table in order to detect the event.

Sometimes a primitive event may not directly trigger any rules, but it may be a component of a composite event. The composite event may not occur until a later time. In such cases, the event detector at the level of the rule associated with the event must read the incident table and copy this information into a table at its own level. The table onto which this information is copied is referred to as an *event table*. Since an event can be associated with rules at different security levels, we can have multiple event tables at different security levels for the same event.

Event tables for primitive events are needed when they are part of a composite event. Sometimes a composite event is made up of other composite events. For each event that is part of a composite event, we have an event table that records its parameters. Another data structure that is needed for detecting composite events is an *event tree*. An example of an event tree for the composite event $(E_1; E_2) \vee E_3$ is given in Figure 2.

Definition 4 (Event Tree). *An event tree $\mathcal{ET}_e = (N, E)$ corresponding to a composite event e is a directed tree where each node e_i represents either event e or one of its constituent. The root node corresponds to event e, and the leaf nodes correspond to the primitive events that make up node e. The edge (e_i, e_j) signifies that node e_i is a constituent of the composite event e_j. e_i in this case is referred to as the child node and e_j as the parent.*

An event can trigger multiple rules. Thus, different event trees can have nodes corresponding to the same event. In such cases, to save storage space, the event trees can be merged to form an event graph. One points need to be mentioned. Only event trees at the same security level can be merged. An event graph may contain event belonging to different rules. The nodes corresponding to events which fire one or more rules are labeled with the rule-ids of the corresponding rule.

Definition 5 (Event Graph). *An* event graph $\mathcal{E}G = (N, E)$ *is a directed graph where node e_i represents an event e_i and edge (e_i, e_j) signifies that the event corresponding to node e_i is a constituent of the composite event corresponding to node e_j. Each node e_i is associated with a label $label_{e_i}$. $label_{e_i}$ is a set of rule-ids (possibly empty) that indicate the rules that will fire when the event corresponding to node e_i happens.*

We now give the algorithms for event detection. The first one focuses on primitive event detection at security level L. The input to this algorithm is the event graph $\mathcal{E}G$ for level L, the set of incident and event tables corresponding to primitive events of $\mathcal{E}G$, and the set of incident tables for level L. The output is the updated event tables and updated incident tables at its own level. The algorithm checks for incidents occurring at level L. This information gets stored in the incident tables at level L. The algorithm also checks whether new rows have been added to the incident tables that correspond to primitive events of $\mathcal{E}G$. If so, it implies new events that are of interest to level L have occurred and it calls the procedure *ProcessEvent* to process these events.

Algorithm 1

Detecting Primitive Events for Rules at Security Level L

Input: (i) $\mathcal{E}G$ – event graph for security level L, (ii) **ET** – Set of event tables where each table corresponds to a primitive event in $\mathcal{E}G$, (iii) **IT** – Set of incident tables for each primitive event in $\mathcal{E}G$ and also for other incidents at level L

Output: (i) **ET** – Set of updated event tables for each primitive event in $\mathcal{E}G$ and (ii) **IT** – Set of updated incident tables.

Procedure *DetectPrimitiveEvents*($\mathcal{E}G$, **ET**, **IT**)
begin
    while *true* **do**
        if an incident e_x occurs at level L
            store its parameters in a new row in incident table it_{e_x}
        for each primitive event e_i corresponding to leaf nodes in $\mathcal{E}G$
            if L dominates $L(e_i)$
                if there is any new entry in incident table it_{e_i}
            begin
                copy the new row in it_{e_i} to event table et_{e_i}
                ProcessEvent(e_i, $\mathcal{E}G$, **ET**)
            end
    end while
end

Algorithm 2

Processing Event e_i for Rules at Security Level L

Input: (i) $\mathcal{E}G$ – event graph for security level L and (ii) **ET** – Set of event tables where each table corresponds to an event in $\mathcal{E}G$

Output: ET – Set of updated event tables for each event in $\mathcal{E}G$.

Procedure $ProcessEvent(e_i, \mathcal{E}G, \mathbf{ET})$
begin

      for each rule-id $r \in label_{e_i}$
      begin

            send event parameters to condition evaluator at level L
            mark node e_i as *occurred*

      end
      for each node e_j such that (e_i, e_j) is an edge of $\mathcal{E}G$
      begin

            /* propagate parameters from node e_i to node e_j and detect composite event */
            $DetectCompositeEvent(\mathcal{E}G, \mathbf{ET}, e_i, param_i, e_j)$

      end
      Delete row containing parameters of instance of e_i from table et_{e_i}

end

The above algorithm *ProcessEvent* describes the actions taken when an event e_i has been detected. Recall that $label_{e_i}$ contains the set of rules that are triggered by e_i. The parameters of e_i are then passed on to the condition evaluator which determines whether the rules listed in $label_{e_i}$ can be triggered or not. The node e_i is marked as *occurred* indicating that this event has taken place. The parameters of event e_i are then passed onto its parents and the *DetectCompositeEvent* procedure is called. The parameters of event e_i are then removed from the event table et_{e_i}.

Algorithm 3
Detecting Composite Event e_i for Rules at Security Level L

Input: (i) $\mathcal{E}G$ – event graph for security level L, (ii) $\mathbf{ET}$ – Set of event tables where each table corresponds to an event in $\mathcal{E}G$, (iii) e_i – child event that has occurred, (iv) $param_i$ – parameters of event e_i, and (v) e_j – parent event
Output: ET – Set of updated event tables for each event in $\mathcal{E}G$.

Procedure $DetectCompositeEvent(\mathcal{E}G, ET, e_i, param_i, e_j)$
begin

      case node e_j

            $\vee$: store $param_i$ in a new row in the table corresponding to the composite event
                $ProcessEvent(e_j, \mathcal{E}G, \mathbf{ET})$
            ;: **if** $e_i = $ *left child* of e_j

                insert a new row for this event instance and store $param_i$ in the composite event t
                if $e_i = $ *right child* of e_j
                    if *left child* of e_j is marked as occurred
                    begin

                        store $param_i$ in the row for this event instance in the composite event tab
                        $ProcessEvent(e_j, \mathcal{E}G, \mathbf{ET})$

                    end
      end case

end

The above algorithm shows how composite events are detected for two kinds of event composition operators – $\vee$ and ;. When the parent node $e_j = \vee$, then occurrence of child

e_i signals the occurrence of the composite event. In such a case, a new row is inserted in the event table corresponding to the composite event. The values inserted in this row correspond to parameters of the child e_i. The composite event is now processed by calling the procedure *ProcessEvent*. When the parent node $e_j =;,$ the event detection is a little more complex. If e_i is the left child, then a new row is inserted in this composite event table. The parameters of e_i are recorded in this row. The event corresponding to the right child must occur before this composite event can take place. If e_i is the right child and the left child has already occurred, then the parameters of e_i are inserted in the corresponding row created by the left child, and the composite event is signaled. The composite event is then processed by calling *ProcessEvent*.

6   Related Work

Related Work in Multilevel Secure Active Databases: Very little work appears in the area of multilevel secure active databases. The major work in this area is by Smith and Winslett [24]. The authors show how an MLS relational model can be extended to incorporate active capabilities. The underlying MLS relational model supports polyinstantiation: that is, all MLS entities in this model can exist at multiple security levels simultaneously. An MLS rule being an MLS entity can also exist at multiple security levels. Unlike our work is that this work is based on the polyinstantiation model. Moreover, this work also does not discuss the details of event detection. In one of our earlier works [20] we discussed the structure of MLS rules, and what impact such rules have on the execution model of an active database. However, event detection was not discussed in details.

Related Work in Expert Systems: Morgenstern [19] considers the problem of covert channels in deductive databases that are subject to mandatory security requirements. Berson and Lunt [2] describe the problems that must be solved in incorporating mandatory security requirements in a product rule system. Garvey and Lunt [10] extend an MLS object-oriented database system with productions rules. Expert system rules differ from active database rules. Expert system rules are executed upon an explicit request for information; active database rules are executed as side effects. Expert system rules are used for inferencing – the order of rule execution is not important. This is not so with active databases.

Related Work in Active Databases: Many work has been performed in the area of active databases. Most of these work differ in the knowledge model and execution model. Some of these active databases use a relational model as an underlying database and others use an object-oriented one. Some of the prototypes based on the relational model are Starburst [27], Ariel [13], POSTGRES [26]. Notable among the object-oriented models are HiPAC [17, 21], NAOS [7], Chimera [5], Ode [1] , SAMOS [11], Sentinel [6] and REACH [4].

Related Work in Multilevel Secure Databases: A large number of work also appears in multilevel secure database system. Majority of these work [8, 9, 12, 14, 15, 22, 23, 25] are in the area of relational database systems and some [3, 16, 18] are in the area of object oriented database systems.

7 Conclusion and Future Work

The absence of a multilevel secure active database limits the applicability of active technologies to applications that use an underlying MLS database system. Our work makes a small step towards fulfilling this gap. We have identified what kinds of rules can be supported and how these rules can be classified into security levels. An important component of rule processing is event detection. Towards this end, we have shown how events can be detected in an MLS active database without causing illegal information flow. We have not based our work on any relational or object-oriented models; our observations, therefore, will be useful to developers of any MLS active database system. In future, we plan to provide more details about the rule processing mechanism and the other components of an active database system. Our eventual goal is to implement an MLS active database system.

References

1. R. Agarwal and N. Gehani. Ode (Object database and environment): The language and the data model. In *Proceedings of the ACM-SIGMOD International Conference on Management of Data*, pages 36–45, Portland, OR, May 1989.

2. T. A. Berson and T. F. Lunt. Multilevel Security for Knowledge-Based Systems. In *Proceedings of the IEEE Symposium on Research in Security and Privacy*, pages 235–242, Oakland, CA, April 1987.

3. N. Boulahia-Cuppens, F. Cuppens, A. Gabillon, and K. Yazdanian. Virtual View Model to Design a Secure Object-Oriented Database. In *Proceedings of the National Computer Security Conference*, pages 66–76, Baltimore, MD, October 1994.

4. A.P. Buchman, H. Branding, T. Kundrass, and J. Zimmermann. REACH: A REal-time ACtive and Heterogeneous Mediator System. *Bulletin of the IEEE Technical Committee on Data Engineering*, 15(4), December 1992.

5. S. Ceri and R. Manthey. Consolidated specification of Chimera, the conceptual interface of idea. Technical Report IDEA.DD.2P.004, Politecnico di Milano, Milan, Italy, June 1993.

6. S. Chakravarthy, E. Hanson, and S.Y.W. Su. Active data/knowledge base research at the University of Florida. *Bulletin of the IEEE Technical Committee on Data Engineering*, 15(4):35–39, December 1992.

7. C. Collet, T. Coupaye, and T. Svensen. NAOS– efficient and modular reactive capabilities in an object-oriented database system. In *Proceedings of the Twentieth International Conference on Very Large Databases*, pages 132–143, Santiago, Chile, 1994.

8. D. Denning and T. F. Lunt. A multilevel relational data model. In *Proceedings of the IEEE Symposium on Research in Security and Privacy*, pages 220–234, Oakland, CA, May 1987.

9. P. A. Dwyer, G. D. Gelatis, and M. B. Thuraisingham. Multilevel security in database management systems. *Computers and Security*, 6(3):252–260, June 1987.

10. T. D. Garvey and T. F. Lunt. Multilevel Security for Knowledge-Based Systems. In *Proceedings of the Sixth Computer Security Applications Conference*, pages 148–159, Tucson, AZ, December 1990.

11. S. Gatziu, A. Geppert, and K. R. Dittrich. Integrating active concepts into an object-oriented database system. In *Proceedings of the Third International Workshop on Database Programming Languages*, Nafplion, Greece, August 1991.

12. J. T. Haigh, R. C. O'Brien, and D. J. Thomsen. The LDV Secure Relational DBMS Model. In S. Jajodia and C.E. Landwehr, editors, *Database Security IV: Status and Prospects*, pages 265–279. Elsevier Science Publishers B.V. (North-Holland), 1991.

13. E. Hanson. Rule condition testing and action execution in Ariel. In *Proceedings of the ACM SIGMOD International Conference on Management of Data*, pages 49–58, San Diego, CA, June 1992.

14. D. K. Hsiao, M. J. Kohler, and S. W. Stround. Query Modifications as Means of Controlling Access to Multilevel Secure Databases. In S. Jajodia and C.E. Landwehr, editors, *Database Security IV: Status and Prospects*, pages 221–240. Elsevier Science Publishers B.V. (North-Holland), 1991.

15. S. Jajodia and R. Sandhu. Toward a Multilevel Relational Data Model. In *Proceedings of the ACM SIGMOD International Conference on Management of Data*, pages 50–59, Denver, CO, 1991.

16. T. F. Keefe, W. T. Tsai, and M. B. Thuraisingham. A Multilevel Security Model for Object-Oriented Systems. In *Proceedings of the National Computer Security Conference*, pages 1–9, Baltimore, MD, October 1988.

17. D.R. McCarthy and U. Dayal. The architecture of an active database management system. In *Proceedings of the ACM-SIGMOD International Conference on Management of Data*, pages 215–224, Portland, OR, May 1989.

18. J. K. Millen and T.F. Lunt. Security for Object-Oriented Database Systems . In *Proceedings of the IEEE Symposium on Research in Security and Privacy*, pages 260–272, Oakland, CA, May 1992.

19. M. Morgenstern. Security and Inference in Multilevel Database and Knowledge-Base Systems. In *Proceedings of the ACM SIGMOD International Conference on Management of Data*, pages 357–373, San Francisco, CA, May 1987.

20. I. Ray. Multi-level secure active database rules and its impact on the design of active databases. In *Proceedings of the Twentieth British National Conference On Databases*, Coventry, U.K., July 2003.

21. A. Rosenthal, S. Chakravarthy, B. Blaustein, and J. Blakeley. Situation monitoring for active databases. In *Proceedings of the Fifteenth International Conference On Very Large Databases*, pages 455–464, Amsterdam, The Netherlands, August 1989.

22. R. Sandhu and S. Jajodia. Referential Integrity in Multilevel Secure Databases. In *Proceedings of the National Computer Security Conference*, pages 39–52, Baltimore, MD, September 1993.

23. L. M. Schlipper, J. Filsinger, and V. M. Doshi. A Multilevel Secure Database Management System Benchmark. In *Proceedings of the National Computer Security Conference*, pages 399–408, Baltimore, MD, October 1992.

24. K. Smith and M. Winslett. Multilevel secure rules: Integrating the multilevel and the active data model. Technical Report UIUCDCS-R-92-1732, University of Illinois, Urbana-Champaign, IL, March 1992.

25. P. D. Stachour and M. B. Thuraisingham. Design of LDV: A Multilevel Secure Relational Database Management System. *IEEE Transactions on Knowledge and Data Engineering*, 2(3):190–209, June 1990.

26. M. Stonebraker and G. Kemnitz. The POSTGRES Next-Generation Database Management System. *Communications of the ACM*, 34(10):78–92, October 1991.

27. J. Widom. The Starburst Rule System: Language Design, Implementation and Application. *Bulletin of the IEEE Technical Committee on Data Engineering*, 15(4):15–18, December 1992.

Key Management for Multicast Fingerprinting

Jian Wang[1], Lein Harn[2], and Hideki Imai[3]

[1] College of Information Science and Technology,
Nanjing University of Aeronautics and Astronautics, Nanjing, China, 210016
wangjian@nuaa.edu.cn
[2] Computer Networking Department, University of Missouri, Kansas City, USA
harnl@umkc.edu
[3] Institute of Industrial Science, The University of Tokyo, Tokyo, Japan
imai@iis.u-tokyo.ac.jp

Abstract. A secure multicast system allows a sender to send a message over a multicast channel to a dynamically changing group of users. A group key management solution, efficiently accommodating dynamic membership, is desirable. Fingerprinting technique has also been employed to trace traitors who illegally retransmit decrypted content to other unauthorized receivers. But, it makes key management much more challengeable. This paper studies this scenario, advances a notion of "subgroup key management", and indicates it should be collusion-free. Moreover, this paper also studies a general subset notion and employs it in subgroup key management approach. Especially, our dynamic key assignment scheme is a generalized mode of Logical Key Hierarchy (*LKH*). At same time, both symmetric and asymmetric cryptographic approaches for the subgroup key distribution are studied. Our approach can not only handle highly dynamic membership of a multicast session but also own very low overhead of communication, and it is collusion-free. Finally, the paper proves the security of proposed solutions and compares its efficiencies.

1   Introduction

Multicast communication is one of main communication modes for a wide range of Internet services, such as video broadcasting and multi-party teleconferencing. A secure multicast system allows a sender to send a message over an insecure multicast channel to a dynamically changing group of users. A group key management solution, efficiently accommodating dynamic membership, is desirable. Besides, fingerprinting technique has also been employed to trace traitors who illegally retransmit decrypted content to other unauthorized receivers. Thus, both encryption and fingerprinting are essential in most secure multicast sessions. Here, encryption is employed to prohibit eavesdropping from unauthorized receivers while fingerprinting is utilized to trace the pirates who illegally leaked decrypted data out. Without encryption, any user can easily intercept the transmitted data, which make fingerprinting meaningless. Hence, encryption is the basement of fingerprinting. Furthermore, key management is also crucial

S. Jajodia and C. Mazumdar (Eds.): ICISS 2005, LNCS 3803, pp. 191–204, 2005.

component of multicast encryption with fingerprinting. Unfortunately, here is a contradiction: fingerprinting assigns any receiver a copy with different mark but conventional key management shares a session key among a group of receivers. The most straightforward solution to it is to transmit each copy of encrypted message in a secure unicast channel to each receiver. Apparently, it is inefficient due to a very large volume of communication, nearly equal to $n * V$ (where n the number of receivers in a session and V is the volume of a single unicast).

In a data stream, distinct marks are embedded to produce different copies of each frame. In this way, multiple sequences are generated from a sequence of frames. And, through combining such multiple sequences, each authorized receiver may be assigned a distinct sequence and certainly some receivers may possibly share a decrypting key upon a frame. Therefore, all members can be dynamically divided into some subgroups (which must be updated upon next frame) so that members in a subgroup share a common key to get the same copy of a frame. How to distribute common keys to receivers is the motivation of subgroup key management. It should handle both very highly frequent change in each subgroup (nearly the same as the frame rate) and dynamic membership. Stateful schemes like LKH[16,17] are infeasible to be exploited directly in subgroup due to its obligatory of state synchronization especially in the wide-area. And, Stateless protocols, like as subset cover revocation scheme[18,19], are also infeasible because of the dependency of communication volume on the size of whole network.

Subgroup key management is divided into two components, i.e. dynamic key assignment and subgroup key distribution. The former may be implemented in similar way as LKH so as to accommodate dynamic membership change. The latter may be implemented by a stateless protocol because it is easily able to handle highly dynamic subgroup. And, each node in a key tree of LKH corresponds to a key and each member is assigned some node keys. And node key can also be regarded as subset key receivers share. Thus, LKH can be integrated with CS/SD seamlessly. In this way, communication overhead of subgroup key management is just related with the size of membership.

Our Contributions. We indicate unique requirements of key management in the context of multicast with fingerprinting. To our best knowledge, it is the first time to accommodate such problem. This paper intends to take advantage of combining multiple sequences in accordance with a fingerprinting collusion secure code to achieve this goal. For this, this paper further advances a framework to combine LKH algorithm and subset cover revocation algorithm to gain efficient, scalable and flexible solution. Main contributions include:

- Definitely indicate subgroup key management must be collusion-free;
- Propose a framework, denoted as LKH-CS, for subgroup key management;
- Advance a general algorithm of dynamic key assignment with subset notion
- Construct a collusion-free asymmetric approach of LKH-CS based on subset Lagrange interpolation. It performs better than other proposed Lagrange Interpolation key distribution scheme.

Table 1. performance comparisons. Notations: a is percent of data selectively watermarked and encrypted. P is volume of transmitted data. N is the number of members. n is the number of copies. p_1 and p_2 the frequency of membership change and subgroup respectively. Our approach 1 and 2 are based on symmetric and asymmetric approach respectively.

	Comm overhead of data	Encryption?	Comm overhead of key distribution	Collusion security	Need support of routers?
[1]	$aPN + (1-a)P$	yes	0	no	no
[2]	nP	no	0	no	yes
[3]	P	no	0	no	yes
[4,5]	$2P$	yes	N	c-collusion	no
Our approach 1 or 2	$2P$	yes	$p_1 logN + p_2 Poly(logN)$	Collusion -free	no

Construction of This Paper. Next section discusses some related works. Section 3 gives some preliminaries, i.e. subset notion and Lagrange interpolation, which will be used later. Our approach, including dynamic key assignment, symmetric/asymmetric key distribution scheme (they are based on subset notion), is described in section 4. Section 5 and 6 give analysis of security and performance respectively. Finally, section 7 concludes the paper.

2   Related Works

Wu et.al.[1] proposed to selectively encrypt and watermark segments of an MPEG video, unicast these and multicast the remainder. The chosen segments could be from 90% to less than 1% of the original video. There is a strict tradeoff between efficiency and security. As smaller amounts are chosen for encrypting and watermarking, more likely content of video is obtained by persons outside. Contrarily, larger percentage are to be chosen, more security will be hold, but its efficiency will decrease and approaches to the unicast model. Additionally, even if only I frames are selectively watermarked, then I-blocks in P and B frames can still provide video with some degree of quality. Moreover, this method is vulnerable to collusion.

Brown et.al.[2] proposed Watercasting, a distributed watermarking scheme. For a multicast group with a tree of depth d, the source creates n differently watermarked copies of each packet ($n > d$). On receiving a group of packets, each router forwards all but one of the packets. The last hop router then forwards exactly one packet to the subnet with the receiver(s). In this way, each receiver can have a unique stream. As the length of the clip increases, the probability to specify a single receiver increases. But, routers support like reliable multicast is essential, and the state of entire network during the transmission must be kept. Additionally, this approach cannot effectively utilized encryption so it cannot deter unauthorized receiver intercepting the content and thus cannot also recognize the traitors.

Judge et.al.[3] proposed watermarking multicast video with a hierarchy of intermediaries, called as *WHIM*. It places a hierarchy of intermediaries and forms an overlay network between them. Watermark is generated based on the router's location and inserted into the content incrementally as it traverses the network. Like Watercasting, *WHIM* also adds some additional requirements to the network router, and cannot effectively exploited encryption too.

Chu et.al.[4], Parviainen et.al.[5] proposed similar protocols to provide a distinct version of a multicast stream to each member. Two watermarked MPEG streams are firstly created, and a key KEY_i^j is used to encrypt the ith frame in stream j ($j = 0, 1$). Then a user is given either KEY_i^0 or KEY_i^1 (not both) depending on the random binary bit sequence of user. The ability to detect collusion is dependent on the length of the retrieved data stream. Even with a stream of sufficient length, to find a traitor is so complex that there is not a known length of stream that can guarantee c-collusion detection. Moreover, these keys are transmitted to each receiver individually.

Chor et al.[6] proposed to to embed different encryption keys into data. This idea was applied in their Traitor Tracing system for broadcast encryption. Some users can collaborate and change data in an unauthorized way. We call it collusion problem, which first addressed by Blakley et al[7]. Boneh et. al.[8] give a collusion-secure fingerprinting scheme for digital data and proved constructively that if the size of the multicast group is N and the size of the collusion group is c, then the generated key must be at least $O(c^4 \log \frac{N}{\varepsilon} \log \frac{1}{\varepsilon})$ long to assure c-secure with ε error probability. Thus, we need to know the group size N in advance to decide how many keys to generate. Besides, many other schemes had also been focusing on collusion-secure codes [8,9,10,11,12,13,14,15]. Suppose a q-ary collusion secure code is employed. Then, for each frame in a stream, different marks are embedded to produce q copies, corresponding to q characters of this code. q sequences are got after all frames in original stream processed, denoted them as $P_{ij}, i = 1, , length(stream), j = 1, , q$. Accordingly, each copy, e.g. P_{ij}, is encrypted with a encrypting key k_{ij}. It can guarantee each receiver a different sequence in accordance with a collusion-secure code.

The distincts of our approach lie in three folds. First, encryption has been extremely emphasized in such context. Secondly, we indicate the hardness of key management. Moreover, collusion-free requirement of key management scheme to guarantee the functionality of fingerprinting is also definitely pointed out. Thirdly, the paper put forward a framework to combine stateful and stateless approaches for subgroup keys management.

3   Preliminary

3.1   Subgroup Key Management

Suppose that a collusion secure code, $(L, N, D)_q$, is used. Here, L is the code length, N the code number, D the minimal Hamming distance of it, and q the alphabet size. Here, let $N = 2^n$ and $q = 2$ for the sake of simplicity. Assume that membership change is at a lower frequency than subgroup modification.

1. *Dynamic key assignment*: When a member leaves from or enters into the session, some keys should be updated. Renewal keys are securely transmitted to the remainders with stateful key distribution, which should be scalable and efficient:
2. *Subgroup key distribution*: Members are portioned into 2 groups, named as $group_0$ and $group_1$, so that they are able to decrypt two distinct copies of a frame respectively;

   Encryption. $C = E_{pk_i, i \in group}(k_0, k_1, group_0, group_1)$, where k_0 and k_1 are keys of two subgroups ($group_0$ and $group_1$) randomly chosen.

   Decryption. $D_{sk_i}(C)$, if $i \in group_0$, it output k_0 otherwise k_1.
3. *Security requirement*: Any receiver outside cannot get any information of both subgroups keys and secret keys employed in this session. Subgroup key distribution should be collusion-free.(as Claim 1)

In this context, there are two kinds of collusion attacks against fingerprinting and key management respectively. Some collusion-secure code can be employed to resist collusion attack against fingerprinting. But it assumes any receiver can receive the permitted data only, which must then be guaranteed by key management. But, some receivers in a subgroup can possibly collude with their key material to get the key of another subgroup in a frame (Here, collusion attack is against key distribution, not dynamic key assignment). Any coalition of receivers succeeding in colluding attack against key distribution certainly makes fingerprinting useless. Thus, we get Claim 1.

Claim 1. *Subgroup key distribution should be collusion-free.*

3.2   Subset Notion

The Subset approach has been extensively employed by many key distribution schemes in the broadcast encryption, e.g. complete sub-tree (*CS*) and sub-tree difference (*SD*) in Subset cover revocation scheme [18]. To our knowledge, so far, all proposed schemes based on subset cover can achieve collusion-free. The following gives a general description on subset.

Definition 2. (subset structure) *For a set N of users, there exists a set $\mathbf{M}$ of subsets, i.e. $\mathbf{M} = S_1, S_2, \ldots, S_j \subset N, j = 1, 2, \ldots$. Thus, for any set $S(\subset N)$ of users, we can have a minimal cover $S_{i1}, S_{i2}, \ldots, S_{il} \subset \mathbf{M}$ which satisfies $S_{ij} \cap S_{ik} = \phi(j \neq k)$ and $\bigcup_j S_{ij} = S$. Then, $\mathbf{M}$ is a subset structure of N and $S_{i1}, S_{i2}, \ldots, S_{il}$ is a cover of S, l is size of the cover.*

Two trivial ways of key management in multicast/broadcast can be also described by this general subset structure. In the first way, key center securely transmits session key to each legitimate receiver in unicast way. The subset structure is $\mathbf{M} = S_1, S_2, \ldots, S_L$, where $|S_j| = 1$ and L is the number of users. Therefore, the size of subset cover equals to the number of legitimate receivers. Because any user belongs to only one subset in $\mathbf{M}$, each user should keep only one key. To another extreme, the size of cover is always 1 for any set of legitimate receivers. The subset structure can be defined as $\mathbf{M} = 2^N$. Therefore, because a user possibly appears in 2^{N-1} subsets in $\mathbf{M}$, each user should keep 2^{N-1} keys. In order to get a good tradeoff between cover size and key size, some strategies are exploited, e.g. *CS/SD*. Subset structure of *CS* mode is $SS = ST_1, ST_2, \ldots$, where ST_i is defined as a sub-tree lying in the binary tree, and that of *SD* mode is $SD = SD_1, SD_2, \ldots$, where SD_i is defined as a difference between two sub-trees with one containing another. An improvement proposed by [20] defines subset structure based on a-ary tree, where subset may be not only sub-tree but also combinations of sub-trees.

Definition 3. (key dependency) *For a subset structure, we can define a key assignment scheme. Suppose a group of subsets $S_1, S_2, \ldots, S_n$, their corresponding keys $k_1, k_2, \ldots, k_n$. If $\exists S \in M, s.t. S \cap S_1 \cup S_2 \cup \ldots \cup S_n = \phi$, with key k. If k can be derived from $k_1, k_2, \ldots, k_n$ with any possible methods, this kind of key assignment is key dependent.*

A key assignment not containing such group of keys defined in definition 2 at all, is key independent. Apparently, the characteristic of key independency is necessary in the key assignment in order to guarantee the collusion-free of key distribution.

Claim 4. *Key independency is a necessary condition of collusion-free in the subset based key distribution scheme.*

Naor [18] proposed the key-indistinguishability assumption and employed it to prove the security of subset cover (*CS/SD*) revocation scheme.

Claim 5. *If a key management satisfies the key-indistinguishability assumption then its key assignment is surely key independent.*

In fact, key independence is equivalent to key indistinguishability with ignorance of deployed encryption algorithm. But key independency can separate key assignment from encryption algorithm. Furthermore, pseudorandom number generator and one-way hash function can be used to reduce the volume of keys associated with subsets under a definition of subset hierarchy. Suppose f is a one-way hash function. Then construct a hash chain for key derivation: a receiver $u \in S1 \subset S2, S1, S2 \in \mathbf{M}$, and suppose u holds the key of S_1, denoted as k_1. Then, u can derive k_2 (key of S_2) with f from k_1, i.e. $k_2 = f(k_1)$.

Proposition 6. *Subset hierarchy also still satisfies key independency with this kind of key derivation.*

Proof. First suppose it is key dependency, which means a group of keys $k_1, k_2, \ldots, k_n$ and corresponding subsets $S_1, S_2, \ldots, S_n$, then $\exists S \in M, s.t. S \cap S_1 \cup S_2 \cup \ldots \cup S_n = \phi$, and its associated key k can be derived from $k_1, k_2, \ldots, k_n$. We can certainly find a minimal subset SM containing $S, S_1, S_2, \ldots, S_n$. k can be derived from key of SM. With predefined f, the key of SM can also be derived from k. Apparently, it is contradicted with the one-wayness of f.

◇

3.3 Lagrange Interpolation

Definition 7. (Lagrange interpolation in the exponent) *Let q be a prime and $f(x)$ a polynomial of degree z over Z_q; Let $j_0, \ldots, j_z$ be distinct elements of Z_q, and $f_0 = f(j_0), \ldots, f_z = f(j_z)$. Define the Lagrange interpolation as:* $LI(j_0, \ldots, j_z; f_0, \ldots, f_z)(x) = \sum_{i=0}^{z}(f_i \times \lambda_i(x))$, *where* $\lambda_i(x) = \prod_{0 \leq i \neq t \leq z} \frac{j_i - x}{j_i - j_t}, t \in [0, z]$.

Now, consider any cyclic group **G** of order q and a generator g of it. For any distinct $j_0, \ldots, j_z \in Z_q$ and $v_0, \ldots, v_z \in G$, define the Lagrange interpolation operator in the exponent as: $EXP - LI(j_0, \ldots, j_z; \log_g v_0, \ldots, \log_g v_z)(x) = g^{LI(j_0, \ldots, j_z; f_0, \ldots, f_z)(x)} = \prod_{t=0}^{z} g^{\log_g v_t \times \lambda_t(x)} = \prod_{t=0}^{z} v_t^{\lambda_t(x)}$. It shows that the function $EXP - LI$ is poly-time computable. And, $EXP - LI(j_0, \ldots, j_z; v_0^r, \ldots, v_z^r)(x) = EXP - LI(j_0, \ldots, j_z; v_0, \ldots, v_z)(x)^r$. In the follows, we will refer to a function of the form $g^{f(x)}$, where $f(x)$ is a polynomial.

4 Our Approach

4.1 Basic Model

Firstly, build a subset structure for N members where each subset is allocated a key and each user is assigned keys of subset it belongs to. In order to get a better tradeoff between cover size (ciphertext size) and key size (user's repository), we take advantage of a d-ary ($d = 2$ in the most cases) key tree to construct the subset hierarchy. Each member is placed in a leaf node of tree and is assigned some key material in accordance with its position in the tree so that it can derive key of any subsets it belongs. In fact, during dynamic key assignment, subset hierarchy is employed to update subset keys upon membership change. During subgroup key distribution, subset structure is utilized to construct a cover for each subgroup so that subset cover based key distribution scheme like CS/SD or its variants can be used. In subsection 4.3 and 4.4, we will discuss two methods of subgroup key distribution: symmetric and asymmetric approaches, both are based on subset notion. In fact, any subset structure can also be used in our schemes if it is key independent.

4.2 Dynamic Key Assignment

With definition of subset hierarchy, dynamic key assignment can run in the same procedure for both symmetric and asymmetric approaches. We try to implement dynamic key assignment using general subset notion. Here, member addition and member removal are processed in the same way. Member removal: Suppose receiver u leaves the session, so that subset structure will be updated.

1. Assume key set assigned to u is $K_u = k_1, k_2, \ldots, k_f$ and corresponding subsets are $S_u = S_1, S_2, \ldots, S_f$. Without loss of generality, we assume $|S_1||S_2| \ldots |S_f|$, $S_1 = u$ and $S_f = allmembers$.

2. S_2 can be expressed as a cover, i.e. $Cover(S_2) = S_{21}, S_{22}, \ldots, S_{2t_2}$. Apparently, $S_1 \in Cover(S_2)$, let $S_{21} = S_1$.

3. S_1 is excluded and S_2 is replaced by S'_2 where $S'_2 = S_{22} S_{23} \cdots S_{2t_2}$. Key center randomly chooses a new key, k'_2, to replace k_2 and securely transmits k'_2 to those members contained in S'_2 with $Cover(S'_2)$.

4. S_3 can be expressed as a cover, i.e. $Cover(S_3) = S_{31}, S_{32}, \ldots, S_{3t_3}$. Apparently, S_1 or $S_2 \in Cover(S_3)$, let $S_{31} = S_2$, and S_3 is replaced by S'_3, where $S'_3 = S'_2 \bigcup S_{32} \bigcup \cdots \bigcup S_{3t_3}$ ($Cover(S'_3) = S'_2, S_{32}, S_{33}, \cdots, S_{3t_3}$). Key center randomly chooses a new key, k'_3, to replace k_3 and securely transmits k'_3 to members contained in S'_3 using $Cover(S'_3)$

5. continue on until S_f, where S_f is replaced by S'_f and k_f by k'_f.

6. Thus, all keys known by removed user are updated in this way.

When a user enters into the session, the subset structure and associated keys should also be updated in the same process as member removal. Dynamic key assignment is nearly the same as *LKH* with subset notion. Next 2 sections will describe symmetric and asymmetric approaches for subgroup key distribution respectively, both are based on the subset notion.

Proposition 8. *Overhead of communications for dynamic key assignments upon a membership change using CS and SD are $d \log_d n$ and $d \log^{1+\varepsilon} n$, respectively. Here, n is the number of members in the multicast session and they are placed in a d-ary tree.*

4.3   Symmetric Encryption Approach

Here, for sake of simplicity, we describe it based on *CS/SD* mode. This is implemented through a key tree like LKH and in a similar way as *CS* mode in the subset cover revocation scheme. Let $U = U_1, U_2, \ldots, U_n$ be a set of n members.

For a frame of data securely transmitted, all members are divided into two subgroups, *group*$_0$ and *group*$_1$, on-the-fly. Members in one subgroup are revoked from another subgroup. Key center will generate a subset cover of a subgroup with the same approach as *CS* mode. Suppose a subset cover $(S_1, S_2, \ldots, S_m)$, then message is $(E_{k_1}(k_s), E_{k_2}(k_s), \ldots, E_{k_m}(k_s)), E_{k_s}(M)$. Here, k_i is the key of subset S_i respectively, k_s is the subgroup session key and M is the data transmitted. In the same way, two session keys are on-the-fly updated in two subgroups. For these two subgroups, *CS* covers are firstly generated for these two subgroups. Assume smaller cover as *CSmin* and the size of it as m and both subgroups employ *CS* mode. The size of these two covers is greater than $t = m + h - max h_i$, where h stands for the height of the tree and h_i the height for subtree.

CS and *SD* mode can also be combined and employed simultaneously, i.e. a subgroup employs *CS* while another employs *SD*. Then, the size of these two covers, $\sum (2^{h_i - h_j} - 1), T_{ij} \in SD, h_j \neq empty + h - max h_i$, is smaller than t. If both subgroups employ SD to distribute subgroup key, the number of subsets will also be smaller than t.

Certainly, other subset structures can also be used, e.g. [20]. Key distribution based on subset hierarchy can be collusion-free, and communication consumption is super-logarithm in average and will approach to $O(n)$ in the worst case where both subgroups have $n/2$ members that are distributed in one-by-one fashion (any two adjacent nodes belong to different subgroups respectively).

Symmetric approaches make key center in charge of all data transmission and thus a point of failure. Additionally only a few trusted nodes can be a sender, but in some time, untrusted nodes also want to send some data. Hence, we exploit asymmetric encryption to solve this problem.

4.4   Asymmetric Encryption Scheme

This paper improves Kurnio et.al. scheme [21] with general subset notion to implement subgroup key distribution, which is described as follows.

Key Generation. The group controller, GC, is in charge of the system setup and does the following.

1. Choose two large primes p ($\approx 1024bits$), q ($\approx 160bits$), $q|p-1$, and a generator g of the multiplicative group of $GF(p)$. Then, publishes p, q and g.
2. Let $\mathbf{M}$ denote the set of subsets and $m = |\mathbf{M}|$ be the total number of subsets in the structure. Each subset is assigned a label i.
3. Generate a set of secret keys, $K = k_i \in GF(q)|i \in \mathbf{M}$, and a set of public keys, $Y = y_i = g^{k_i} \pmod{p}|i \in \mathbf{M}$.
4. Publishe all the public keys and securely sends assigned set of secret keys, $K_j \subset K$, to user U_j.

Proposition 9. *With CS subset in a d-ary tree, the storage size for GC and members are $(dn-1)/(d-1)$ and $\log_d n + 1$ secret keys, respectively. There are $(dn-1)/(d-1)$ public keys. n is the number of members in the multicast session.*

Proposition 10. *With LSD mode in a binary tree, the storage size for GC and members are $2n-1$ and $\log^{1+\varepsilon} n + 1$ secret keys, respectively. There are $2n(\log n - 1) + 2$ public keys. (according to works of Halevi and Shamir[19])*

Key Distribution. Suppose a group controller GC will transmit a subgroup key to a subgroup $U_L \subset U$. For this subgroup, a subset cover can be constructed and denote as C. Assume $|C| = s$.

1. GC randomly chooses an element r of $GF(q)$ and multicasts $Y = g^r \pmod{p}$.
2. GC chooses a set I of $s-1$ distinct elements of $GF(q)$ such that $0 \notin I$ and $C \bigcap I = \phi$. Then, calculates

$$y_c = \prod_{a \in C} (y_a)^{L(C,a,c)} \pmod{p}, \ forall \ c \in I \qquad (1)$$

where

$$L(C, a, c) = \prod_{b \in C, b \neq a} \frac{c - b}{a - b} \pmod{q} \tag{2}$$

Then, multicasts $Y_c \| c, \forall c \in I$, where $Y_c = (y_c)^r$ and $\|$ means concatenation.

3. A member $U_j \in U_L$, with a secret key $k_e \in K_j$, where $e \in C \cap N_{U_j}$, (N_{U_j}, a set of subsets U_j belonging to) and the multicast data, calculates the subgroup key GK as follows.

$$GK = (Y^{k_e})^{L(I \cup \{e\}, e, 0)} \times \prod_{c \in I} (Y_c)^{L(I \cup \{e\}, c, 0)} \pmod{p} \tag{3}$$

Theorem 11. *In the above scheme, anyone in U_L is able to compute GK.*

Proof. Without loss of generality, assume $C = 1, 2, \ldots, s$. Let the secret keys and public keys associated with C be $k_a | a \in C$ and $y_a = g^{k_a} \pmod{p} | a \in C$, respectively. Notice that there implicitly exists a unique polynomial $f(x)$ of degree at most $s - 1$ such that $g^{f(a)} = g^{k_a}, \forall a \in C$. Using these public keys, one can calculate $y_c = g^{f(c)}, \forall c \in I$, as follows,

$$y_c = g^{f(c)} = g^{\sum_{a \in C} f(a) \times L(C, a, c)} = \prod_{a \in C} (y_a)^{L(C, a, c)} \pmod{p} \tag{4}$$

So, each user in U_L computes the subgroup key as

$$GK = (Y^{k_e})^{L(I \cup \{e\}, e, 0)} \times \prod_{c \in I} (Y_c)^{L(I \cup \{e\}, c, 0)}$$

$$= (g^{r \times f(e)})^{L(I \cup \{e\}, e, 0)} \times \prod_{c \in I} (g^{r \times f(c)})^{L(I \cup \{e\}, c, 0)}$$

$$= \prod_{c \in I \cup \{e\}} (g^{r \times f(c)})^{L(I \cup \{e\}, c, 0)} = g^{r \times \sum_{c \in I \cup \{e\}} f(c) \times L(I \cup \{e\}, c, 0)}$$

$$= g^{r \times f(0)} \pmod{p}$$

This completes the proof.   ◇

5   Security Analysis

Subgroup key management is consisted of two parts, i.e. dynamic key assignment and subgroup key distribution. Therefore, we should consider two kinds of attacks, i.e. attacks from expelled members and from participating members. Some expelled members can try to collude with key materials they hold to produce a decoder to get the secret data within the session. On the other hand, some participating members can probably collude to get that subgroup key unassigned to them. The former security is related to dynamic key assignment while the latter is related to subgroup key distribution.

5.1   Security of Dynamic Key Assignment

Firstly, let us look at dynamic key assignment. When a member leaves, those keys he knew will be updated in a similar way as LKH so that those keys become useless. We assume that the dynamic key assignment satisfies the key-independency property. This assumption can be easily satisfied only when all used keys are chosen randomly and irrelevant with each other. Usually, ciphertext series for each member in LKH way may be $E_{k_{n-1}}(k_n), E_{k_{n-2}}(k_{n-1}), \dots, E_{k_0}(k_1)$, where $E_{k_{i-1}}(k_i)$ means that encrypting k_i with k_{i-1}. Hence, remaining members who hold k_{i-1} can decrypt this series so as to do key-update. This security depends completely on the employed encryption scheme.

Claim 12. *If new key is randomly chosen, dynamic key assignment is also collusion-free and the key independency can be reserved.*

Claim 13. *Security of dynamic key assignment is completely equivalent to the employed encryption scheme with the Key-independency. This means that if the employed encryption scheme is CPA, CCA1, CCA2, gCCA-secure then LKH encryption is also correspondingly CPA, CCA1, CCA2, gCCA-secure.*

5.2   Security of Symmetric Key Distribution

In the framework of *LKH-CS*, CS (*SD*) mode proposed by Naor[18] is exploited to distribute the subgroup key to members. As pointed out in that paper, the security of CS (SD) is also based on the key-indistinguishable assumption. As pointed out in claim 5, this assumption is equal to key independency with ignoring deployed encryption algorithm and furthermore is true when all keys are randomly chosen. Naor has indicated that *CS* (*SD*) can resist collusion attack from any coalition of members.

5.3   Security of Asymmetric Key Distribution

CDH Problem. *Input g, g^{x_1} and g^{x_2}, computing $g^{x_1 x_2}$.*

Theorem 14. *If the CDH problem is hard, any coalition in another subgroup can find GK with negligible possibility.*

Proof. Our proof uses a reduction argument. It is sufficient to show that if there exists a probabilistic polynomial-time algorithm G that on inputs $g^r, g^{rf(c), \forall c \in I}$ and $g^{f(a)}, a \in M$, outputs $g^{rf(0)}$ with a non-negligible probability, where $f(x)$ is a polynomial of degree at most $s - 1$, then G can be used to solve the *CDH* problem. Let $I = c_1, c_2, \dots, c_{s-1}$. Choose randomly $a_1, a_2, \dots, a_{s-1} \in GF(q)$ and construct a unique polynomial $h(x)$ of degree at most $s - 1$ so that $h(c_i) = a_i, 1 \leq i \leq s - 1$, and $g^{h(0)} = g^{x_2}$. It can calculate $g^{h(c_i)} = g^{a_i}, 1 \leq i \leq s - 1$, and also $g^{h(\alpha)}, \forall \alpha \in GF(q)$, and hence $g^{h(a)}, \forall a \in M$. Furthermore, we can compute $(g^{x_1})^{a_i} = g^{x_1 f(c_i)}, c_i \in I$ with knowing a_i. Now if G is given the input,$g^{x_1}, (g^{x_1})^{a_i}, i = 1, \dots, s-1$ and $g^{h(a)}, a \in M$, it will output $g^{x_1 x_2} = g^{x_1 f(0)}$. This means that G can solve the *CDH* problem and so contradicts the hardness assumption of the *CDH* problem.

5.4   Collusion Resistance

As described in section 3, key distribution should be collusion-free in the scenario of subgroup key management. Both the proposed symmetric and asymmetric key distribution schemes based on subset hierarchy are collusion-free, shown in subsection 5.2 and 5.3.

6   Performance Analysis and Comparisons

6.1   Metrics of Subset

In this paper, the subset notion becomes the center for both dynamic key assignment and subgroup key distribution (including symmetric and asymmetric approaches). Therefore, the parameters of subset definition determine the performance of subgroup key management in this paper. The number of subsets a receiver belonging to determines both repository in each receiver and Overhead of communication in dynamic key assignment. The size of a cover also determines Overhead of communication in subgroup key distribution.

Apparently, with different definition of subset, subgroup key management has different performance. Thus, in the following, we discuss the performance based on CS/SD definition because of their simplicity and broad usage. In fact, receiver can derive keys of subset it belongs to with the method (one-way hash function) described in section 3 so that the secret repository can be further reduced. Key derivation will not be considered in the following discussion.

6.2   Storage

In the symmetric schemes, $\log n$ keys are kept in each member for CS-type key distribution and $\log^{1+\varepsilon} n$ keys for SD-type key distribution. (n: # of members)

In the asymmetric scheme, $\log n$ keys are kept secret in each member and $2n-1$ in key center for CS-based Lagrange interpolation and $\log^{1+\varepsilon} n$ and $2n(\log n - 1) + 2$ keys for SD-based Lagrange interpolation. At the same time, public keys of $2n - 1$ and $2n(\log n - 1) + 2$ are stored in bulletin board, which is required by sender only. Any member can get subgroup key authorized to it with the dynamically assigned private key, no need any public key. This reduces repository or communication volumes.

6.3   Communication Overhead

Dynamic Key Assignment. $O(\log n)$ ciphertexts is needed for each membership change in both symmetric and asymmetric scheme with CS or SD mode.

Subgroup Key Distribution. Assume that the sizes of subset cover in CS mode are n_1 and n_2 for two subgroups, where $n_1 \leq n_2$. In the symmetric approach, overload of $n_1 + n_2$ are required in both-CS mode and $< 3n_1 - 1$ in both-SD mode. In asymmetric approach, both-CS and both-SD require overhead of $n_1 + n_2 - 2$ and $< 3n_1 - 3$ respectively. In fact, $1 \leq n_1 \leq n/2$, and n_1 is in poly-logarithmic level ($O(Poly(\log n))$) in the average.

6.4   Comparisons

Certainly, key management schemes of both multicast and broadcast may be also applied in the subgroup key management. LKH[16,17] and subset cover revocation schemes[18,19] are the most prominent in these two fields respectively. Hence, we compare them (directly employed in subgroup key management) and our scheme in the scenario of multicast with fingerprinting.

Communication Overhead. When LKH is directly employed in the subgroup key management, it is $O(\log n)$ for each frame due to subgroup change. When subset cover revocation scheme is directly employed, it is $O(Poly(\log L))$ (L: # of receivers within a network) in the average. For our scheme, it is $O(p_1 \log n + p_2 \times Poly(\log n))$ (p_1 is the frequency of membership change in this session and p_2 is the frame rate, and assume $p_1 < p_2$) that becomes $O(Poly(\log n))$ (much smaller than $O(Poly(\log L))$ due to $n \ll L$) in the average.

In term of communication overhead, utilizing directly LKH in the context of subgroup is optimal, but this scheme is still not suitable for subgroup key management because state synchronization makes it incapable of accommodate highly dynamic change of subgroup especially within wide-area (Frequency of subgroup change, LKH can support, must be smaller than $1/RTT$ (RTT stand for round trip time)). Furthermore, retransmission will make the frequency it can support to be doubly reduced in distinct probability even with reliable transmission techniques like proactive FEC.

7   Concluding Remarks

This paper discusses influences of fingerprinting on key management in the secure multicast session and indicates some special requirements of key management. Fingerprinting can be implemented in secure multicasting with combining multiple sequences in accordance with some collusion secure code. Based on it, we model this associated key management as subgroup key management. A framework, denoted as LKH-CS, is proposed to solve the problem (Here, LKH is used for dynamic key assignment and CS/SD mode is used for subgroup key distribution and both can be integrated seamlessly), which can not only accommodate highly frequent change of subgroup but also possess good performance of communication, and additionally, subgroup key distribution of it is collusion-free. This paper also generalizes subset notion in the context of subgroup key management and proposes a dynamic key assignment, and symmetric and asymmetric subgroup key distribution based on it. Both symmetric cryptosystem and asymmetric approaches possess the similar communication overhead.

This work still needs further improvement. We still look for better algorithm of subgroup key distribution, because communication overhead of our scheme is possibly proportional to the size of membership in the worst case (even if it happens in very low possibility). Certainly, subset structure in the subgroup key management still needs careful study.

References

1. Wu, T. and Wu, S.: Selective encryption and watermarking of mpeg video, Tech. Rep., North Carolina State Univ
2. Brown, I., Perkins, C., and Crowcroft J.: Watercasting: distributed watermarking of multicast media, in Proc. of the First Intl workshop on Networked Group Communication, 1999.
3. Judge, P. and Ammar, M.: WHIM: Watermarking Multicast Video with a hierarchy of Intermediaries, Computer Networks 39(6): 699-712, 2002.
4. Chu, H., Qiao, L., and Nahrstedt, K.: A secure multicast protocol with copyright protection, in ACM SIGCOMM Comp. Comm. Review, Vol. 32, No. 2, pp.42-60, Apr. 2002.
5. Parviainen, R. and Parnes, P.: Large Scale Distributed Watermarking of Multicast Media Through Encryption, Intl. Fed. for Info. Proc., Comm. and Multimedia Sec. Joint working Conf. IFIP Tc6 and TC11, May 21-22, 2001.
6. Chor, B. A., Fiat, A., and Naor, M.: Tracing Traitors, In Proceedings of CRYPTO'94, LNCS 839, pp. 257-270, Springer-Verlag, 1994.
7. Blakley, G. R., Meadows, C., and Purdy, G. B.: Fingerprinting long forgiving messages, In Proceedings of CRYPTO'85, LNCS 218, pp.180-189, 1986.
8. Boneh, D. and Shaw, J.: Collusion-secure Fingerprinting for digital data, IEEE Trans. on Info. Theory, 44(5):1897-1905, Sept 1998.
9. Domingo-Ferrer, J. and Herrera-Joancomarti, J.: Short collusion-secure fingerprints based on dual binary hamming codes, Electronics Letters, Vol. 36, No. 20, pp.1697-1699, 2000.
10. Safavi-Naini, R. and Wang, Y.: Collusion secure q-ary fingerprinting for perceptual content. Security and Privacy in Digital Rights Management2001, LNCS 2320, pp.57-75, 2002.
11. Staddon, J. N., Stinson, D. R., and Wei, R.: Combinatorial properties of frameproof and traceability codes, IEEE trans. on Info. Theory, Vol.47, No.3, pp.1042-1049, 2001.
12. Guth, H. and Pfitzmann, B.: Error- and collusion-secure fingerprinting for digital data, Information Hiding'99, LNCS 1768, pp.134-135, 2000.
13. Safavi-Naini, R. and Wang, Y.: New results on frameproof codes and traceability schemes, IEEE Trans. on Info. Theory, Vol.47, No.7, pp.3029-3033, 2001.
14. To, V.D., Safavi-Naini, R. and Wang, Y.: A 2-secure Code with Efficient Tracing Algorithm, INDOCRYPT 2002, LNCS 2551, pp.149-163, 2002.
15. Cohen, G., Litsyn, S. and Zemor, G.: Binary Codes for Collusion-Secure Fingerprinting, ICICS 2001, LNCS 2288, pp.178-185, 2002.
16. Wallner, D. M., Harder, E. J. and Agee, R. C.: Key Management for Multicast: Issues and Architectures, IETF draft wallner-key, July 1997.
17. Wong, C. K., Gouda, M. and Lam, S.: Secure Group Communications Using Key Graphs, IEEE/ACM Trans. on Networking, Vol. 8, No. 1, 2000, pp.16-30.
18. Naor, D., Naor, M. and Lotspiech, J.: Revocation and Tracing Schemes for Stateless Receivers, Proc. of Crypto 2001, pp. 41-62, 2001.
19. Halevi, D. and Shamir, A.: The LSD Broadcast Encryption Scheme, Crypto 2002, LNCS 2442, pp. 47-60, 2002.
20. Asano, T.: A Revocation Scheme with Minimal Storage at Receivers, Y. Zheng(Ed.): ASIACRYPT 2002, LNCS 2501, pp.433-450, 2002.
21. Kurnio, H., Safavi-Naini, R., and Wang, H.: Efficient Revocation Schemes for Secure Multicast, K. Kim(Ed.): ICICS 2001, LNCS 2288, pp. 160-177, 2002.

A Key Reshuffling Scheme for Wireless Sensor Networks

Ashok Kumar Das

Department of Computer Science and Engineering,
Indian Institute of Technology, Kharagpur 721 302, India
akdas@cse.iitkgp.ernet.in

Abstract. In this paper, we propose an improved alternative for the path key establishment phase of the bootstrapping protocol in a sensor network. This scheme has better connectivity than the path key establishment. The communication overhead for our scheme is comparable with that for the path key establishment. Moreover, the guarantee of good connectivity allows us to start with bigger key pools, thereby improving the resilience against node capture.

1 Introduction

Recent advances in wireless communications and electronics have enabled the development of low-cost, low-power, multifunctional sensor nodes that are small in size and communicate untethered in short distances. These tiny sensor nodes, which consist of sensing, data processing, and communicating components, leverage the idea of sensor networks. Thus, the sensor networks give a significant improvement over the traditional sensors.

A sensor network consists of many tiny computing sensor nodes that are scattered in an area for the purpose of sensing some data and transmitting data to nearby *base stations* for further processing. The transmission between the sensor nodes is done by short range radio communications. The base station is assumed to be computationally well-equipped whereas the sensor nodes are resource-starved. Such networks are used in many applications including tracking of objects in an enemy's area for military purposes, distributed seismic measurements, pollution tracking, monitoring fire and nuclear power plants, tacking patients, engineering and medical explorations like wildlife monitoring, etc. Mostly for military purposes, data collected by the sensor nodes need to be encrypted before transmitting to the neighboring nodes and the base stations.

Each sensor node contains a primitive processor featuring very low computing speed and only small amount of programmable memory. Sensor node is battery-powered and is expected to operate for only few days. Moreover, sensor nodes have the ability to communicate with each other and the base stations by short range wireless radio transsimission at low bandwidth and over small communication ranges (typical example is at most 30 meters i.e., 100 feet).

Due to the above limitations of a sensor network it is not feasible to use public-key routines [1,2,3]. [4] says that RSA is almost 1000 times slower than the DES [5,6,7]. Now-a-days RC5 [8] is much more faster than the DES. Hence, a symmetric cipher is the only viable option for encryption/decryption of secret data. As a result, one can use

S. Jajodia and C. Mazumdar (Eds.): ICISS 2005, LNCS 3803, pp. 205–216, 2005.

RC5 algorithm for secret communications between the sensor nodes. But setting up the symmetric keys among communicating nodes is a challenging job in a sensor network.

Several sensor nodes are deployed throughout a sensor field very densely. Therefore, careful handling of topology maintenance is required. However, the topology changes due to the three phases. In *predeployment and deployment phase*, sensor nodes can be deployed from a truck or a plane in the sensor field. In *post-deployment phase*, topology may change after deployment because of irregularities in the sensor field like obstacles or due to jamping, noise, available energy of the nodes, malfunctioning, addition of new sensor nodes, mobility of the sensor nodes, etc. In *redeployment of additional nodes phase*, additional sensor nodes can be redeployed due to the faulty or rogue sensor nodes.

The rest of the paper is organized as follows. We briefly discuss the overviews of some existing key pre-distribution schemes in Section 2. In this section, we focus our discussion on the basic random key pre-distribution scheme (the EG scheme) [9] proposed by Eschenauer and Gligor and the polynomial-pool based key pre-distribution scheme (the poly-pool scheme) [10] proposed by Liu and Ning. The EG scheme supports a large network, but it is not quite resilient against node capture. On the other hand, the poly-pool scheme supports reasonable network size and provides better security than the EG scheme. Some other schemes include the q-composite scheme [11], the random pairwise keys scheme [11] proposed by Chan et al. and the matrix-pool based scheme due to Du et al. [12]. The q-composite scheme is an improved version of the EG scheme and it is slightly more resilient against node capture than the EG scheme. The random pairwise keys scheme does not support a big network, whereas it is perfectly secure against node capture. The matrix-based scheme has performance comparable with the poly-pool scheme. In Section 3, we propose a new scheme which is considered as an alternative for the path key establishment phase. We call our scheme as the *key reshuffling scheme*. In this section, we first develop our scheme and after that we provide a theoretical analysis for our scheme over the EG scheme as well as the poly-pool scheme. In Section 4, we report our simulation results of the network connectivity measurement over the EG scheme as well as the poly-pool scheme. In Section 5, we compare our scheme with the path key establishment. Section 6 highlights some advantages achieved from our scheme. Finally, Section 7 concludes the paper.

2   Background : Overview of the Key Predistribution Schemes

Key pre-distribution in sensor networks has received considerable research attention in recent years [9,11,10,13,14,12]. After a brief overview, we concentrate on the basic random key pre-distribution scheme (the EG scheme) [9] and the polynomial pool-based scheme (the poly-pool scheme) [10].

2.1   The Basic Bootstrapping Framework

Key establishment in a sensor network is effected by a three-phase process called *bootstrapping*. The three stages of bootstrapping are as follows:

- *Key predistribution:* This step is done before the deployment of the sensor nodes in a particular target field (i.e., a deployment area). A key set-up server chooses a pool $\mathcal{K}$ of randomly generated keys and assigns to each node u a subset K_u of $\mathcal{K}$. K_u is called the key ring of sensor node u.

- *Direct key establishment:* Immediately after deployment, each sensor node tries to locate all other sensor nodes with which it can communicate directly and secretly. Two nodes u and v are called *physical neighbors* if they are within the communication ranges of one another. u and v are called *key neighbors* if they share one or more key(s) in their key rings K_u and K_v. Sensor nodes u and v can secretly and directly communicate with each other if and only if they are both physical neighbors and key neighbors, and they are called as *direct neighbors*. In direct key establishment phase, each sensor node u locates its direct neighbors. For this, u broadcasts its own id and the ids of the keys in its key ring.

- *Path key establishment:* This is an optional stage and, if executed, adds to the connectivity of the network. Let two physical neighbors u and v fail to establish a direct link between them in the direct key establishment phase. But there exists a path, say, $< u = u_0, u_1, u_2, \ldots, u_{h-1}, u_h = v >$ in the network such that each u_i a direct neighbor of u_{i+1} ($i = 0, 1, 2, \ldots, h - 1$). u generates a random key k, encrypts k with the key shared between $u = u_0$ and u_1 and transmits this encrypted key to u_1. u_1 retrieves k by decrypting the encrypted key using the shared key between u and u_1 and encrypts k by the key shared between u_1 and u_2 and transmits it to u_2. This process is continued until the key k reaches the desired destination v. Therefore, u and v can communicate secretly and directly using k and thereby become direct neighbors. However, the main difficulty in this process is the discovery of a path between u and v. The communication complexity increases significantly with the number h of hops. In practical situations, h is restricted to a small value, say 2 or 3.

2.2   The Basic Random Key Predistribution Scheme (EG Scheme)

Eschenauer and Gligor in their seminal paper [9] bootstrap the era of research of bootstrapping in sensor networks. This method, henceforth referred to as the EG scheme, is essentially the basic bootstrapping method just described above.

The key set-up server starts with a pool $\mathcal{K}$ of randomly generated keys. The number $|\mathcal{K}| = M$ is taken to be a small multiple of the network size n. For each sensor node u to be deployed, a random subset of m keys is selected and given to u as its key ring K_u. Upon deployment, each node discovers its direct neighbors as specified in the basic bootstrapping framework.

2.3   The Polynomial Pool-Based Key Predistribution Scheme

Liu and Ning's polynomial-pool based key distribution scheme (the poly-pool scheme) [10] can be described as follows. Let $F_q = GF(q)$ be a finite field with a q (either a prime or 2^m for some positive integer m) just big enough to accomodate a symmetric encryption key. Let $f(X, Y) \in F_q[X, Y]$ be a t-degree bivariate symmetric polynomial i.e., $f(X, Y) = f(Y, X)$. A *polynomial share* of f is a univariate polynomial $f_\alpha(X) = f(X, \alpha)$ for some $\alpha \in F_q$. Thus, we have:

$$f_\alpha(\beta) = f(\beta, \alpha) = f(\alpha, \beta) = f_\beta(\alpha). \tag{1}$$

If two shares f_α and f_β of the same polynomial f are given to two nodes, they can come up with the common value $f(\alpha, \beta) \in F_q$ as a shared key between them. If $(t+1)$ or more shares of f are known, one can easily reconstruct $f(X, Y)$ uniquely just by using the *Lagrange's Interpolation formula*. Thus, the disclosure of upto t shares does not reveal the polynomial f to an adversary and uncompromised shared keys based on f remains completely secure. If $t = 0$, then this scheme degenerates to the EG scheme.

The key set-up server selects a random pool $\mathcal{K}$ of s symmetric bivariate polynomials in $F_q[X, Y]$ each of degree t in X and Y. Some ids $\alpha_1, \alpha_2, \ldots, \alpha_n \in F_q$ are also generated for the sensor nodes in the network, where n is the network size. For each sensor node u in the network, s' polynomials $f_1, f_2, \ldots, f_{s'}$ are randomly picked up from $\mathcal{K}$ and the polynomial shares $f_1(X, \alpha), f_2(X, \alpha), \ldots, f_{s'}(X, \alpha)$ are loaded in the key ring K_u of u, where α is the id of u. Upon deployment, each sensor u transmits the ids of the polynomials, the shares of which reside in its key ring. Two physical neighbors u and v having shares of some common polynomial(s) can establish a pairwise key between them.

3   Key Reshuffling Scheme

It is seen that due to random selection of keys for the key rings of the sensor nodes from a big pool of keys $\mathcal{K}$, the key rings remain some unused keys which are no longer useful for establishing a pairwise key with the physical neighbors. Hence, it is necessary to find a proper destination alongwith a path with which the source node can share its unused key(s) with the destination(s). Our scheme provides two sensor nodes which are not physical neighbors to establish a key so that they can communicate secretly.

This is accomplished by the following algorithm as follows.

3.1   Algorithm KeyReshuffling

1. *for each node u in the sensor network* **do**
2.   *for each unused key k in its key ring* **do**
3.   Transmit k securely to u's all direct neighbors.
4.   Each direct neighbor transmits k to its direct neighbors.
5.   Continue this process until the key k is found for a destination v in less than or equal to a pre-determined hop threshold.
6.   If k is found in v's key ring, then v transmits an acknowledgement to u by indicating the matching key k and its id.

Since the network communication overhead of the key reshuffling scheme increases as the number of hops increases, the number of hops of the key reshuffling scheme may be restricted to 2 or 3.

3.2   Analysis of the Key Reshuffling Scheme

We analyze our scheme over the EG scheme [9] and the poly-pool scheme [10].

Network Connectivity of the Key Reshuffling Scheme over the EG Scheme: Let M and m be the key-pool size and the key-ring size respectively. Let the key neighborhood graph $G_{key} = (V, E)$ on n sensor nodes ($| V |= n$) in which a link $(u, v) \in E$ exists between the two nodes u and v if and only if these nodes be key neighbors.

Let p' denote the probability that a link exists between two randomly selected sensor nodes of this graph G_{key}. Due to Erdös and Rényi [15], the probability that the G_{key} is connected is given by

$$P_c = e^{-e^{-\gamma}} \tag{2}$$

where γ is any real constant and $p' = \frac{\ln n}{n} + \frac{\gamma}{n}$ as $n \to \infty$. When we fix P_c with a very high value, say, 0.99999, the expected degree of each node in G_{key} is

$$d' = p'(n - 1) = \frac{(n - 1)}{n}[\ln n - \ln(-\ln(P_c))]. \tag{3}$$

P_c is known as the *global connectivity*.

But in practice, the direct neighborhood graph $G = G_{direct}$ is not random, because it depends on the geographical area where the sensor nodes are distributed. However, if we assume that the above results for random graphs hold for G also, then we get:

$$d' = n'p \tag{4}$$

where n' is the expected number of physical neighbors of each node, and p is the probability that two physical neighbors share one or more keys from their key rings. p is called the *local connectivity*.

For the derivation of p, we have the total number of ways to select m keys of a key ring from the pool $\mathcal{K}$ of size M is $\binom{M}{m}$. Now, for a fixed key ring K_u of node u, the total number of ways to select K_v of a node v such that K_v does not share a key with K_u is $\binom{M - m}{m}$. Thus, we have, $p = 1-$ prob[two nodes do not share a key] and hence,

$$p = 1 - \frac{\binom{M - m}{m}}{\binom{M}{m}} = 1 - \prod_{i=0}^{m-1} \frac{M - m - i}{M - i}. \tag{5}$$

Let d denote the average number of neighbor nodes that each node can contact. Consider any one of these d neighbors. Let h be the number of hops which be less than or equal to a maximum value, known as *hop_threshold* (i.e., a predetermined limit). The probability that an intermediate node shares a pairwise key with both the source u and the destination v is p^2. As long as one of the d nodes can act as an intermediate node, the source u and the destination v can establish a common key. So the probability that two nodes u and v establish a pairwise key is

$$P_s = 1 - (1 - p)(1 - p^2)^d. \tag{6}$$

This equation is true for $h = 1$.

Let us consider $h = 2$. Consider y as any one of the d neighbors of v. The probability that y does not share a pairwise key with u and v via d possible intermediate nodes is $(1 - p^3)^d$. By considering all d possible neighbors of v, we obtain the probability that two nodes establish a pairwise key is

$$P_s = 1 - (1 - p)(1 - p^2)^d(1 - p^3)^{d^2}. \tag{7}$$

Thus, applying the *principle of mathematical induction*, we finally obtain the probability that the two sensors share a key in h hops ($\leq hop\_threshold$) is given by the following formula:

$$P_{keyreshuffling} = 1 - (1 - p)(1 - p^2)^d \ldots (1 - p^{h+1})^{d^h}. \tag{8}$$

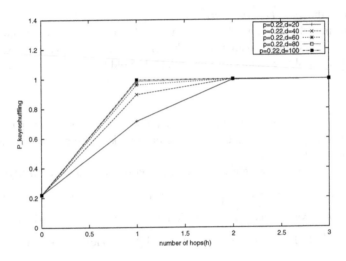

Fig. 1. Key Reshuffling over the EG scheme. Assume $M = 40000, m = 100$ so that $p = 0.22$.

We have considered $M = 40000, m = 100$ so that $p = 0.22$ for our analysis. From Figure 1, it is very clear that when the average number of neighbors increases then the connectivity also increases. Moreover, we have succeeded in obtaining 100% connectivity in $h \geq 2$ hops. Thus, the network remains highly connected after the key reshuffling scheme in $h = 2$ hops.

Network Connectivity of the Key Reshuffling Scheme over the Polynomial Pool-Based Scheme: Like the EG scheme [9], the poly-pool scheme can be analyzed under the framework of random graphs. Let s be the polynomial pool size of the symmetric bivariate polynomials in $F_q[X, Y]$ where q is a large prime such that it is suitable to fit in sensor's memory and each polynomial is of degree t in X and Y. Let s' be the number of polynomial shares per each node. The local connectivity p is computed as

$$p = 1 - \prod_{i=0}^{s'-1} \frac{s - s' - i}{s - i}. \tag{9}$$

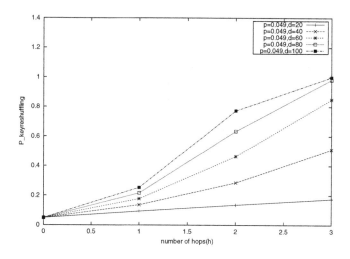

Fig. 2. Key Reshuffling over the poly-pool scheme. Assume $s = 500$, $s' = 5$ so that $p = 0.049$.

Given constraints on the network and the nodes, the desired size s of the polynomial pool can be determined from the above formula.

Now, the probability of two sensor nodes establishing a pairwise key in h hops ($\leq$ *hop_threshold*) for the key reshuffling scheme can be determined similar to the derivation for the EG scheme and hence, it is given by

$$P_{keyreshuffling} = 1 - (1-p)(1-p^2)^d \ldots (1-p^{h+1})^{d^h}. \tag{10}$$

For analysis, we have taken $s = 500$ and $s' = 5$. Then, $p = 0.049$, that is, the network is likely to remain disconnected initially with high probability. From Figure 2, it is clear that after executing our scheme we have the high network connectivity figures when the average number of neighbors increases and $h \geq 2$. In other words, the network becomes connected with high probability.

4   Simulation

In this section, we discuss the simulation results of the network connectivity achieved by our scheme over the EG scheme as well as the poly-pool scheme.

We have simulated our scheme for several random deployment models two of which are shown in Figures 3 and 4. Each dot in the figures represents the deployment location of a sensor node. Our simulation suggests that the results of our scheme are not much sensitive with respect to different deployment models.

For the EG scheme, we have taken the standard parameters $n = 10000$, $M = 40000$, $m = 100$. Then, we have the local connectivity as $p = 0.23$, whereas the actual value is 0.22. Figure 5 clearly shows that both the simulation as well as actual network connectivity of our scheme over the EG scheme are very closed.

Fig. 3. A random deployment model

For the poly-pool scheme, we have considered the parameters as $s = 500$, $s' = 5$ and $n = 10000$. The actual local connectivity becomes 0.0492, while the simulated value is 0.0484. Figure 6 clearly also shows that both the simulation as well as actual network connectivity of our scheme over the poly-pool scheme are very closed with respect to both the random deployment models.

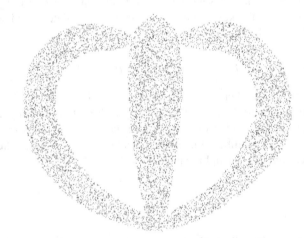

Fig. 4. A random deployment model

5   Comparison

In this section, we compare our scheme with the path key establishment over the EG scheme as well as the poly-pool scheme.

For the poly-pool scheme, we have considered the parameters: $s = 500$, $s' = 5$, and $n = 10000$. Then, we have simulated with respect to the random deployment models

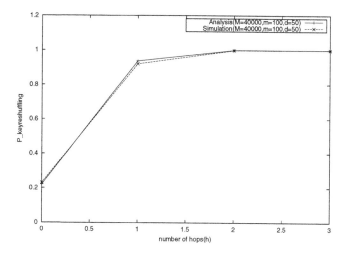

Fig. 5. Simulation v.s. actual results of network connectivity for the key reshuffling scheme over the EG scheme. Assume $M = 40000, m = 100, n = 10000$.

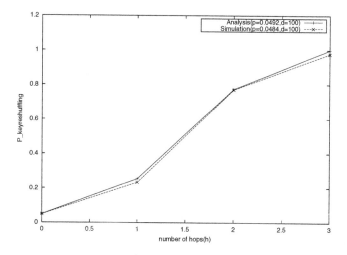

Fig. 6. Simulation v.s. actual results of network connectivity for the key reshuffling scheme over the poly-pool scheme. Assume $s = 500, s' = 5, n = 10000$.

shown in Figures 3 and 4. Figure 7 shows that our scheme has better connectivity than what the path key establishment guarantees.

Similarly, for the EG scheme we have the parameters: $M = 40000, m = 100, n = 10000$, and $d = 50$. Again, Figure 8 clearly tells us that our scheme has better performance than the path key establishment with respect to both random models shown in Figures 3 and 4.

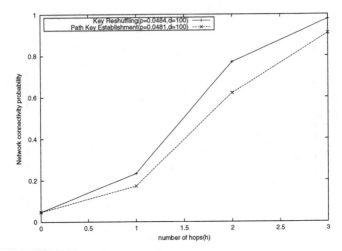

Fig. 7. Comparison of network connectivity between the key reshuffling and the path key establishment over the poly-pool scheme. Assume $s = 500, s' = 5, n = 10000$.

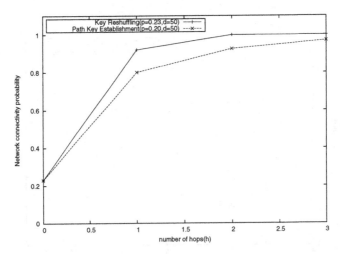

Fig. 8. Comparison of network connectivity between the key reshuffling and the path key establishment over the EG scheme. Assume $M = 40000, m = 100, n = 10000$.

6   Advantages of the Key Reshuffling Scheme

In this section, we highlight some advantages achieved from our scheme.
   Some advantages of our scheme are as follows:

1. *Network connectivity*
   From the above results we conclude that our key reshuffling scheme produces excellent performances over the EG scheme as well as the poly-pool based scheme with respect to network connectivity than the path key establishment.

2. *Network resilience against node capture*

The resilience figures against node capture are given in the EG scheme [9] and the poly-pool scheme [10]. To establish a path between a source and a destination for key sharing network communication overhead due to extra transmission of unused keys is necessary. Thus, this scheme improves security at the cost of network communication overhead.

3. *Routing decisions*

Since our scheme increases connectivity of the network, so each sensor node can route encrypted sensing data to a proper destination using a predetermined number of hops path instead of sending to its neighbors. Hence, this allows us to reduce the overhead cost of routing in the sensor network.

7   Conclusion

We have shown that our proposed scheme produces better performances with respect to the network connectivity, the network resilience against nodes capture and the routing decisions between sensor nodes. This scheme, however, improves the security at the cost of network communication overhead. Thus, our scheme would be a more attractive choice than the path key establishment.

References

1. Rivest, R.L., Shamir, A., Adleman, L.M.: A method for obtaining digital signatures and public-key cryptosystems. Communications of the ACM **21** (1978) 120–126
2. Diffie, W., Hellman, M.E.: New directions in cryptography. IEEE Transactions on Information Theory **22** (1976) 644–654
3. Gamal, E.: A public key cryptosystem and a signature scheme based on discrete logarithms. IEEE Transactions on Information Theory **31** (1985) 469–472
4. Brassard, G.: Modern Cryptology. Springer-Verlag, New York, Berlin (1988)
5. Stallings, W.: Cryptography and Network Security: Principles and Practices. 3rd edn. Prentice Hall (2002)
6. Schaefer, E.: A simplified data encryption standard algorithm. In: Cryptologia. (1996)
7. Merkle, R., Hellman, M.: On the security of multiple encryption. Communications of the ACM (1981)
8. Rivest, R.: The rc5 algorithm. Dr. Dobb's Journal (1995)
9. Eschenaur, L., Gligor, V.D.: A key management scheme for distributed sensor networks. In: 9th ACM Conference on Computer and Communication Security. (2002) 41–47
10. Liu, D., Ning, P.: Establishing pairwise keys in distributed sensor networks. In: Proceedings of 10th ACM Conference on Computer and Communications Security (CCS), Washington DC, USA (2003) 52–61
11. Chan, H., Perrig, A., Song, D.: Random key predistribution for sensor networks. In: IEEE Symposium on Security and Privacy, Berkely, California (2003) 197–213
12. Du, W., Deng, J., Han, Y.S., Varshney, P.K.: A pairwise key pre-distribution scheme for wireless sensor networks. In: ACM Conference on Computer and Communications Security (CCS'03), Washington DC, USA (2003) 42–51

13. Du, W., Deng, J., Han, Y.S., Chen, S., Varshney, P.K.: A key management scheme for wireless sensor networks using deployment knowledge. In: 23rd Conference of the IEEE Communications Society (Infocom'04), Hong Kong, China (2004)
14. Perrig, A., Szewczyk, R., Wen, V., Culler, D., Tygar, J.D.: Spins : Security protocols for sensor networks. In: Proceedings of the 7th Annual ACM/IEEE International Conference on Mobile Computing and Networking (MobiCom), Rome, Italy (2001) 189–199
15. Erdos, P., Renyi, A.: On random graphs. Publ. Math. (1959) 290–297

CCMEA: Customized Cellular Message Encryption Algorithm for Wireless Networks

Debdeep Mukhopadhyay[1,*], Abhishek Chaudhary[2,**],
Arvind Nebhnani[2,**], and Dipanwita RoyChowdhury[3,***]

[1] Department of Computer Sc. and Engg, IIT Kharagpur, India
debdeep@vlsi.iitkgp.ernet.in
[2] Department of Electrical Engineering, IIT Kharagpur, India
{achaudhary, arvind}@ee.iitkgp.ernet.in
[3] Department of Computer Sc. and Engg, IIT Kharagpur, India
drc@cse.iitkgp.ernet.in

Abstract. Cellular Message Encryption Algorithm (CMEA) has been widely used for wireless security and the breaking of the scheme proves the requirement of alternatives. In the current paper the properties of the CMEA, which has lead to the successful cryptanalysis, has been identified. Accordingly the algorithm has been modified to prevent the attacks. Finally the customized CMEA has been subjected to standard linear and differential cryptanalysis to evaluate its security margin. The endeavour demonstrates that with appropriate modifications the CMEA can be transformed into a strong cipher, which is essential for wireless security.

1 Introduction

Cellular Message Encryption Algorithm (CMEA) [1] has been developed by the Telecommunications Industry Association (TIA) to encrypt digital cellular phone data. CMEA is one of the four cryptographic primitives specified in a Telecommunications Industry Association (TIA) standard, and is designed to encrypt the control channel, rather than the voice data. It is a block cipher which uses a 64 bit key and operates on a variable block length. CMEA is used to encrypt the control channels of cellular phones. It is distinct from ORYX, an also insecure stream cipher that is used to encrypt data transmitted over digital cellular phones.

In March 1997, Counterpane Systems and UC Berkeley jointly [2] published attacks on the cipher showing it had several weaknesses. In the paper the authors have presented several attacks on CMEA which are of practical threat to the security of digital cellular systems. The authors describe an attack on CMEA which requires $40 - 80$ known plaintexts, has time complexity about $2^{24} - 2^{32}$, and finishes in minutes or hours of computation on a standard workstation. The

---

[*] Phd student.
[**] BTech Final Year Students.
[***] Associate Professor.

S. Jajodia and C. Mazumdar (Eds.): ICISS 2005, LNCS 3803, pp. 217–227, 2005.

authors point out that the cryptanalysis of CMEA underscores the need for an open cryptographic review process. Thus having faith on new algorithms which are designed close door is always dangerous. The use of such algorithms can lead to a total collapse of the cellular telephonic industry. CMEA is used to protect sensitive control data, such as the digits dialed by the cellphone user. A successful break of CMEA might reveal user calling patterns. Finally compromise of the control channel contents could lead to the leaking of any confidential data (like credit card numbers, bank account numbers and voice mail PIN numbers) that the user types on the keypad.

Following the revelation of the weakness of CMEA, a patchup algorithm called ECMEA was standardised by TIA. A further enhancement of ECMEA, called SCEMA, is also developed [1]. However according to [2] the previous cryptanalysis of all the crypto-algorithms proposed by TIA clearly demonstrate that there is a need of explicitly stating security assumptions during every step of the design. Also security components should not be reused without thouroughly examining the implications of reuse. Although it has been proposed that the future generation cellular networks (CDMA 2000 1X Revision A) will use AES(Rijndael)[3], the implementation constraints of a wireless network might prove to be a concern. This motivates the design of special ciphers for wireless telephones (networks) but at the same time which are evaluated meticulously. The security margins of such algorithms must be stated so as to increase confidence in the ciphers. In other words, dedicated as well as standard block cipher security analysis should be presented for the ciphers which are used to prevent frauds in such important networks. In these lines, the present paper revisits the CMEA algorithm. The algorithm has been analysed to understand the reasons of its insecurity. Based upon the analysis the CMEA has been modified to CCMEA. The new algorithm has been analysed and it has been shown that the original attacks do not work against the cipher. The security of CMEA depends on the strength of the T-Box. Hence, security margins have been presented to establish that the T-Box provides sufficient security margins against linear and differential cryptanalysis.

The paper is organised as follows. In *section 2* the preliminaries have been stated which details the original CMEA algorithm. In *section 3* the attacks against the CMEA algorithm have been analysed. *Section 4* presents the customized CMEA with necessary modifications to plague the existing weaknesses of CMEA. *Section 5* performs a security analysis of CCMEA. Finally *section 6* concludes the work.

2   The CMEA Algorithm

This section describes the CMEA algorithm. CMEA is a byte-oriented variable width block cipher with a 64 bit key. Block sizes may be any number of bytes. CMEA is optimized for 8-bit microprocessors with severe resource limitations.

CMEA has three layers. The first layer performs one non-linear pass on the block, affecting left-to-right diffusion. The second layer is a purely linear, unkeyed operation intended to make changes in the opposite direction. One can think of the second step as exoring the right half of the block onto the left half. The third layer performs a final non-linear pass on the block from left to right. In fact, it is the inverse of the first layer.

CMEA obtains its non-linearity in the first and third layer from a 8-bit keyed lookup table known as the T-Box. The T-Box calculates its 8-bit output as $T(x) = C((((C(((C(((C((x \oplus K_0) + K_1) + x) \oplus K_2) + K_3) + x) \oplus K_4) + K_5) + x) \oplus K_6) + K_7) + x$ given input byte x and 8-byte key $K_{0,...,7}$. In this equation C is an unkeyed 8-bit lookup table known as the CaveTable. All the operations are 8 bit operations. The algorithm encrypts a n-byte message $P_{0,...,n-1}$ to a ciphertext $C_{0,...,n-1}$ under the key $K_{0...7}$ as follows:

$y_0 = 0$
$for(i = 0; i < n; i++)$
{
$\quad P_i' = P_i + T(y_i \oplus i\})$
$\quad y_{i+1} = y_i + P_i'$
}

$\quad for(i = 0; i < \lfloor n/2 \rfloor; i++)$
$\quad\quad P_i'' = P_i' \oplus (P_{n-i-1}' \bigvee 1)$

$z_0 = 0$
$for(i = 0; i < n; i++)$
{
$\quad z_{i+1} = z_i + P_i''$
$\quad C_i = P_i'' - T(z_i \oplus i)$
}

Recovering the values of all the 256 T-Box entries is equivalent to the breaking of CMEA even if the keys are not recovered. The values of $T(0)$ occupies a position of special importance. $T(0)$ is always used to obtain C_0 from P_0. Without $T(0)$ one cannot trivially predict where other T-Box entries are likely to be used. Knowing $T(0)$ lets us learn the inputs to the T-Box lookups that modify the second byte in the message. The CAVE Table has very skewed statistical distribution. 92 of the possible 256 eight bit values never appear.

3   Analysis of the Attacks on CMEA Algorithm

The original CMEA algorithm has been attacked using both chosen plaintext and known plaintext attack [2]. CMEA is weak against chosen-plaintext attacks; one can recover all the T-Box entries with about 338 chosen texts (on average) and very little work. The work [2] also shows that the cipher is weak under a known plaintext attack due to the skewed nature of the Cave Table.

A detailed study of the CMEA algorithm gives reason as to why CMEA is susceptible to chosen plaintext and known plaintext attacks. In this section the properties of the algorithm which make the cipher weak have been identified.

The CMEA algorithm shall be developed to a new algorithm named CCMEA plaguing the weaknesses of the existing CMEA. The security of CCMEA has been analyzed in the following section. Recovery of all values of the 256 T-Box entries is equivalent to the breaking of the cipher, so the strength of the T-Box requires special attention and hence has been treated subsequently in details.

- **Property 1.** If the plaintext is of the form $P = \{1-x, 1-x, \ldots, 1-x\}$ and the ciphertext is of the form $C = \{-x, \ldots\}$ then with very high probability $T(0) = x$.

  Analysis: $P'_0 = P_0 + T(0) = 1 - x + T(0)$.
  If $T(0) = x$, we have $P'_0 = 1$.
  Thus, $y_1 = y_0 + P'_0 = 0 + 1 = 1$.

  Likewise, $P'_1 = P_1 + T(1 \oplus 1) = 1 + 1 = 2$.
  Thus, $y_2 = y_1 + P_1 = 1 + 1 = 2$.
  Thus continnuing we have $P'_{n-1} = 1$.
  So, $P''_0 = P'_0 \oplus (P'_{n-1} \vee 1) = 1 \oplus 1 = 0$.
  Hence, $C_0 = P''_0 - T(0) = -T(0) = -x$.

  The probability when using the CaveTable is dependent on the fact that the initial guess for $T(0)$ is correct and the possible number of trials is thus only $(256\text{-}92)/2 = 82$ on the average.

- **Property 2.** If the plaintext is of the form $P = \{1 - T(0), 1 - T(0), \ldots, 1 - T(0), k - T(0), 0\}$ and the ciphertext is $C = \{t - T(0), \ldots\}$ where $k = ((n-1) \oplus j) - (n-2)$ then with very high probability $t = T(j)$.

  Analysis: It has been shown that $P'_i = 1$ and $y_i = i$, where $0 \le i \le (n-3)$.
  Now, $P'_{n-2} = P_{n-2} + T(y_{n-2} \oplus n - 2)$
  $\qquad\qquad = P_{n-2} + T(0)$, since $y_{n-2} = n - 2$
  $\qquad\qquad = k - T(0) + T(0) = k$.
  Using this fact, $y_{n-1} = y_{n-2} + P'_{n-2}$
  $\qquad\qquad\qquad = (n-2) + k = (n-1) \oplus j$.
  Therefore, $P'_{n-1} = P_{n-1} + T(y_{n-1} \oplus n - 1)$
  $\qquad\qquad\qquad = 0 + T(j)$.
  Thus, $C_0 = t - T(0)$
  $\qquad\quad = P''_0 - T(0)$
  $\qquad\quad = P'_0 \oplus (P'_{n-1} \vee 1) - T(0)$.
  Thus, $t = 1 \oplus (T(j) \vee 1)$
  $\qquad = T(j)$ with a very high probability, with some confusion with the LSB.

- **Property 3.** The CMEA algorithm uses a skewed CAVE Table[2]. The CAVE Table is not a permutation and 92 of the possible 256 values does not occur.

– **Property 4.** The CMEA algorithm uses a four round T-Box which can be subjected to meet-in-the-middle attack[2].

Using the above properties one can explain why the CMEA algorithm is weak against the chosen plaintext and known plaintext attacks. The causes of the attacks are enlisted below:

1. Chosen Plaintext Attack: The CMEA algorithm is weak against chosen plaintext attack because of properties 1 and 2.
2. Known Plaintext Attack: The known plaintext attack is powerful against the CMEA algorithm because of properties 3 and 4.

4   CCMEA : Customized Cellular Message Encryption Algorithm

Analyzing the above properties the CMEA algorithm has been modified. The resultant cipher is presented in this section.

– **Modification 1.** Clearly the update equation of P_1 needs to be changed so that properties 1 and 2 work no more. The modified equation is of the form:
$P_i' = P_i + T(y_i \oplus f(i, n))$
such that as we vary i from 0 to $(n - 1)$ (where n is the number of byte blocks in the plaintext) the T-Box is not predictably accessed. In the original CMEA property 1 exists because for a particular nature of the input plaintext and key the T-Box was always referred at the point 0. So, the function $f(i, n)$ should be such that the T-Box is accessed at different points. After considering several forms of the function $f(i, n)$ the proposed function is $f(i, n) = 2i\%n$, hence the update equation is:

$$P_i' = P_i + T(y_i \oplus 2i\%n)$$

Thus the algorithm is transformed into:

$y_0 = 0$
$for(i = 0; i < n; i + +)$
{
$\quad P_i' = P_i + T(y_i \oplus 2i\%n)$
$\quad y_{i+1} = y_i + P_i'$
}

$$for(i = 0; i < \lfloor n/2 \rfloor; i + +)$$
$$P_i'' = P_i' \oplus (P_{n-i-1}' \bigvee 1)$$

$z_0 = 0$
$for(i = 0; i < n; i + +)$
{
$\quad z_{i+1} = z_i + P_i''$
$\quad C_i = P_i'' - T(z_i \oplus 2i\%n)$
}

- **Modification 2.** The CAVE Table is replaced with the AES S-Box which can be efficiently implemented[4]. Thus the distribution is no more skewed and all the possible 256 values appear as a possibility.
- **Modification 3.** The T-Box previously had 4 rounds. The number of rounds of the T-Box has been increased to 8 rounds to prevent meet-in-the-middle attack. The output of the 4 round T-Box is recycled again through the T-Box.

5   Cryptanalysis of the Customized CMEA

In this chapter we use the two most powerful cryptanalysis techniques applied to symmetric-key block ciphers, namely linear and differential cryptanalysis. Linear cryptanalysis was introduced by Matsui [5] in 1993 as a theoretical attack on the Data Encryption Standard (DES) and later successfully used in the practical cryptanalysis of DES; differential cryptanalysis was first presented by Biham and Shamir to attack DES. Although the early target of both the attacks was DES, the wide applicability of both attacks to numerous other block ciphers has solidified the preeminence of both cryptanalysis techniques in the consideration of the security of all block ciphers. For example, many of the candidates submitted for the recent Advanced Encryption Standard process undertaken by the National Institute of Standards and Technology were designed using techniques specifically targeted at thwarting linear and differential cryptanalysis. This is evident, for example, in the Rijndael cipher, the encryption algorithm selected to be the new standard. Although both Linear and Differential Cryptanalysis are world wide accepted standards to test the security of any encryption algorithm, how the attacks are to be carried out depends upon the algorithm. In fact, applying the two forms of attacks to a new algorithm is in itself a challenge. The next section shows how to cryptanalyze CCMEA using linear and differential cryptanalysis.

First, we shall compare the strength of the Cave Table used in CMEA with the Rijndael S-Box used in CCMEA under the light of linear and differential analysis.

5.1   Comparision of the Strengths of Cave Table and AES S-Box

Linear Cryptanalysis of the non-linear Cave Table or AES S-Box (an S-Box in general) involves forming a linear approximation table (LAT). For, an input $X_1, X_2, \ldots, X_8$ the output of the S-Box is represented by $Y_1, Y_2, \ldots, Y_8$. The S-Box is approximated with linear equations of the form:

$$a_1 X_1 \oplus a_2 X_2 \oplus \ldots \oplus a_8 X_8 \oplus b_1 Y_1 \oplus b_2 Y_2 \oplus \ldots \oplus b_8 Y_8 = 0.$$

Here, $a_i, b_i \in 0, 1$. The linear analysis observes the non-linearity by observing the deviation of the actual output from the output of the linear expressions. That is, we form a table which shows the number of cases in which the linear

Table 1. LAT Comparision of AES S-Box and the Cave Table

Deviation	Frequency (Cave)	Frequency (AES)
22	286	0
23	0	0
24	162	0
25	0	0
26	72	0
27	0	0
28	30	0
29	0	0
30	11	0
31	0	0
32	3	0

expression can relate the input and output bits of the S-Box. In a strong cipher the probability that any linear expression will hold is $1/2$. Thus, the deviation or bias from $1/2$ measures the security of the S-Box. The rows and columns of the S-Box are represented by hexadecimal numbers, encoding the values of $a_1, a_2, \ldots, a_8$ and $b_1, b_2, \ldots, b_8$. In the LAT for the CMEA Cave Table and the AES S-Box we have also observed the number of cases in which various linear expressions hold. The deviation is calculated from 128 (corresponding to the probability $1/2$). The deviation in the table is a measure of the probability bias,

Probability Bias = Deviation/128.

The LAT shows that the deviations in the Cave Table have greater frequency as compared to the AES S-Box (which is infact zero for the values shown). This indicates that the AES S-Box is more secure compared to the Cave Table S-Box under the light of linear cryptanalysis.

The Difference Distribution Table (DDT) of an S-Box gives us the security of the S-Box. The table stores the number of cases where the output difference (dy) is a particular value, given an input pair (dx). A high value in the difference distribution table indicates a weakness of the S-Box of the cipher. Since, it is not possible to draw (due to space) the DDT for an 8-bit S-Box and the AES S-Box, we represent a snap-shot of the output in a different way.

The table below shows the comparisions of the DDT of both the boxes. In the table we record the number of $dx - dy$ sets and their corresponding frequency. For example the first record shows that there are 39898 cases where the value in the actual DDT table is zero. We see that in the Cave table the DDT has some higher frequencies for $dx - dy$ pairs. For example we see that there are 18 cases where the number of a particular $dx - dy$ pair is 10. The AES box on the other hand, has no occurence of such a high DDT value. This indicates weakness, while the AES S-Box does not show any. The above observations justify the replacement of the Cave Table with the Rijndael S-Box.

The T-Box plays a central role in the cipher structure of CMEA. One can gather information about the T-Box entries from the known CMEA encryptions.

Table 2. DDT Comparision of AES S-Box and the Cave Table

No. of dx-dy sets	Frequency (Cave)	Frequency (AES)
0	39898	33150
1	0	0
2	19709	32130
3	0	0
4	5007	255
5	0	0
6	787	0
7	0	0
8	115	0
9	0	0
10	18	0
11	0	0
12	1	0
13	0	0
14	0	0
15	0	0

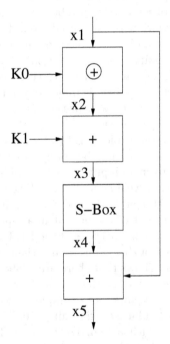

Fig. 1. One round T-Box

Also if the T-Box is compromised and all the T-Box outputs can be identified then the CMEA algorithm is also broken. So, the problem reduces to the cryptanalysis of the T-Box algorithm, given information about the input and output of some of the elements. More formally in this section we shall inspect given the T-Box input and outputs for some values is it possible to obtain the other T-Box elements or to recover the key. We analyze the T-Box algorithm under linear and differential attacks [5].

5.2   Linear Cryptanalysis of the Modified T-Box

Figure 1 shows the single round of the T-Box. The linear expression relating the bits of $x1$ and the keys $K0$ and $K1$. The expression may be derived as follows:

$$x_5[0] = x_4[0] \oplus x_1[0] \text{ , with probability 1,}$$
$$= f(x_3[i_1], x_3[i_2], \ldots, x_3[i_k]) \oplus x_1[0],$$

where f is a linear approximation of the S-Box, the probability of such an expression is say upper bounded by p_{RD}.

It must be noted that such an expression will have the largest probability bias. All other linear approximations will have a smaller bias and hence we have considered this expression. The fact can be established using the following logic:

The bias of other linear expessions can be estimated from the bias of the individual linear expressions by using the Piling-Up lemma [5]. Thus if we combine l linear equations of the form $x_5[i] = x_4[i] \oplus x_1[i]$ each with a bias $(1/2)^{i+1}$, (we prove this later in lemma1) the bias of the combined equation is

$$2^{l-1} \prod_{i=i_1}^{l} (1/2)^{i+1}$$
$$= 2^{l-1}[(1/2)^{i_1+1}.(1/2)^{i_2+1}.\ldots.(1/2)^{i_l+1}]$$
$$= 1/2^{(i_1+i_2+\ldots+i_l+1)} < 1/2.$$

Note that $1/2$ is the bias of the equation with which we have started with viz. $x_5[0] = x_4[0] \oplus x_1[0]$. So, all other linear approximations have a lesser bias. Hence, all the other linear equations which are developed from other starting equations have a lesser bias and also a lesser probability. Thus we compute the probability of the linear trail with the maximum probability, to give us the upper bound of linear probability values of the T-Box.

Now to obtain linear expressions where $x_3[i_1]$ is expressed in terms of $x_1[i_1]$ and $K_0[i_1]$ we have

$$x_3[i_1] = x_2[i_1] \oplus K_1[i_1], \text{ with probability } p_i \text{ and bias } \epsilon_i.$$
$$= x_1[i_1] \oplus K_0[i_1] \oplus K_1[i_1], \text{ with bias } \epsilon_i. \text{ Thus,}$$
$$x_5[0] = f(x_1[i_1], x_1[i_2], \ldots, x_1[i_k], K_0[i_1], K_0[i_2], \ldots, K_0[i_k], K_1[i_1], K_1[i_2],$$
$$\ldots, K_1[i_k]) \oplus x_1[0],$$

with bias $\epsilon_{i1}.\epsilon_{i2}.\ldots.\epsilon_{ik}.\epsilon_{RD}$. Hence the bias of the linear trail is given by $\epsilon_{i1}.\epsilon_{i2}.\ldots.\epsilon_{ik}.\epsilon_{RD}$. It can be proved that for given n bit inputs, x and K, the output y, denoted by $y = x + k$, can be represented by the linear equation $y = x \oplus k$, with bias ϵ_i. Then, $\epsilon_i = (1/2)^{i+1}$.

The proof can be obtained by tracing the probability of the carry from the previous bit positions. Combining the above results one can obtain the maximum bias of a linear trail in the T-Box of the block cipher: $(1/2)^{i_1+1}.(1/2)^{i_2+1}.....$ $(1/2)^{i_k+1}.\epsilon_{RD}$. Thus the bias becomes exponentially small compared to that of a linear approximation of the AES Rijndael S-Box.

5.3   Differential Cryptanalysis of the Modified T-Box

We first observe the security that a single round of the T-Box provides against a differential attack. Figure 1 shows the single round T-Box. Given $x1$ and $x5$ (the input and output pairs at any point) one can calculate $x3$. Thus the problem reduces to the cryptanalysis of the Portion of the T-Box shown in figure 2. In the figure, $dx1$ and $dx2$ are same and do not depend upon the key.

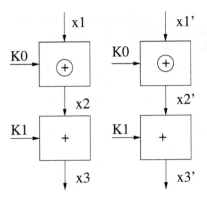

Fig. 2. One round T-Box

Once we know $dx1$ and $dx2$ and observe the differential property of the addition block to obtain information about $K1$ we can also obtain $K0$. Analysis of one round of the T-Box brings the following observations to the surface. We have created tables for the entire key space and noted how many keys are possible for each pair of $(dx2,dx3)$. The table shows that the distribution is very sparse and there are a large number of cases where a $(dx2,dx3)$ pair is not possible for any key. There are instances for which certain keys can be immediately ruled out. The remaining set of possible keys vary in sizes and range from as low as 2 to 254(except the $(0,0)$ pair where all keys are possible). Thus in such a worst case scenario a random search over only 2 values will reveal $K1$ and hence $K0$. Hence one round of the T-Box shows weaknesses. So we need to increase the number of rounds.

Let us calculate the maximum probability of a differential to pass through one round of the T-Box. It was found that there exist weak keys for each possible $dx1$. The weak key is defined to be a key for which there is a $dx3$ which always occurs for a particular dx1 and the key. Next the $dx3$ which serves as the input to the S-Box was considered. The corresponding output differential $dx4$ with the highest probability was observed. Next for all these $dx1$'s and $dx4$'s the possible $dx5$'s was found which had the highest probability. The above steps were done for all possible $dx1$'s and their corresponding weak keys. The analysis results in the worst case maximum probability of obtaining a $dx5$ for any given $dx1$. The probability worked out to be around 0.0078, so for 8 rounds of the T-Box the probability is around 1.37×10^{-17}, which is negligible. If we do not use weak keys then the worst case probability of the passing of differential reduces to around 0.0039. But this reduces the key space. So we see that the T-Box is quite resistant to Differential Cryptanalysis as well. Any attack on the modified CMEA, must start from the cryptanalysis of the T-Box since it will not be possible to break the algorithm without getting the T-Box entries first.

6   Conclusion

In the present paper the original CMEA algorithm has been modified into CCMEA. The paper shows how the existing cryptanalysis of CMEA fails to break CCMEA. It has been shown that the T-Box provides sufficient security margin to the cipher CCMEA in the face of linear and differential cryptanalysis. In short, the paper demonstrates that with suitable modifications the original CMEA algorithm can be made strong and hence can be an important choice for wireless security.

References

[1] TIA Telecommunications Industry Association, "Common Cryptographic Algorithms, Revision D.1, Publication Version, September 13, 2003," http://ftp. tiaonline.org/TR-45/TR45AHAG/Public/ComCryptAlgD1.pdf.

[2] David Wagner, Bruce Schneier and John Kelsey, "Cryptanalysis of the Cellular Message Encryption Algorithm," in *Crypto 1997*, 2002, Also a NESSIE report, pp. 526–537.

[3] Joan Daemen and Vincent Rijmen, *The Design of Rijndael*, Springer-Verlag, 2002.

[4] V. Rijmen, "Efficient Implementation of the Rijndael Sbox," http://www.esat.kul euven.ac.be/ rijmen/rijndael.

[5] Howard M. Keys, "A Tutorial on Linear and Differential Cryptanalysis," www.engr. mun.ca/~howard/PAPERS/ldc_tutorial.ps.

A Hybrid Design of Key Pre-distribution Scheme for Wireless Sensor Networks

Dibyendu Chakrabarti, Subhamoy Maitra, and Bimal Roy

Applied Statistics Unit, Indian Statistical Institute,
203 B T Road, Kolkata 700 108
{dibyendu_r, subho, bimal}@isical.ac.in

Abstract. Here a scheme is presented for key pre-distribution in wireless sensor networks. A transversal design is considered to construct a (v, b, r, k) configuration. Then properly chosen blocks are merged to form sensor nodes such that there is no intra-node common key. The choice of blocks in merging is currently made heuristically in a randomized manner. The scheme is called hybrid as a combinatorial design followed by a heuristic is applied. Detailed analysis is presented regarding the number of nodes, number of keys per nodes and the probability that a link gets affected if certain number of nodes are compromised. It is also argued how the scheme compares favourably with the state of the art proposals. Towards the end we also present a result to find out the lower bound on the number of nodes given a certain combinatorial design.

Keywords: Combinatorial Design, Sensor Network, Key Pre-distribution, Random Merging.

1 Introduction

Key pre-distribution schemes in private key based secure encrypted communication among sensor nodes has become an active area of research as evident from [2,4,6,10,11,13,7]. One may refer to [8] for broader perspective in the area of sensor networks.

Let us first describe the area of application. Consider N number of sensor nodes where the geographical positioning of the nodes cannot be decided a priori. Any two nodes in RF range (geometrically adjacent) are expected to be able to communicate securely. One option is to maintain different secret keys for each of the pairs. Then each of the nodes needs to store $N - 1$ keys. Given (i) the huge number of sensor nodes generally deployed, (ii) the memory constraint of the sensor nodes, this solution is not practicable. On the other hand, on-line key exchange is also not possible since implementation of public key framework demands processing power beyond that of present day sensor nodes. Thus the thrust area of research is key pre-distribution to each of the sensor nodes before deployment and the most used mathematical tool for key pre-distribution is combinatorial design. Each of the sensor nodes contains M many keys and each key is shared by Q many nodes, (thus fixing M and Q) such that the encrypted

S. Jajodia and C. Mazumdar (Eds.): ICISS 2005, LNCS 3803, pp. 228–238, 2005.

communication between two nodes may be decrypted by at most $Q - 2$ other nodes if they fall within the RF range of the two communicating nodes. Similarly one node can decrypt the communication between any two of at most $M(Q-1)$ nodes if it lies within the radio frequency range of all the nodes who share a key with it.

The goal in this paper is to present a randomized block merging based design strategy that originates from Transversal Design. We differ from the existing works where it is considered that any two nodes will have either 0 or 1 common key and motivate a design strategy with more number of common keys. This is important from resiliency consideration in an adversarial framework since if certain nodes are compromised, the proportion of links that becomes unusable can be kept low, i.e., the connectivity of the network is less disturbed. We compare our scheme with a very recently proposed scheme [11] that uses basic combinatorial design strategy. Our contribution is the use of proper merging of blocks after this basic design.

Note that in one of our earlier papers [3] we have considered the block merging strategy in a completely randomized fashion. In that case there was a possibility that the constituent blocks of a sensor node, may share common keys among themselves. This is a loss in terms of the connectivity in the designed network as no shared key is needed since there is no necessity for 'intra-node communication'. In this endeavour, we consider the merging such that there is no common key among the blocks that are being merged and that makes the work distinct (and improved too) from our earlier paper.

The computation to find out a shared key under this framework is of very low time complexity [11,3], which basically requires calculation of the inverse of an element in a finite field. Note that Blom's scheme [1] has been extended in recent works for key pre-distribution in wireless sensor networks [6,10]. The problem with these kinds of schemes is the use of several multiplication operations (as example see [6–Section 5.2]) for key exchange.

The randomized key pre-distribution is another strategy in this area [7]. However, the main motivation is to maintain a connectivity (possibly with several hops) in the network. As example [7–Section 3.2], a sensor network with 10000 nodes has been considered and to maintain the connectivity, it has been calculated that it is enough if one node can communicate with only 20 other nodes. Note that the communication between any two nodes may require a large number of hops. However, as we discussed earlier, only the connectivity criterion (with too many hops) can not suffice in an adversarial condition. Further in such a scenario, the key agreement between two nodes requires exchange of the key indices.

The use of combinatorial and probabilistic design (also a combination of both – termed as hybrid design) in the context of key distribution has been proposed in [2]. In this case also, the main motivation was to have low number of common keys as in [11]. On the other hand we propose the idea of good number of common keys between any two nodes. The novelty of our approach is to start from a combinatorial design and then apply a probabilistic extension in the form of random merging of blocks (such that the merged blocks do not share any common key) to form the sensor nodes and in this case there is good flexibility in adjusting the number of common keys between any two nodes. Our scheme can also be called a hybrid one as it combines deterministic design idea with randomized block merging.

Further a lower bound on the number of nodes given a (v, b, r, k) design is presented. The merging strategy adapted for this looks promising for further investigation.

2   Preliminaries

2.1   Basics of Combinatorial Design

Let A be a finite set of subsets (also known as blocks) of a set X. A *set system* or *design* is a pair (X, A). The degree of a point $x \in X$ is the number of subsets containing the point x. If all subsets/blocks have the same size k, then (X, A) is said to be uniform of rank k. If all points have the same degree r, (X, A) is said to be regular of degree r.

A regular and uniform set system is called a $(v, b, r, k) - 1$ design, where $|X| = v, |A| = b$, r is the degree and k is the rank. The condition $bk = vr$ is necessary and sufficient for existence of such a set system. A $(v, b, r, k) - 1$ design is called a (v, b, r, k) configuration if any two distinct blocks intersect in zero or one point.

A (v, b, r, k, λ) BIBD is a $(v, b, r, k) - 1$ design in which every pair of points occurs in exactly λ many blocks. A (v, b, r, k) configuration having deficiency $d = v - 1 - r(k - 1) = 0$ exists if and only if a $(v, b, r, k, 1)$ BIBD exists.

Let g, u, k be positive integers such that $2 \leq k \leq u$. A group-divisible design of type g^u and block size k is a triple $(X, \mathcal{H}, \mathcal{A})$, where X is a finite set of cardinality gu, $\mathcal{H}$ is a partition of X into u parts/groups of size g, and $\mathcal{A}$ is a set of subsets/blocks of X. The following conditions are satisfied in this case:

1. $|H \bigcap A| \leq 1 \ \forall H \in \mathcal{H}, \ \forall A \in \mathcal{A}$,
2. every pair of elements of X from different groups occurs in exactly one block in $\mathcal{A}$.

A Transversal Design $TD(k, n)$ is a group-divisible design of type n^k and block size k. Hence $H \bigcap A = 1 \ \forall H \in \mathcal{H}, \ \forall A \in \mathcal{A}$.

Let us now describe the construction of a transversal design. Let p be a prime power and $2 \leq k \leq p$. Then there exists a $TD(k, p)$ of the form $(X, \mathcal{H}, \mathcal{A})$ where $X = \mathbb{Z}_k \times \mathbb{Z}_p$. For $0 \leq x \leq k - 1$, define $H_x = \{x\} \times \mathbb{Z}_p$ and $\mathcal{H} = \{H_x : 0 \leq x \leq k - 1\}$.

For every ordered pair $(i, j) \in \mathbb{Z}_p \times \mathbb{Z}_p$, define a block $A_{i,j} = \{x, (ix+j) \bmod p : 0 \leq x \leq k - 1\}$. In this case, $\mathcal{A} = \{A_{i,j} : (i, j) \in \mathbb{Z}_p \times \mathbb{Z}_p\}$. It can be shown that $(X, \mathcal{H}, \mathcal{A})$ is a $TD(k, p)$.

Now let us relate a $(v = kr, b = r^2, r, k)$ configuration with sensor nodes and keys. X is the set of $v = kr$ number of keys distributed among $b = r^2$ number of sensor nodes. The nodes are indexed by $(i, j) \in \mathbb{Z}_r \times \mathbb{Z}_r$ and the keys are indexed by $(i, j) \in \mathbb{Z}_k \times \mathbb{Z}_r$. Consider a particular block $A_{\alpha, \beta}$. It will contain k number of keys $\{(x, (x\alpha + \beta) \bmod r) : 0 \leq x \leq k - 1\}$. Here $|X| = kr = v$, $|\mathcal{H}_x| = r$, the number of blocks in which the key (x, y) appears for $y \in \mathbb{Z}_r$, $|A_{i,j}| = k$, the number of keys in a block. For more details on combinatorial design refer to [12,11].

Note that if r is a prime power, we will not get an inverse of $x \in \mathbb{Z}_r$ when x is not a unit of $\mathbb{Z}_r$ i.e., $\gcd(x, r) > 1$. This is required for key exchange protocol. So basically we should consider the field $GF(r)$ instead of the ring $\mathbb{Z}_r$. However, there is no problem when r is a prime by itself. In this paper we generally use $\mathbb{Z}_r$ since in our examples we consider r to be prime.

2.2   Lee-Stinson Approach [11]

Let there be a $(v = rk, b = r^2, r, k)$ configuration. The following correspondence may be noted:

Number of distinct keys $= v = rk$, number of sensor nodes $= b = r^2$, number of distinct keys per node $= k$ and replication of each key occurs $= r$ times, i.e. each key repeats itself in r nodes.

It is easy to check that $bk = vr$ and $v - 1 > r(k - 1)$.

Thus there are either 0 or 1 common key between two nodes. The design $(v = 1470, b = 2401, r = 49, k = 30)$ has been used as an example in [11]. The important parameters of the design are as follows:

Expected number of common keys between two nodes $= p_1 = \frac{k(r-1)}{b-1} = \frac{k}{r+1} = \frac{30}{49+1} = 0.6$.

For an intermediate node, there is a good proportion of pairs (40%) of nodes that share no common key, and two such nodes will communicate via an intermediate node, i.e. the paths connecting these nodes are essentially two hop paths. Given a random geometric deployment, the example in [11] shows that the expected proportion such that two nodes that are able to communicate either directly or through an intermediate node is as high as 0.99995.

A resiliency measure of such an arrangement is also presented in [11]. Under adversarial situation, if a few sensor nodes are compromised, then all the keys present in those nodes have to be discarded. Given the number of compromised nodes, one needs to calculate the proportion of links which are rendered unusable. The expression for this proportion is shown to be $fail(s) = 1 - \left(1 - \frac{r-2}{b-2}\right)^s$, where s is the number of nodes compromised. In this particular example, $fail(10) \approx 0.17951$. That is, given a large network comprising as many as 2401 nodes, a compromise of only 10 nodes may render almost 18% of the links unusable.

3   Our Strategy: Merging Blocks in Combinatorial Design

We use the concept of merging blocks to form a sensor node. For the time being, we do not specify any merging strategy. The only constraint is that the blocks that will be merged to form a node will not have any common key among themselves. For this we use the following heuristic.

Heuristic 1

1. *flag = true; count = 0; all the blocks are marked as unused;*
2. *an array node[...] is available, where each element of the array can store z many blocks;*
3. *while(flag){*
   (a) *choose a random block, mark it as used and put it in node[count];*
   (b) *for (i = 1; i < z; i + +){*
      i. *search the unused blocks in random fashion and put the first available one in node[count] which has no common key with the existing blocks already in node[count];*
      ii. *mark this block as used;*
      iii. *if such a block is not available then break the for loop and assign flag = false;*
   (c) *} (end for)*
   (d) *if flag = true then count = count + 1;*
4. *} (end while)*
5. *report that N = count many nodes are available as the output;*

It is very clear that given (v, b, r, k) configuration with $b = r^2$, if one merges z many blocks to get each node then the maximum possible nodes that are available could be $N \leq \lfloor \frac{b}{z} \rfloor$. However, it is not clear at this stage whether given any configuration one can really achieve the upper bound $\lfloor \frac{b}{z} \rfloor$ with the constraint that the blocks constituting a node can not have any common key among themselves. However, using Heuristic 1, we could achieve the upper bound in certain cases and could reach very close to the upper bound in the other cases. These results will be available in the following sections. At this point we assume that such a merging is possible to get the number of nodes reaching very close to the the upper bound $\lfloor \frac{b}{z} \rfloor$ given a (v, b, r, k) configuration and z. This is the issue where we differ from our earlier paper [3] where the issue of no common key among the constituent blocks of a node has not been discussed.

Theorem 1. *Consider a $(v = rk, b = r^2, r, k)$ configuration. We merge z many randomly selected blocks to form a sensor node such that the blocks that will be merged will not have any common key among themselves.*

1. *There will be $N \leq \lfloor \frac{b}{z} \rfloor$ many sensor nodes.*
2. *The number of shared keys between any two nodes approximately follow the binomial distribution $\mathcal{B}\left(z^2, p_1\right)$, where $p_1 = \frac{k}{r+1}$.*
3. *The probability that any two nodes share no common key is $(1 - p_1)^{z^2}$.*
4. *The expected number of keys shared between two nodes is $z^2 p_1$.*
5. *Each node will contain $M = zk$ many distinct keys.*

Proof. The first item is easy to see.

Now consider the item 2. Consider the basic (v, b, r, k) configuration. Each block corresponds to a sensor node. If one considers the average number of common keys between a given node and any other node, the expression is 'number of nodes that share a common key with the given node' divided by 'total number of nodes -1' which is $\frac{k(r-1)}{r^2-1} = \frac{k}{r+1}$. This can also be seen as a probability $p_1 = \frac{k}{r+1}$ that two randomly chosen blocks share a common key. If the blocks are merged randomly, then one block of one node (z many options) can share a common key with another block in another node (again z many options) with a probability p_1. Thus there are in total z^2 many ways of choosing one block each from two distinct nodes. In each of the z^2 cases (number of trials), the probability of sharing a key between the blocks (success probability) is p_1. Thus the number of shared keys between any two nodes follows the binomial distribution $\mathcal{B}(z^2, p_1)$. The only deviation from the assumptions of Binomial distribution in our case is the constraint that the blocks are merged in a manner such that they do not share a common key. However, as z is very small compared to r^2, this does not disturb assumptions of the binomial distribution significantly. We have also run sufficient number of experiments to confirm this justification. Hence the number of shared keys between any two nodes approximately follows the binomial distribution $\mathcal{B}(z^2, p_1)$.

The proof of items 3, 4 are easy to see and are also available in [3].

As the blocks in a node do not share a common key among themselves, the number of keys in a node is exactly zk. This proves item 5.   □

Note that if one merges z blocks to get a node without any restriction (as it has been studied in [3]), then according to the previous discussion, the z blocks will share $\binom{z}{2}p_1$ many keys among themselves on an average. Thus if there are N many nodes, the expected number of links, that will be wasted for intra-node common keys, is $N\binom{z}{2}\frac{k}{r+1}$. Thus in the method proposed in this paper, we gain $N\binom{z}{2}\frac{k}{r+1}$ many secret links in the overall sensor network than what proposed in [3]. That is the gain in number of secret links per node is $\binom{z}{2}\frac{k}{r+1}$ with this strategy than what was described in [3].

Note that with the Heuristic 1 it is not always possible to get the merging so that we get exactly $\lfloor \frac{b}{z} \rfloor$ many sensor nodes. Consider a $(v = 101 \cdot 7, b = 101^2, r = 101, k = 7)$ configuration and merging of $z = 4$ blocks to get a node. Thus there will be $N = 2550$ many nodes at maximum. We attempted 1000 many runs for this merging to get the maximum number of nodes, i.e., $N = 2550$, and we got success in 909 many cases. The rest of the 91 cases, where the heuristic was not successful, we could reach very close to 2550, in fact in all the cases we could reach at least up to 2547.

Next we like to calculate the proportion of links disturbed if s nodes are compromised. This can also be seen as the probability that a random link cannot be used after compromise of s many random nodes. This is referred as $fail(s)$ in [11]. We refer to this here as $Fail(s)$ as the way we calculate this is different than that of [11].

The following example illustrates the experimental results and we show that using our technique we get better (lower) $Fail(s)$ value than [3] as evident from Table 1. Consider a $(v = 101 \cdot 7, b = 101^2, r = 101, k = 7)$ configuration and merging of $z = 4$ blocks to get a node. Thus there will be 2550 many nodes. In such a situation we present the proportion of links disturbed if s many $(1 \leq s \leq 10)$ nodes are compromised, i.e., this can also be seen as the probability that two nodes get disconnected which were connected earlier (by one or more links). In Table 1 we present the comparison. The experimental results are the average of 100 runs for each s.

Table 1. Comparison of experimental $Fail(s)$ values

s	1	2	3	4	5	6	7	8	9	10
Expt. ([3])	0.022987	0.045345	0.068904	0.090670	0.114853	0.135298	0.158633	0.181983	0.203342	0.222167
Expt.(our)	0.022595	0.044146	0.067136	0.091243	0.112162	0.133693	0.157884	0.178895	0.200226	0.219273

In the experiments, s number of nodes are selected at random and all the keys contained therein are discarded. The changed situation is evaluated afresh, in particular, the increase in the number of nodes disconnected is noted and the relative increase is calculated. This is in fact the definition of $Fail(s)$.

3.1   Comparison with [11]

In the example presented in [11], the design $(v = 1470, b = 2401, r = 49, k = 30)$ has been exploited to get $N = 2401, M = 30, Q = 49, p_1 = 0.6, 1 - p_1 = 0.4$.

Table 2. Comparison with an example presented in [11]

Comparison	our (experimental)	[11]
Number of nodes	2550	2401
Number of keys per node	28	30
Probability that two nodes don't share a common key	0.309916	0.4
$Fail(s)$	0.219273	0.185714

Now we consider the $(v = 101 \cdot 7 = 707, b = 101^2 = 10201, r = 101, k = 7)$ configuration to attain a comparable design after merging. Note that in this case $p_1 = \frac{k}{r+1} = \frac{7}{102}$. We take $z = 4$. Thus $N = \lfloor \frac{10201}{4} \rfloor = 2550$. Considering the binomial distribution presented in Theorem 1(3), the theoretical probability that two nodes will not have a common key is $(1 - \frac{7}{102})^{16} = 0.32061$. Experimentally with 100 runs we find the average value as 0.309916 which is little less (better) than the theoretically estimated value. Note that this is considerably lesser than the value 0.4 presented in [11]. The average number of common keys between any two nodes is $z^2 p_1 = z^2 \frac{k}{r+1} = 16 \frac{7}{102} = 1.098039$. Experimentally with 100 runs we get it as 1.098362 on an average which is a higher (improved) value than the theoretical estimate. The values presented over here are experimental, whereas the values presented in our earlier paper [3] were theoretical.

The $Fail(s)$ value is little worse in our case than what has been achieved in [11]. The comparison in Table 2 is only to highlight the performance of our design strategy with respect to what is described in [11] and that is why we present a design with low number of common keys between any two nodes on an average. However, we will present a practical scenario in the next section where there are more number (≥ 5) of common keys (on an average) between any two nodes and consequently the design achieves much less $Fail(s)$ values.

4   A Practical Design with More Keys Shared Between Two Nodes (on an Average)

The are quite a few obvious problems in the example presented in [11] where ($v = 1470, b = 2401, r = 49, k = 30$) configuration was used to get the parameters $N = 2401, M = 30, Q = 49, p_1 = 0.6, 1 - p_1 = 0.4$.

First, the communication between any two nodes can take place in a single hop in 60% of the cases. For the rest 40%, the communication takes place in two hops (i.e., via an intermediate node). Thus the average path length between any two nodes becomes 1.4. However, had there been a common key between any two nodes, it would have remained 1 only.

Secondly, the involvement of a third node as described above increases the vulnerability to eavesdropping of the communication by a factor of 2; in the former case, the number of nodes that can decrypt the communication is $Q - 2$ and in the latter, it is $2(Q - 2)$.

Last, but not the least, the compromise of s many nodes render $1 - (1 - \frac{Q-2}{N-2})^s$ proportion of links unusable. Specifically, if there are 2401 nodes and $s = 10$, link failure is as high as 17.95%.

An increase in the number of common keys between two nodes solves these problems. However, there are also a few caveats:

1. Number of keys per node will increase subject to the constraint of storage space. If one considers 4 Kbyte of memory for key storage, 256 keys of size 128 bit (16 byte) may be stored in a sensor node. In [11–Page 4], it has been commented that storing 150 keys in a sensor node may not be practical. On the other hand, in [6–Page 47], [10–Section 5.2], scenarios have been described with 200 many keys.

2. Determining key pre-distribution schemes using combinatorial designs with a certain pre-specified number of common keys (say for example 5) between any two nodes may not be easy [5,14]. In the literature, a sensor node corresponds to a block in combinatorial design [2,11]. If a few blocks are merged to form a sensor node, the key space at each node is increased and the number of common keys between any two nodes can also be increased as per requirement. It will be demonstrated that a much better control is exercised over the design parameters in key pre-distribution algorithms by this technique.

That is, we differ from the existing works where it is considered that any two nodes will have either 0 or 1 common key and motivate a design strategy with more number of common keys. This is important from resiliency consideration in an adversarial framework since if certain nodes are compromised, the proportion of links that becomes unusable can be kept low, i.e., the connectivity of the network is less disturbed.

We start with the idea that a node can contain 128 keys and as we like to compare the scenario with [11], we will consider the number of sensor nodes ≥ 2401, as it has been used in the examples in [11].

Consider a $(v = rk, b = r^2, r = 101, k = 32)$ configuration. If one merges $z = 4$ blocks (chosen at random with the restriction that the blocks constituting a node can not share any common key among themselves) to construct a node, the following scheme is obtained (refer to Theorem 1).

1. There can be $\leq \lfloor \frac{10201}{4} \rfloor = 2550$ sensor nodes. However, we reduce the number to 2500 nodes only and found success using Heuristic 1 in all the 100 runs.
2. The probability that two nodes do not share a common key is approximately $\left(1 - \frac{32}{102}\right)^{16} = 0.002421$. The experimental value on an average is 0.002139 with 100 runs which is lesser (better) than the theoretically estimated value.
3. Expected number of keys shared between two nodes $= \frac{16 \cdot 32}{102} \geq 5.019608$. The experimental value with 100 runs is 5.021085 on an average, little better than the theoretically estimated value.
4. Each node will contain exactly 128 many distinct keys.

In the following table we present the experimental value for $Fail(s)$, where we take the average over 100 runs for each s.

Table 3. Experimental $Fail(s)$ values

s	1	2	3	4	5	6	7	8	9	10
$Fail(s)$	0.000746	0.001725	0.002888	0.004397	0.005967	0.008107	0.010413	0.013100	0.016239	0.020162

This example clearly uses more keys (128) per sensor node than the value 30 in the example of [11]. Note that directly from a (v, b, r, k) configuration, it is not possible to have $k > r$. However, in a merged system this is possible. Moreover, the average number of keys shared between any two nodes is ≥ 5. It is not easy to get a combinatorial design [12] to achieve such a goal directly. This shows the versatility of the design proposed by us.

5   A Lower Bound on Number of Merged Nodes

In order to obtain a bound on the number of nodes that can be formed by coalescing disjoint blocks, a simple strategy is proposed here. Consider a $(v = rk, b = r^2, r, k)$ configuration which essentially comprises of r^2 number of blocks, arranged in the form of a $r \times r$ matrix. The rows and columns are indexed by

$0, 1, \cdots, r - 1$. It is easy to see that all the blocks belonging to the same row are disjoint since there is no repetition of any key and each key occurs exactly once in each row (see also [3–Section 4] for more details). So if one fixes a row and chooses z number of blocks to form a node, then there will not be any common key among the blocks forming the node. Thus one gets $\lfloor \frac{r}{z} \rfloor$ number of nodes from each row and $r \bmod z$ number of blocks will be left over in each row. So, at least $r \lfloor \frac{r}{z} \rfloor$ many sensor nodes will be formed such that no node will contain intra-node key(s). Thus given a (v, b, r, k) design, it is always possible to construct at least $r \lfloor \frac{r}{z} \rfloor$ many sensor nodes under the constraint we propose here and we have the following result.

Theorem 2. *Referring to Theorem 1 $N \geq r \lfloor \frac{r}{z} \rfloor$.*

It may be noted that the lower bound on N is independent of k.

After that one may additionally try to form other nodes by using the residual $r(r \bmod z)$ number of blocks ($r \bmod z$ number of blocks in each row and there are r rows. This we have done by trial and error and we could be successful in reaching $N = \lfloor \frac{b}{z} \rfloor$ (the upper bound) for the $(v = kr, b = r^2, r = 101, k)$ configurations with $k = 7, 32$ and merging value $z = 4$. We have experimented with 100 runs for each of the two cases $k = 7, 32$. The parameters are almost same for this strategy as the case of outputs from Heuristic 1 except the following parameter.

Note that this technique suffers from a limitation viz. all the $\lfloor \frac{r}{z} \rfloor$ many nodes formed from a single row won't share any common key among themselves. This gives an immediate lower bound for the parameter "proportion of nodes that do not share any common keys among themselves" as there will be no common key among $\binom{\lfloor \frac{r}{z} \rfloor}{2}$ many nodes formed from a single row and further there are r such rows. Thus the lower bound is $\frac{r \binom{\lfloor \frac{r}{z} \rfloor}{2}}{N}$ which is again independent of k. Moreover, apart from these, there may be other nodes generated from blocks belonging to different rows. This is the reason we find that this strategy is worse than the Heuristic 1 as k increases. In this strategy, for $k = 7$, this parameter is 0.314226 with $N = 2550$ (Heuristic 1 gives 0.309916, $N = 2550$) and for $k = 32$, this parameter is 0.016083 with $N = 2550$ (Heuristic 1 gives 0.002421, $N = 2500$).

Currently we are attempting to devise some modified merging strategy that will result in minimum number of disjoint blocks.

6   Conclusion

The contribution of this paper is the proposal of a heuristic improvement of the randomized block merging strategy in proposing a key pre-distribution scheme for secure communication among the sensor nodes [3]. In this case we present a strategy for merging blocks in a (v, b, r, k) configuration in such a manner that the blocks constituting a node will not share any common key among themselves. This provides a better (secure) connectivity in the network than our existing scheme [3]. Obviously, non-availability of combinatorial designs that meets user requirements is the prime mover of this merging strategy. We present approximate theoretical analysis and supporting experimental results to justify our claims. The central idea of our strategy is to have more number of common keys among sensor nodes to provide secure communication than the idea of low number of common keys that have been presented in [11]. Towards the end we also present some lower bound results on the number of nodes generated from a specific combinatorial design obeying the constraints we mention. We are currently working on getting an improved strategy from this idea so that any pair of nodes can share at least one common key.

References

1. R. Blom. An optimal class of symmetric key generation systems. Eurocrypt 84, pages 335–338, LNCS 209, 1985.
2. S. A. Camtepe and B. Yener. Combinatorial design of key distribution mechanisms for wireless sensor networks. Eurosics 2004.
3. D. Chakrabarti, S. Maitra and B. Roy. A Key Pre-distribution Scheme for Wireless Sensor Networks: Merging Blocks in Combinatorial Design. To be presented in *8th Information Security Conference, ISC'05*, Lecture Notes in Computer Science, volume 3650, Springer Verlag.
4. H. Chan, A. Perrig, and D. Song. Random key predistribution schemes for sensor networks. IEEE Symposium on Research in Security and Privacy, pages 197–213, 2003.
5. C. J. Colbourn, J. H. Dinitz. The CRC Handbook of Combinatorial Designs. CRC Press, 1996.
6. W. Du, J. Ding, Y. S. Han, and P. K. Varshney. A pairwise key pre-distribution scheme for wireles sensor networks. Proceedings of the 10th ACM conference on Computer and Communicatios Security, Pages 42–51, ACM CCS 2003.
7. L. Eschenauer and V. B. Gligor. A key-management scheme for distributed sensor networks. Proceedings of the 9th ACM conference on Computer and Communicatios Security, Pages 41–47, ACM CCS 2002.
8. J. M. Kahn, R. H. Katz and K. S. J. Pister. Next century challenges: Mobile networking for smart dust. Proceedings of the 5th annual ACM/IEEE international conference on mobile computing and networking, pages 483–492, 1999.
9. D. Stinson. Cryptography: Theory and Practice (Second Edition). Chapman & Hall, CRC Press, 2002.
10. J. Lee and D. Stinson. Deterministic key predistribution schemes for distributed sensor networks. SAC 2004.
11. J. Lee and D. Stinson. A combinatorial approach to key predistribution for distributed sensor networks. IEEE Wireless Computing and Networking Conference (WCNC 2005), 13–17 March, 2005, New Orleans, LA, USA.
12. A. P. Street and D. J. Street. Combinatorics of experimental design. Clarendon Press, Oxford, 1987.
13. D. Liu, and P. Ning. Establishing pairwise keys in distributed sensor networks. Proceedings of the 10th ACM conference on Computer and Communicatios Security, ACM CCS 2003.
14. D. R. Stinson. Combinatorial Designs: Constructions and Analysis. Springer, New York, 2003.

Detecting ARP Spoofing: An Active Technique

Vivek Ramachandran[1] and Sukumar Nandi[2]

[1] Cisco Systems, Inc., Bangalore India
[2] Indian Institute of Technology, Guwahati, Assam, India

Abstract. The Address Resolution Protocol (ARP) due to its stateless-
ness and lack of an authentication mechanism for verifying the identity
of the sender has a long history of being prone to spoofing attacks. ARP
spoofing is sometimes the starting point for more sophisticated LAN
attacks like denial of service, man in the middle and session hijacking.
The current methods of detection use a passive approach, monitoring
the ARP traffic and looking for inconsistencies in the Ethernet to IP address mapping. The main drawback of the passive approach is the time
lag between learning and detecting spoofing. This sometimes leads to
the attack being discovered long after it has been orchestrated. In this
paper, we present an active technique to detect ARP spoofing. We inject ARP request and TCP SYN packets into the network to probe for
inconsistencies. This technique is faster, intelligent, scalable and more
reliable in detecting attacks than the passive methods. It can also additionally detect the real mapping of MAC to IP addresses to a fair degree
of accuracy in the event of an actual attack.

1 Introduction

The ARP protocol is one of the most basic but essential protocols for LAN communication. The ARP protocol is used to resolve the MAC address of a host given
its IP address. This is done by sending an ARP request packet (broadcasted) on
the network. The concerned host now replies back with its MAC address in an
ARP reply packet (unicast). In some situations a host might broadcast its own
MAC address in a special Gratuitous ARP packet. All hosts maintain an ARP
cache where all address mappings learnt from the network (dynamic entries) or
configured by the administrator (static entries) are kept. The dynamic entries
age out after a fixed interval of time, which varies across operating systems.
After the entry ages out it is deleted from the cache and if the host wants to
communicate with the same peer, another ARP request is made. The static entries never age out. A more detailed discussion of the ARP protocol is available
at [1].

The ARP protocol is stateless. Hosts will cache all ARP replies sent to them
even if they had not sent an explicit ARP request for it. Even if a previous un-
expired dynamic ARP entry is there in the ARP cache it will be overwritten by
a newer ARP reply packet on most operating systems. All hosts blindly cache
the ARP replies they receive, as they have no mechanism to authenticate their
peer. This is the root problem, which leads to ARP spoofing.

S. Jajodia and C. Mazumdar (Eds.): ICISS 2005, LNCS 3803, pp. 239–250, 2005.

ARP spoofing is the process of forging ARP packets to be able to impersonate another host on the network. In the most general form of ARP spoofing the attacker sends spoofed ARP responses to the victim periodically. The period between the spoofed responses is much lesser than the ARP cache entry timeout period for the operating system running on the victim host. This will ensure that the victim host would never make an ARP request for the host whose address the attacker is impersonating. Following subsection briefly discuss the current detection and mitigation techniques.

1.1 Current Mitigation and Detection Techniques

Existing ARP spoofing detection techniques are discussed next sequentially.

1.1.1 Secure ARP Protocol (S-ARP)

This has been proposed as a replacement for the ARP protocol in [10]. The S-ARP protocol is definitely a permanent solution to ARP spoofing but the biggest drawback is that we will have to make changes to the network stack of all the hosts. This is not very scalable as going for a stack upgrade across all available operating systems is something both vendors and customers will not be happy about. As S-ARP uses Digital Signature Algorithm (DSA) we have the additional overhead of cryptographic calculations though the authors of the paper have claimed that this overhead is not significant.

1.1.2 Static MAC Entries

Adding static MAC addresses on every host for all other hosts will not allow spoofing but is not a scalable solution at all and managing all these entries is a full time job by itself. This can fail miserably if mobile hosts such as laptops are periodically introduced into the network. Also some operating systems are known to overwrite static ARP entries if they receive Gratuitous ARP packets (GARP).

1.1.3 Kernel Based Patches

Kernel based patches such as Anticap[11] and Antidote[12] have made an attempt to protect from ARP spoofing at a individual host level. Anticap[11] does not allow updating of the host ARP cache by an ARP reply that carries a different MAC address then the one already in the cache. This unfortunately makes it drop legal gratuitous ARP replies as well, which is a violation to the ARP protocol specification [1]. Antidote [12] on receiving an ARP reply whose MAC address differs from the previously cached one tries to check if the previously learnt MAC is still alive. If the previously learnt MAC is still alive then the update is rejected and the offending MAC address is added to a list of banned addresses.

Both the above techniques rely on the fact that the ARP entry in the cache is the legitimate one. This creates a race situation between the attacker and the victim. If the attacker gets his spoofed ARP entry into the hosts cache before the real host can, then the real MAC address is banned. This can only be undone by administrative intervention. Thus we can conclude that wrong learning may cause these tools to fail in detecting ARP spoofing.

1.1.4 Passive Detection

In Passive Detection we sniff the ARP requests/responses on the network and construct a MAC address to IP address mapping database. If we notice a change in any of these mappings in future ARP traffic then we raise an alarm and conclude that an ARP spoofing attack is underway. The most popular tool in this category is ARPWATCH [9].

The main drawback of the passive method is a time lag between learning the address mappings and subsequent attack detection. In a situation where the ARP spoofing began before the detection tool was started for the first time, the tool will learn the forged replies in it's IP to MAC address mapping database. Now only after the victim starts communicating with some other host the inconsistency will be detected and an alarm raised. The attacker may have made his getaway because of this delay. Also a spoofed entry learned as in the above scenario would have to be manually undone by the network administrator. The only solution to this problem is to manually feed the correct address mappings into the database before starting the tool or create an attack free learning traffic. Both of these are unreasonable due to scalability and mobility issues. An ideal example would be mobile hosts e.g. laptops brought in by customers or visitors to a company. This slow learning curve makes it impossible to install passive tools on a large network (1000+ hosts) and expect them to identify attacks instantaneously.

The passive techniques do not have any intelligence and blindly look for a mismatch in the ARP traffic with their learnt database tables. If an ARP spoofing is detected than there is no way of ascertaining if the newly seen address mapping is because of a spoofing attempt or the previously learnt one was actually a spoofed one. Our technique will determine the real MAC to IP mapping during an actual attack to a fair degree of accuracy.

The passive learning technique is also very unreliable. A new address mapping is learnt when ARP traffic is seen from them. Thus a switch ARP Cache table overflow attempt by the generation of random ARP reply packets per second with arbitrary MAC and IP addresses will just result in new stations being discovered instead of being reported as attack traffic. To overcome problems in earlier techniques, we present a new ARP spoofing detection technique. Our technique uses an active approach to detect ARP spoofing. We send out ARP request and TCP SYN packets to probe the authenticity of the ARP traffic we see in the network. The approach is faster, intelligent, scalable and more reliable in detecting attacks than the passive methods. It can also additionally detect the real mapping of MAC to IP addresses to a fair degree of accuracy in the event of an actual attack. A description of the technique in detail is reported in following sections.

2   The Proposed Active Detection Technique for ARP Spoofing

The proposed technique actively interacts with the network to gauge the presence of ARP spoofing attacks. We will henceforth assume the following about the network we desire to protect.

2.1   Assumptions

1. The attacker's computer has a normal network stack. This assumption will hold for most of the attacks as "ready to use" ARP spoofing tools [8] have always been the attacker's most popular choice. If the attacker does use a customized stack then our technique will still detect ARP spoofing but will not be able to predict the correct address mappings anymore. We will discuss performance in the presence of a customized stack in section 2.5.
2. The individual hosts we desire to protect on the network may use a personal firewall but at least one TCP port should be allowed through the firewall. This is to allow our probe packets (TCP SYN packets) to go through. This is a reasonable assumption as even if a firewall is installed some LAN based services such as NETBIOS etc are normally allowed through it for LAN communication.
3. We assume that all devices, which we protect, have a TCP/IP network stack up and running.

2.2   Terminology

We now introduce the terminology used in the rest of this paper.

1. *Threshold interval*: ARP replies to an ARP request must be received within a specified time interval. After this time has elapsed we will consider the ARP request to have "expired". We will call this interval as the *"Threshold Interval"*. This will be administratively configurable on any tool using our technique.

2. *Host Database*: This is the mapping of all legitimate IP and MAC pairs on the network verified and learnt by our technique.

The ARP packets consist of the MAC header and the ARP header. Based on the value of the source and destination MAC addresses in the MAC header and as advertised in the ARP header we can divide the all ARP packets into 2 categories.

1. *Inconsistent Header ARP packets*: The MAC addresses in the MAC and ARP header differ i.e. Source MAC address in MAC header! = Source MAC address in ARP header (in ARP requests/responses) and/or Destination MAC address in MAC header! = Destination address in ARP header (only for ARP replies).
2. *Consistent Header ARP packets*: These are the compliment of the *Inconsistent Header ARP packets*. The MAC addresses in the MAC and ARP headers match in these packets.

Note that *Inconsistent Header ARP packets* are guaranteed spoofed packets, as such an anomaly is only possible in attack traffic. Based on the above classification we can further bunch the *Consistent Header ARP packets* into three groups:

1. *Full ARP Cycle*: An ARP request and it's corresponding ARP replies seen within the *threshold interval*.

2. *Request Half Cycle*: An ARP request for which no replies are sent as seen within the *threshold time*.

3. *Response Half Cycle:* An ARP reply generated without an ARP request.

These three categories form the basis of our input to the ARP spoofing detection mechanism. The following subsection discusses the Architecture of the proposed technique in detail.

2.3   Architecture

Please refer to Figure 1 for the architecture discussion. We have adopted a modularized approach and have divided our spoof detection into the following modules:

1. *ARP Sniffer module*: This sniffs all ARP traffic from the network.

2. *MAC - ARP header anomaly detector module*: This module classifies the ARP traffic into *Inconsistent Header ARP packets* and *Consistent Header ARP packets.*

3. *Known Traffic Filter module*: This filters all the traffic, which is already learnt. It will either drop the packet if the Ip to MAC mapping is coherent with the learnt Host Database or raise an alarm if there are any contradictions. All the new ARP packets with unknown addresses are sent to the *Spoof Detection Engine* for verification.

4. *Spoof Detection Engine module:* This is the main detection engine. We feed the *Consistent Header ARP packets* to it as input. The design of this module will be discussed in Section 2.4.

5. *Add to Database Module*: Legitimate ARP entries verified by the *Spoof Detection Engine* are added to the *Host Database* by this module.

6. *Spoof Alarm Module*: This module raises an alarm on detection of ARP spoofing by sending a mail, SMS etc to the administrator.

As shown in Figure 1, the *ARP Sniffer* module sniffs all the ARP traffic in its LAN segment and passes it to the *MAC – ARP Header Anomaly Detector*. This module passes the entire *Consistent Header ARP packets* to the *Known Traffic Filter* module. The entire *Inconsistent Header ARP packets* are sent to the Spoof Alarm. This is done because the *Inconsistent Header ARP packets* are all spoofed packets as discussed earlier. The *Known Traffic Filter* module will remove all traffic coherent with the already learnt addresses by consulting the

Host Database. If there is a contradiction in the ARP traffic for already learnt addresses then it raises a *Spoof Alarm.* All new ARP traffic is passed to the *Spoof Detection Engine.*

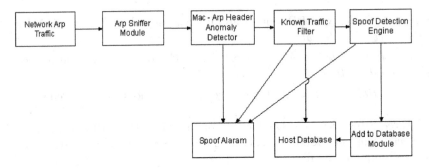

Fig. 1. Inter-relation between various Modules used by the ARP Spoof Detection Algorithm

The *Spoof Detection Engine* applies our detection algorithm to detect ARP spoofing. The newly seen Consistent *Header ARP packets* are input to this module. The engine now internally bunches these packets into the three categories discussed in Section 2.2 namely *Full ARP Cycle, Request* and *Response Half Cycle*packets. The detection algorithm applied by the engine will be discussed in the section 2.4. After applying the detection algorithm the *Spoof Detection engine* either sends the ARP entry to the *Add to Database* module or the *Spoof Alarm* module. The *Add to Database* module will add these verified MAC and IP address mapping to the *Host Database.* The *spoof detection engine* is discussed in detail next.

2.4   The Spoof Detection Engine

The *Spoof Detection Engine* is the heart of the whole system. The three different ARP Cycle packets as discussed in Section 2.2 are treated in slightly different ways by the *Spoof Detection Engine* to detect an attempted spoofing. The *Spoof Detection Engine* works based on the following Rules:

Rule A: "The network interface card of a host will accept packets sent to its MAC address, Broadcast address and subscribed multicast addresses. It will pass on these packets to the IP layer. The IP layer will only accept IP packets addressed to its IP address(s) and will silently discard the rest of the packets. If the accepted packet is a TCP packet it is passed on to the TCP layer. If a TCP SYN packet is received then the host will either respond back with a TCP SYN/ACK packet if the destination port is open or with a TCP RST packet if the port is closed".

Rule B: "The attacker can spoof ARP packets impersonating a host but he can never stop the real host from replying to ARP requests (or any other packet) sent to it. The valid assumption here is that the real host is up on the network."

It should be noted that these rules have been derived from the correct behavior that a host's network stack should exhibit when it receives a packet. To exemplify Rule A, let a host have MAC address = X and IP address = Y. If this host receives a packet with destination MAC address = X and destination IP address = Z then even though the network interface card would accept the packet as the destination MAC address matches, the host's network stack will silently discard this packet as the destination IP address does not match, without sending any error messages back to the source of the packet.

Based on Rule A, we can conceive of two types of probe packets from a host's network stack point of view which we will use to detect ARP spoofing.

a. *Right MAC – Wrong IP packet:* The destination MAC address in the packet is of the host but the IP address is invalid and does not correspond to any of the host's addresses. The destination host will silently drop this packet.

b. *Right MAC – Right IP packet:* The destination MAC address and IP addresses pairs are of the host's and its network stack accepts it.

We will henceforth assume that the attacker is using an unmodified network stack. The performance of our technique in the presence of a modified network stack will be evaluated in Section 2.5. Based on the above observation we will construct our own packets based on *Rule A* and send them on the network. We will use the address information in the ARP response packet sent by the host whose authenticity is to be verified. We will use the MAC and IP addresses used in the ARP response packet to construct a TCP SYN packet i.e. the destination MAC and IP in the TCP SYN packet will be the source MAC and IP address advertised in the ARP response packet and the source MAC and IP in the TCP SYN packet would be of the host running the *Spoof Detection Engine*. The TCP destination port will be chosen based on the presence/absence of packet filtering firewalls on the network hosts. If there is a firewall installed on the hosts we will choose the "allowed TCP port" (as in section 2.1) and if no firewalls are there then we can choose any TCP port. The rest of the header values in the TCP SYN packet will be set as usual.

When a TCP SYN packet as constructed above is sent to the source of the ARP reply packet, the host's response will be based on Rule A. If the ARP response was from the real host its IP stack will respond back with either a TCP RST packet (If the destination port is closed) or a TCP SYN/ACK packet (if the destination port is open).

If the ARP response had been from a malicious host then its network stack would silently discard the TCP SYN packet in accordance with Rule A. Thus based on the fact that the *Spoof Detection Engine* does/does not receive any TCP packets in return to the SYN packet it sent, it can judge the authenticity of the received ARP response packet.

We will now discuss how Rules A and B can be used together to detect ARP spoofing attempts in a network. Please refer to Figure 2 for a diagrammatic representation of the algorithm in the form of a flow chart. As we had mentioned earlier the ARP packets are classified into the 3 cycles namely *Full ARP Cycle, Request* and*Response Half Cycles* and then fed as input to the *Spoof Detection Engine*. We will now discuss the application of the above discussed technique to these 3 Cycles to detect ARP spoofing.

2.4.1 Full ARP Cycle

A *Full ARP Cycle* will consist of an ARP request and one or more responses. We will send TCP SYN packet(s) constructed using the MAC and IP address information in the ARP reply packet(s) to the source host(s) as mentioned previously in Section 2.4. Based on *Rule A* only the real host will reply back with either a TCP SYN/ACK or RST packet. We will add this entry into our *Host Database* as a legitimate MAC to IP address mapping. All other ARP replies which were part of the recorded *Full ARP Cycle* are spoofed replies and the module will raise a *Spoof Alarm* for their addresses.

Note that not only we have detected spoofing but also have successfully detected the MAC to IP address mapping of the true host on the network, as only the true host's network stack replies to TCP SYN probes as per *Rule A*.

2.4.2 Request Half Cycle

A *Request half cycle* might arise when either the destination host is down on the network. If the source IP of the ARP request packet is unknown and not in our *Host Database* then we will send a TCP SYN packet constructed as mentioned in Section 2.4 from the source MAC and IP address information advertised in the ARP request packet. If we get a TCP SYN/ACK or RST packet in response then the host is authentic else we raise a *Spoof Alarm*. As an alternative way of detecting spoofing we also send an ARP Request packet to the sender of the *Request Half Cycle* and we will raise a *Spoof Alarm* if we do not get the same MAC address in the ARP Response packet from the host in return. We will use both these mechanisms simultaneously to detect spoofing. The latter method will come in handy when the attacker uses a customized stack which we will discuss in Section 2.5. Figure 1 only contains the TCP method flow for simplicity.

2.4.3 Response Half Cycle

A *Response Half Cycle* could arise because of two situations:

1. It is an ARP spoofing attempt by a malicious attacker. This is one of the most common ways of orchestrating an ARP spoofing by sending periodic spoofed ARP response packets to the victims so that the spoofed address entry never expires in the victim's ARP cache.

2. We may have missed the ARP request. This may happen if the detection tool just came online after the ARP request was sent and so we could only

sniff the ARP response. Another remote possibility is we missed a packet because of a huge number of packets coming in and inadequate buffer space in the input queue.

To probe the authenticity of the sender of the ARP response we first send an ARP request packet corresponding to the ARP response packet i.e. the destination IP address in the constructed ARP request = the source IP address of the received ARP response and the source IP address of the constructed ARP request = *Spoof Detection Engine's* host's IP address. The Source MAC address of the constructed ARP request = *Spoof Detection Engine's* host's MAC address and the destination MAC address will be the broadcast address.

By *Rule B* even if an attacker is spoofing ARP packets on the network he cannot stop the real host from replying to an ARP request sent to it. As the destination MAC address of an ARP request is the broadcast address so every host will receive it. Thus when we send the above packet out to the network there could be two possible responses:

1. *One or more ARP responses:* We will now consider our ARP request and these ARP responses as a single Full ARP Cycle. This Full ARP Cycle will now be dealt with as in Section 2.4.1 to detect spoofing.

2. *No ARP responses:* If we do not receive any ARP responses than most probably the real host is down and the ARP responses we see are by an impersonating attacker. To detect this we send a TCP SYN packet constructed as in Section 2.4 based on the information in the received ARP response packet. We will find that the impersonating host will not reply to this TCP packet as its network stack will discard it according to *Rule A* and we will raise a Spoof Alarm.

Thus we have successfully shown how we can detect ARP spoofing attacks in a network using our active injection technique. Till now we have assumed that the attacker is using a normal network stack and orchestrates all these attacks with ready to use tools such as ARP-SK [8]. We will now discuss the performance of our technique in the presence of a customized network stack used by the attacker.

2.5   Attacker Uses a Customized Stack

Let us assume that the attacker is aware of our proposed method and has customized his network stack to reply to the TCP SYN packets and ARP request packets destined for the real host, he desires to impersonate. Even in such a scenario we will be able to detect ARP spoofing successfully using *Rule B*. The only limitation now would be that we would not be able to detect the real MAC and IP address as in the previous case.

Almost all ARP spoofing techniques continuously send spoofed ARP response packets to the victims. This is done so that the victim never needs to raise an ARP request, as the ARP cache entry for the host who's MAC is being spoofed never ages out. But if we send an ARP request on the network, requesting for

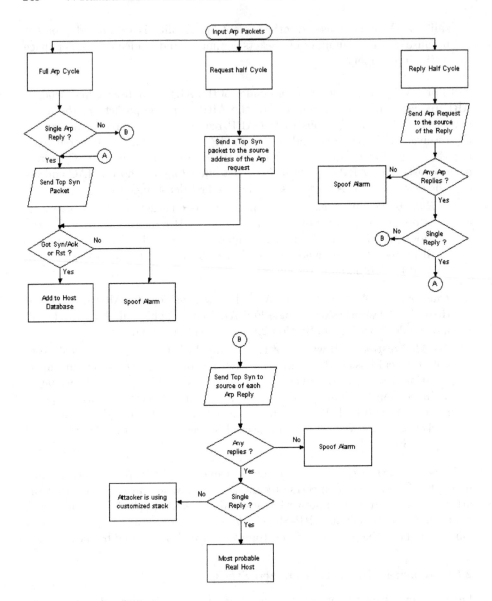

Fig. 2. Flow Chart Representation of the Spoof Detection Engine

the MAC address of the host (whose address is being spoofed) the host will reply with an ARP response packet (Rule B). Now we will have a MAC address mismatch for the same IP as the spoofed replies sent by the attacker previously will carry a different MAC address.

We will now discuss our performance for a customized network stack in the light of the ARP Cycles:

1. *Full ARP Cycle*: If spoofing is on then, both the Attacker and the real host will reply to the original ARP request and we can detect a conflict in the MAC address for the same IP. Also if we send a TCP SYN packet to the source address of both the ARP replies than we will receive two TCP packets in response as the attacker's customized stack replies as well along with the real host. This makes it very easy to detect spoofing.

2. *Request Half Cycle*: As outlined in Section 2.4.2 we will try to authenticate the sender of the request by sending an ARP request packet back to the sender and check the reply(s) for spoofing. If the source MAC addresses in the ARP reply packet received for the injected ARP request does not match the MAC address in the ARP *Request Half Cycle* packet then we will raise a *Spoof Alarm*.

3. *Reply Half Cycle*: If a customized stack is used we will get multiple replies to the ARP request we send as in Section 2.4.3. Also when we send out TCP SYN packets to the sources of the ARP request we will get multiple TCP (SYN/ACK or RST) packets in return with different MAC addresses. This is enough to conclude that a spoofing is going on.

Note that though we can detect ARP spoofing even in the presence of an attacker aware of our methods and using a customized stack we cannot predict the correct MAC to IP address mapping. This is the only limitation of our method in the presence of a customized stack.

3   Comparison with Passive Techniques

Our technique is clearly much faster and reliable than the passive detection techniques. This technique can be used in a large network and it will immediately detect ARP spoofing attacks even if the attack had begun before the tool using our technique was operational. This is because the time lag between learning and detection is very less as we probe the authenticity of hosts as soon as we see ARP traffic from them. Also our technique verifies the authenticity of the ARP traffic on the network and does not blindly add newly seen traffic to its database. Even in the event of an actual attack our technique can detect the correct IP to MAC address mapping of the real host in the absence of the attacker using a customized network stack. If the attacker uses a customized stack, which replies to our probes we are still able to detect ARP spoofing but will not be able to predict the real MAC to IP address mapping. So even in our worst-case scenario (in the presence of a customized stack) our performance is still better than using a Passive detection technique.

4   Conclusion

This paper proposed an active technique to detect ARP spoofing. We have shown that our technique is much faster, intelligent and scalable compared to passive detection techniques. Our technique also detects the correct MAC to IP address mapping during an actual attack. In presence of a customized stack, our detection algorithm will still detect ARP spoofing, though it is not be able to infer the correct address mapping. As we are using an active method to probe the authenticity of ARP traffic on a per packet basis, the time lag between learning new addresses and detecting spoofing is minimum. The network overhead due to the packet injection by us is fairly minimal as we send one ARP request and one TCP SYN packet per host on the network and then infer their authenticity based on the replies to our packets. Also as these packets are sent out only once for every host, for the entire lifetime of the tool, it makes it very scalable even for large networks.

References

1. D Plummer, "An Ethernet Address Resolution Protocol", RFC-826, USC Information Science Institute, California, November 1982. http://www.ietf.org/rfc/rfc0826.txt
2. Stevens, W. Richard. "TCP/IP Illustrated, Volume 1. The Protocols". Addison Wesley Longman, Inc, 1994. ISBN: 0201633469.
3. R.Wagner, "Address Resolution Protocol Spoofing and Man in the Middle Attacks" http://rr.sans.org/threats/address.php,2001.
4. A. Ornaghi and M. Valleri, "A multipurpose sniffer for switched LANs" http://ettercap.sf.net.
5. AtStake.com. Etherleak: Ethernet frame padding information leakage.http://www.atstake.com/ research/advisories/2003/a010603-1.txt, 2003.
6. Althes. "The IP Smart spoofing", InterOp Paris 2002. http://www.althes.fr/ressources/avis/smartspoofing.htm
7. Yuri Volobuev. "Redir games with ARP and ICMP". http://lists.insecure.org/lists/bugtraq/1997/Sep/0059.html
8. Fredric Raynal, Eric Detoisien, Cedric Blancher, "ARP-SK: a swiss knife tool for ARP". http://www.ARP-sk.org/
9. Lawrence Berkeley National Laboratory , "ARPWATCH tool": ARP Spoofing Detector. ftp://ftp.ee.lbl.gov/ARPwatch.tar.gz
10. Danilo Bruschi, Alberto Ornaghi, Emilia Rosti , "S-ARP: a Secure Adderess Resolution Protocol" 19th Annual Computer Security Applications Conference, 2003, www.acsac.org/2003/papers/111.pdf
11. M. Barnaba, "Anticap" http://cvs.antifork.org/cvsweb.cgi/anticap, 2003
12. I. Teterin , "Antidote" http://online.securityfocus.com/archive/1/299929

Episode Based Masquerade Detection

Subrat Kumar Dash, Krupa Sagar Reddy, and Arun K. Pujari

AI Lab, University of Hyderabad, Hyderabad - 500 046, India
techno_subrat@yahoo.co.in, krupa.sagar@gmail.com,
akpcs@uohyd.ernet.in

Abstract. Masquerade detection is one of major concerns of system security research due to two main reasons. Such an attack cannot be detected at the time of access and any detection technique relies on user's signature and even a legitimate user is likely to deviate from its usual usage pattern. In the recent years, there have been several proposals to efficiently detect masquerader while keeping the false alarm rate as low as possible. One of the recent technique, Naive Bayes with truncated command line, has been very successful in maintaining low false alarm rate. This method depends on probability of individual commands. It is more appropriate to consider meaningful groups of commands rather than individual commands. In this paper we propose a method of masquerade detection by considering episodes, meaningful subsequences of commands. The main contributions of the present work are (i) an algorithm to determine episode from a long sequence of commands, and (ii) a technique to use these episodes to detect masquerade block of commands. Our experiments with standard datasets such as SEA dataset reveal that the episode based detection is a more useful masquerade detection technique.

1 Introduction

One of the challenges in computer security is masquerade attack where an illegitimate entity poses as (and assumes the identity of) a legitimate entity. The illegitimate user, called *masquerader*, hides his/her identity by impersonating a legitimate user in a computer system or network and may maliciously damage the system. Masquerade attack can occur in varieties of ways such as by obtaining a legitimate user's password, accessing an unattended and unlocked workstation, forging email address in messages, overtaking a computer via a network access. It is not possible to detect such attacks by any type of detection at the time of accessing. It is also hard to detect this type of security breach at its initiation because the attacker appears to be a normal user with valid authority and privileges. Masquerader can be either an insider with malicious intent trying to hide his identity by impersonating other users or an outsider, who generally try to gain access to the account of the super-user. The broad range of damage that can be caused via masquerade attacks makes this as one of the most serious threats to computer and network infrastructure.

S. Jajodia and C. Mazumdar (Eds.): ICISS 2005, LNCS 3803, pp. 251–262, 2005.

The detection of a masquerader relies on a user signature, a sequence of commands collected from a legitimate user. The underlying assumption is that the signature captures detectable patterns in a user's sequence of commands. This signature is compared to the current user's session. A sequence of commands produced by the legitimate user should match well with patterns in the user signature, whereas a sequence of commands of a masquerader should match poorly with the user's signature. Based on this premise, there have been numerous attempts at successfully detecting masquerade attacks (minimizing false negatives) without degrading the quality of a user's session (minimizing false positives). The detection becomes difficult when the masquerader perfectly mimics original user's behavior. There is also a chance that the legitimate user may be detected as a masquerader if the user's behavior change, which may cause annoying false alarms.

Most of the masquerade detection techniques that are proposed in recent years depend on truncated or enriched command lines. It is assumed that individual commands play a very important role in determining legitimate or questionable behaviour of a user. But to the contrary, the usage consists of a set of commands for a particular task, rather than isolated commands. For example, dvips and gview can be viewed as one interrelated pair of commands and natural to occur together. Thus, identifying an user to be legitimate or masquerader based on individual commands is robust enough for successful identification but may generate many false positives. Thus it is more natural to have a masquerade detection technique based on episodes rather than with individual commands. To accomplish this, it is necessary to determine meaningful subsequence of commands that may define a single task or purpose.

In this paper we propose a masquerade detection technique based on episodes. We propose a novel method of determining meaningful episode from the continuous stream of commands. Our algorithm is based on boundary entropy method proposed for text segmentation in [2]. The episodes, so identified, are subjected to Naive Bayes Classification to determine masquerade episodes. When number of commands in masquerade episodes exceeds a specified count, we identify the user to be a masquerader. We demonstrate that for SEA dataset the performance of our technique is better than many earlier methods.

In Section 2 we briefly outline the existing techniques of masquerade detection. In section 3, we discuss about the standard data sets which are used for performance evaluation of this attack. Section 4 outlines a motivating example to illustrate the underlying principle of the proposed method. We propose a novel scheme based on frequency and entropy to detect meaningful episodes in Section 5. In Section 6, the masquerade detection based on episodes is described. Section 7 is concerned with the experimental details.

2   Earlier Work

In this section we review the different known techniques proposed for the purpose of masquerade detection. Schonlau et al., in [13], study various masquerade detection methods like *Bayes 1-Step Markov, Hybrid Multi-Step Markov, Incremental*

Probabilistic Action Modeling (IPAM), Uniqueness, Sequence-Match, and *Compression.* Bayes 1-Step Markov method is based on single-step transitions from one command to the next, and it determines the consistency of the observed transition probabilities with historical probabilities. Hybrid Multi-Step Markov method is a hybrid model of Markov model and a simple independence model, depending on the proportion of commands in the test data that are not observed in the training data. IPAM is based on single-step command transition probabilities, estimated from the training data. Uniqueness approach, is based on ideas about command frequency. Commands not seen in the training data may indicate a masquerade attempt and the more infrequently a command is used by the user community as a whole, the more indicative that command is of being a masquerade. Sequence-Match method computes a similarity match between the most recent user commands and a user profile. The idea behind the compression approach is that new data from a given user compresses at about the same ratio as old data from that same user, and that data from a masquerading user will compress at a different ratio and thereby be distinguished from the legitimate user.

In [10], Maxion and Townsend propose *Naive Bayes with updates* model which assumes that the user generates a sequence of commands, one command at a time, each with a fixed probability that is independent of the commands preceding it. In spite of the unrealistic assumption of independence of individual commands, the success of this technique is the best. In [11] the same author shows that valuable information is lost when *truncated* command line data is used and proposes to use *enriched* command line data which yields better results than the earlier data set of truncated commands.

In [3] Coull et al. propose a novel technique based on pair-wise sequence alignment (a variation of the classic Smith-Waterman algorithm [15] for biological sequence). In [16], it is proposed to profile a user by modeling his data exclusively, without using examples from other users. Recently, in [7], a new and efficient masquerade detection technique based on SVM is proposed. It is based on two novel concepts of *common commands* and *voting engine*. The common commands are sets of commands used frequently by more than X number of users at the rate exceeding Y%. In order to extract features, the blocks of 100 commands are further viewed as smaller blocks by sliding a smaller window within the block. SVM predictor determines whether each sub-block is normal or not. A *"Voting engine"* decides if the total block is to be considered as being anomalous. If the number of masquerade sub-blocks exceeds threshold value, the block is considered as masquerade block.

3 Data Sets

At this stage, it is apt to study the data sets that are considered to be standard for the study of command line based attacks. There are three standard datasets available for studying the characteristics of masquerade attack.

One is provided by Schonlau et al. [13], which is a truncated command dataset, commonly called as SEA dataset. Most of the techniques described above use this

Table 1. Results from previous approaches to masquerade detection

Method	Hit Rate	False Positive
SVM (1v49 configuration)	94.8%	0.0%
SVM (SEA configuration)	80.1%	9.7%
Semi-Global Alignment	75.8%	7.7%
Recursive Data Mining	75.0%	10.0%
Bayes one-step Markov	69.3%	6.7%
Naive Bayes (no updating)	66.2%	4.6%
POMDP	63.8%	1.0%
Naive Bayes (updating)	61.5%	1.3%
Hybrid Markov	49.3%	3.2%
IPAM	41.1%	2.7%
Uniqueness	39.4%	1.4%
Sequence Matching	36.8%	3.7%
Compression	34.2%	5.0%

dataset. This data is collected by UNIX *acct* auditing mechanism and consists of 15,000 "truncated" commands of 50 users. Maxion [10] proposes another configuration called *1v49 configuration*. In this configuration, the first 5,000 commands were used to build a model, and the first 5,000 commands entered by each of the rest of group, 49 users, were used as test data. This is contrary to SEA configuration where each user's rest 10,000 commands containing simulated masquerade blocks are used as test data.

Lane and Broadly [8] generated another dataset, which contains 9 sets of sanitized user data drawn from the command histories of 8 UNIX computer users over the course of up to 2 years (USER0 and USER1 were generated by the same person, working on different platforms and different projects). The data is drawn from *tcsh* history files.

Another dataset is collected by Greenberg [5], which contains data of 168 different users of University of Calgary. The users are divided into 4 groups (Novice Programmers, Experienced Programmers, Computer Scientists & Non-programmers) according to their computer experience and needs.

The performance of the methods discussed above for SEA and 1v49 configurations is summarized in Table 1.

4   Motivating Example

While experimenting with the existing techniques for different datasets, we found many interesting cases that motivated the current research. Let us consider the following example. For the User 10 of SEA dataset, the training set contains many unique commands – commands which are unique to this user. These are op-newus, pg, where, fls_star, arch_uni, op_mko, test.m2., m3_flse etc. Interestingly, in the 24th block in the test data of this user none of these commands appears. It is, however, a legitimate block for this user. On the other hand, this block contains commands like netscape and telnet, which are used by this user (in the training

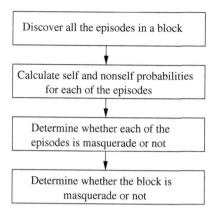

Fig. 1. Block Diagram of episode based masquerade detection algorithm

set) much less frequently than other users' use. It may be noted that `netscape` is used 9 times (6 times in a row) by User 10 and `telnet` is used 7 times (4 times in a row). Thus, the ratios of *self-probability* to *nonself-probability* of these two commands are very low and because of their repeated use, Naive Bayes technique identifies this as a masquerade block – a false positive – even when there is strong evidence of user 10 signature in commands like `launchef`.

It can be concluded that a command with low ratio, if used repeatedly for as low as 10% times, may drag the overall probability of the block to a low value yielding a false positive. This may happen even if there are other commands which have reasonably high ratio. On the other hand, if we identify episodes, the continuous stream of 6 `netscape` commands can be an episode. This subsequence would be detected as a masquerade episode. There may be nearly 20 episodes for 24th block of User 10 and only few of them are detected as masquerade. One such masquerade episode is the consecutive sequence of `netscape`. The total number of commands in all masquerade episodes is much less in proportion to the full length of the block and hence the block is recognized as a legitimate block. Thus, if a user deviates from its usual commands and uses the less frequent commands for few times, then existing algorithms may raise a false alarm. On the other hand, it would be better to recognize the episode as masquerade and if the user does not deviate too much from his own pattern set of episodes then episode based technique can still recognize the block as a legitimate one.

The proposed method is based on the foregoing discussion. We give in figure 1 the block diagram outlining the major modules of the proposed method.

5   Episode Discovery Algorithm

In this section we propose an algorithm to extract meaningful subsequences, *episodes*, from a continuous sequence of commands. We adopt the *Voting-Experts* paradigm proposed in [2]. The proposed episode discovery is concerned with assigning score to every element of the sequence so that higher value of the score indicates more likelihood of the element being the end point of an episode. The scores for each element are accumulated for each position of a sliding window of fixed length. While the window slides from left to right, the *boundary-expert* scores for a position by computing boundary entropy and the *frequency-expert* votes for the position based on the frequency of occurrence of the subsequence in the whole sequence. The main intuition behind the boundary entropy is the following.

In a subsequence, if any element precedes many distinct elements then it is difficult to determine any pattern of occurrence of the pair of elements. Hence, the entropy at this element has a very high value. On the other hand, if there is any specific pattern of occurrence then the entropy would be low. Similarly, the frequency-expert assigns high score when the subsequence is very frequent, which is attributed to being more meaningful. In order to complete these scores efficiently, it is proposed to compile the sequence data in the form of a trie of ngrams. This data structure is then used to determine the scores at every location. We describe below the construction of trie from the sequence data.

Construction of trie: The trie can be viewed as a pre-fix tree of depth d, so that each distinct subsequence of length $d - 1$ is a path from root node to a leaf node in this tree. Two subsequences having common prefix share common ancestors representing the prefix fragment. At every node, the frequency indicates the frequency of the subsequence represented by the path from root to the current node. We describe in figure 2 the algorithm for construction of the trie.

Algorithm: to construct an ngram of depth $(n + 1)$ from a command sequence C.
Input: Sequence of commands C, depth d
Initialize: root = NULL
$\qquad\qquad n = d - 1$
do for each $c_i \in C$
$\quad$ if root has a child node labelled c_i then
$\quad\quad$ increment frequency of node c_i by 1
$\quad$ else
$\quad\quad$ add new child node labeled c_i with frequency 1
$\quad$ endif
$\quad$ do for $j = i - n + 1$ to $i - 1$
$\quad\quad$ if $j > 0$ then
$\quad\quad\quad$ do for each subsequence S_k comprising of commands c_j to c_{i-1}
$\quad\quad\quad\quad$ if S_k has a child node with labeled c_i then
$\quad\quad\quad\quad\quad$ increase frequency of this node by 1.
$\quad\quad\quad\quad$ else
$\quad\quad\quad\quad\quad$ add a new child node to the subsequence S_k labeled c_i with frequency 1.
$\quad\quad\quad\quad$ endif
$\quad\quad\quad$ enddo
$\quad\quad$ endif
$\quad$ enddo
enddo

Fig. 2. The algorithm for construction of trie

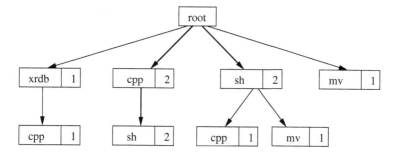

Fig. 3. Trie for Example 1 with d=3. The thickness of edges indicates the frequency.

We illustrate the concept with the following example.

Example 1: Let us consider the sequence of six commands: xrdb, cpp, sh, cpp, sh, mv. The trie with depth 3 can be generated using the algorithm as depicted in figure 3.

We can observe that the leaf node labeled sh (second from left) represents the sequence {cpp, sh} and hence the number 2 at this node indicates the frequency of the subsequence. And each of the sequences {xrdb, cpp}, {sh, cpp} and {sh, mv} is present once. The two sequences {sh, cpp} and {sh, mv}, have a common prefix {sh}, which is also the common ancestor for the corresponding nodes.

Calculation of boundary entropy using the trie: The entropy of a node refers to the entropy of the sequence from the root node to the concerned node. Let $f(x)$ be the frequency of the node x. Let x_0 be a node and $parent(x_0)$ be the parent node of x_0. Let us assume that $x_1, x_2, ..., x_m$ are the other child nodes of $parent(x_0)$.

The probability of the subsequence represented at node x_0, denoted as $p(x_0)$, is given by

$$P(x_0) = \frac{f(x_0)}{f(parent(x_0))}$$

The entropy of $parent(x_0)$ is given by

$$e(parent(x_0)) = -\sum_{i=0}^{m} p(x_i) \log p(x_i)$$

It can be noted that the entropy for the leaf nodes is zero.

Each node of the ngram trie has two parameters, one is frequency and the other is entropy (of course except the root node). Level 1 onwards, for each level, we calculate the mean frequency (f_l), mean entropy (e_l), standard deviation taking f_l (σ_{fl}), and standard deviation taking e_l (σ_{el}). These are calculated by taking the parameters of each node belonging to the same level. Now, for each node belonging to the same level we standardize its frequency (f) and entropy (e) as,

$$f = \frac{f - f_l}{\sigma_{fl}}, \text{ and } e = \frac{e - e_l}{\sigma_{el}}$$

Finding episodes using the ngram trie structure: To find episodes from the given command stream, it is necessary to find the correct boundary in the stream. We achieve this, by using the above ngram trie with two parameters: frequency and entropy. Both the parameters contribute equally in finding the possible boundary by assigning scores to the probable boundary positions.

The above trie data structure helps us in efficiently computing the entropy and frequency of a subsequence. We take a window of size n ($n+1$ is the depth of the trie) and examine different subsequences within the window. For instance, if x_0, x_1, x_2, ..., and x_{n-1} are the elements falling in the window, then we examine the entropy at each location as follows.

The entropy at location i is the entropy of the node x_i at level $i+1$ along path x_0, x_1, ..., x_i. The location corresponding to the highest entropy is identified and its score is incremented by 1.

The frequency at location i is calculated by the sum of the frequencies of subsequences $(x_0 \ldots x_{i-1})$ and $(x_i \ldots x_{n-1})$. The score at the location with highest frequency is incremented by 1. In this case, our goal is to maximize the sum of the frequencies of the left and right subsequences of the probable boundary.

We take a sliding window of length n. There are n possible boundary positions inside the window. After sliding the window across the whole command sequence, we end up with scores for each location in the sequence. In a stream of $|C|$ commands, there are $|C| - 1$ positions within the sequence. If a position is repeatedly voted for boundary by different windows then it is likely to accrue a locally-maximum score. We choose the position with local maximum of score as boundary of the episode.

Example 2: We consider the 51st block of 100 commands of user 1 of SEA dataset consisting of the following 100 commands.

```
java, .java_wr, expr, expr, dirname, basename, egrep, egrep, egrep,
egrep, egrep, java, aacdec, cat, aiffplay, sh, aacdec, cat, aiffplay, sh,
aacdec, cat, aiffplay, sh, netscape, netscape, netscape, netscape,
netscape, netscape, netscape, aacdec, cat, aiffplay, sh, netscape,
netscape, netscape, netscape, netscape, netscape, netscape, netscape,
netscape, netscape, netscape, netscape, netscape, netscape, netscape,
hostname, id, nawk, getopt, true, grep, date, lp, find, mkdir, expr,
generic, cat, file, post, awk, cat, post, rm, generic, ln, ln, generic,
lp, sh, getpgrp, LOCK, true, ls, sed, FIFO, cat, date, generic, generic,
date, generic, gethost, download, tcpostio, tcpostio, tcpostio, tcpostio,
cat, generic, ls, generic, date, generic, rm.
```

Taking depth of the trie as 5, 16 episodes are obtained as follows.

1. java, .java_wr, expr, expr, dirname, basename
2. egrep, egrep, egrep, egrep, egrep
3. java, aacdec, cat, aiffplay, sh

4. aacdec, cat, aiffplay, sh
5. aacdec, cat, aiffplay, sh
6. netscape, netscape, netscape, netscape
7. netscape, netscape, netscape
8. aacdec, cat, aiffplay, sh
9. netscape, netscape, netscape, netscape, netscape, netscape, netscape, netscape, netscape, netscape, netscape, netscape, netscape, netscape, netscape
10. hostname, id, nawk, getopt, true, grep, date, lp, find, mkdir, expr, generic, cat, file, post, awk, cat, post
11. rm, generic
12. ln, ln, generic, lp, sh, getpgrp, LOCK, true
13. ls, sed, FIFO, cat, date, generic
14. generic, date, generic
15. gethost, download, tcpostio, tcpostio, tcpostio, tcpostio
16. cat, generic, ls, generic, date, generic, rm

It can be seen that it has correctly identified {aacdec, cat, aiffplay, sh} to be an episode which occurs three times in the given sequence. The second episode in the list groups all the egrep commands occurring continuously forming a meaningful episode.

6   Masquerade Detection Based on Episodes

We also know that the behaviour of the masquerader cannot be identified just by one single command or instantaneously. Even a legitimate user may deviate from his normal behaviour for sometime. Thus, it is more appropriate to doubt a user who is consistently deviating from the normal signature rather than a user who deviates momentarily and returns to the normal pattern. Thus it is necessary to detect the episodes which may be masquerade and take into account the length of such episodes to determine the block to be masquerade. We make use of Naive Bayes algorithm given in [10] for detecting masquerade episodes.

Let C be the set of unique commands. Let C_j be the set of unique commands used by the user u_j during training and $f(c, u_j)$ be the frequency with which the command c is entered by the user u_j during training. We define following probability,

$$P(c, u_j) = \frac{f(c, u_j) + \alpha}{\sum_{c_i \in C_j} f(c_i, u_j) + \alpha|C|}$$

Similarly, we define probability of use of command c for a group of users except user u_j as

$$P(c, U_{\neq j}) = \frac{\sum_{u_k \in U \wedge k \neq j} f(c, u_k) + \alpha}{\sum_{u_k \in U \wedge k \neq j} \sum_{c_i \in C_j} f(c_i, u_k) + \alpha|C|}$$

where α is a pseudocount, and $|C|$ is the number of distinct commands in the data.

The pseudocount can be any real number larger than zero (0.01 in this study), and is added to ensure that there are no zero counts. The lower the pseudocount, the more sensitive the detector is to previously unseen commands. The pseudocount term in the denominator compensates for the addition of a pseudocount in the numerator.

Training Phase :
do for each user $u_j \in U$
    do for each unique command c_i in the training data of user u_j
        calculate $P(c_i, u_j)$ and $P(c_i, U_{\neq j})$
    enddo
enddo

Testing Phase :
For each block b_i in the testing set of a user u_j we find the set of episodes e in the block b_i. For each of the episode $e_k \in e$, we calculate the *self* and *nonself* probability of e_k as,

$$Self(e_k, u_j) = \prod_{c \in e_k} P(c, u_j)$$

$$Nonself(e_k, u_j) = \prod_{c \in e_k} P(c, U_{\neq j})$$

Then, we decide whether the episode is masquerade or legitimate depending upon the ratio of the self and nonself part calculated above, as follows,

$$Masq(e_k) = \begin{cases} 1, & \text{if } \frac{Self(e_k, u_j)}{Nonself(e_k, u_j)} \leq \lambda \\ 0, & \text{otherwise} \end{cases}$$

where, λ is a threshold. Then we compute the score of the block b_i as,

$$score(b_i) = \sum_{e_k \in b_i} |e_k| Masq(e_k)$$

If $score(b_i) > \theta$, then the block b_i is declared as a masquerade block.

7   Experimental Results

We experimented our algorithm with SEA dataset for different values of λ and the ROC curve is given in figure 4. Each of the blocks of 100 commands are segmented to determine the episodes. Each episode is tested for masquerade using the Naive-Bayes technique. Then based on the number of commands in masquerade blocks we determine whether a block is masquerade or not. The threshold λ, the ratio of self vs non-self probabilities, is used to determine whether an episode is masquerade or not. A block of 100 commands is detected to be masquerade if total commands in masquerade episodes exceed 40. Thus the θ is taken to be 40%. It can be seen from the ROC curve that our algorithm outperforms many of the earlier algorithms. Our best result is the detection rate of 88.31% with a false alarm rate of 14.49%. None of the earlier algorithms has achieved this level of accuracy so far.

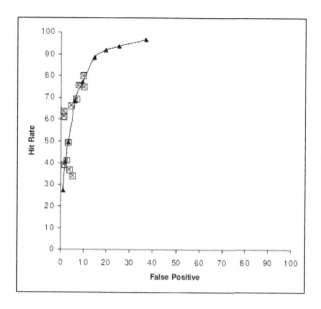

Fig. 4. ROC of the episode based Naive Bayes Algorithm and comparison with other algorithms

8   Conclusions

In this paper, we propose a new algorithm for masquerade detection based on episodes. Our method emphasizes on finding meaningful and frequent episodes in a block and based on the legitimacy of the episodes, terms the block to be normal or masquerade. A valid user may sometime deviate from its normal usage pattern. Any small deviation in the command sequence is localized to episodes and thus its effect to the legitimacy of the entire block is reduced. This results in an improved detection rate and reduced false alarm. As indicated by our experimental results, our algorithm performs better than many standard methods. Moreover, our method is more realistic in the sense that it does not generate false alarm for any momentary deviations.

Acknowledgment

This research is supported by Ministry of Communication and IT, Govt of India under the grant no. 12(22)/04-IRSD dated: 04.02.2004.

References

1. Chinchani, R., Muthukrishnan, A., Chandrasekaran, M., Upadhyaya, S.: RACOON: Rapidly generating user command data for anomaly detection from customizable templates. 20th Annual Computer Security Applications Conference (ACSAC), Tucson, AZ , December (2004)

2. Cohen, P., Heeringa, B., Adams, N. M.: An unsupervised algorithm for segmenting categorical timeseries into episodes. In: Proceedings of the ESF Exploratory Workshop on Pattern Detection and Discovery, London, UK. September (2002) 49-62
3. Coull, S., Branch, J., Szymanski, B., Breimer, E.: Intrusion detection: A bioinformatics approach. In: 19th Annual Computer Security Applications Conference, Las Vegas, Nevada, December 8-12. (2003)
4. Davison, B. D., Hirsh, H.: Predicting sequences of user actions. Predicting the Future: AI Approaches to Time-Series Problems. AAAI Technical Report WS-98-07, AAAI Press, Menlo Park, California, (1998)
5. Greenberg, S.: Using Unix: Collected traces of 168 users. Technical Report 88/333/45, Department of Computer Science, University of Calgary, Canada, (1988)
6. Killhourhy, K. S., Maxion, R. A.: Investigating a possible flaw in a masquerade detection system. Technical Report CS-TR: 869, School of Computing Science, University of Newcastle. (2004)
7. Kim, H.-S., Cha, S.-D.: Empirical evaluation of SVM-based masquerade detection using UNIX commands. Computers & Security, Vol. 24, March. (2005) 160-168
8. Lane, T., Brodley, C. E.: Temporal Sequence Learning and Data Reduction for Anomaly Detection. In: Proceedings of the Fifth ACM Conference on Computer and Communications Security, San Francisco, California, November 3-5. (1998) 150-158
9. Maxion, R. A., Townsend, T. N.: Masquerade detection augmented with error analysis. IEEE Transactions on Reliability, 53(1) March (2004) 124-147
10. Maxion, R. A., Townsend, T. N.: Masquerade detection using truncated command lines. In: Proceedings of the International Conference on Dependable Systems and Networks (DSN-02), Washington, D.C. 23-26 June (2002) 219-228
11. Maxion, R. A.: Masquerade detection using enriched command lines. In: International Conference on Dependable Systems and Networks (DSN-03), San Francisco, CA, USA, June (2003)
12. McCallum, A., Nigam, K.: A comparison of event models for Naive-Bayes text classification. In AAAI-98 Workshop on Learning for Text Categorization, Madison, Wisconsin (1998)
13. Schonlau, M., DuMouchel, W., Ju, W., Karr, A. F., Theus, M., Vardi, Y.: Computer intrusion: Detecting masquerades. Statistical Science, 16(1) February (2001) 58-74
14. Schonlau, M., Theus, M.: Detecting masqueraders in intrusion detection based on unpopular commands. Information Processing Letters, 76(1-2) November (2000) 33-38
15. Wagner, R. A., Fisher, M. J.: The string-to-string correction problem. Journal of the ACM, Vol.21 (1974) 168-173
16. Wang, K., Stolfo, S. J.: One-class training for masquerade detection. In: 3rd ICDM Workshop on Data Mining for Computer Security (DMSEC), Florida, November (2003)

A Game-Theoretic Approach to Credit Card Fraud Detection

Vishal Vatsa[1], Shamik Sural[2], and A.K. Majumdar[1]

[1] Department of Computer Science & Engineering
[2] School of Information Technology,
Indian Institute of Technology, Kharagpur, India
vishalvats@yahoo.com, {shamik@sit, akmj}@cse.iitkgp.ernet.in

Abstract. Intrusion prevention mechanisms are largely insufficient for protection of databases against Information Warfare attacks by authorized users and has drawn interest towards intrusion detection. We visualize the conflicting motives between an attacker and a detection system as a multi-stage game between two players, each trying to maximize his payoff. We consider the specific application of credit card fraud detection and propose a fraud detection system based on a game-theoretic approach. Not only is this approach novel in the domain of Information Warfare, but also it improvises over existing rule-based systems by predicting the next move of the fraudster and learning at each step.

1 Introduction

Intrusion detection is a critical part of the measures implemented for maintaining an attack tolerant database system. Though database management systems can provide intrusion prevention up to a certain extent by virtue of traditional access control mechanisms, they would not be sufficient for protection against syntactically correct but semantically damaging transactions [1]. Chung et al bring out that misuse detection in database systems has not been adequately addressed and propose DEMIDS, which can derive user profiles from database audit logs [2]. Lee et al suggest tagging the data objects with "time semantics" and monitor behavior at the level of sensor transactions [3]. Hu and Panda concentrate on analyzing the dependencies among data items in a database [4].

Consider a database system in an organization and a set of authorized users who have access rights on the database such as in banking services, credit card companies,etc. There always exists the possibility of legitimate and even non-legitimate transactions, what we hereby term as *fraudulent transactions*, being attempted by the authorized users or more typically, by adversaries posing as authorized users. The primary objective of any defense mechanism monitoring such an application would be to identify these fraudulent transactions as early as possible while limiting the possibility of raising too many false alarms. This form of Intrusion Detection in databases is an essential component of Information Warfare. The situation can be visualized as two adversaries playing against each other, the attacker launching attacks against the database system and the

S. Jajodia and C. Mazumdar (Eds.): ICISS 2005, LNCS 3803, pp. 263–276, 2005.

detection system countering it. The problem effectively models as a typical game with each player trying to outdo the other and Game theory has long been used to tackle such problems.

The field of Game theory has been explored for problems ranging from auctions to chess and its application to the domain of Information Warfare seems promising. Samuel et al bring out the role of Game theory in Information Warfare [5]. They highlight that one can utilize well-developed Game theory algorithms to predict future attacks and the differences and challenges in this domain as compared to traditional games like chess, such as limited examples, multiple simultaneous moves and no time constraints [6]. Liu and Li have presented a game-theoretic attack prediction model for attacks on IDS-protected systems [7]. The authors have considered choosing a threshold by the detection system dependent on the profile of the customer and the availability weight provided by the system. It is clear that if the threshold is low, it may result in the genuine transactions being rejected causing a negative payoff to the cardholder, which is considered as zero by the authors. Further, in a real-world scenario, the genuine cardholder cannot be expected to choose his action according to Nash Equilibrium and any deviations can only be suspected. As the detection system increases the availability weight, to avoid denial of service to the customer, there is no pure strategy equilibrium and the thief can act to maximize his payoff. Our model is not limited by these assumptions and we also improvise by including the possibility of 'learning' in our system, which takes place at every step of the multi-stage game. This was also validated by our experimental study.

The rest of the paper is organized as follows. Section 2 describes the work related to credit card fraud detection. Section 3 describes the Game-theoretic model and the architecture of the proposed fraud detection system (FDS). In Section 4, we describe the experiment conducted and analyze the results. We conclude in Section 5 of the paper.

2   Related Work

Fraud, as in the Encyclopedia, is defined as "willful misrepresentation intended to deprive another of some right" and is a major source of concern in a number of applications such as e-commerce, telecommunication industry, computer intrusion, etc. Credit card fraud is a growing problem in the credit card industry. In the USA, the online retail sales were reported to be $ 144 billion in 2004, which was a 26% increase over 2003 [8]. It is also estimated that 87% of purchases made over the Internet are paid by credit card [9]. The Association of Payment and Clearing Services (APACS) report showed that the cost of credit card fraud reached $ 966.74 million in 2004, which was an increase of 20% as compared to 2003 [10]. Another survey of over 160 companies revealed that online fraud (committed over the Web or phone shopping) is 12 times higher than offline fraud (committed by using a stolen physical card) [11]. The growing number of credit card users worldwide provides more opportunities for "thieves" to steal credit card details and subsequently commit fraud. A notion that rule-based systems, which take into account attributes like shipping address, product type, IP address, etc, should suffice for fraud prevention would be misleading. Labeling any transaction as 'fraudulent' is difficult for any static rule-based FDS due to a variety of reasons such as orders being shipped to an address different from billing address, genuine orders consisting of sale-able items like jewelry, etc. Confirming every suspected transaction from the genuine cardholder is not always possible or even practical due to the cost factor involved.

Though there are a variety of ways in which credit card fraud can be perpetrated, we classify them into two broad categories. This brings out the difference in the way frauds are carried out and also in the detection techniques used against them.

Physical Card. The cardholder either loses the card or his card is stolen and is then used by somebody else. This is the most fundamental type of fraud. In this case a substantial financial loss would occur only if the cardholder does not realize the loss of his card. Intuitively, the fraudster would attempt large volume or large value purchases in the shortest possible time. This should not be too difficult to detect by the fraud detection system in place.

Virtual Card. The second type of fraud, which is more difficult to tackle, can take place if the cardholder does not realize that someone else is in possession of his card details. This would also encompass the fraud that takes place due to counterfeit cards. These kinds of frauds may or may not get noticed, which depends on the strength of the fraud detection system in place. Further, the genuine cardholder in this case, will be able to detect the fraudulent transactions on his card only when he receives the credit statement at the end of the month.

Some of the common ways by which a fraudster can obtain the credit card details of an unsuspecting cardholder are shoulder surfing, dumpster diving, packet intercepting and database stealing [12]. We also add that unscrupulous employees at merchant establishments, restaurants, gas stations, etc, can note credit card details and possibly pass them on to an organized group of fraudsters. A variety of secure payment systems have been proposed to thwart credit card fraud such as Address Verification Service (AVS), Card Verification Value, Secure Electronic Transactions (SET) protocol, Secure Socket Layer (SSL), etc [13]. Even if we disregard the problems that may be peculiar to a particular payment system, it may be noted that in general, they will be ineffective against shoulder surfing, dumpster diving and database stealing, where the credit card details are known to the fraudster.

Credit card fraud detection has drawn lot of interest and a number of techniques, with special emphasis on data mining and neural networks, have been proposed to counter fraud in this field. Low et al described a method to implement a credit card system that would protect person's identity using simple cryptographic blocks [14]. Ghosh and Reilly carried out a feasibility study for Mellon

Bank to determine the effectiveness of neural network for credit card fraud detection [15]. The neural network used for this study is the P-RCE (Restricted Coulomb Energy) neural network. The authors concluded that it was possible to achieve a reduction of 20% to 40% in the total fraud losses. Aleskerov et al presented CARDWATCH, a database mining system based on a neural network learning module [16] . The system trains a neural network with the past data of a particular customer, which can then be used to process the current spending behavior and detect anomalies and they assume that since the normal behavior of the thief is to purchase as much as possible in limited time, the anomaly in transactions will most probably be detected. Chan et al divide a large data set of transactions into smaller subsets and then apply the mining techniques in parallel in a distributed data mining approach [17]. The resultant base models are then combined to generate a meta-classifier. More recently, Syeda et al have discussed the use of parallel granular neural networks for fast credit card fraud detection [18]. The parallel granular neural network (GNN) aims at speeding up the data mining and knowledge discovery process. The above-mentioned techniques, in general, attempt to either train a neural network with training data and then classify fraudulent/legitimate transactions or detect anomalies from the large amount of data using data mining techniques. These approaches would largely be static in nature and hence, would suffer from the limitation that the methodology being employed can be figured out by the fraudster. In contrast, we present a Game-theoretic approach for credit card fraud detection and propose the model of a FDS. The FDS improvises by using Game-theoretic techniques for fraud detection in addition to the existing ones and learns at each step of the game. This enables the FDS to predict the next move of the fraudster and switch to a counter- strategy at any stage to minimize the opponent's payoff.

3   Proposed Fraud Detection System

The proposed FDS is modeled with a two-tiered architecture. We aim at including some of the useful features available in commercial Fraud Detection systems while we improve upon it by including a layer working on Game-theoretic strategies. In our proposed system, the first line of defense is an intelligent rule-based system while the second uses Game-theoretic techniques for fraud detection. It may be noted that though we have considered transaction amount as an attribute for prediction, any other feature such as 'duration between transactions' can also be similarly considered.

3.1   Game-Theoretic Model

The presence of *two parties with conflicting goals* provided us with the initial impetus to use Game theory as an approach for fraud detection. In our quest to develop a Game-theoretic model for credit card fraud detection, the problem was compared with some well-known games such as "Bridges Problem", "D-day game" and "Inspection Game" to find similarity and differences in comparison. Our initial motivation was the classic "Bridges Problem" [19] . It is safe to assume that the fraudster is likely to have a pre-conceived notion about the system trying to judge transactions based, at least, on the amount range. The fraudster, hence, faces the option of choosing between two, three or more bridges (depending on the ranges), each associated with a certain amount of risk. The problem also draws similarity to the D-day game, which is a situation involving the Invasion of France during World War II [20]. The game involves the Allies and Germany, with three possible sites for the Allies to invade. In order to win, the Allies need to choose a site where the Germans are not expecting them. Another possible model is that of the Inspection Game between a customs inspector and a smuggler [21]. The Inspection Game is played in n stages wherein the smuggler may choose one of the stages to attempt an illegal act. Murali and Laxman proposed detecting network intrusions via sampling with a game-theoretic approach [22]. The problem requires detecting an intruding packet in a communication network and has been modeled as a two-person zero-sum game.

We realized subtle differences these games had when compared to the situation we intended to work upon. For example, in the Bridges Problem, the thief is aware about the risks/uncertainty associated with a bridge while we would have to consider the risks to be implicit. Further, the thief is unaware about the ranges specified by the IDS and also, he may be working with completely different payoffs as compared to those assumed by IDS. Assumptions like, the smuggler learns of each inspection as it is made or that the inspector may announce his mixed strategy would be too weak in the case of fraud detection [23]. The study of these games and a variety of others helped us in devising a new model for the credit card detection system and introducing some strategies in our experimental setup.

We model the situation as a game between two players, the thief and the FDS. As stated earlier, it is safe to assume that the thief is likely to attempt a fraudulent transaction with a belief that his transaction may be monitored on the basis of transaction amount. For example, a very high value transaction is likely to raise an alarm. Hence, the aim of the thief is to avoid suspicion/detection by the FDS and try to maximize his payoff, either in the long run or in a short time (for fear of the fraud being detected before long). On the other hand, the aim of the FDS is to minimize its loss by detecting the fraud at an early stage. In our model, the loss can be minimized if the system is able to predict the next move of the thief correctly. In such a scenario, we say that the thief has been 'caught'. The dilemma for the thief, on the other side, is to be able to choose a transaction range that has not been predicted by the FDS.

The game, in case of three transaction ranges, can be modeled as shown in Figure 1. The thief, oblivious of the ranges or the strategies used by the FDS, needs to choose the ith range from the possible 'n' ranges. The FDS, in contrast, is unaware of the thief's choice and hence, the possible choices form the information set for the FDS. A correct prediction of the ith range by the FDS results in the thief being caught.

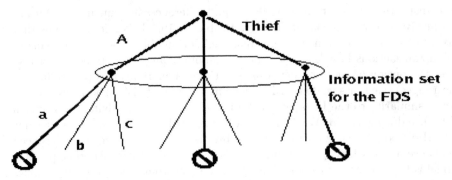

Fig. 1. Modeling the game

3.2   Architecture

The Fraud Detection System comprises of two layers, the 'Rule-based component' and the 'Game-theoretic component'. We discuss the two components separately.

The First Layer. We felt the necessity of the first layer not only for inclusion of certain features from available systems but also because we do not want to tackle millions of transactions with the Game theory rules, most of which are carried out due to routine use of credit cards. This layer would have rules like average daily/ monthly buying, shipping address being different from billing address, etc. In addition, customer-specific rules can also be incorporated. Intuitively, the first layer can filter out seemingly genuine transactions as is being done by the existing systems.

In an application such as credit card fraud detection, it is very difficult to conclusively declare that a given transaction is fraudulent. One may initially only suspect a transaction to be fraudulent with a certain probability. Consider the most basic of the checks which is used in many of the commercial systems and by various credit card companies, namely, billing and shipping address mismatch. However, such a mismatch could be either due to a fraudster aiming to get items delivered at an address or the actual cardholder gifting an item to a friend. In view of this, the First Layer of our proposed architecture uses generic as well as customer-specific rules to calculate the overall suspicion score for a transaction that is submitted. To amplify the idea, consider assigning weights to the different attributes of a transaction or better still, to a series of transactions on the same card number. Transactions scoring high due to attributes such as 'high value', 'sale-able item', 'address mismatch', etc, may trigger an alarm albeit the possibility of it being false cannot be ruled out. The main idea is that given a transaction and a specific user, what confidence measure can be assigned for the transaction to be from the genuine cardholder. Hence, the First Layer flags a transaction as 'suspect' if it crosses a user-defined threshold level. This introduces a trade-off between false positives (when the threshold is low) and more seriously, false negatives (when the threshold is high). We introduce the Second Layer in order to tackle this issue.

The Second Layer. The second tier is the Game-theoretic component of the model. We consider the game between the fraudster and the FDS to be a multi-stage repeated game. This is essential because, firstly, the fraudster is likely to try again even if he fails with one card and secondly, no effective learning can take place if the game is considered to be a one-shot one.

It is also worthwhile to mention that the game being played between the FDS and the fraudster is one of incomplete information since the fraudster would be completely unaware of the modus operandi of the Detection System. However, the fraudster is likely to have some notions or beliefs about the strategy of the FDS, as stated earlier. For example, it may be intuitive for him to believe that the FDS may raise an alarm if he carries out a very high-valued transaction or if he attempts a high value transaction of a saleable item like jewelry. Further, since we assume that the situation is one of repeated games, the fraudster can use his past experience to build upon his belief about the FDS strategy. This phenomenon, called 'learning' in game-theoretic terms, will help him to realize and then play according to a Nash Equilibrium (NE) such that he cannot play anything better given the strategy of the FDS. The FDS, as the other player, needs to choose its own best strategy to counter this. One may realize that the advantage of this approach is that this component is not one-time rule-based but will anticipate the next move of the opponent using Game-theoretic strategies. In the realm of Information Warfare, anticipating the next move correctly is a definite advantage to either player. The architecture of the proposed Credit Card Fraud Detection System is depicted in Figure 2.

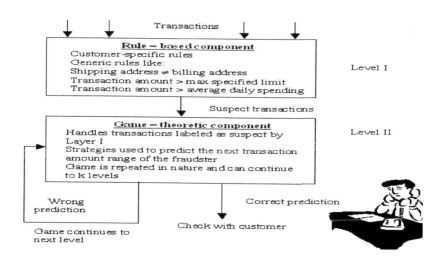

Fig. 2. Architecture of the proposed fraud detection system

The flow of events as would occur in the FDS have been depicted in Figure 3. The transaction for a particular card number is checked at Layer I. If it clears the checks at Level I, it is logged in the master database, failing which it is passed to the Game-theoretic component and the card is marked as suspect. This signifies

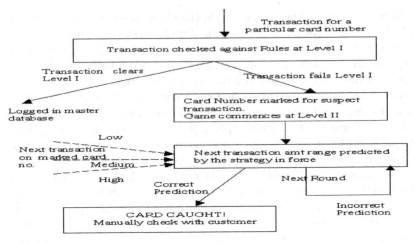

Fig. 3. Flow of events

the beginning of the game between the thief and the FDS. Layer II predicts the next move of the thief and in the event of the prediction being correct, the card is declared as caught.

4   Experimental Results

Our work is primarily focused on the design of a credit card FDS based on a Game-theoretic approach, but unavailability of real credit card data proved to be a serious handicap for testing our system. This was anticipated since real credit card data is treated as confidential by credit card institutions and not released to the public. As one of the solutions to this problem, we invited students from our institute, hereby termed as volunteers, to interact with the system. This was beneficial because firstly, the interaction by the users of the system helped us to capture real data that would be expected in a credit card transaction database. Secondly, it is difficult to model human behavior, whether of genuine cardholder or fraudster, in the absence of real data. The experiment provided us with an opportunity to do so. Lastly, the experiment enabled us to try out the efficacy of our Game-theoretic algorithms.

The three different prediction strategies that were implemented to work in parallel are as follows.

4.1   Tit-for-Tat Strategy

The Tit-for-Tat strategy works well in a wide variety of environments and won the worldwide competition for the well-known "Prisoner's Dilemma", played repeatedly [24]. Since the fraudster is playing a game in which he has no notion of the strategies being used by the opponent, he is likely to be guided by the outcomes of the preceding rounds. For example, if he is successful in carrying out a particular type/range of transaction, it is likely that he may try a similar transaction again.

4.2 Mixed Strategy

The second strategy implemented in the FDS was a mixed strategy. Though the payoffs are not common knowledge, we propose that the FDS assigns arbitrary payoffs when the game is initiated and predicts the next move according to the mixed strategy derived from these payoffs. This constitutes the initial belief of the FDS and will be strengthened/weakened as the game proceeds in a repeated game scenario. For example, consider that the FDS assigns a very high payoff for the thief to carry out a high value transaction at step k. Therefore, the FDS will predict that the fraudster is likely to undertake a high value transaction with a high probability. Assume that contrary to this, the fraudster opts for a low value transaction instead, at step k + 1, and repeats it at step k + 2. Thus, we can say that, the FDS may need to re-work its belief after x unsuccessful predictions. We assigned the thief's payoffs proportional to the transaction amount and a comparatively large negative payoff for getting caught as shown in Figure 4.

FDS

		I	II	III
		I	**II**	**III**
Thief	**I**	-80,80	10,-10	10,-10
	II	20,-20	-80,80	20,-20
	III	50,-50	50,-50	-80,80

Fig. 4. Payoff matrix for mixed strategy

4.3 Strategy Based on Markov Models of Game

The Tit-for-Tat strategy is strictly pure since it predicts the last move of the opponent as the next predicted move. We propose that though there is a high probability of a fraudster repeating his last move (as would be predicted correctly by Tit-for-Tat), there is a finite probability for the fraudster to attempt a transaction in a different range, like possibly to increase his payoff. This can be modeled as a Markov chain, in which we model the different transaction amount ranges as distinct states. The last suspicious transaction submitted to Layer II is said to be the present state of the fraudster. A fraudster can be expected to stay in his present state with probability p1 but can also be expected to transit to the other two states each with probability p2, where p1 >> p2, as shown in Figure 5.

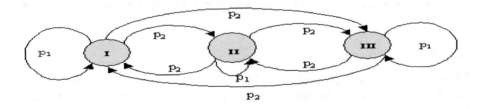

Fig. 5. Strategy based on Markov Models of game

4.4 Results

The volunteers participating in the game were issued with randomly generated credit card details required for an online transaction. Each volunteer was supposed to have 'stolen' these details. The volunteers could carry out online purchases at an intranet site hosted specifically for this purpose. The volunteers were issued with a new card number, if the previous turned invalid, in order to validate that learning can happen in a repeated game scenario.

To evaluate the results, we state that, given the application of credit card fraud detection, a strategy can be said to be efficient if it meets the following criteria.

(a)Predicts the next move of the opponent correctly in the least number of rounds. This ensures that the card is flagged or turned 'invalid', thus, minimizing the losses.

(b)Minimizes the false negatives, that is, accurately predicts the next transaction amount range, for a suspected card number.

The Game-theoretic prediction strategies were tried out in two phases. In the first phase of the study, we classified the online purchases into three ranges. Thus, any submitted transaction could classify either as a low value, a medium value or a high value transaction. The Game-theoretic component would predict the next transaction amount range for a particular card number, if classified as suspect. In the event of the next transaction amount range being the same as the prediction, the transaction was classified as fraudulent and the card number declared invalid. A notion of the opponent's behavior for his move in the second round and a comparison of the three strategies in the first phase of the experiment, with respect to efficacy in predicting that move correctly, have been shown in Figure 6. For this phase, mixed strategy proved to be more efficient in predicting the next move of the opponent. It was also observed that the volunteers were not able to learn the strategies easily especially because the information is imperfect both in terms of strategies and the ranges.

After our initial experiment, we decided to reduce the ranges to two, instead of three, and give the opponent's a better chance of learning the strategy of the FDS. Note that the ranges for the second and third strategy were not changed.

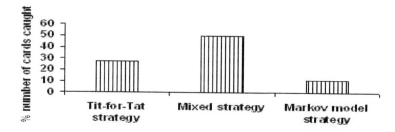

Fig. 6. Second move prediction comparison – first phase

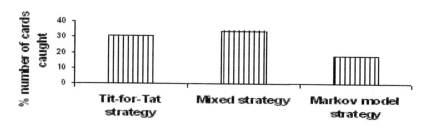

Fig. 7. Second move prediction comparison - second phase

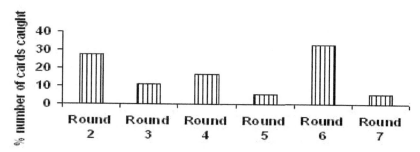

Fig. 8. Performance of Tit-for-Tat strategy - first phase

A comparison of the three strategies, in the second phase of the experiment has been shown in Figure 7.

We used the Tit-for-Tat strategy to return results to the volunteers and to observe their ability to learn the same. Figures 8 and 9 depict the number of cards that were caught in each round in the first phase and the second phase of the experiment, respectively. It was observed that the performance of Tit-for-Tat was better in the initial rounds but the volunteers who learnt the strategy (approximately, if not exactly) were successful in playing longer.

The performance of the three strategies, with respect to failure in predicting a fraudulent transaction correctly, that is, the number of false negatives is shown in Figure 10. It may be noted that since the players were effectively playing

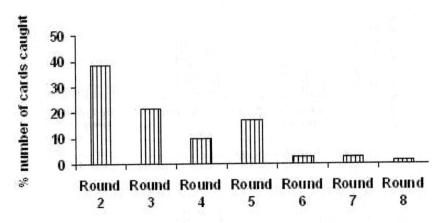

Fig. 9. Performance of Tit-for-Tat strategy - second phase

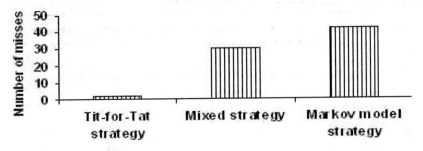

Fig. 10. Comparison of number of misses

with Tit-for-Tat strategy, it was possible that the transaction was predicted to be fraudulent correctly earlier by this strategy as compared to the other two strategies, resulting in a miss by the other two.

The number of volunteers who were able to successfully learn the strategy as a percentage of the total number of volunteers who played is depicted in Figure 11(a). Though a majority of the volunteers were not able to learn the strategy, 40% of them were able to do so. This proved to be an interesting result since it validated the hypothesis that learning does take place in the scenario being considered. For a fixed set of strategies of the FDS, the thief may initially be able to carry out a few transactions but eventually, he will be able to learn his best strategy (or the Nash Equilibrium strategy) against the FDS and can carry out 'n' transactions. The effect of playing with NE strategy, which was LHLHLH or HLHLHL for the second phase of the experiment, vis-a-vis other strategies has been depicted in Figure 11(b). It is pertinent to note that while we demonstrate 'learning' for the fraudster, we intend to build upon the approach by way of learning for the FDS. This would enable the FDS to strengthen its belief about the fraudster and switch to an alternate counter-strategy during the course of play.

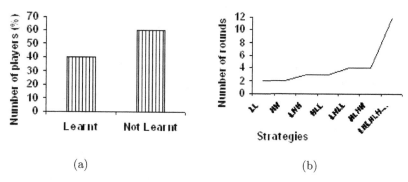

Fig. 11. (a) 'Learnt' vs. 'Not Learnt' (b) Payoff of thief with different strategies

5   Conclusions

The functional approach for most of the intrusion detection systems are rule-based mechanisms, however, they suffer from the limitation that the fraudster may eventually learn the methodology being employed. We have discussed a novel approach of using Game theory in the domain of credit card fraud detection and described the proposed architecture of such a system. We observed that though learning is slower with complex strategies, it does take place in a multi-stage game. We have demonstrated that the approach was validated by the thief being able to learn the strategy of the FDS. Conversely, in a two-player game, between the thief and the FDS, it is indeed also possible for the FDS to learn the strategy of the thief at every step and adopt a counter strategy so as to minimize his payoff. Our approach is not strategy-specific and other heuristic game-theoretic strategies can be included to further improvise the system. Though we have tackled a specific application, we feel that Game theory can be effectively used to counter intrusion in databases in general. We intend to develop a simulator to model the different behaviors of genuine cardholders as well as the fraudster and test the performance of the proposed system on a larger-scale with the simulated data.

Acknowledgements

This work is partially supported by a research grant from the Department of Information Technology, Ministry of Communication and Information Technology, Government of India, under Grant No. 12(34)/04-IRSD dated 07/12/2004.

References

1. T. Chiueh, D. Pilania, *Design, Implementation and Evaluation of a Repairable Database Management System*, Proceedings of ACSAC 2004, 179-188, 2004.

2. C.Y. Chung, M. Gertz, K. Levitt, *DEMIDS: A Misuse Detection System for Database Systems*, Third International IFIP TC-11 WG11.5 Working Conference on Integrity and Internal Control in Information Systems, 159-178, 1999.

3. V.C.S. Lee, J.A. Stankovic, H.S. Son, *Intrusion Detection in Real-Time Database Systems via Time Signatures*, Proc. Sixth IEEE Real Time Technology and Applications Symposium (RTAS 2000), 124-133, 2000.

4. Y. Hu, B. Panda, *Identification of Malicious Transactions in Database Systems*, Seventh Int. Database Engineering and Applications Symposium (IDEAS), China, 329-335, 2003.

5. S.N. Hamilton, W.L. Miller, A. Ott, O.S. Saydjari, *The Role of Game Theory in Information Warfare*, Fourth Information Survivability Workshop, 2002.

6. S.N. Hamilton, W.L. Miller, A. Ott, O.S. Saydjari, *Challenges in Applying Game Theory to the Domain of Information Warfare*, Fourth Information Survivability Workshop, 2002.

7. P. Liu, L. Li, *A Game-Theoretic Approach for Attack Prediction*, Technical Report, PSU-S2-2002-01, Penn State University, 2002.

8. http://www.haveninternet.com/welcome.htm, Complete Website and e-commerce solutions, (20 Apr 05).

9. http://www.aaa-merchant-account.com/, Merchant account credit card processing, (20 Apr 05).

10. http://www.clearlybusiness.com/cb/articles/, Clearly Business âĂŞ Card Fraud, (20 Apr 05).

11. http://sellitontheweb.com/ezine/news0434.shtml, Online fraud is 12 times higher than offline fraud, (20 Apr 05).

12. Y. Li, X. Zhang, *A Security-Enhanced One-Time Payment Scheme for Credit Card*, 14th International Workshop on RIDEâĂŹ04, 40-47, 2004.

13. M.E. Peters, *Emerging eCommerce Credit and Debit Card Protocols*, Proc. 3rd International Symposium on Electronic Commerce, 39-46, 2002.

14. S.H. Low, N.F. Maxemchuk, S. Paul, *Anonymous credit cards and their collusion analysis*, IEEE/ACM Transactions on Networking, 809-816, 1996.

15. S. Ghosh, D.L. Reilly, *Credit card fraud detection with a neural network*, Proc. 27th Annual Hawaii International Conference on System Sciences, 621-630, 1994.

16. E. Aleskerov, B. Freisleben, B. Rao, *CARDWATCH: A Neural Network Based Database Mining System for Credit Card Fraud Detection*, Proc. Computational Intelligence for Financial Engineering (CIFEr), 220-226, 1997.

17. P.K. Chan, W. Fan, A.L. Prodromidis, *S.J. Stolfo, Distributed Data Mining in Credit Card Fraud Detection*, IEEE Intelligent Systems, 67-74, 1999.

18. M. Syeda, Y.Q. Zhang, Y. Pan, *Parallel Granular Neural Networks for Fast Credit Card Fraud Detection*, Proc. FUZZ-IEEE 2002 Int. Conference, 572-577, 2002.

19. http://plato.stanford.edu/entries/game-theory/, Game Theory, (26 Apr 05).

20. A. Kydd, Formal Theory for Political Science âĂŞ Lecture Notes, 2002.

21. T.S. Ferguson, C. Melolidakis, *On the Inspection Game*, Naval Research Logistics 45, 327-334, 1998.

22. M. Kodialam, T.V. Lakshman, *Detecting network intrusions via sampling: A Game-theoretic Approach*, Proc. IEEE INFOCOM 2003, 1880-1889, 2003.

23. M. Maschler, *A price leadership method for solving the inspectorâĂŹs non-constant sum game*, Naval Research Logistics Quarterly 13, 11-33, (1966).

24. http://www.abc.net.au/science/slab/tittat/story.htm, âĂIJTit for TatâĂİ, (28 Apr 05).

Modifications of SHA-0 to Prevent Attacks

Roshni Chatterjee, Moiz A. Saifee, and Dipanwita RoyChowdhury

Dept. of Computer Science & Engineering,
Indian Institute of Technology Kharagpur, India-721302
{roshni, drc}@cse.iitkgp.ernet.in

Abstract. One of the most popular hash algorithms is the SHA-0, proposed by NIST. However, researchers have already found security flaws in SHA-0, thereby also posing a threat against other algorithms of the SHA family. In this paper we present two simple modifications which can be easily incorporated into the original SHA-0 algorithm to make it secure against one of its most basic attack methodologies. We further show that the modified algorithm performs equally well as the original one when compared against standard metrics that are used to evaluate hash functions. We have developed a prototype tool to compare and evaluate the modified and the original SHA-0 algorithm.

1 Introduction

An increased demand, in recent years, for devising systems which are critical and secure has led to an increased awareness for developing secure and reliable systems, which maintain correctness and conform to performance models. This, in turn, has catalyzed the emergence of several security standards , of which the Secure Hash Standard (SHS) [17, 18, 19] proposed by NIST, is one of the most notable one. Several hashing algorithms, which conform to SHS, have been developed over the years.

A large fraction of research activities on hashing has focused on the development of one way hash functions which are tough to invert. One such hash function is the cryptographic one way hash function, which is expected to be *irreversible* and *collision resistant*. A hash function H takes a variable length string input and produces a fixed length string output. Here, H is called a *one-way* hash function when it is irreversible. This means, it is easy to compute the hash value Y for a given input X (Y = H(X)), but hard to calculate the inverse, i.e., the input from the hash output ($X = H^{-1}(Y)$). If the one way hash function possesses the property that it is computationally infeasible to find 2 inputs (messages) which hash to the same value (message digest), then the hash function is said to be collision resistant. These two properties (*irreversibility* and *collision resistance*) make the cryptographic one-way hash function suitable for a variety of applications in message authentication, digital signatures and password storage. Some of the most widely used hash algorithms include MD4 [22], MD5 [24], SHA-0 [17] and SHA-1 [18].

However, with the increase in computational power, these two desirable properties of any existing standard hash algorithm get constantly threatened. Lack of collision resistance is considered to be a weakness of a cryptographic hash algorithm since it implies that an attacker can find two different messages that hash to the same value, and

S. Jajodia and C. Mazumdar (Eds.): ICISS 2005, LNCS 3803, pp. 277–289, 2005.

thereby, replace the correct message with the incorrect one. Recently, collisions have been reported for SHA-0 and SHA-1 [4, 8, 14, 21, 27]. In reaction, NIST has hinted at a possible migration from the SHA-1 to the SHA-2 by 2010 [20], while searches for a completely new hash algorithm are also being pursued.

While existing research has focused on the development of new hash algorithms and in the improvement of existing ones, not much work has been done in modifying a hash algorithm to strengthen it against a specific attack. In this paper, we propose one such approach by suggesting two modifications to SHA-0 to make it resilient against the recent attack methodology [8]. Though SHA-1 is more widely used than SHA-0, our work has focused on SHA-0 because collisions for full 80 round SHA-0 have been published [14, 27]. Further, since, SHA-1 and SHA-2 are basically structured on SHA-0, a threat to SHA-0 is a potential threat to all the other SHA algorithms. On the one hand, therefore, switching to the higher SHA algorithms (i.e., SHA-2) may not be a good solution, while on the other hand, implementing a completely new algorithm will involve a huge resource overhead. In this context, our work is of major importance.

In particular, we have the following contributions:

- Instead of proposing a new algorithm, we suggest modifications to make SHA-0 resilient against the most recent well-known attack.
- We further show that our proposed modification can be seamlessly integrated into any SHA-based framework by maintaining all the desirable characteristics and with very small resource overhead.

This paper is organized as follows: Section 2 describes the basics, while in Section 3, our proposed modifications for SHA-0 have been stated and explained. Section 4 presents the experimental results.

2   Basic Overview

In this section, we briefly define a few concepts and notations for explaining our work.

2.1   A Brief History of Cryptographic Hash Algorithms

Among the various hash algorithms like MD2 [16], MD4 [22, 23], MD5 [24], RIPEMD-160 [12], HAVAL [28], Tiger [1], and the SHA algorithms [17, 18, 19], the MD and the SHA-family of algorithms are the most widely used hash algorithms. MD4, a member of the MD family of hash algorithm, was widely used till security flaws [6, 9] were found in it. As a result MD5, an extension of MD4, was proposed by R.Rivest. However, collisions for MD5 [3, 7, 10, 11] were published soon, which made SHA the obvious choice as a standard hash algorithm. Now, SHA-1, a strengthened version of SHA-0, is the most commonly used hash algorithm.

Until 1998, the SHA algorithm was considered to be secure against the known attack methods. However in 1998, for the first time, collisions for 35 rounds SHA-0 was published by Chabaud and Joux in [8], where the attack method is based on the differential cryptanalysis of block ciphers [5]. The complexity of their attack is 2^{61}. Again in [4] Biham and Chen reported collisions for 65 round and "near collisions" for 80 round SHA-0. In [4] they identified an extra weakness in the SHA-0 algorithm, called the "neutral bits". The report [27] states that collisions for 80 round SHA-1 will be published soon.

2.2 SHA-0 Algorithm

The various pre-requisites for SHA-0 are as follows:

- "+" $\Rightarrow$ addition modulo 2^{32}
- $ROL_i(X)$ means left rotation of a 32-bit word X by i bits
- $A^{(m)}$, $B^{(m)}$, $C^{(m)}$, $D^{(m)}$, $E^{(m)}$, $W^{(n)}$, temp are all 32 bit variables where $0 \leq n \leq 79$ and $0 \leq m \leq 80$
- $W_{(j)}^{(i)}$ represents the jth bit of $W^{(i)}$, where $0 \leq i \leq 79$ and $0 \leq j \leq 31$ and we use a similar notation for A, B, C, D, and E.
- The constants $K^{(i)}$ and functions $f^{(i)}$ for the different rounds are as follows:

Table 1. Functions and Constants for Original SHA-0

Round(i)	Function $f^{(i)}$	Constant $K^{(i)}$
0-19	IF:$(X \wedge Y) \vee (\neg X \wedge Z)$	0x5a827999
20-39	XOR:$(X \oplus Y \oplus Z)$	0x6ed9eba1
40-59	MAJ:$(X \wedge Y) \vee (X \wedge Z) \vee (Y \wedge Z)$	0x8f1bbcdc
60-79	XOR:$(X \oplus Y \oplus Z)$	0xca62c1d6

The SHA-0 algorithm takes as input a message M of length $\leq 2^{64}$. The algorithm can be divided into two main stages:

- **Preprocessing Stage:**
  - **Step 1:** Message padding - Pad M such that its length is congruent to 448 modulo 512. The padding consists of a '1' followed by as many '0's as required.
  - **Step 2:** Represent length of M (before padding) by a 64 bit block and append to the padded message.
  - **Step 3:** Divide padded M into 512 bit blocks.
  - **Step 4:** Initialization - Five 32 bit variables $A^{(0)}$, $B^{(0)}$, $C^{(0)}$, $D^{(0)}$, $E^{(0)}$ are initialized as follows:
    $A^{(0)} = $ 0x67452301, $B^{(0)} = $ 0xefcdab89, $C^{(0)} = $ 0x98badcfe,
    $D^{(0)} = $ 0x10325476, $E^{(0)} = $ 0xc3d2e1f0

- **Computation Stage:** For each 512 bit block X of M, do the following: Store X as sixteen 32 bit blocks denoted by $W^{(0)}$, $W^{(1)}$, ..., $W^{(15)}$.
  - **Step 1:** Expansion/Message Schedule - Expand X to 2560 bits using the following recursion formula: $\forall i$, $16 \leq i \leq 79$
    $W^{(i)} = W^{(i-3)} \oplus W^{(i-8)} \oplus W^{(i-14)} \oplus W^{(i-16)}$
  - **Step 2:** for i= 0 to 79
    temp = $ROL_5(A^{(i)}) + f^{(i)}(B^{(i)}, C^{(i)}, D^{(i)}) + K^{(i)} + W^{(i)} + E^{(i)}$;
    $E^{(i+1)} = D^{(i)}$;

$D^{(i+1)} = C^{(i)}$;
$C^{(i+1)} = ROL_{30}(B^{(i)})$;
$B^{(i+1)} = A^{(i)}$;
$A^{(i+1)} = $ temp;

- **Step 3:** Evaluation of Final Values:
  A = $A^{(0)} + A^{(80)}$, B = $B^{(0)} + B^{(80)}$, C = $C^{(0)} + C^{(80)}$,
  D = $D^{(0)} + D^{(80)}$, E = $E^{(0)} + E^{(80)}$

The values A,B,C,D,E for the ith 512 bit block act as the initial variables ($A^{(0)}$, $B^{(0)}$, $C^{(0)}$, $D^{(0)}$, $E^{(0)}$) for the next (i.e.,$(i + 1)^{th}$) 512-bit block of the message. The final hash value, after all the 512 bit blocks have been processed, is the concatenation of the values in the 5 registers: A,B,C,D,E.

The following subsection discusses the first and perhaps the most important collision attack on SHA-0 till date.

2.3   Collision Search Method of Chabaud and Joux

This section gives a brief overview of the basic collision search method against SHA-0 proposed by Chabaud and Joux in [8].

The Method: For finding collisions for 2 different messages, two identical messages M and M' represented as $W^{(0)},W^{(1)},W^{(2)},...,W^{(79)}$, and $W'^{(0)},W'^{(1)},W'^{(2)},$ ..., $W'^{(79)}$ respectively, have been considered. A single bit difference is introduced (by negating $W_1'^{(i)}$) which results in two different message digests[1]. The difference in the two message digests is corrected by changing five more bits $W_6'^{(i+1)}$, $W_1'^{(i+2)}$, $W_{31}'^{(i+3)}$, $W_{31}'^{(i+4)}$, $W_{31}'^{(i+5)}$ of the message M'. This results in a collision. The authors have argued that the success probability of this correction method, that is, the probability of finding a collision is $\frac{1}{2^{61}}$. However, if all the nonlinear functions in the SHA-0 are replaced by XOR then the above method can deterministically find a collision. The collision search algorithm can be formally explained as below. To find such a collision for 2 messages M and M', represented as $W^{(0)}, W^{(1)}, ... , W^{(79)}$, and $W'^{(0)}, W'^{(1)}, ...$, $W'^{(79)}$ respectively, the authors in [8] have formulated the following steps:

- **Error Vector Generation:** An 80 bit *error vector* is defined, where $W_1'^{(i)}$ is negated if bit i of the error vector = 1; else it is left unchanged
- **Calculation of Masks:**
  - Calculate the *perturbative mask* from the error vector. This mask M_0 must satisfy the given equation: [8]
    $$M_0^{(i)} = M_0^{(i-3)} \oplus M_0^{(i-8)} \oplus M_0^{(i-14)} \oplus M_0^{(i-16)} \qquad \forall 11 < i < 80$$
  - Calculate the 5 *corrective masks:* from the *perturbative mask.*
  - Calculate the *global differential mask* from the above six masks.
- **Final Pattern Computation:** Evaluate a pattern of 0s and 1s from the "global differential mask". Certain constraints are to be considered for this computation as described below:

---

[1] The output of a hashing algorithm is called the message digest.

1. Due to the characteristic of the IF function, no two successive perturbations can occur in the rounds 0-16.
2. For the above method of correction to work, the last five rounds can have no perturbations, i.e., the last 5 bits of the pattern should be zeroes.

When this final pattern is applied to the message M', then there is a probability $(=\frac{1}{2^{61}})$ of finding collisions between M and the changed M'.

To counter this method of attack, we have suggested two modifications to the basic SHA-0 algorithm, which are explained in the subsequent section.

3   Our Proposed Modifications

This section discusses the two modifications proposed by us and the justification of using these modifications and how well they are able to withstand the method of attack given in [8].

3.1   Replacement of XOR by a Nonlinear Function NF

The Proposal: In SHA-0 the XOR appears as the $f^{(i)}$ function for rounds 20-39 and rounds 60-79 (Table 1). This XOR is replaced by the nonlinear function [2] as defined below:

$$NF:(\neg X \wedge Y) \vee (X \wedge Z)$$

After this replacement, Table 1 (Section 2.3) for the SHA-0 algorithm gets modified as shown in Table 2.

Table 2. Functions and Constants for Modified SHA-0

R(i)	Function $f^{(i)}$	Constant $K^{(i)}$
0-19	IF:$(X \wedge Y) \vee (\neg X \wedge Z)$	0x5a827999
20-39	NF:$(\neg X \wedge Y) \vee (X \wedge Z)$	0x6ed9eba1
40-59	MAJ:$(X \wedge Y) \vee (X \wedge Z) \vee (Y \wedge Z)$	0x8f1bbcdc
60-79	NF:$((\neg X \wedge Y) \vee (X \wedge Z))$	0xca62c1d6

Justification for Choosing NF: The XOR is replaced by a nonlinear function to decrease the probability of the attack method described in [8]. As discussed in [8], since XOR is a linear function, the probability that the corrections will result in a collision, is 1. However, if this XOR is replaced by any nonlinear function then the probability becomes less than 1. In the following subsection we explain the basic characteristics of *NF* which makes it a suitable candidate for the replacement.

---

[2] In [13] nonlinear feedback functions have been used in the design of a family of hash algorithms FSR-255.

1. For the rounds where NF is used, if the 1st bits of two adjacent words i.e., $W_1^{(i)}$ and $W_1^{(i+1)}$ are changed, then the probability that the correction will succeed is zero. Thus, while calculating the pattern of 0s and 1s for finding collisions, no two successive perturbations can be allowed for the rounds where NF is being used. In addition to the above constraint, other constraints for the calculation of the global pattern remains the same as described in Section 2.3. The pattern construction method as described in Section 2.3 is applied while considering all the constraints. We have experimentally shown that no such pattern is possible after replacing XOR by NF. Since no pattern can be found, it can be claimed that no two colliding messages using the method described in [8] can be found. Thus, the attack methodology proposed in [8] fails.

2. Evidently NF has an equal distribution of 0s and 1s. This equal distribution in turn guarantees the desirable high probability of equal distribution of 1s and 0s in the output of the compression function $f^{(i)}$.

3. The $f^{(i)}$ is a function of the B, C and D values. Since, the function $f^{(i)}$ works parallely on all 32 bits (Section 2.3), analysis for one bit applies to all the other bits. Thus, for the analysis we consider one bit only. According to the method in [8] (Section 2.3), the one bit difference in the input messages M and M' gives rise to the following three possibilities:

   (a) $B_1^{(i)} \neq B_1'^{(i)}$, while $C_1^{(i)} = C_1'^{(i)}$, $D_1^{(i)} = D_1'^{(i)}$.
   (b) $C_{31}^{(i)} \neq C_{31}'^{(i)}$, while $B_{31}^{(i)} = B_{31}'^{(i)}$, $D_{31}^{(i)} = D_{31}'^{(i)}$.
   (c) $D_{31}^{(i)} \neq D_{31}'^{(i)}$, while $B_{31}^{(i)} = B_{31}'^{(i)}$, $C_{31}^{(i)} = C_{31}'^{(i)}$.

   From the truth table, we see that for all $2^3 = 8$ possible cases if the nth bit of any of the three registers differ, then the outputs of $f^{(i)}$ and $f'^{(i)}$ will also differ in that particular n^{th} bit. However, when XOR is replaced by NF then for half of the cases (i.e. 4 out of 8 possibilities) the outputs differ in the nth bit while for the remaining half of the cases the outputs do not differ. Because of this characteristic of NF, it cannot be approximated by any linear function (like XOR) and hence, is resistant to an attack.

3.2   Introducing Redundancy in the Algorithm

By using each message block twice in a round, we propose to introduce redundancy in every round of the SHA-0 algorithm. This redundancy is introduced in the step 2 of the computation stage of SHA-0 (Section 2.2). The step 2 of the computation stage gets modified as follows:

Step 2: for i= 0 to 79
$temp = ROL_5(A^{(i)}) + f^{(i)}(B^{(i)}, C^{(i)}, D^{(i)}) + K^{(i)} + W^{(i)} + E^{(i)};$
$E^{(i+1)} = D^{(i)};$
$D^{(i+1)} = C^{(i)};$
$C^{(i+1)} = ROL_{30}(B^{(i)});$
$B^{(i+1)} = A^{(i)} \oplus ROL_1(W^{(i)});$
$A^{(i+1)} = temp;$

All the other steps remain the same. The symbols and constants also have the same meanings as in SHA-0. In each round (i) of Step 3 the input message block $W^{(i)}$ is used twice: Once while calculating the value of temp and once while calculating the value of B. At the same time, we have also introduced a 1 bit left rotation to interleave the bits. This redundancy is introduced to counter the correcting block attack[3]. Though the philosophy of the attack proposed in [8] is based on differential attack, it can be inferred as a correcting block attack.

How Our Modification Counters the Attack Proposed in [8]:
After this modification is introduced, the collision search method described in [8] is applied as follows: As in the method in [8], two identical messages M and M' are considered and 1 bit of M' is negated ($W_1'^{(i)}$). This results in two different message digests. To correct this difference, the method in [8] suggests the change of five more bits of M' so that the values of the registers A and A' for the two messages M and M' in the 5 successive rounds (i+1),(i+2), ..., (i+5) are equal. We apply this method to the modified algorithm and it is shown in Table 3 that the correction method fails to correct the difference at the end of five rounds. In fact, as the number of rounds increase the difference between the two messages increases, thus eliminating the possibility that the attack method [8] will work.

Table 3. Perturbations and Corrections

Rounds	i	i+1	i+2	i+3	i+4	i+5
Perturbations	W_1					
Corrections		W_2, W_6	W_0, W_1, W_3, W_7	$W_0, W_2, W_4, W_5, W_8, W_{31}$	W_0, W_2, W_3, W_9	$W_0, W_1, W_2, W_5, W_6, W_7, W_{10}, W_{30}, W_{31}$
Differing bits in reg A		A_1				
Differing bits in reg B		B_2	B_1, B_3, B_7	B_1, B_2, B_4, B_8	$B_0, B_1, B_3, B_5, B_6, B_9$	B_1, B_3, B_4, B_{10}
Differing bits in reg C			C_0	C_1, C_5, C_{31}	C_0, C_2, C_6, C_{31}	$C_1, C_3, C_4, C_7, C_{30}, C_{31}$
Differing bits in reg D				D_0	D_1, D_5, D_{31}	D_0, D_2, D_6, D_{31}
Differing bits in reg E					E_0	E_1, E_5, E_{31}

Table 3 is explained as follows: *Perturbations* refer to the initial change of a bit in M'. *Corrections* indicate those bits in the message M' which need to be changed to make the variables A and A' of M and M' respectively, equal in rounds (i+1), (i+2), ..., (i+5). *Differing bits* refer to those bits in the two messages which are different even after applying the necessary corrections. Table 3 illustrates how the modified algorithm counters the attack methodology described in [8] for a specific case, where initially the input messages M and M' are all 0s. For other messages also, the correction method

---

[3] Correcting block attack is an attack in which the opponent uses a pre-existing [message digest] pair, and tries to change one or more message blocks such that the resulting digest remains intact [2].

in [8] fails to correct the difference at the end of 5 rounds, thereby countering the attack proposed in [8].

4   Experimental Results

This section discusses the experimental results, which show that the modified SHA-0 algorithm while being resistant against the commonly known attacks for hashing algorithms retains the good hashing properties of the original SHA-0 as well. All the experiments were performed on a 2.4Ghz Pentium workstation with 256MB memory.

4.1   Robustness of Modified SHA-0 Against Various Attacks

- **Attack 1: Birthday Attack:** Birthday attack is a cryptographic attack where the theory of birthday paradox is used. The attack is explained as follows: Let H be a cryptographic hash algorithm which outputs n bits. The level of effort required to find two random messages X and Y such that H(X)=H(Y), is proportional to $2^{\frac{n}{2}}$, where n is the length of the message digest produced by H. Since our modified algorithm produces 160 bits output the effort required for this attack is 2^{80}, which is computationally infeasible [26]. Therefore, the modified algorithm is secure against the birthday attack.
- **Attack 2:** A common cryptographic attack is one which tests the difference in the message digests for two almost similar messages. The attack is described as follows: Let M be an arbitrary message of length n and M' be derived from M by flipping a randomly chosen bit of M. Let the corresponding message digest pair be $H_k(M)$ and $H_k(M')$ respectively. If the differing bits between the two message digests is on an average $\frac{n}{2}$, then the hash algorithm is said to be secure against this attack. In Table 4, the average result is given for a run of all possible cases of 1 bit difference. Results show that for the modified SHA-0 the difference (that is, XOR between $H_k(M)$ and $H_k(M')$) has on an average equal number of zeroes and ones (i.e., = 80). Therefore, it can be inferred that the modified SHA-0 is resistant against the above attack. 3 different files of size 768 bytes and 3 different files of 4800 bytes have been taken for the experiment.
- **Attack 3: Differential Attack:** Though differential cryptanalysis [5] is a common cryptographic attack against the block ciphers, it is also used to attack hash algorithms. The attack is explained as follows: For example, if the difference between

Table 4. Results for Attack Method 2

Input Message Size(bytes)	No. of ones for $H_k(M) \oplus H_k(M')$	
	Original SHA-0	Modified SHA-0
768	87	82
768	75	82
768	82	80
4800	73	72
4800	83	86
4800	79	80

Table 5. Results for Differential Attack

Input File Size (bytes)	Avg. standard deviation of XOR Distribution	
	Original SHA-0 (D=1)	Modified SHA-0
768	8.0008	7.9981
4800	8.000319	8.000413
48000	8.006675	8.007985
	Original SHA-0 (D=2)	Modified SHA-0
64	5.65669	5.65836

2 messages be 2 bits, (i.e.,say,D=2) then the message digest pair difference D' for the corresponding 2 message digests can be calculated. From the distribution of D' corresponding to different message pairs, the standard deviation(σ) is calculated. The experiments were run for all possible 1 and 2 bit differences for an input message. For 1 bit difference three different file sizes and for each file size 3 different input files were considered. However, for 2 bit difference, due to inadequate memory the experiments could not be run on file sizes greater than 64 bytes. The results in Table 5 show that both the modified SHA-0 algorithm and the original SHA-0 have the same resistance against the differential attack.

The original SHA-0 is resistant to all the above common attacks against a cryptographic hash algorithm. The above results indicate that our modified algorithm is also secure against these common attacks . Thus, we can conclude that the introduced modifications in SHA-0 do not make it vulnerable to the attacks against which the original SHA-0 was secure.

4.2   Evaluation of the Modified SHA-0 as a Hashing Algorithm

In this section, the original SHA-0 and the modified version are evaluated against the metrics

1. Bit variance test
2. Entropy test

proposed in [15]. The authors in [15] give a test suite to evaluate the quality of a hash algorithm. We evaluate the quality of both the original SHA-0 and the modified SHA-0 against the following tests [15]:

1. **Bit Variance Test:** The bit variance test [15] consists of measuring the impact on the digest bits by changing input message bits. Bits of an input message are changed and the corresponding message digests (for each changed input) are calculated. Finally from all the digests produced, the probability (P_i) for each digest bit to take on the value of 1 and 0 is measured. If $P_i(1) = P_i(0) = \frac{1}{2}$ for all digest bits i ($i \leq 1 \leq n$) where n is the digest length, then the one way hash function under consideration has attained maximum performance in terms of the bit variance test. For this test, it is difficult to check for all possible bit changes on the input message. Therefore, only 1 and 2 bit changes have been considered.

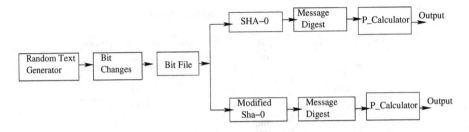

Fig. 1. Tool for the Bit Variance Test

Tool for the Test: The tool consists of a random text generator which produces English text. On this English text, all possible 1 and 2 bit changes are applied to produce a bit file from which the corresponding message digests are generated. From all the message digests, P_calculator calculates the probabilities, $P_i(0)$ and $P_i(1)$ for each bit of the 160 bit message digest. The experiments were performed for 10 different messages. Results given in Table 6 show that for both the algorithms the condition $P(f(X) = f(X + \alpha)) = \frac{1}{2}$ $\forall \alpha$ having Hamming weight $\leq$ 2 have been satisfied. (Here α is a Boolean vector of length 160 bits, X is the input message of length 512 bits and f is a Boolean function mapping the set of all n length Boolean vectors to the set $\{0, 1\}$). Thus, both the algorithms (original and modified) pass the bit variance test.

2. **Entropy Test:** Entropy measures the amount of information content of a message and is maximum when it equals the total number of bits in the message. Since, it is infeasible to calculate the entropy of the message digest, an approximate method is used.

Approximate Entropy Assessment Method: Let the message digest be composed of blocks where each block is equal to 1 byte. By taking all possible combinations of byte pairs a set of 16 bit numbers (0-65535) are obtained for each message di-

Table 6. Results for Bit Variance Test

Input Messages	Avg Probability $P(f_k(X) = f_k(X \oplus \alpha))$, for all digest bits	
	Original SHA-0	Modified SHA-0
X_1	0.500148	0.500154
X_2	0.4999837	0.500723
X_3	0.499871	0.500021
X_4	0.500247	0.500124
X_5	0.500066	0.499740
X_6	0.499574	0.500221
X_7	0.50022	0.500038
X_8	0.499871	0.499630
X_9	0.500201	0.500006
X_{10}	0.499657	0.500346

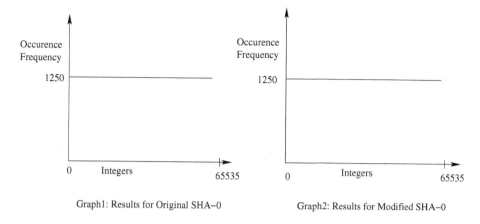

Fig. 2. Results of Entropy Test

gest. For a large number of message digests if the frequencies of occurrences of these numbers (0-65535) are equal, then the approximate entropy for the 16 bit subblocks of the message digest is 16. For the *entropy test*, all possible combinations of 8-bit numbers from each 160 bit message digest, (=20*(20-1)) are taken to form 16 bit numbers. The test is carried out for 200000 messages. Thus, there are 20000*20*(20-1) 16-bit number occurrences in the digest pool.

The results given in Fig 2 (Graph1 and Graph2) show that for both the original SHA-0 and the modified version the approximate entropy for 16-bit subblock is 16, since the occurrence frequencies of all the numbers (0-65535) are almost equal.

5   Conclusion

In this paper, we have proposed two modifications of the original SHA-0 algorithm to make it resilient against the recent attack methodology and thereby save the overhead of designing and implementing a completely new hash algorithm. We have also shown that that the introduced modifications in SHA-0 do not make it vulnerable to the attacks against which the original SHA-0 was secure. We believe that the basic philosophy of our approach may be extended to combat similar attacks against other members of the SHA family. Further, as future work, we propose to analyze another identified weakness of SHA-0, namely *neutral bits* [4] and suggest modifications to overcome this weakness.

Acknowledgments

The work is partially supported by the DIT sponsored project "Design and implementation of cryptosystems resistant to vulnerabilities and side-channel attacks (SCA)".

References

1. Anderson, R., Biham, E., Tiger: A Fast New Hash Function, Fast Software Encryption - FSE'96, LNCS 1039, Springer-Verlag (1996), pp. 89–97
2. Bakhtiari,S.,Safavi-Naini,R., Pieprzyk,J., Cryptographic Hash Functions: A Survey. http://www.securitytechnet.com/resource/crypto/algorithm/Symmetric/bakhtiari95cryptographic.pdf
3. Berson, T., Differential Cryptanalysis Mod 2^{32} with Applications to MD5. Proceedings, EUROCRYPT May 1992, New York, Springer Verlag, Ed. R.A. Rueppel, pp. 71-80
4. Biham, E., Chen,R., Near-Collisions of SHA-0 -2004. Advances in Cryptology-CRYPTO '04, LNCS, M. Franklin, Ed., Springer Verlag, vol 3152, pp 290-306
5. Biham, E., Shamir, A., Differential Cryptanalysis of DES-like Cryptosystems. Journal of Cryptology, Vol 4,No 1, pp. 3-72, 1991
6. Boer, B., Bosselaers, A., An attack on the last two rounds of MD4, Advances in Cryptology - Crypto '91, Springer-Verlag (1992), pp. 194-203
7. Boer, B., Bosselaers, A., Collisions for the Compression Function of MD5. Proceedings, EUROCRYPT 1993, New York, Springer Verlag, pp. 293-305
8. Chabaud, F.,Joux,A., Differential Collisions in SHA-0. Lecture Notes in Computer Science: Vol 1462. Proceedings of the 18th Annual International Cryptology Conference on Advances in Cryptology, pp 56-71, 1998
9. Dobbertin,H., Cryptanalysis of MD4. Journal of Cryptology, vol.11, no.4, pp 253-271, Springer Verlag, 1998
10. Dobbertin, H., Cryptanalysis of MD5 Compress. Presented at the Rump Session of EUROCRYPT'96, May 1996
11. Dobbertin, H., The Status of MD5 After a Recent Attack. CryptoBytes, Summer 1996
12. Dobbertin, H., Bosselaers, A., Preneel, B., RIPEMD-160, a strengthened version of RIPEMD, Fast Software Encryption, LNCS 1039, Ed. D. Gollmann, Springer-Verlag, 1996, pp. 71-82
13. Gajewski, T.A., Janicka-Lipska, I., Stoklosa, J., The FSR-255 family of hash functions with a variable length of hash result, Artificial Intelligence and Security in Computing Systems, Kluwer Academic Publishers, 2003, pp. 239-248
14. Joux,A., Collisions in SHA-0. Short Talk presented at CRYPTO 2004 Rump Session, 2004
15. Karras, D.A., Zorkadis, V.,A Novel Suite for Evaluating One-Way Hash Functions for Electronic Commerce Applications. Proceedings of the 26th EUROMICRO'00, Vol 2, pp. 2464-2468
16. Kaliski Jr, B.S., RFC 1319: The MD2 Message-Digest Algorithm, RSA Laboratories, April 1992.
17. National Institute of Standards and Technology, Secure Hash Standard, FIPS Publication-180, 1993
18. National Institute of Standards and Technology, Secure Hash Standard, FIPS Publication-180-1, 1995.
19. National Institute of Standards and Technology, Secure Hash Standard, FIPS Publication-180-2, 2002
20. NIST Brief Comments on Recent Cryptanalytic Attacks on Secure Hashing Functions and the Continued Security Provided by SHA-1. http://csrc.nist.gov/news.highlights/NIST-brief-Comments-on- SHA1-attack.pdf
21. Rijmen,V., Oswald,E., Update on SHA-1. A.J.Menezes(ed.), CT-RSA 2005, LNCS 3376, pp 58-71, 2005, Springer Verlag
22. Rivest,R., The MD4 Message Digest Algorithm. S.Vanstone(Ed.) Advances in Cryptology-CRYPTO'90, LNCS 537, pp. 303-311, Springer Verlag, 1991

23. Rivest, R.L., RFC 1320: The MD4 Message-Digest Algorithm, Network Working Group, 1992
24. Rivest,R., The MD5 Digest Algorithm, Network Working Group Request for Comments: 1321, April 1992. http://theory.lcs.mit.edu/ rivest/Rivest-MD5.txt
25. Schneier,B., Applied Cryptography, 2nd Ed., John Wiley and Sons, Inc.
26. Stallings,W., Cryptography and Network Security Principles and Practice, 3rd ed., Prentice Hall India
27. Wang,X., Yin, Y.L., Yu,H., Collision Search Attacks on SHA-1, Feb 13,2005. http://theory.csail.mit.edu/ yiqun/shanote.pdf
28. Zheng, Y., Pieprzyk, J., and J. Seberry, HAVAL - A One-Way Hashing Algorithm with Variable Length of Output, Advances in Cryptology - AusCrypt'92, Lecture Notes in Computer Science, Vol. 718, pp. 83-104, Springer-Verlag, Berlin, 1993

How to Solve Key Escrow and Identity Revocation in Identity-Based Encryption Schemes*

JoongHyo Oh[1], KyungKeun Lee[2], and SangJae Moon[2]

[1] Digital Certification Center,
Korea Financial Telecommunications and Clearings Institute(KFTC), Korea
jhoh@kftc.or.kr
[2] School of Electrical Engineering & Computer Science,
Kyungpook National Univ., Korea
honeyy@ee.knu.ac.kr, sjmoon@knu.ac.kr

Abstract. In identity-based cryptography, a user's public key is easily derived from the user's identity and a corresponding private key is generated for the user by a trusted third party, known as a Key Generation Center (KGC). The direct derivation of public keys in identity-based cryptography can eliminate the need for certificates and can solve certain public key management problems. Identity-based cryptography has many advantages for public key management, but it has two drawbacks that prevent its practical application in the real world: key escrow problems and lack of support for a fine-grained revocation of identity. At present, there is no solution that can simultaneously solve both problems; schemes that can solve the key escrow problem still have the identity revocation problem, and vice versa. In this paper, we consider a secure identity-based encryption scheme to support a fine-grained revocation without key escrow and also present a mediated key agreement protocol based on the same setting. Using the proposed scheme, we can apply identity-based cryptography more securely and practically in the real world.

Keywords: Mediated identity-based encryption, Identity revocation, Key escrow, Mediated key agreement protocol.

1 Introduction

The concept of identity-based public key cryptography was first proposed in 1984 by Adi Shamir [1]. In identity-based cryptography, a user's public key is easily derived from its identity, for example, an IP address or an e-mail address. The corresponding private key is generated for the user by a trusted third party called the Key Generation Center (KGC). The direct derivation of public keys in identity-based cryptography can eliminate the need for certificates and can solve certain public key management problems. Boneh et al. recently presented the first

---

* This research was supported by University IT Research Center Project of Korea.

S. Jajodia and C. Mazumdar (Eds.): ICISS 2005, LNCS 3803, pp. 290–303, 2005.

practical and secure identity-based encryption scheme, and many proposals for identity-based cryptographic schemes have followed [2,6,7,8,14,18,20,23,24,25].

Identity-based cryptography has many advantages in public key management, but it has two drawbacks that prevent it from being practically applied in the real world. One of these problems is key escrow, which seems to be inevitable because of the scheme's dependence on a KGC that uses a single master key to generate private keys for users. Key escrow may be essential in circumstance where an audit trail is required. However, It is undesirable mainly in personal communications. Another significant problem with current identity-based cryptographic schemes is that there is a lack of support for the fine-grained revocation of identity. An identity-based cryptographic scheme aims to simplify public key management by deriving public keys from identities, which makes it difficult to control a user's security privileges for identity revocation. For example, if a user's private key corresponds to its identity and it is compromised, then a ciphertext intended for the user may be decrypted and disclosed by a malicious user. A method for controlling the security privileges of users in an identity-based cryptosystem is essential.

At present, no solutions exist that solve both key escrow and identity revocation problems; schemes that solve the key escrow problem still face the identity revocation problem, and vice versa. In this paper, we consider a secure identity-based encryption scheme that supports a fine-grained revocation without incurring key escrow.

Related Works. An identity-based cryptosystem has an inherent key escrow because of its dependence on a KGC that uses a single master secret key to generate a user's private key. Key escrow enables the KGC to decrypt all of the ciphertext in its domain. Many schemes have been proposed to eliminate the problem of key escrow [2,12,6,8,9,10,11]. Boneh et al. and Chen et al. both proposed a multiple authority scheme to tackle the problem of key escrow [2,12]. Boneh et al.'s solution was to distribute a master key to multiple authorities using a secret sharing method in which users computed the private key in a threshold manner. Chen et al.'s scheme prevented key escrow by using multiple authorities, each with its own independent master key [12]. However, the schemes of both Boneh et al. and Chen et al. are cumbersome and inefficient as they require multiple identification by each authority.

An alternative approach to tackling the issue of key escrow is to utilize the user's chosen private information [6,8,10]. These types of schemes are similar to a certificate-based system and require the management of each user's public information due to the user's chosen private information. They can eliminate key escrow, but they lose the advantage of identity-based cryptography in which the public key is directly derived from the identity. Recently, Lee et al. proposed a secure key issuing protocol in which a private key is issued by a single key generation center, and its privacy is protected by multiple key privacy agents [9]. This scheme solves the problem of key escrow and greatly reduces the cost of user identification. However, it is complicated and requires quite a lot of computation and communication. Note that none of the schemes discussed above are able to support a fine-grained revocation of identity.

Few identity-based cryptosystems are able to check the status of an identity. This is an inherent drawback caused by the system's focus (the goal of the scheme is only to avoid the use of public key certificates). As in traditional PKI, a user's private key may be compromised with some reason. So, an efficient solution to revoke identity in identity-based cryptosystems must be provided. Boneh et al. introduced a method, called mediated RSA (mRSA), for obtaining the instantaneous revocation of a user's public key privileges [3]. The idea behind this scheme was to give one piece of the user's private key to a semi-trusted security mediator (SEM) and the other piece to a user; The user is unable to decrypt a ciphertext without a ciphertext-dependent token, which is given by the SEM. Public key revocation is achieved by forcing the SEM to stop issuing tokens for the revoked user's public key. Building on this idea, Ding and Tsudik proposed a method that transforms mRSA into an identity-based mediated RSA scheme (IB-mRSA)[5]. However, because all the users in an IB-mRSA have a common modulus, the system is completely broken if an attacker knows a user's full private key, or if a malicious user colludes with the SEM. Libert et al. proposed a more secure and efficient scheme than IB-mRSA, one that is based on Boneh and Franklin's IBE [13].

This mediated architecture eliminates the need to check the status of a public key before it is used. The sender does not have to worry about the validity of the recipient's public key before encrypting a message with the recipient's public key. The recipient will not be able to decrypt a ciphertext if his public key has been revoked; the mediator simply withholds the necessary information. In particular, in an identity-based cryptosystem, the sender cannot know the validity of the recipient's private key because the sender uses only a public key that is directly derived from the recipient's identity to encrypt the plaintext. Thus, in this environment, a mediated scheme is a good possible solution for identity revocation. With this type of mediated scheme, the ciphertext is not disclosed even if the sender uses a revoked identity to encrypt a message. Note, however, that the key escrow problem is still an issue in this mediated identity-based scheme. At present, there is no identity-based encryption scheme that supports the fine-grained revocation of identity without incurring key escrow.

Our Contribution. In this paper, to solve both key escrow and identity revocation, we propose a mediated identity-based encryption scheme that does not suffer from inherent key escrow. Our proposed scheme eliminates key escrow by using a online security mediator that provides a privacy service to each user who receives a piece of a private key from KGC and also supports a fine-grained revocation of identity simultaneously. Our scheme is the first to avoid key escrow and to also support a fine-grained identity revocation. We argue that identity-based cryptography can be applied more securely and practically in the real world if it is used in conjunction with our scheme. In addition, we sketch an application of our mediated identity-based encryption scheme ; a mediated authenticated key agreement protocol with the same system parameters and keys as the proposed mediated encryption scheme. With this protocol, users who wish to share a secret session key in the identity-based scheme do not need to worry about the validity of each other's identity and a secure session key share is possible.

The rest of this paper is organized as follows. Section 2 gives some background definitions for bilinear maps and associated computational problems. In Section 3, we give our concrete mediated identity-based encryption scheme without key escrow and, in Section 4, we show that our scheme is secure against a weak chosen ciphertext attack. Section 5 sketches a mediated authenticated key agreement protocol as an application of our encryption scheme and discusses a mediated digital signature scheme based on our mediated encryption scheme. Section 6 concludes the paper and discusses challenges for future research.

2 Background Definitions

In this section, we briefly review some of the properties of bilinear maps, which are very useful to build the identity based cryptosystems with pairing and our scheme.

Bilinear Pairings. Let $\mathbb{G}_1$ be an additive group and let $\mathbb{G}_2$ be a multiplicative group of the same prime order q. We let P denote a generator of $\mathbb{G}_1$. We assume that the discrete logarithm problem is hard in both groups. A bilinear pairing is a map $\hat{e} : \mathbb{G}_1 \times \mathbb{G}_1 \to \mathbb{G}_2$ with the following properties:

1. Bilinear : $\hat{e}(P, Q + R) = \hat{e}(P, Q) \cdot \hat{e}(P, R)$ and $\hat{e}(P + Q, R) = \hat{e}(P, R) \cdot \hat{e}(Q, R)$ for all $P, Q, R \in \mathbb{G}_1$. In particular $\hat{e}(aP, bQ) = \hat{e}(P, Q)^{ab}$ for all $P, Q \in \mathbb{G}_1$ and for all $a, b \in \mathbb{Z}_q^*$.
2. Non-degenerate : $\hat{e}$ does not send all pairs in $\mathbb{G}_1 \times \mathbb{G}_1$ to the identity in $\mathbb{G}_2$ and, if P is a generator of $\mathbb{G}_1$, then $\hat{e}(P, P)$ is a generator of $\mathbb{G}_2$.
3. Computable : There is an efficient algorithm to compute $\hat{e}(P, Q)$ for any $P, Q \in \mathbb{G}_1$.

Typically, the modified Weil or Tate pairing on an elliptic curve over a finite field can be used to build such bilinear maps. We refer to [21,2,22] for a more detailed description on how these groups, pairings, and other parameters should be selected for efficiency and security.

Bilinear Diffie-Hellman Problem (BDHP). Given two groups $\mathbb{G}_1$ and $\mathbb{G}_2$ of the same prime order q, a bilinear map $\hat{e} : \mathbb{G}_1 \times \mathbb{G}_1 \to \mathbb{G}_2$ and a generator P of $\mathbb{G}_1$, $BDHP$ is to compute $\hat{e}(P, P)^{abc}$ given (P, aP, bP, cP).

BDH Parameter Generator. As in [2], a randomize algorithm $\mathcal{IG}$ is a BDH parameter generator if $\mathcal{IG}$ takes a security parameter $k > 0$, runs in polynomial time in t, and outputs the description of groups $\mathbb{G}_1, \mathbb{G}_2$ of same prime order q and a pairing $\hat{e} : \mathbb{G}_1 \times \mathbb{G}_1 \to \mathbb{G}_2$.

3 Our Mediated Identity-Based Encryption Scheme Without Key Escrow (mIBEwe)

In this section we describe our proposed scheme, which is a secure mediated identity-based encryption scheme that does not have key escrow and that also provides a fine-grained revocation of identity. The main idea behind our scheme is using a security mediator, which we call a Privacy and Revocation Authority (PRA), to provide a private key privacy service. This PRA provides privacy service for users by authenticating them and acting as a mediator to control users' security privileges. Three entities participate in our scheme, and their roles are as follows.

- **Key Generation Center (KGC):** The KGC identifies users and generates private keys for users. It splits the private key of each user into two pieces, sending one piece to the user and the other to the PRA.
- **Privacy and Revocation Authority (PRA):** The PRA acts as an online security mediator, as in [3], and also provides a privacy service to authenticated users in order to tackle key escrow. The PRA authenticates a user by verifying if a user has a valid partial private key issued from the KGC. It should be a semi-trusted third party.
- **User:** A user is an entity that uses identity-based encryption scheme. Any user who wants to be issued a private key must be identified by the KGC. A user has a private key which is composed two partial keys issued by the KGC and the PRA.

Once a user's identity is confirmed by the KGC, the user receives a partial private key from the KGC. The PRA authenticates the user by verifying that the user is in possession of the partial private key from KGC, and then the PRA provides the authenticated user with a private key privacy service to eliminate key escrow. Fine-grained identity revocation is obtained by applying a mediated architecture [3]. Our scheme consists of 5 algorithms, Setup, KeyGenerate, PrivacyProtect, Encrypt, and Decrypt, which are concretely described below.

Setup: This algorithm takes security parameter k and returns the system parameters and the master key. This algorithm is usually run by the KGC with the PRA. We assume that parameters are publicly and authentically available.

1. The KGC runs $\mathcal{IG}$, BDH parameter generator, on input k, to generate output groups $\mathbb{G}_1, \mathbb{G}_2$ of prime order q, a generator P of $\mathbb{G}_1$, a bilinear map $\hat{e} : \mathbb{G}_1 \times \mathbb{G}_1 \to \mathbb{G}_2$ and a master-key $s \in \mathbb{Z}_q^*$. It then computes its public key, $P_{kgc} = sP$ and chooses hash functions $H_1 : \{0,1\}^* \to \mathbb{G}_1^*, H_2 : \mathbb{G}_2 \to \{0,1\}^n, H_3 : \{0,1\}^n \times \{0,1\}^n \to \mathbb{Z}_q^*, H_4 : \{0,1\}^n \to \{0,1\}^n$, where n denotes the size of the plaintext.
2. The PRA chooses its private key $t \in \mathbb{Z}_q^*$ and then computes public key, $P_{pra} = tP$. It publishes P_{pra} and keeps t secure.
3. The KGC publishes the system parameters: params $= \langle q, \mathbb{G}_1, \mathbb{G}_2, \hat{e}, n, P, P_{kgc}, P_{pra}, H_1, H_2, H_3, H_4 \rangle$.

The master-key s is only known to the KGC and the private key t is kept secure by the PRA.

KeyGenerate: A user with identity ID_A chooses a random $r \in \mathbb{Z}_q^*$ and computes $R = rP \in \mathbb{G}_1$. The user is identified by the KGC and requests the KGC to issue a private key. The KGC gives a partial private key to the user as follows.

1. A user requests the KGC to issue a private key by sending R and ID_A.
2. The KGC computes the hash value $Q_A = H_1(ID_A)$ and private key $D_A^k = sQ_A$. Then it chooses a random point $d_{A,user}^k \in \mathbb{G}_1$ and computes $d_{A,pra}^k = D_A^k - d_{A,user}^k$.
3. The KGC computes $T_1 = sR + d_{A,user}^k$ and $K_1 = \hat{e}(d_{A,pra}^k, R)$, and then gives blinded partial private key T_1 and K_1 to the user, while $d_{A,pra}^k$ is given securely to the PRA. We assume that there is a secure channel between the KGC and the PRA.
4. The user computes $d_{A,user}^k = T_1 - rP_{kgc}$ and checks the partial private key by verifying $\hat{e}(d_{A,user}^k, R) \cdot K_1 = (Q_A, P_{kgc})^r$. If the verification is successful, the user then keeps it secure. Because $rP_{kgc} = sR = rsP$ acts as a sort of DH-type session key, the KGC and a user are able to communicate securely without any secure channel.

PrivacyProtect: To be provided privacy service which is able to tackle key escrow, the user must convince the PRA that he (or she) has the valid partial private key from the KGC. If possession of the partial private key is proved, the PRA provides the key privacy service as follows.

1. The user chooses a random value $x \in \mathbb{Z}_q^*$ and computes $X = xP$, $Y = \hat{e}(X, d_{A,user}^k)$, $Z = \hat{e}(P_{kgc}, Q_A)^x$.
2. The user sends (X, Y, Z) and his identity ID_A to the PRA.
3. By verifying $Z = Y \cdot \hat{e}(X, d_{A,pra}^k)$, the PRA verifies the user's possession of the partial private key. If the verification is unsuccessful, then the PRA sends an 'Error' message and terminates the protocol. The verification of the partial signature of the user is easily computed as follows by a bilinear map property.

$$
\begin{aligned}
Y \cdot \hat{e}(X, d_{A,pra}^k) &= \hat{e}(X, d_{A,user}^k) \cdot \hat{e}(X, d_{A,pra}^k) \\
&= \hat{e}(X, d_{A,user}^k + d_{A,pra}^k) \\
&= \hat{e}(X, D_A^k) \\
&= \hat{e}(xP, sQ_A) \\
&= \hat{e}(sP, Q_A)^x = Z
\end{aligned}
$$

4. The PRA computes $Q_A = H_1(ID_A)$ and $D_A^p = tQ_A$. Then the PRA chooses a random point $d_{A,user}^p \in \mathbb{G}_1^*$ and computes $d_{A,pra}^p = D_A^p - d_{A,user}^p$.
5. The PRA computes $T_2 = tX + d_{A,user}^p$ and $K_2 = \hat{e}(d_{A,pra}^p, X)$, then gives a blinded partial private key T_2 and K_2 to the user. The PRA computes $D_{A,pra} = d_{A,pra}^k + d_{A,pra}^p$ and keeps it securely with ID_A as a PRA's half of the user's private key.

6. The user computes $d^p_{A,user} = T_2 - xP_{pra}$ and checks the partial private key by verifying $\hat{e}(d^p_{A,user}, X) \cdot K_2 = (Q_A, P_{pra})^x$. If the verification is successful, then he computes $D_{A,user} = d^k_{A,user} + d^p_{A,user}$ and stores it securely as his final (partial) private key.

Encrypt: This is almost the same as in the scheme originally proposed by Boneh and Franklin [2]. Given a plaintext M and recipient's identity ID_A

1. Compute $Q_A = H_1(ID_A) \in \mathbb{G}_1$,
2. Choose a random $\sigma \in \{0,1\}^n$ and compute $a = H_3(\sigma, M)$.
3. Compute $U = aP$, $g = \hat{e}(P_{kgc} + P_{pra}, Q_A)^a \in \mathbb{G}_2$. Note that $P_{kgc} + P_{pra}$ can be stored with pre-computation.
4. The ciphertext is $C = \langle U, V, W \rangle = \langle aP, \sigma \oplus H_2(g), M \oplus H_4(\sigma) \rangle$.

Decrypt: After receiving the ciphertext $C = \langle U, V, W \rangle$, the recipient forwards it to the PRA. The PRA computes the partial information to decrypt the ciphertext and sends it to the recipient.

1. The PRA checks if the recipient's identity ID_A is revoked. If it is, it returns an 'ID revoked' error message.
2. If it is not revoked, the PRA computes $g_{pra} = \hat{e}(U, D_{A,pra})$ and sends it to the recipient.
3. The recipient computes $g_{user} = \hat{e}(U, D_{A,user})$.
4. When receiving g_{pra} from the PRA, the recipient computes $g = g_{pra} \cdot g_{user}$.
5. The recipient computes $\sigma = V \oplus H_3(g)$ and then $M = W \oplus H_4(\sigma)$.
6. Then the recipient computes $a = H_3(\sigma, M)$ and tests that $U = aP$. If not, the ciphertext is rejected.
   It is easy to verify the consistency from bilinear properties .

$$\begin{aligned}
g_{user}g_{pra} &= \hat{e}(U, D_{A,user}) \cdot \hat{e}(U, D_{A,pra}) \\
&= \hat{e}(U, D_{A,user} + D_{A,pra}) \\
&= \hat{e}(U, d^k_{A,user} + d^p_{A,user} + d^k_{A,pra} + d^p_{A,pra}) \\
&= \hat{e}(U, D^k_A + D^p_A) \\
&= \hat{e}(U, D^k_A)\hat{e}(U, D^p_A) \\
&= \hat{e}(sP, Q_A)^a \hat{e}(tP, Q_A)^a \\
&= \hat{e}(sP + tP, Q_A)^a \\
&= \hat{e}(P_{kgc} + P_{pra}, Q_A)^a = g
\end{aligned}$$

The KGC can't learn the PRA's private key and, likewise, the PRA can't know the master key of the KGC. Note that the KGC and the PRA are two distinct authorities and do not collude with each other. The user's partial private key consists of two half pieces, one from the KGC and one from the PRA. So, the KGC and PRA never know both halves of the user's private key. They are therefore unable to decrypt ciphertexts intended for the user. If key escrow is required in case of need such as audit trail, the KGC can obtain the user's half private key from the SEM with legal treatment.

Additionally, users never know the PRA's partial private key and cannot compute ciphertext dependent token to decrypt a ciphertext anywhere without the PRA's assistance. As well, because users can decrypt with only the PRA's help, the PRA can control the security privilege of the user on identity revocation; a ciphertext which was encrypted with revoked identity is not able to decrypt at all, so fine-grained revocation of an identity is provided. Even though the KGC's master key is compromised, a ciphertext of a user is not disclosed and, similarly, though the PRA is attacked, attacker cannot decrypt ciphertexts of users and he is just able to revoke a unrevoked user or unrevoke a revoked user. The only way for a attacker to completely break our scheme is to take control of both the KGC and the PRA.

The KGC is responsible for identifying users. After a successful identification, the KGC issues a private key to the user. The PRA simply provides a privacy service to an authenticated user who already has a partial private key from the KGC. The PRA should be a semi-trusted third party. Users are identified only by the KGC. Our scheme can provide fine-grained identity revocation without incurring key escrow and, also, it does not require a secure channel because it uses a DH-type blinding information.

4   Security

We will now show that our mediated identity-based encryption scheme without key escrow (mIBEwe) is weakly semantically secure against insider attack when the attacker does not have the user's partial private key, which corresponds to the target identity. We will prove the security of our scheme by the same method as was used in [15].

Definition 1. *We say that our mediated identity based encryption scheme without key escrow (mIBEwe) is weakly semantically secure against insider attack if no polynomially bounded adversary has a non-negligible advantage in the following game. IND-mIBEwe-wCCA denotes the security notion of indistinguishability against weak Chosen Ciphertext Attacks in our mediated identity-based encryption scheme.*

Game Setup: The challenger takes a security parameter k and runs the Setup procedure of mIBEwe, which gives the adversary $\mathcal{A}$ the resulting system parameters.

Phase 1: $\mathcal{A}$ issues a sequence of queries, each one being either a decryption query, a partial user key extraction query, a partial PRA key extraction query, a partial user privacy key extraction query, a partial PRA privacy key extraction query, or a PRA decryption query. Each query may be adaptive based on information gained from the previous query.

- Decryption query : $\mathcal{A}$ produces an identity ID_i and a ciphertext C_i. For a decryption query of $\mathcal{A}$, the challenger generates both pieces of the private key and privacy key corresponding to ID_i and sends the result of the decryption of C_i to $\mathcal{A}$.

- Partial user key extraction query (q_1) : $\mathcal{A}$ chooses an identity ID_i and receives the user part of the private key issued by KGC($d_{i,user}^k$).
- Partial PRA key extraction query (q_2) : $\mathcal{A}$ chooses an identity ID_i and receives the PRA part of the private key generated by the KGC($d_{i,pra}^k$).
- Partial user privacy key extraction query (q_3) : From this query, $\mathcal{A}$ receives the user's part of the privacy key corresponding to $ID_i(d_{i,user}^p)$.
- Partial PRA privacy key extraction query (q_4) : $\mathcal{A}$ chooses an identity ID_i and receives the part of the privacy key that belongs to the PRA($d_{i,pra}^p$).
- PRA decryption query (q_d) : $\mathcal{A}$ chooses an identity ID_i and a ciphertext C_i, and receives a token allowing the user of identity ID_i to decrypt the ciphertext.

Challenge: Once $\mathcal{A}$ decides that Phase 1 is over, $\mathcal{A}$ chooses two plaintexts $m_0, m_1 \in \mathcal{M}$ and an identity ID_c on which it wishes to be challenged. It is not allowed to choose an identity for which it made queries during Phase 1. The challenger now picks a random bit $b \in \{0,1\}$ and computes C, the ciphertext of m_b with the ID_c that is sent to $\mathcal{A}$.

Phase 2: $\mathcal{A}$ issues a second sequence of queries as in Phase 1. This time, $\mathcal{A}$ cannot ask the plaintext corresponding to C nor the partial private key corresponding to ID_c. But $\mathcal{A}$ is allowed to make a PRA decryption on C for the identity ID_c.

Guess: $\mathcal{A}$ outputs a guess $b' \in \{0,1\}$ and wins the game if $b = b'$.

We define $\mathcal{A}$'s advantage in this game to be $Adv(\mathcal{A}) := |2 \cdot Pr[b' = b] - 1|$.

Theorem 1. *Suppose that H_1, H_2 and H_3 are random oracles and that there exists* IND-mIBEwe-wCCA *adversary $\mathcal{A}$ against our mediated identity based encryption scheme without key escrow. Suppose $\mathcal{A}$ has advantage ϵ, runs in polynomial time t, makes at most q_1 partial user key extraction query, q_2 partial PRA key extraction query, q_3 partial user privacy key extraction query, q_4 partial PRA privacy key extraction query and q_d PRA decryption query. Then we have an adversary $\mathcal{B}$ that is able to win the IND-ID-CCA2 game against the Boneh-Franklin's FullIdent scheme with the same advantage ϵ. $\mathcal{B}$ runs in time $t' = t + O(q_1 t_s + q_d t_\epsilon)$ where t_s denotes the time to compute the key simulate procedure and t_ϵ is the computation time of the pairing $\hat{e}$.*

Proof. We use the attacker $\mathcal{A}$ to build an algorithm $\mathcal{B}$ that is able to distinguish ciphertexts produced by the Boneh-Franklin's FullIdent scheme. At first, $\mathcal{B}$ is given the Boneh-Franklin FullIdent scheme's system parameters, params $= \langle q, \mathbb{G}_1, \mathbb{G}_2, \hat{e}, n, P, P_{pub}, H_1, H_2, H_3, H_4 \rangle$, produced by the challenger[2]. $\mathcal{B}$ simulates the Setup of mIBEwe to create the PRA's private key t and computes $P_{pra} = tP$. Then, $\mathcal{B}$ computes $P_{kgc} = P_{pub} - P_{pra}$ and provides the new system parameters, params $= \langle q, \mathbb{G}_1, \mathbb{G}_2, \hat{e}, n, P, P_{kgc}, P_{pra}, H_1, H_2, H_3, H_4 \rangle$ to $\mathcal{A}$ as parameters of mIBEwe. $\mathcal{B}$ will act as $\mathcal{A}$'s challenger in the IND-mIBEwe-wCCA game and controls the PRA. It maintains a list $\mathcal{K}_l$ of tuples $\langle ID_i, d_{i,user}^k, d_{i,user}^p, d_{i,pra}^k, d_{i,pra}^p \rangle$. The list is initially empty.

Phase 1: $\mathcal{A}$ launches Phase 1 of its attack by making a series of queries. $\mathcal{B}$ answers these queries as follows.

1. In the case of every query made by $\mathcal{A}$ to random oracles H_1, H_2 and H_3, $\mathcal{B}$ simply forwards the query to its challenger and sends the answer back to $\mathcal{A}$.
2. If the query is to decrypt C_i under the private key for ID_i then $\mathcal{B}$ relays the decryption query to the challenger and simply relays the plaintext derived from the challenger to $\mathcal{A}$ directly.
3. For a partial user key extraction query on an ID_i, $\mathcal{B}$ first checks whether the list $\mathcal{K}_l$ already contains an entry for ID_i. If the query ID_i already appears on the list $\mathcal{K}_l$ in a tuple $\langle ID_i, d^k_{i,user}, d^k_{i,pra}, d^p_{i,user}, d^p_{i,pra} \rangle$, then $\mathcal{B}$ simply sends $d^k_{i,user}$ on the list to $\mathcal{A}$. If no such entry is found in the list $\mathcal{K}_l$, $\mathcal{B}$ forwards ID_i to its challenger and receives a private key D_i. Then, $\mathcal{B}$ performs a key simulate procedure using D_i as follows.

> key simulate : $\mathcal{B}$ computes $D^p_i = tH_1(ID_i)$ and $D^k_i = D_i - D^p_i$. $\mathcal{B}$ chooses random $d^k_{i,user}, d^p_{i,user} \in \mathbb{G}_1$ and computes $d^k_{i,pra} = D^k_i - d^k_{i,user}$ and $d^p_{i,pra} = D^p_i - d^p_{i,user}$.

   $\mathcal{B}$ sends $d^k_{i,user}$ to $\mathcal{A}$ and puts the entry $\langle ID_i, d^k_{i,user}, d^k_{i,pra}, d^p_{i,user}, d^p_{i,pra} \rangle$ into the list $\mathcal{K}_l$.
4. When $\mathcal{A}$ issues a partial PRA key extraction query with ID_i, $\mathcal{B}$ first searches in the list $\mathcal{K}_l$ for an entry containing ID_i. If such an entry is found, it returns $d^k_{i,pra}$ on the list to $\mathcal{A}$. Otherwise, $\mathcal{B}$ forwards ID_i to the challenger and receives a private key D_i. $\mathcal{B}$ performs key simulate procedure with D_i as above step 3. $\mathcal{B}$ sends $d^k_{i,pra}$ to $\mathcal{A}$ and puts the entry $\langle ID_i, d^k_{i,user}, d^k_{i,pra}, d^p_{i,user}, d^p_{i,pra} \rangle$ into the list $\mathcal{K}_l$.
5. When $\mathcal{A}$ issues a partial user privacy key extraction query, $\mathcal{B}$ first searches in the list $\mathcal{K}_l$ for an entry containing ID_i. If such an entry is found, it returns $d^p_{i,user}$ on the list to $\mathcal{A}$. Otherwise, $\mathcal{B}$ forwards ID_i to the challenger and receives a private key D_i. $\mathcal{B}$ performs key simulate procedure with D_i as step 3. $\mathcal{B}$ sends $d^p_{i,user}$ to $\mathcal{A}$ and puts the entry $\langle ID_i, d^k_{i,user}, d^k_{i,pra}, d^p_{i,user}, d^p_{i,pra} \rangle$ into the list $\mathcal{K}_l$.
6. For a partial PRA privacy key extraction query on an ID_i, $\mathcal{B}$ first checks whether the list $\mathcal{K}_l$ already contains an entry for ID_i. If such an entry is in the list $\mathcal{K}_l$, $\mathcal{B}$ simply returns $d^{pra}_{i,pra}$ on the list to $\mathcal{A}$. Otherwise, $\mathcal{B}$ forwards ID_i to the challenger and receives a private key D_i. $\mathcal{B}$ performs key simulate procedure with D_i as step 3. $\mathcal{B}$ sends $d^p_{i,pra}$ to $\mathcal{A}$ and puts the entry $\langle ID_i, d^k_{i,user}, d^k_{i,pra}, d^p_{i,user}, d^p_{i,pra} \rangle$ into the list $\mathcal{K}_l$.
7. For a PRA decryption query on a ciphertext $C_i = (U, V, W)$ and an identity ID_i, $\mathcal{B}$ first searches in the list $\mathcal{K}_l$ for an entry containing ID_i. If such an entry is found, it recovers the $d^k_{i,pra}$ and $d^p_{i,pra}$ in the list $\mathcal{K}_l$. Then $\mathcal{B}$ computes the pairing $\hat{e}(U, d^k_{i,pra} + d^p_{i,pra})$ and sends it to $\mathcal{A}$. If no such entry exists, $\mathcal{B}$ forwards ID_i to the challenger and receives a private key D_i. $\mathcal{B}$ performs key simulate procedure with D_i as step 3. $\mathcal{B}$ computes $\hat{e}(U, d^k_{i,pra} + d^p_{i,pra})$, sends it to $\mathcal{A}$, and puts the entry $\langle ID_i, d^k_{i,user}, d^k_{i,pra}, d^p_{i,user}, d^p_{i,pra} \rangle$ into the list $\mathcal{K}_l$.

Challenge: At some point, $\mathcal{A}$ decides to end Phase 1 and outputs the challenge identity ID_c and two equal length plaintexts $m_0, m_1 \in \mathcal{M}$. In particular, ID_c cannot be an identity for which the partial private key has been extracted.

When $\mathcal{B}$ receives the challenge plaintext, it forwards m_0 and m_1 to its challenger and chooses ID_c as its challenge identity. It then receives a ciphertext from its challenger and forwards a ciphertext as a challenge to $\mathcal{A}$.

Phase 2: $\mathcal{A}$ continues to issue a series of queries as in Phase 1 and $\mathcal{B}$ responds to it in the same way as in Phase 1.

Guess: At the end of the game, $\mathcal{A}$ makes a guess b' for b. Then $\mathcal{B}$ outputs b' as its own guess to its challenger. It is clear that $\mathcal{B}$ wins the IND-ID-CCA2 game if and only if $\mathcal{A}$ wins the IND-mIBEwe-wCCA game that it plays with $\mathcal{B}$. $\mathcal{B}$'s advantage is the same as $\mathcal{A}$'s. It takes time $t' = t + O(q_1 t_s + q_d t_\epsilon)$ for reduction, where t_s denotes the time to compute the key simulate procedure and t_ϵ is the computation time of the pairing $\hat{e}$.   □

5   An Application to Key Agreement Protocol and Digital Signature

In this section, we sketch a mediated key agreement protocol based on the mediated identity-based encryption scheme given in Section 3 and discuss a challenging issue of a mediated digital signature based on our encryption scheme. This protocol may be quite useful when viewed as part of a complete package with the same mediated system architecture.

In traditional PKI, key agreement protocols rely on the parties obtaining each other's certificates, extracting each other's public keys, checking certificate chains and, finally, generating a shared secret. The technique of identity-based cryptography greatly simplifies this process. However, in identity-based key agreement protocols, the identity of the user may be revoked for some reason. For example, the user's private key could be compromised. In this case, the status of the identity must be checked. In this section, we present a mediated key agreement protocol without key escrow based on Smart's scheme [18]. Smart's protocol has inherent key escrow. With our mediated protocol, the problems of identity revocation and key escrow can be eliminated in identity-based key agreement protocols.

The system Setup, KeyGenerate and PrivacyProtect are the same as in mIBEwe scheme outlined in section 3. Suppose two users A and B wish to share a secret key. Each user has one piece of the private key($D_{A,user}$ or $D_{B,user}$) and the PRA has the other part, as stipulated in the KeyGenerate and PrivacyProtect procedure in Section 3. A and B both generate an ephemeral private key, a and b, in $\mathbb{Z}_q^*$ and compute $T_A = aP$ and $T_B = bP$, respectively. They send an ephemeral public key to each other as follows to agree to a secret key.

User A		User B
$a \in \mathbb{Z}_q^*$		$b \in \mathbb{Z}_q^*$
compute $T_A = aP$		compute $T_B = bP$
	$\xrightarrow{\quad T_A \quad}$	T_A
T_B	$\xleftarrow{\quad T_B \quad}$	

Then user A sends T_B to the PRA and receives $\hat{e}(D_{A,pra}, T_B)$ in exchange. A computes a session key, $K_{AB} = \hat{e}(aQ_B, P_{kgc}+P_{pra})\hat{e}(D_{A,pra}, T_B)\hat{e}(D_{A,user}, T_B)$. B also is able to compute $K_{BA} = \hat{e}(bQ_A, P_{kgc}+P_{pra})\hat{e}(D_{B,pra}, T_A)\hat{e}(D_{B,user}, T_A)$ in the same way. We can show that the secret shared keys agree,

$$
\begin{aligned}
K_{AB} &= \hat{e}(aQ_B, P_{kgc} + P_{pra})\hat{e}(D_{A,pra}, T_B)\hat{e}(D_{A,user}, T_B) \\
&= \hat{e}(Q_B, P_{kgc} + P_{pra})^a \hat{e}(D_{A,pra} + D_{A,user}, T_B) \\
&= \hat{e}(Q_B, P_{kgc})^a \hat{e}(Q_B + P_{pra})^a \hat{e}(D_A^k + D_A^p, T_B) \\
&= \hat{e}(sQ_B, aP)\hat{e}(tQ_B, aP)\hat{e}(D_A^k, T_B)\hat{e}(D_A^p, T_B) \\
&= \hat{e}(sQ_B + tQ_B, aP)\hat{e}(sQ_A, bP)\hat{e}(tQ_A, bP) \\
&= \hat{e}(D_B^k + D_B^p, T_A)\hat{e}(bQ_A, sP + tP) \\
&= \hat{e}(D_{B,user} + D_{B,pra}, T_A)\hat{e}(bQ_A, P_{kgc} + P_{pra}) \\
&= \hat{e}(D_{B,user}, T_A)\hat{e}(D_{B,pra}, T_A)\hat{e}(bQ_A, P_{kgc} + P_{pra}) \\
&= K_{BA}
\end{aligned}
$$

If the identity of a user was revoked, the PRA does not send a partial computation to complete key agreement. Therefore, each party needs not worry about the validity of the other's identity. The KGC and the PRA cannot find out a private key of a user and cannot compute a partial computation of a user by one-self. Key escrow does not exist if the KGC does not collude with the PRA. Each user who participates in the protocol computes two bilinear pairing computation and this is the same in original Smart's protocol [18]. It is trivial to add a key confirmation property to our mediated key agreement protocol, making a three pass protocol as [16,18]. Additionally, to ensure forward secrecy, A and B can instead use the shared key $H(K_{AB}\|abP)$, where H is a suitable hash function [16]. With our mediated key agreement protocol, we can share easily a secure key without key escrow and worry about the identity revocation.

Now, we discuss an application to a mediated digital signature based on our mediated encryption scheme in Section 3. A mediated pairing-based digital signature scheme was presented in [15] but this is not identity-based scheme. There is no mediated pairing-based identity-based digital signature scheme. Several identity-based digital signature schemes with pairing were proposed[23,24,20,25]. However, these schemes seem unable to transform a mediated version based on our mediated encryption scheme. It is owing to that private key computation of signature algorithms consists of a simple multiplication with hash value. This results that a user finds out the part of the private key that belongs to the PRA. We argue that simple transformation of existing identity-based signature schemes with pairing is impossible. To keep secure the part of the private key that belong to the PRA in a pairing-based mediated identity-based digital signature scheme, we think that the PRA's partial computation should be a form of bilinear pairing and more researches in this issue are needed.

6   Conclusions

In this paper, we considered how to solve both key escrow and identity revocation in identity-based encryption schemes. In order to eliminate key escrow of the

KGC, we subdivided the key issuing authority into two parties; KGC and SEM which provides a fine-grained identity revocation. With this separation, we could consider eliminating key escrow and fine-grained identity revocation in the proposed scheme. The proposed scheme will be a practical solution to consider both key escrow and identity revocation simultaneously in identity-based encryption schemes. We also presented a mediated authenticated key agreement protocol as an application of our mediated encryption scheme. This simple protocol may be quite useful when viewed as part of a complete package with the proposed mediated encryption scheme. By using our mediated schemes, the identity-based cryptography can be applied more securely and practically in the real world. As a future work, we intend to develop a distributed model of our mediated architecture and appropriate digital signature scheme based on our proposed mediated encryption scheme.

Acknowledgement

The authors would like to thank the anonymous reviewers for their helpful comments.

References

1. A.Shamir, "Identity-based cryptosystems and signature schemes," *CRYPTO'84*, LNCS 196, Springer-Verlag, pp.47-53, 1984.
2. D.Boneh and M.Franklin, "Identity-based encryption from the Weil pairing," *CRYPTO'01*, LNCS 2139, Springer-Verlag, pp.213-229, 2001.
3. D.Boneh, X.Ding, G.Tsudik, and C.M.Wong, "A method for fast revocation of public key certificates and security capabilities," In *10th USENIX Security Symposium*, Washington, D.C., 2001.
4. D.Boneh, X.Ding, and G.Tsudik, "Identity based encryption using mediated rsa," In *3rd Workshop on Information Security Application*, Jeju Island, 2002.
5. X.Ding and G.Tsudik, "Simple Identity-Based Cryptography with Mediated RSA," In *Proceedings of CT-RSA'03*, LNCS, Springer-Verlag, 2003.
6. C.Gentry, "Certificate-based encryption and the certificate revocation problem," *EUROCRYPT 2003*, LNCS 2656, Springer-Verlag, pp.272-293, 2003.
7. K.G.Paterson, "Cryptographic from pairings: a snapshot of current research," *Information Security Technical Report*, 7(3), pp.41-54, 2002.
8. S.Al-Riyami and K.G.Paterson, "Certificateless public key cryptography," *Asiacrypt 2003*, LNCS 2894, Springer-Verlag, pp.452-473, 2003.
9. B.Lee, C.Boyd, E.Dawson, K.Kim, J.Yang and S.Yoo, "Secure Key Issuing in ID-Based Cryptography," *ACM Second Australasian Information Security Workshop*, New Zealand, pp.69-74, 2004.
10. Z.Cheng, R.Comley and L.Vasiu, "Remove Key Escrow from The Identity-Based Encryption System," In *Foundations of Information Technology in the Era of Network and Mobile Computing*, 2004.
11. Ai-fen,et.al, "Separable and Anonymous Identity-Based Key Issuing without Secure Channel," Cryptology ePrint Archive, Report2004/322, 2004.

12. L.Chen, K.Harrison, N.Smart and D.Soldera, "Applications of multiple trust authorities in pairing based cryptosystems," *InfraSec 2002*, LNCS 2437, Springer-Verlag, pp.260-275, 2002.

13. B.Libert and J.Quisquater, "Efficient Revocation and Threshold Pairing Based Cryptosystems," *Principle of Distributed Computing(PODC) 2003*

14. J.Baek and Y.Zheng, "Identity-Based Threshold Decryption," Cryptology ePrint Archive, Report2003/164, 2003.

15. B.Libert and J.Quisquater, "What is Possible with Identity Based Cryptography for PKIs and What Still Must Be Improved," *EuroPKI 2004*, LNCS 3093, Springer-Verlag, pp.57-70, 2004.

16. L.Chen and C.Kudla, "Identity Based Authenticated Key Agreement Protocols from Pairings," *16th IEEE Computer Security Foundations Workshop - CSFW 2003* pp.219-233, 2003.

17. W.Junior and R.Terada, "An IBE Scheme to Exchage Authenticated Sceret Keys," Cryptology ePrint Archive, Report2004/071, 2004.

18. N.P.Smart, "An Identity based authenticated key agreement protocol based on the Weil pairing," *Electronic Letters*, vol.38, pp.630-632, 2002.

19. N.McCullagh and P.Barreto, "A New Two-Party Identity-Based Authenticated Key Agreement," Cryptology ePrint Archive, Report2004/122, 2004.

20. F.Hess, "Efficient Identity Based Signature Schemes based on Pairings," *Selected Areas in Cryptography 9th Annual International Workshop, SAC2002*, LNCS 2595, Springer-Verlag, pp.310-324, 2003.

21. P.Barreto, H.Kim, B.Lynnn and M.scott, "Efficient algorithms for pairing-based cryptosystems," *CRYPTO2002*, LNCS 2442, Springer-Verlag, pp.354-368, 2002.

22. S.Galbraith, "Supersingular curves in cryptography," *AsiaCrypt2001*, LNCS 2248, Springer-Verlag, pp.495-513, 2001.

23. J.C. Cha and J.H. Cheon, "An Identity-Based Signature from Gap Diffie-Hellman Groups," *Public key Cryptography-PKC 2003*, LNCS 2567, Springer-Verag, pp.18-30, 2003.

24. K.G.Paterson, "ID-based signatures from pairings on elliptic curves," *Electronics Letters*, vol.38, no.18, pp.1025-1026, 2002.

25. J.A. Solinas, "ID-based Digital Signature Algorithms," *7th Workshop on Elliptic Curve Cryptography-ECC 2003*, 2003.

On Broadcast Encryption with Random Key Pre-distribution Schemes

Mahalingam Ramkumar

Department of Computer Science and Engineering,
Mississippi State University, Mississippi State, MS 39762
ramkumar@cse.msstate.edu

Abstract. Broadcast encryption (BE) deals with the problem of establishing a secret, shared by $g = G - r$ *privileged* nodes, among a set G nodes. Specifically, a set of r *revoked* nodes are denied access to the secret. Many schemes to address this problem, based on key pre-distribution schemes (KPS), have been proposed in the literature. Most state-of-the-art methods employ tree-based techniques. However, *random* key pre-distribution schemes (RKPS), which have received a lot of attention in the recent past (especially in the context of ad hoc and sensor network security), also cater for BE. In this paper we analyze the performance of BE using RKPSs. While in most tree-based methods the source of the broadcast is assumed to be the root of the tree (unless asymmetric cryptographic primitives can be used), BE using RKPSs caters for BE by *peers* - without the need for asymmetric cryptography. Furthermore, unlike most BE schemes where the identities of the revoked nodes have to be explicitly specified, BE using RKPSs allow for protecting the identities of the revoked nodes, which could be a useful property in application scenarios where privacy is a crucial issue.

1 Introduction

Broadcast encryption (BE) [1] provides a means of establishing shared secret between g privileged nodes, among of a set of G nodes, where $g + r = G$, and the r nodes which are *not* provided with the secret are usually referred to a revoked nodes. For situations where $g << G$ it may be more efficient to set-up a shared secret between g nodes using g unicast transmissions. However, for scenarios where $r << G$ (or $g \approx G$) such an approach is very inefficient. BE schemes provide a very satisfactory solution for cases where $r << G$.

In many application scenarios [2], BE may assume a slightly different form. The universe, or the set $\mathbb{U}$, consists of all nodes in the system. Out of $\mid \mathbb{U} \mid = N$ nodes, there may exist a subset $\mathbb{G}_0 \in \mathbb{U}$ of G nodes. Typically, the G nodes share a secret (a priori), privy only to the nodes in the set $\mathbb{G}_0$. The problem that BE needs to address in this case, is the efficient dissemination of a secret to all nodes in $\mathbb{G}_0$ - except a subset $\mathbb{G}_R \in \mathbb{G}_0$ of r nodes. At the end, this results in a new subset $\mathbb{G}_1 = \mathbb{G}_0 \setminus \mathbb{G}_R$ of $g = G - r$ nodes, which now share a secret (not available to nodes not in $\mathbb{G}_1$).

Typically, BE is realized using some form of key pre-distribution, where a set of k secrets are distributed to each node in the universe of N nodes (before the system is deployed). The source of the broadcast then

S. Jajodia and C. Mazumdar (Eds.): ICISS 2005, LNCS 3803, pp. 304–316, 2005.

1. chooses a broadcast secret K_b (intended for the set $\mathbb{G}_0$),
2. encrypts K_b using n keys $K_{e1} \cdots K_{en}$, and
3. transmits n values $E_{K_{ei}}(K_b), 1 \leq i \leq n$.

The keys $K_{e1} \cdots K_{en}$ are chosen in such a way that none of the r nodes in $\mathbb{G}_R$ can (using their preloaded secrets) "discover" *any* of the keys $K_{e1} \cdots K_{en}$, while the remaining $G - r$ nodes in $\mathbb{G}_1 = \mathbb{G}_0 \setminus \mathbb{G}_R$ may be able to discover *at least one* of the secrets $K_{e1} \cdots K_{en}$, and thereby gain access to the secret K_b. Typically, the source of the broadcast does *not care* if the nodes in $\mathbb{U} \setminus \mathbb{G}_0$ gain access to K_b. For example, if the G nodes shared a secret K_{N_0} *before* the broadcast, the shared secret between the nodes in $\mathbb{G}_1$ *after* the broadcast may be $K_b \oplus K_{N_0}$ - which neither the explicitly revoked nodes in $\mathbb{G}_R$ or the other nodes $\mathbb{U} \setminus \mathbb{G}_0$ can gain access to - the former do not have access to K_b and the latter do not have access to K_{N_0}.

The efficiency of BE schemes is usually measured in terms of:

1. The bandwidth needed for the broadcast. More specifically, the number of encryptions needed to securely convey the broadcast secret, and overheads, if any.
2. Resilience of the scheme to collusion of revoked nodes.
3. Storage complexity at the receivers of the broadcast.
4. Computational complexity for recovering the broadcast secret for each receiver.
5. Computational complexity involved in choosing the keys $K_{e1} \cdots K_{en}$ by the source of the broadcast.

Efficient solutions to the problem of broadcast encryption has received a lot of attention since the problem was defined by Fiat and Noar in Ref. [1]. Most current state of the art solutions [3] - [8] are tree-based, where the source of the broadcast is assumed to be the trusted authority (TA) at the root of the tree, who distributes the secrets in the first place. However, such schemes can generally be extended to permit broadcast by parties other than the TA - if asymmetric cryptographic primitives are employed.

In this paper we consider BE using random key pre-distribution schemes (RKPS). Though RKPSs can also be deployed in a tree-like hierarchy, we restrict ourselves to a "flat" deployment. We argue that BE using RKPS schemes offers many advantages over the better known tree-based BE schemes for many application scenarios. Specifically, the two primary advantages offered by RKPSs (over tree-based schemes) are:

1. they permit *any* node to perform BE, *without* the use of asymmetric cryptographic primitives
2. they permit revocation of nodes without *explicitly specifying* the identities of revoked nodes - which is potentially very useful when privacy is a concern.

The rest of this paper is organized as follows. In Section 2 we briefly review KPSs, with an emphasis on RKPSs. In Section 3 we provide a quantitative analysis of the efficiency of BE using RKPSs. Discussions, interpretations and comparisons with other BE schemes, and some potential applications is the topic of Section 4. Conclusions are offered in Section 5.

2   Key Pre-distribution

A key distribution scheme (KDS) is a mechanism for distributing secrets to all nodes in a network. The secrets provided to each node facilitate establishment of cryptographic bonds or associations between the nodes. KDSs can be broadly classified into two categories. In the first category are schemes where the secrets distributed to[1] each node are *independent*. In other words, secrets of a node do not provide any information about secrets of other nodes. Examples of KDSs in this category include schemes based on the symmetric Needham-Schroeder protocol [9] (or Kerberos-like schemes), and the public key infrastructure (PKI).

For schemes in the second category, key pre-distribution schemes (KPS) [10], the secrets distributed to each node are *not* completely independent. The primary advantage of KPSs is that they cater for ad hoc authentication of nodes *without* the involvement of the TA, and *without* the use of asymmetric cryptography. Typically KPSs consist of a trusted authority (TA) who chooses a set of P secrets, and N nodes with unique IDs. Each node is provided with a "key ring" consisting of k secrets. The set of secrets provided to each node is a function of the P secrets chosen by the TA and the unique ID of the node. However, by exposing secrets from a finite number of nodes, it may be possible to determine all P secrets of the TA and thus compromise the KPS entirely. There is thus a concept of n-secure KPS. An n-secure KPS can "resist" coalitions of up to n nodes. More specifically, up to n nodes pooling their secrets together cannot compromise a n-secure KPS. Typically, for most KPSs $k \propto n$. Thus KPSs are inherently trade-offs between security (coalition size n that can be resisted) and complexity (of secure storage, k).

2.1 Random KPS

The concept of n-secureness of a KPS is however not an adequate description of *random* key pre-distribution schemes (RKPS). For any RKPS, by exposing secrets from n nodes an attacker could discover *shared secrets* between arbitrary nodes with a some probability p. Thus a more appropriate characterization of RKPSs is as (n, p)-secure.

RKPSs exploit two fundamental "dimensions"

1. *the uniqueness of intersections of large subsets* consisting of *independent* keys, and
2. *generating many keys* from each independent key.

Many RKPS schemes that exploit the first dimension, uniqueness of intersections, have been proposed in literature. We refer to all such schemes as RPS (random preloaded subsets). RPS schemes are extensions of *subset intersection* schemes [11] - [13], with the twist that the allocation of keys is random or pseudo-random. Dyer et al [14] (in 1995) was the first to point out the simplicity and effectiveness of *random subset allocations* in the literature. The idea of random subsets has received substantial attention in the recent past in the context of sensor networks [15] - [20] and ad hoc networks [21].

Leighton and Micali (LM) [22] (in 1993) proposed a elegant random KPS (LM-KPS) that exploits[2] the "second dimension." In the LM-KPS each node gets a hashed version of *all* $P = k$ TA's keys. Each of the $P = k$ independent keys are however hashed repeatedly to derive many *dependent* keys.

In HARPS [23], Ramkumar and Memon proposed a RKPS which utilizes both dimensions. In (P, k, L) HARPS, the TA chooses P keys $K_1 \cdots K_P$, and each node is

---

[1] Or chosen by the nodes in case asymmetric cryptographic primitives are used.

[2] The LM-KPS was the first KPS proposed in literature with probabilistic assurances.

loaded with a *hashed* subset of k keys. The TA has an indexed set of P secrets, a cryptographic hash function $h()$ and a public random function $F_H()$. For a node A,

$$F_H(A) = \{(\alpha_1, a_1), (\alpha_2, a_2), \ldots, (\alpha_k, a_k)\}, \text{ and } \mathbb{A} = \{{}^{a_1}K_{\alpha_1}, {}^{a_2}K_{\alpha_2}, \ldots, {}^{a_k}K_{\alpha_k}\},$$

where the notation ${}^{i}K_j$ represents the result of *repeatedly* hashing of K_j, i times, using a (public) cryptographic hash function $h()$. The first coordinate $\{\alpha_1, \alpha_2, \ldots, \alpha_k\}$, $1 \leq \alpha_i \leq P$, and $\alpha_i \neq \alpha_j \forall i \neq j$, represents the index of the keys chosen to be preloaded in node A. The second coordinate $\{a_1, a_2, \ldots, a_k\}$, where the a_is are iid and uniformly distributed integer values between 1 and L, represent the number of times each chosen key is hashed (using cryptographic hash function $h()$) before they are preloaded in the node A. LM-KPS and RPS are actually special cases of HARPS. LM is HARPS with $P = k$, and RPS is HARPS with $L = 0$ (or keys are not hashed before pre-loading).

3 Broadcast Encryption Using Random KPSs

As HARPS is a generalization of LM and RPS we shall only consider broadcast encryption using HARPS (the special cases easily follow). For BE using HARPS, the sender employs a subset of all secrets not covered by the union of the r revoked nodes. If we represent by $\mathbb{R}$ the entire set of secrets that the source has access to, and by $\mathbb{S}_r$ the secrets covered by the union of r nodes, each of the *independent* secrets in $\mathbb{R} \setminus \mathbb{S}_r$ can be used to encrypt the broadcast secret K_B. Consider the illustrative example below with $P = 8, k = 4, L = 4$.

i	1	2	3	4	5	6	7	8
A	4	2	x	1	x	3	x	x
B	x	3	1	x	3	2	x	x
d_i	3	1	x	x	2	1	4	4
C	x	3	4	1	x	x	2	x
D	2	x	x	x	3	1	4	x

The TA chooses $P = 8$ keys $K_1 \cdots K_8$, and $k = 4, L = 4$. Node A has keys with indexes $i = 1, 2, 4, 6$ at hash depths 4, 2, 1 and 3 respectively (or keys ${}^{4}K_1, {}^{2}K_2, {}^{1}K_4$ and ${}^{3}K_6$). d_i is the hash depths the TA can employ for each $1 \leq i \leq P$ for encrypting K_b which revokes A and B. TA can use keys ${}^{3}K_1, {}^{1}K_2, {}^{2}K_5, {}^{1}K_6, {}^{4}K_7$, and ${}^{4}K_7$. Node C uses ${}^{4}K_7$ for decrypting the secret. Node D can use ${}^{3}K_1$ or ${}^{1}K_6$ or ${}^{4}K_8$.

If C is the *source* of the broadcast (revoking A and B) C could choose ${}^{4}K_8$ for encrypting K_b.

3.1 Analysis of Efficiency of Broadcast Encryption

Let us first consider the case of BE by the TA. The TA has access to all secrets $K_1 \cdots K_P$ (at hash depth 0). Each of the r (to-be-revoked) nodes have $k < P$ keys each. The hash depths of the keys are uniformly distributed between 1 and L. The union of indexes of keys in all r nodes may still *not* contain some of the P indexes. Obviously such keys can be used by the TA for encrypting the broadcast secret (as none of the r nodes can decrypt them). For example if the key index i is not present in the union of r nodes, the broadcast secret can be encrypted safely with ${}^{L}K_i$.

Now consider a key indexed i, which however, u of the r nodes have. Let us assume that the hash depths of those u keys are $d_1 \cdots d_u$, with $d_{min} = \min(d_1 \cdots d_u)$. The TA could still use key ${}^{d_{min}-1}K_i$ to encrypt the broadcast secret. Proceeding in this fashion, the TA could now use *on an average*, some n_j keys at each hash depth $1 \leq j \leq L$, for encrypting the broadcast secret.

With these $n = \sum_{j=1}^{L} n_j$ keys the TA hopes to "reach" *every* privileged node. Some of the transmitted keys may be useful to many nodes. Most may not be useful for a *particular* node. Once again, while the TA can encrypt the broadcast secret with keys $K_1 \cdots K_P$ (at hash depth 0), they are not useful for the purpose of reaching the nodes - none of the nodes can decipher them. Thus key indexes, where the corresponding $d_{min} = 1$ in the union of the r nodes, cannot be used by the TA for encrypting the broadcast secret.

However, while it is guaranteed that none of the r nodes (even if they pool all their secrets together) can decipher the broadcast secret, there is a possibility that some of the $g = G - r$ privileged nodes too may *not* be able to decrypt *any* of the n encryptions. We shall represent by p_o, the probability that an arbitrary node among the group of g privileged nodes *cannot* use *any* of the n keys. In such an event, on an average, gp_o privileged nodes may not be able to decrypt the broadcast secret. As long as $p_o << \frac{1}{g}$, this may not be a serious issue.

Note that it is also possible to trade-off p_o for bandwidth (n, the number of encryptions needed). For instance, the TA may decide to send only a subset of the encrypted secrets in order to meet a *target* p_o. For the gp_o nodes (on an average) that may be missed, the TA could send the broadcast secret using the secret the TA shares with every node (the secret shared between the TA and any node can be a function of *all* k keys in the node - as the TA has access to all secrets).

The question now is, how many secrets (on an average) does the TA need to transmit? But prior to that, we need an estimate the number of keys $n_j, 1 \leq j \leq L$ that the TA can use. It is easy to see that for $j = L$, the n_j keys correspond to the keys that none of the r nodes have (at *any* hash depth). The probability that any node has a key indexed i is $\xi = \frac{k}{P}$. Thus the probability that none of the r nodes have key i is $(1 - \xi)^r$. In other words

$$n_L = P(1 - \xi)^r. \tag{1}$$

Now let us evaluate the expression for n_j for a general j. Let us assume that u out of r nodes have some key index i (the probability that exactly $u > 0$ out of r nodes have the ith key is $\binom{r}{u}\xi^u(1 - \xi)^{(r-u)}, 1 \leq u \leq r$), with corresponding hash depths $d_1 \cdots d_u$. Under this condition, the TA can employ hash depth j for the key i if $d_{min} = \min(d_1 \cdots d_u) = j+1$. As each $d_l, 1 \leq l \leq u$ is uniformly distributed between 1 and L. Noting that $\Pr\{d_{min} = j + 1\} = \Pr\{d_{min} > j\} - \Pr\{d_{min} > j + 1\}$, we have

$$\Pr\{d_{min} = j+1\} = \frac{(L - j)^u - (L - j - 1)^u}{L^u}$$

Thus, if we represent by ν_{ij} the probability that the TA employs hash depth j for key indexed i, we have

$$n_j = P\nu_{ij} \text{ where } \nu_{ij} = \sum_{u=1}^{r} \binom{r}{u}\xi^u(1 - \xi)^{(r-u)} \frac{(L - j)^u - (L - j - 1)^u}{L^u}. \tag{2}$$

In order to decrypt a secret encrypted with key index i at depth j, the node should have the secret i (probability ξ) at depth $d \leq j$ (probability $\frac{j}{L}$). Encryption keys that use higher hash depths are thus "more useful." Thus for a particular encryption key at hash depth j (or any one of the n_j keys) the probability of outage is $p_{o_i} = (1 - \xi\frac{j}{L})$.

The TA does not have to use *all* $n = \sum_{j=1}^{L} n_j$ keys. The TA may instead only use a subset $m = \sum_{j=q}^{L} n_j$ keys. In the case the probability of outage for any node (or the probability that it cannot decipher *any* of the $\sum_{j=q}^{L} n_j$ encryptions) is p_o^*, and the total number of encryption needed to convey the secret to all $g = G - r$ nodes is

$$n_e = \left(\sum_{j=q}^{L} n_j \right) + gp_o^* \text{ where } p_o^* = \prod_{j=q}^{L} (1 - \xi\frac{j}{L})^{n_j}. \tag{3}$$

The source (TA in this case) would first try to use all keys at depth $j = L$. If that does not yield a satisfactory p_o the TA would then try adding the keys at depth $j = L - 1$, and so on. Thus if the broadcast uses a minimum depth of q it implies all possible encryption keys *above* depth q *will be chosen*. However, it is *not* generally necessary that *all* possible keys *at* depth q are chosen. Out of the n_q possible keys only n_q^* keys may be chosen.

If the probability of outage is p_o' after all possible keys $\sum_{j=q+1}^{L} n_j$, above depth q are chosen (or $p_o' = \prod_{j=q+1}^{L} (1 - \xi\frac{j}{L})^{n_j}$), then the choice of $n_q^* \leq n_q$ would result in an overall bandwidth of

$$n_e = \left(\sum_{j=q+1}^{L} n_j \right) + n_q^* + gp_o' \left(p_{o_q} \right)^{n_q^*}, \tag{4}$$

where $p_{o_q} = (1 - \xi\frac{q}{L})$. The optimal choice of n_q^*, and the corresponding minimum bandwidth (n_e^* - the number of encryptions of the broadcast secret needed for the broadcast) required are therefore

$$n_q^* = \frac{\log\left(\frac{-1}{gp_o' \log\left(p_{o_q} \right)} \right)}{\log\left(p_{o_q} \right)} \qquad n_e^* = \left(\sum_{j=q+1}^{L} n_j \right) + n_q^* + gp_o' \left(p_{o_q} \right)^{n_q^*}. \tag{5}$$

As HARPS is a generalization of RPS [21] and LM [22], extension of the results above to LM and RPS are trivial. For LM, $\xi = 1$. Which implies $n_L = 0$ and

$$n_j = \frac{(L - j)^r - (L - j - 1)^r}{L^r} \quad \text{(for LM scheme)} \tag{6}$$

For RPS, all KPS keys (the P TA's secrets and the k secrets in each node) have the same hash depth. so only keys that none of the r nodes have (which occurs with probability $(1 - \xi)^r$ can be used - or $n = P(1 - \xi)^r$. The probability of outage in this case is $p_o = (1 - \xi)^n$. Once again, not all n keys may be needed. Only $q < n$ keys may be chosen in order to minimize

$$n_e^* = q + g(1 - \xi)^q \implies q = \min\left(\frac{\log\left(\frac{-1}{g \log(1-\xi)} \right)}{\log(1 - \xi)}, n = P(1 - \xi)^r \right). \tag{7}$$

Extension of the analysis above to broadcast encryption by *peers* is also trivial. Note that if the source is a peer, it may not be able to use all possible n_j keys at depth j that the TA can. It can use a key at depth j only if the source node *has* the key (probability ξ) *and* even if has a key for that index, the hash depth of the key should be less than or at least equal to j. Thus all we need to do is to replace n_j in all the equations above by

$$n_{j_p} = n_j \frac{\xi j}{L}. \tag{8}$$

4   Performance Evaluation

Table 1 shows the performance of HARPS, RPS and LM for broadcast encryption (both by TA and by peers) for 3 different values of the group sizes (roughly a thousand, million and billion) for $k = 500$. For LM and HARPS, $L = 64$ (the largest hash depth permissible). For HARPS and RPS we assume that an optimal value of $\xi = \frac{k}{P}$ is chosen for each case ((for a given r and G) - the optimal value of ξ is also indicated within parenthesis for the case of $G = 1024$.

Table 1. Performance of broadcast encryption in terms of number of encryptions necessary *per revoked node*) for various values of r using random KPSs, for group sizes $G = 2^{10}, 2^{20}, 2^{30}$ (roughly a thousand, million and billion), for $k = 500$ and $L = 512$. For RPS and HARPS the corresponding optimal choice of ξ, are also indicated within parenthesis.

	Broadcast Encryption By TA								
r	$G = 2^{10}$			$G = 2^{20}$			$G = 2^{30}$		
	HARPS	RPS	LM	HARPS	RPS	LM	HARPS	RPS	LM
2	1.456(0.994)	1.710(0.926)	1.457	2.886	3.548	2.888	4.504	5.638	4.511
4	1.456(0.867)	1.687(0.700)	1.485	3.065	3.666	3.173	4.924	6.010	5.168
8	1.393(0.593)	1.586(0.442)	1.528	3.102	3.644	3.605	5.095	6.098	6.247
32	0.139(0.189)	1.272(0.137)	1.645	2.887	3.333	5.873	4.951	5.825	21.56
64	0.988(0.099)	1.096(0.073)	1.714	2.721	3.128	17.667	4.777	5.600	1.1e4
128	0.829(0.052)	0.912(0.039)	1.749	2.544	2.914	267.07	4.580	5.355	2.7e5
	Broadcast Encryption By Peers								
2	1.464(0.996)	1.738(0.923)	1.469	2.915	3.625	2.9174	4.571	5.910	4.579
4	1.521(0.862)	1.833(0.667)	1.558	3.299	4.248	3.455	5.453	7.459	5.865
8	1.596(0.667)	1.961(0.368)	1.863	3.894	5.348	5.898	7.017	11.452	315

Some of the points worth noting are the following:

1. For small group sizes the efficiency of BE using RKPSs is significantly better than tree-based methods (the most efficient of which requires about 1.25 encryptions per revoked node.
2. The same keys can be used for various group sizes with increasing efficiency as group size reduces. For tree-based schemes the number of secrets provided to each node would depend on the *maximum* possible group size. Even though the same secrets can be used for smaller group sizes, they cannot be used with greater efficiency. In the example above we have used the same $k = 500$ for all group sizes.

Table 2. Performance of HARPS and RPS designed for $r = 64$, $G = 2^{20}$, for other values of r. For HARPS, $P = 6080, k = 500, L = 512$. For RPS $P = 8435, k = 500$. The figure represent the *total* number of encryptions needed to revoke r nodes.

r	1	2	4	8	16	32	64	72	128
n_H	145	145	145	145	145	145	174	195	375
n_R	197	197	197	197	197	197	203	1972	8.5e5

However, the efficiency of BE with RKPSs depends on the size of r. For HARPS and RPS, for each r we have chosen the optimal value of ξ (the optimal value of ξ also depends on the group size G, but to a much smaller extent). For LM (by definition), ξ is always one. As it is not practical to change the value of ξ after deployment, for any deployment of RPS / HARPS (with some k, ξ), there would be an *optimal* choice of r.

For instance, consider a HARPS deployment optimized for $r = 64$ with $k = 500, P = 6080, L = 64$, for a group size of 1 million. While the number of revocations per node is only about 2.721 encryptions per node if $r = 64$, in practice smaller sizes of r need to be catered for. In general, HARPS or RPS designed for large r would perform very poorly for small r. Table 2 lists the number of encryptions needed for revoking r nodes for $r = 1, 2, 4, 8, 16, 32, 64$ and 128 (in terms of *total number of encryptions - not number of encryptions per revoked node*). Note that the *same* number of encryptions are needed for revoking 1 to 32 nodes! This is due to the fact that a minimum number of encryptions (145 for HARPS and 197 for RPS in this case) have to be transmitted to achieve the desired probability of outage - irrespective of the number of revoked nodes. The loss in efficiency is very high especially for small r. However, HARPS designed for some r degrades much more gracefully for larger r when compared to RPS.

While the LM scheme does not have this problem, it does not perform very well for large r (especially for large group sizes). It might appear at first sight that revocation can always be performed in smaller *batches* using LM (where a subset of nodes is revoked in each batch) with small batch sizes, without any loss of efficiency[3]. However, this is not desirable. While the tree-based schemes by Noar et al [3] and Halevy et al [4], are resistant to collusion of all revoked nodes *even if they were revoked in different "batches"*, for broadcast encryption using random KPSs, the system is resistant only to collusion of *all nodes in a batch*.

Thus a solution to this problem may be to use many systems in parallel with different values of ξ (in practice 2 systems with $xi = 1$ and $\xi = 0.1$ may be sufficient) could be used. For example, we could use $k_1 = k_2 = k_3 = k_4 = k_5 = 200$, and $P_1 = 200, P_2 = 400, P_3 = 800, P_4 = 1600, P_5 = 3200$), or effectively $k = 400 \times 5 = 2000$ and $P = 400 + 800 + 1600 + 3200 + 6400 = 12400$). Alternately a system could have P keys $K_1 \cdots K_P$, and the probability that key i is assigned to any node could be $\xi_i = \mu f(i)$ where μ is appropriately chosen such that $0 < \mu f(i) \leq 1$ and $f(i)$ is a monotonic function of i. Figure 1 (left) plots the bandwidth required vs r (from 1 to 200) for such a hybrid HARPS deployment with $k = 200 \times 5 = 1000$, and $P = 200 + 250 + 800 + 1600 + 3200 = 6050$, and $L = 512$, for group sizes of roughly a thousand, million and a billion. There is however a *soft* upper bound on the size of r

---

[3] The results in Table 1 are in terms of number of encryptions *per* revoked node.

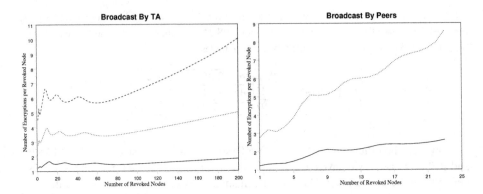

Fig. 1. Performance of broadcast encryption using a hybrid HARPS scheme employing $k = 5 \times 200 = 1000$, $P = 200 + 250 + 800 + 1600 + 3200 = 6050$, and $L = 512$, for broadcasts by TA (left) and by peers (right). Dashed line (only in the left figure) is for $G = 2^{30}$. Dotted lines and unbroken lines (in both figures) are for $G = 2^{20}$ and $G = 2^{10}$ thousand respectively.

(which also depends on the group size G). As r increases, it may not be possible for the TA to find enough keys to use for encrypting the broadcast, and thus will not be able to attain a low enough p_o to ensure that all intended nodes can be reached.

Figure 1 (right) is the plots for broadcast encryption by peers, for group sizes of a thousand and a million Broadcast encryption by peers is impractical for large group sizes and r - the number of keys a source can employ is substantially less than the number of keys the TA can.

4.1   Overheads

Apart from the encryptions of the secrets, for BE schemes the source should also indicate the identities of the revoked nodes. For revocation using random KPSs (while this can also be done), it is more efficient (both in terms of bandwidth needed and computational complexity at the receiver) to instead provide the *indexes of the keys used* for encryption (and additionally, their corresponding hash depths in case of HARPS and LM).

The expression for the overheads can be obtained easily by considering the entropies of the indexes and the hash depths. Let o_I be the entropy of overheads for transmitting indexes of the subset of P keys that are used for encrypting the broadcast secret (n_e out of P keys are used). If we define $\mathbb{H}(x) = -x \log_2(x)$, we have

$$o_I = P \left\{ \mathbb{H}\left(\frac{n_e}{P}\right) + \mathbb{H}\left(\frac{P - n_e}{P}\right) \right\} \text{ bits.}$$

Let O_d be the entropy of the hash depths for the n_e encryption keys used. Or

$$o_d = n_e \sum_{j=q}^{L} \mathbb{H}\left(\frac{n_j}{n_e}\right) \text{ bits.}$$

Typically, the overheads range between 10 to 40 bits per revoked node. However, more important than the reduced overhead (compared to tree-based schemes) is the fact that this caters for privacy - *by protecting the identities of the revoked nodes.*

4.2   Broadcast Authentication

In practice, broadcasts meant for revoking nodes need to be authenticated. This calls for the ability to cater for broadcast authentication. Various techniques for broadcast authentication (without employing asymmetric cryptography[4]) have been considered in the literature. Such techniques can be divided into two main classes:

1. Instantaneous authentication techniques
2. Authentication using delayed disclosure

With the first class of methods (based on key pre-distribution), broadcast authentication can be achieved by appending many key based message authentication codes (MAC) [14], [24] - [25], - one corresponding to each of the k keys the source node it has in its key ring (all random KPSs cater for broadcast authentication). Any verifier may be able to verify a subset of the MACs. However, such approaches have the disadvantage of large bandwidth requirements (the number of appended authentication codes, k may be high).

The second class of methods, based on one-way hash chains [26] have been investigated by various researchers [27] - [29]. With this approach, the source creates a one-way hash chain and uses a value from the hash chain to calculate the message authentication code for a message to be authenticated. Later the pre-image of the value used is made public. At this point the verifiers are assured that the source that transmitted the first message was the one who released the pre-image (as no one else can, in practice compute the pre-image of a disclosed value). However, such methods typically need to be *bootstrapped* from a pre-authenticated value[5].

Thus a satisfactory solution may be to use RKPSs for bootstrapping hash-chain based techniques. In other words, the more bandwidth expensive authentication using RKPSs could be used for the first broadcast to authenticate the "commitment" key in the hash chain, and subsequent broadcasts can be authenticated by releasing pre-images of the commitment.

4.3   Pros and Cons

A summary of advantages and disadvantages of broadcast encryption using RKPSs (as opposed to state-of-the-art tree-based schemes in [3] and [4]) are as follows

1. Advantages:
   (a) broadcast by peers without the use of asymmetric cryptography
   (b) higher efficiency for smaller group sizes

---

[4] If asymmetric cryptography is feasible, broadcast authentication can be achieved using digital signatures which can be verified by any receiver.
[5] The first class of methods - methods based on key pre-distribution - do not need to be bootstrapped.

(c) flexible group / universe size - no hard limit on the maximum size of groups or the total number of nodes.
(d) ability to protect identity of revoked nodes.
(e) lower bandwidth for overheads
(f) the secrets used for broadcast encryption can also be used for mutual authentication and broadcast authentication.

2. Disadvantages:
(a) Limit (though soft) on the size of total number of nodes that can be revoked while still catering for resistance against collusion of *all* revoked nodes.
(b) For very large group sizes (say a billion or above) it may be impractical for the source of the broadcast to *verify* if *all* privileged nodes can decipher the broadcast. Thus
  i. the source may have to sacrifice the bandwidth efficiency (by using more keys for encrypting the broadcast secret) and target a value of outage probability p_o that is considerably lower than the inverse of the group size ($p_o << \frac{1}{G}$), in order to render the probability of such an event very low, *or*
  ii. the system should cater for such "accidentally" missed nodes to approach the source and receive the secret through alternate channels (the second approach is perhaps more practical for large group sizes).

4.4   Potential Applications

Wireless Ad Hoc Network Security. Security solutions for (wireless) mobile ad hoc networks could benefit greatly if nodes in a vicinity could establish shared secrets while *selectively excluding* some nodes. As an example, it could be very useful in many ad hoc routing protocols if nodes could establish a shared secret with all their 2-hop neighbors - which are not provided to 1-hop neighbors [30], [31]. This could for instance, help nodes authenticate their messages to their 2-hop neighbors and ensure that one-hop neighbors do not modify the contents of the packet they forward. This could be easily realized by a broadcast which "revokes" all one hop neighbors.

In such scenarios, it is more important that the explicitly revoked nodes are *denied* access to the secret, than ensuring that all other nodes actually receive the secret. Obviously, the set of excluded nodes need not be based just on hop counts - there may be other reasons to choose the set of revoked nodes. For instance, in scenarios where nodes maintain a "neighborhood watch" [32] and rate the trust-worthiness of each node, nodes may need to exchange information, while shielding it from the node (or nodes) with "questionable morals".

Publish-Subscribe Systems. In publish-subscribe (pub-sub) [33], [34] systems broadcast encryption will be very useful for distributing secrets to a set of subscribers (or more specifically revoking a set of current subscribers by providing continuing subscribers with a new secret). With the possibility of broadcast encryption by peers, any node has the ability to become a publisher, and distribute secrets to other nodes. In pub-sub systems one very important issue is protection of the privacy of publisher-subscriber relationships. Thus tree-based broadcast encryption schemes (even when they are used with asymmetric cryptographic primitives to facilitate broadcasts by peers) which need to explicitly specify the identities of the revoked nodes may not be very suitable for this purpose.

5 Conclusions

We discuss the applicability of random key pre-distribution schemes for broadcast encryption and argue that this may be a useful paradigm in many application scenarios. One of the main shortcoming of broadcast encryption using random KPSs is the limit on the number of nodes that can be revoked. While BE can still be performed in batches to overcome this "soft" limit, the collusion resistance holds only for nodes within each batch.

However, in scenarios where privacy is an important issue, and / or it may be infeasible to employ asymmetric cryptographic primitives, BE using random KPSs can be a very useful tool - especially since the same secrets used for BE can also be used for mutual authentication and broadcast authentication.

References

1. A. Fiat, M. Noar, "Broadcast Encryption," Lecture Notes in Computer Science, Advances in Cryptology, Springer-Verlag, **773**, pp 480–491, 1994.
2. R. Canetti, T. Malkin, K. Nissin, "Efficient Communication-Storage Tradeoffs for Multicast Encryption," EUROCRYPT 1999, pp 459–474.
3. D. Noar, M. Noar, J. Lotspiech, "Revocation and Tracing Routines for Stateless Receivers," Lecture Notes in Computer Science, Advances in Cryptology, Springer-Verlag, **2139**, 2001.
4. D. Halevy, A. Shamir, "The LSD Broadcast Encryption Scheme," Advances in Cryptology - CRYPTO 2002: 22nd Annual International Cryptology Conference, Santa Barbara, California, USA, August 18-22, 2002.
5. C.K. Wong, M. Gouda, S. Lam, "Secure Group Communications using Key Graphs," Proceedings of SIGCOMM 98, pp 68–79, 1998.
6. J. Lotspiech, S. Nusser, F. Pestonoi, "Anonymous Trust: Digital Rights Management using Broadcast Encryption," Proceedings of the IEEE, **92** (6), pp 898–909, 2004.
7. Eli Gafni A1, Jessica Staddon A2, Yiqun Lisa Yin, "Efficient Methods for Integrating Traceability and Broadcast Encryption," Advances in Cryptology - CRYPTO'99: 19th Annual International Cryptology Conference, Santa Barbara, California, USA, August 1999.
8. G. Kreitz, "Optimization of Broadcast Encryption Schemes," Master's Thesis, Royal Institute of Technology, Sweden, Feb 2005.
9. R. Needham and M. Schroeder, "Using encryption for authentication in large networks of computers," Communications of the ACM, 21(12), December 1978.
10. R. Blom, "Non-Public Key Distribution" CRYPTO 1982, pp 231–236, 1982.
11. L. Gong, D.J. Wheeler, "A Matrix Key Distribution Scheme," *Journal of Cryptology*, **2**(2), pp 51-59, 1990.
12. C.J. Mitchell, F.C. Piper, "Key Storage in Secure Networks," *Discrete Applied Mathematics*, **21** pp 215–228, 1995.
13. P. Erdos, P. Frankl, Z. Furedi, "Families of Finite Sets in which no Set is Covered by the Union of *r* Others," *Isreal Journal of Mathematics*, **51**, pp 79–89, 1985.
14. M. Dyer, T. Fenner, A. Frieze and A. Thomason, "On Key Storage in Secure Networks," *Journal of Cryptology*, **8**, 189–200, 1995.

15. L. Eschenauer, V.D. Gligor, "A Key-Management Scheme for Distributed Sensor Networks," Proceedings of the Ninth ACM Conference on Computer and Communications Security, Washington DC, pp 41-47, Nov 2002.

16. H. Chan, A. Perrig, D. Song, "Random Key Pre-distribution Schemes for Sensor Networks," IEEE Symposium on Security and Privacy, Berkeley, California, May 2003.

17. R. Di Pietro, L. V. Mancini, A. Mei, "Random Key Assignment for Secure Wireless Sensor Networks," 2003 ACM Workshop on Security of Ad Hoc and Sensor Networks, October 2003.

18. S. Zhu, S. Xu, S. Setia S. Jajodia, "Establishing Pair-wise Keys For Secure Communication in Ad Hoc Networks: A Probabilistic Approach," Proc. of the 11th IEEE International Conference on Network Protocols (ICNP'03), Atlanta, Georgia, November 4-7, 2003.

19. W. Du, J. Deng, Y.S. Han. P.K.Varshney, "A Pairwise Key Pre-distribution Scheme for Wireless Sensor Networks," Proceedings of the 10th ACM Conference on Computer and Communication Security, pp 42–51, 2003.

20. D. Liu, P.Ning, "Establishing Pairwise Keys in Distributed Sensor Networks," Proceedings of the 10th ACM Conference on Computer and Communication Security, Washington DC, 2003.

21. M. Ramkumar, N. Memon, R. Simha, "Pre-Loaded Key Based Multicast and Broadcast Authentication in Mobile Ad-Hoc Networks," Globecom-2003.

22. T. Leighton, S. Micali, "Secret-key Agreement without Public-Key Cryptography,"*Advances in Cryptology* - CRYPTO 1993, pp 456-479, 1994.

23. M. Ramkumar, N. Memon, "An Efficient Random Key Pre-distribution Scheme for MANET Security," IEEE Journal on Selected Areas of Communication, March 2005.

24. N. Alon, "Probabilistic Methods in External Finite Set Theory," in *Extremal Problems for Finite Sets*,, pp 39-57, 1991.

25. R. Canetti, J. Garay, G. Itkis, D. Micciancio, M. Naor, B. Pinkas, "Multicast Security: A Taxonomy and Some Efficient Constructions," INFOCOMM'99, 1999.

26. L. Lamport, "Password Authentication with Insecure Communication," Communications of the ACM, 24(11):770-772, November 1981.

27. S. Cheung, "An Efficient Message Authentication Scheme for Link State Routing", Proceedings of the 13th Annual Computer Security Applications Conference, San Diego, California, December 1997, pp. 90-98.

28. R.J. Anderson, F. Bergadano, B. Crispo, J.H. Lee, C. Manifavas and R.M. Needham, " A New Family of Authentication Protocols," ACM Operating Systems Review, vol. 32, n. 4, pp. 9-20, October 1998, ACM Press.

29. A. Perrig, R. Canetti, D. Song, D. Tygar, "Efficient and Secure Source Authentication for Multicast," in Network and Distributed System Security Symposium, NDSS '01, Feb. 2001.

30. P-W Yau, C. J. Mitchell, "2HARP: A Secure Routing Protocol for Mobile Ad Hoc Networks," 5th World Wireless Congress (WWC 2004), San Francisco, USA, May 2004,

31. X. Du, Y. Wang, J. Ge, Y. Wang, "A Method for Security Enhancements in AODV Protocol," 17 th International Conference on Advanced Information Networking and Applications (AINA), Xian, China, 2003.

32. S. Buchegger, J-Y. Le Boudec, "Nodes Bearing Grudges: Towards Routing Security, Fairness and Robustness in Mobile Ad Hoc Networks," Proceedings of Tenth Euromicro Workshop on Parallel Distributed and Network-based Processing, 2002.

33. P.T. Eugster, P.A. Felber, R. Guerraoui, A-M. Kermarrec, "The Many Faces of Publish/Subscribe," Technical Report, URL citeseer.ist.psu.edu/649723.html.

34. C. Wang, A. Carzaniga, D. Evans, A. L. Wolf, "Security Issues and Requirements for Internet-Scale Publish-Subscribe Systems," Hawaii International Conference on System Sciences, January, 2002.

A Framework for Examining Skill Specialization, Gender Inequity, and Career Advancement in the Information Security Field⋆
(An Ongoing Project Report)

Sharmistha Bagchi-Sen[1], JinKyu Lee[2],
H. Raghav Rao[2], and Shambhu Upadhyaya[3]

[1] University at Buffalo, Dept. of Geography, Buffalo, NY 14260
[2] University at Buffalo, MIS, School of Management, Buffalo, NY 14260
[3] University at Buffalo, Dept. Computer Science and Eng., Buffalo, NY 14260
{geosbs, jklee2, mgmtrao, shambhu}@buffalo.edu

Abstract. This paper presents an ongoing research project that examines career advancement barriers to women information security professionals. The study proposes to identify the skill sets critical for success in the information security area and to examine gender differences in specialized skill sets. The paper provides a brief review on IT workforce studies with a special focus on gender inequity problems. The research design and analytical methods are also presented.

1 Introduction

This study proposes to identify the skill sets required for various job responsibilities and successful career advancement in the information security area and examine gender differences in the area of specialization. Recently, cyber security has become a major area of IT application across industrial sectors and regions [1], [2]. In spite of the decline in investment and employment in IT in the past several years, and the outsourcing of IT jobs overseas, the subfield of information security has received institutional investment. According to an industry magazine, "the IT security specialist was named the hottest job for 2003 and 2004, and the post of chief privacy officer just got the nod for the highest-paying hot job, bringing in an average salary of $122,360. An IT manager or security manager came in ninth on the list of high-paying hot jobs with an average salary of $91,470." The Department of Homeland Security also identified Cyber security as one of the critical areas of the national strategy for homeland security. The national strategy to secure cyberspace[1] articulates national cyber security awareness and training programs as one of its five national priorities and addressing the shortfalls in the numbers of trained and certified cyber security personnel as one of its important missions. Yet, recent studies pointed out that the mix of

---

⋆ Research supported, in part, by National Science Foundation Grant CNS-0420448.
[1] http://www.whitehouse.gov/pcipb/

S. Jajodia and C. Mazumdar (Eds.): ICISS 2005, LNCS 3803, pp. 317–321, 2005.

skills and other requirements for career advancement in the information security area need to be uncovered. Given these situation, it is important to understand what are the important skills needed by information security professionals and which of them are critical for career advancement in the area.

This study pays a special attention to gender (in)equity in career advancement in information security area. During the IT boom period, shortage of workers, high turnover rates and retention problems drew attention to the importance of attracting women to the international IT labor market [3]. Despite conscious efforts to attract women, retention and advancement issues for women continued to be a problem in the 1980s and 1990s [4]. While a complete solution to this problem is yet to be developed, we are facing a similar problem in the information security labor market. This study tackles this unexplored research area to alleviate the shortage of skilled information security professionals and barriers to women's career advancement in the field. Accordingly, this study attempts to achieve three main objectives: 1) to understand skill requirements for various information security jobs, 2) to test the existence of gender division in specialized skill sets and information security tasks, and if so, 3) to find out the impact of the differentiated specialization on career advancement in information security.

Expected Contributions. Upon successful completion of this research project, the findings will provide an insight that can help educational institutions and governments provide better educational/training program for potential information security professionals and effectively handle the supply-demand discrepancy in the information security job market. The results will also allow potential information security professionals better equipped with necessary skills and experience, while the increased transparency can attract more talented people in the field. Women considering an information security career will realize a large benefit from the results because the findings can enable governments and the industry to promote gender equity in the area.

2   Literature Review

Gender Inequity and Career Advancement. Previous research on gender inequity in the IT area has found that gender inequity persists in senior managerial ranks, even though there is no significant gender differences in job performance [5]. This gender inequity can come from various social and structural barriers that hinder career advancement of women in the IT field [6]. A salient social barrier is employers' and co-workers' expectations on women's role and duty in family. Structural barriers can emerge from institutional characteristics or work culture such as long working hours, extensive travel, and male-dominated organization culture.

Gender Discrimination in Education. The social and institutional barriers start exerting negative effects long before the job search stage. Trauth [7] found that limited educational opportunity for women is a significant obstacle to women IT workforce in some societies. Even in a society where educational opportunity is considered to be fair (e.g., the US), those barriers are observable in the dwindling proportion of women studying computer and information science [8]. According to a report on study area preference, men are three times more likely than women in selecting computer science as their field of study. Some empirical study results suggest that discouraging conditions in educational institutions (e.g., faculty characteristics and behaviors) [9] and environment [10] might have aggravated this gender division in career path.

Gender Difference in Specialized Skill Sets. A related issue to above problem is the disparity between industry needs and academic preparation. Although the needs to improve technical training have been emphasized even in the general IT field, the crucial role of a mix of technical skills and other specific knowledge, skills and abilities in the information security area has not yet attracted enough research interest. Nevertheless, we have seen anecdotal evidence that, in banking industry, women are clustering in low-complexity tasks (e.g., mainframe operation or access control), while men are disproportionately focusing on more sophisticated technical tasks (e.g., firewall configuration). In order to understand career advancement barriers to women information security professionals, we suggest examining gender disparity in specialization area and required skill sets that should have been developed over educational/training period.

3   Research Method and Design

This study uses a structured questionnaire survey method to collect data. The sample group consists of (ISC)2 certified information security professionals. (ISC)2, the research partner of this project, is a non-profit international organization dedicated to training, and certifying information security professionals worldwide. A web-based survey, scheduled in Oct. 2005, will invite (ISC)2 members in the US (n=15,000).

The face validity of the survey instrument has been assessed by two Ph.D. level MIS students, two information security professionals, and two cyber security researchers. Some variables measured in the questionnaire include importance of various skills[2] for the respondent's job, responsibility to information security tasks[3], educational/job experiences, and demographics among others.

Analyses. In addition to descriptive statistics, we adopt polychotomous logistic regression to explore important skill sets for different information security jobs. For this, the respondents will be clustered by their tasks, and then the resulting job category (J_i) will be regressed on the importance levels of IT (T), business (B), soft (S) skill sets, as well as gender (G) and the years in the information security field (E). The logistic regression model can be specified as (Eq. (1)):

---

[2] Adapted from skill lists in http://www.ualr.edu/~itreport/
[3] Extracted from the CISSP Common Body of Knowledge.

$$\hat{J}_i = \alpha + \beta_1 T_i + \beta_2 B_i + \beta_3 S_i + \beta_4 G_i + \beta_5 E_i \tag{1}$$

ANOVA will be used to examine the association between gender and skill/task specialization, while age and work experience are controlled by a randomized blocks design. Skills for career advancement are examined by another logistic regression model (Eq. (2)), where managerial level becomes the proxy measure for career advancement (A_j). The dataset will be grouped by age/job experience and analyzed separately.

$$\hat{A}_j = \alpha + \beta_1 T_j + \beta_2 B_j + \beta_3 SIj + \beta_4 G_j \tag{2}$$

We expect that preliminary results from these analyses become available by December 2005.

4   Discussions

We have presented an ongoing research project that examines gender inequity, education, skill specialization and career advancement in the area of information security. Based on previous research, we argued that different skills are required for different sets of information security tasks, which are also associated with career advancement in the area. Also hypothesized in this study are gender divisions in the specialized skill/responsibility sets and career advancement. Upon completion, this study will provide valuable insight to potential information security workforce, but also to government policy makers and educational institutions.

References

1. H. Kang, S. Bachi-Sen, H.R. Rao, and S. Banerjee, "Internet skeptics: An analysis of intermittent users and net-dropouts," *IEEE Technology and Society Magazine*, vol. 24, 2005.
2. T. Herath, S. Bagchi-Sen, and H.R. Rao, "Gender issues and vulnerability to internet crime," *Trauth, E. (eds.): Gender and Information Technology Encyclopedia*, 2006.
3. A. Maitland, "A long-term solution to the it skills shortage," *Financial Times*, vol. 9, 22 February 2001.
4. S. Pfleeger and N. Mertz, "Executive mentoring: what makes it work?," *Communications of the ACM*, vol. 38, pp. 63–73, 1995.
5. G. Truman and J. Baroudi, "Gender differences in the information systems managerial ranks: an assessment of potential discriminatory practices," *MIS Quarterly*, vol. 18, pp. 129–141, 1994.
6. M. Ahuja, "Women in the information technology profession: a literature review, synthesis and research agenda," *European Journal of Information Sys.*, vol. 11, pp. 20–34, 2002.
7. E. Trauth, S. Nielsen, and L. von Hellens, "Explaining the it gender gap: Australian stories," *Proc. of the 10th Australasian Conf. on Information Systems*, Dec. 2000.

8. T. Camp, "The incredible shrinking pipeline," *Communications of the ACM*, vol. 40, pp. 103–110, 1997.

9. E. Trauth, "Odd girl out: an individual differences perspective on women in the it profession," *Information Technology & People*, vol. 15, no. 2, pp. 98–118, 2002.

10. S. Banerjee, H. Kang, S. Bagchi-Sen, and H.R. Rao, "Gender divide in the use of the internet applications," *International Journal of E-Business Research*, vol. 1, no. 2, 2005.

SPEAR: Design of a Secured
Peer-to-Peer Architecture
(An Ongoing Project Report)

Jaydev Misra[1], Pinakpani Pal[2], and Aditya Bagchi[2]

[1] Kolaghat Engineering College,
West Bengal University of Technology,
Kolkata , India
jsm02@rediffmail.com
[2] Indian Statistical Institute,
203, B.T. Road, Kolkata,
India 700108
{pinak, aditya}@isical.ac.in

1 Background

In a Peer-to-Peer (*P2P*) system, a large number of nodes are pooled together to share their resources, information and services. Here all nodes are considered to be peers and so they should be at the same level with no hierarchy, like clients or servers. An ideal P2P system is supposed to be dynamic, where a node can join or leave the network any time. Exploiting this idea, many systems have already been developed for different application areas. A major concern of a P2P system is the searching of proper resources among different autonomous peers. Two well known P2P systems, Napster and Gnutella, have shown two different approaches. Napster [1] provides a central indexing facility where any search process has to go through the machine that provides the central index. On the other hand, Gnutella [2] is an absolutely open P2P environment where searching is done by flooding and it uses IP for its underlying network service. Kaaza [3] provides a service that may be viewed as a hybrid of Gnutella and Napster. It has nodes distributed in two layers. Some nodes, called super nodes or Super-Peers, act as indexing servers for other nodes. Searching across Super-Peers may be done in Gnutella style. Nodes, other than super-peers, are known as ordinary peers . One ordinary peer is connected to only one Super-Peer. So, each super-peer is connected to many ordinary peers where the super-peer provides the indexing service to its ordinary peers. An ordinary peer, on the other hand, reports to its Super-Peer the resources that it likes to share in the P2P environment. While the communication between a Super-Peer and its ordinary peers may be done in the Napster style, communication among Super-Peers is supposed to adopt the Guntella protocol. In order to make efficient search in a P2P environment, many good search protocols have already been proposed. Development of an efficient P2P architecture is also an interesting area of study. A recent review paper [9] has made a summary of all these research efforts. Security is another

S. Jajodia and C. Mazumdar (Eds.): ICISS 2005, LNCS 3803, pp. 322–327, 2005.

important area of investigation in a P2P environment. [9] and [5] have listed the essential security requirements in a P2P environment. These requirements may be divided into two groups. While the first group includes secure storage, access control, identity management and authentication, the second group deals with secure routing, provisions of anonymity and resilience against denial of service. Individual nodes handle the security requirements in the first group. However, the second set of requirements can be met only by considering the entire network with all the nodes and their interconnections. So the required security measures must be embedded in the network architecture and in the different protocols of peer-to-peer communication. SPEAR is a research effort that ventures to design a secured peer-to-peer architecture. It aspires to provide two-way anonymity, resilience against denial of service and network stability against withdrawal of nodes. Subsequent sections discuss the salient features of the project.

2   Proposed Architecture

Design of a P2P system architecture is centered around achieving good search and update efficiency. It also considers the dynamic nature of the network, i.e. possible withdrawal of nodes. Neither Napster nor Gnutella can meet the requirements. A hybrid approach like super-peer network becomes necessary. "Peers" research group at the Stanford University, USA has suggested different possible hybrid P2P architectures [11] and studied their relative performances. In the same test environment, it has also studied the performance of a super-peer network [12]. From these studies, the research group has made the following conclusions:

- Super-peer networks are effective because they combine the efficiency of the centralized client-server model with the autonomy, load balancing and robustness of distributed search.
- Super-peer redundancy greatly reduce load to individual super-peer and improves reliability.
- Outdegree of each super-peer should be maximized while the TTL of individual super-peer should be minimized.
- A super-peer can shield the identity of the ordinary peers under it and thus can provide anonymity.

In the course of studying different hybrid architectures, "Peers" group has also identified the security requirements in a P2P environment [5] but have not suggested any specific measure to achieve them. Since the earlier study has indicated that in super-peer network, the identity of a group of ordinary peers can be shielded by their super-peer, this type of two layered network has been taken as the basis of SPEAR architecture.

2.1   Arrangement of Nodes

Similar to super-peer network, the SPEAR system also has two layers. The nodes are divided into clusters. Each cluster has a super-peer and a number of ordinary peers connected to it. Inter-cluster connections are only among super-peers. Depending on the application area, the SPEAR system may have two different cluster formation philosophies:

1. Geographical proximity: It involves intranet type arrangement where a LAN is associated with a LAN server. The LAN server, which is the super-peer here, is connected to the Internet. The other nodes of the LAN, the ordinary peers in this case, are automatically shielded from the web.
2. Semantic proximity: In a data-sharing environment, nodes having similar type of data may form a cluster. One member of that cluster may be elected as the super-peer. However, since a super-peer is supposed to provide indexing service to its ordinary peer, it needs to store and update the dynamic hash table (*DHT*) for the peers under it. Depending on the frequency of certain queries, it may also have to cache data from some of its ordinary peers to improve query processing time. So, a super-peer may have more resources than the ordinary peers connected to it. Further discussion would reveal the need of having more than one such super-peer in a cluster.

2.2   Peer to Super-Peer Connections

Similar to Gnutella, SPEAR also plans to use IP as its underlying service protocol and all its nodes may be connected to web (not in case of intranet-internet combination). However, in this P2P environment, a super-peer may not be aware of the ordinary peers connected to another super-peer. The identity, i.e. the IP addresses, of the ordinary peers and even the local DHT that connects the ordinary peers to its super-peer are shielded from the outer world, i.e. other super-peers. The utility of such arrangement will be clear when the anonymity issues are discussed. Distinct protocols will control the planned withdrawal of nodes and particularly the admission of new peers to a cluster. Any new peer joins the system at the ordinary peer level only. Some recent research efforts [6,7] have considered various admission control protocols and their relative merits in a P2P environment. These protocols are applicable to the direct admission of nodes to a P2P system. However in SPEAR, the nodes are added only at the ordinary peer level where the actual P2P environment exists at the interconnected super-peer level. So, here the admission has been planned to be on the basis of local recommendations from existing ordinary peers. Each new applicant is allowed to make data transfer with a group of existing ordinary peers in a cluster. Depending on the quality of the transfer behavior and the relevance of the data the new applicant wants to share, a recommendation cum reputation is computed by each peer. The accumulated recommendations at the super-peer are used to compute local trust value of the possible new entrant and the admission decision is taken. It has also been assumed that the members within a cluster would maximum be passive adversaries(may read others data but won't alter them). This assumption is logical because the ordinary peers can always access the local DHT at the super-peer and can get access to the data of other peers through proper queries. So, no PKI arrangement has been planned at this level. However, each ordinary peer would have a negotiated key with its super-peer. The key negotiation would be done using well known Diffie-Hellman algorithm [8].

2.3   Super-Peer Interconnection

Actual P2P environment exists at the super-peer level. The super-peer network originally proposed by Kaaza, expected that the network at the super-peer level would communicate using Gnutella protocol. However, for a secured P2P architecture, such an open unstructured approach cannot be adopted. In SPEAR, it has been planned that each super-peer would communicate with its trusted neighbors only. So, it calls for a trusted negotiation system and establishment of trusted neighbors. Different trust models [4,10,13] have been studied for this purpose. The effective strategy for the SPEAR model is yet to be designed. However, it has been decided that two trusted neighbors should maintain the DHT of each other and would also share resources e.g. providing storage space for data-sharing applications. The DHT considered here is the super-peer level DHT and not the local DHT, maintained within a cluster, between a super-peer and its ordinary peers. Communication at the super-peer level would be controlled by a public key infrastructure. This super-peer level infrastructure ensures that all nodes at this level are reachable from one another. So, a search from one super-peer would go to its trusted neighbors, which is a set of super-peers. These super-peers in turn would propagate the search through their respective trusted neighbors. It is obvious, if a node at the super-peer level has very few trusted neighbors, it would cover the entire network with too many hops, i.e. a high TTL (Time To Live) value. This would ultimately contribute towards the efficiency of query processing. So, the design constraint would specify an upper bound for TTL value. As a result, each super-peer has to maintain a minimum number of trusted neighbors so that any of its search can cover the network within the TTL upper bound.

2.4   Availability

One of the major problems in a peer-to-peer system is its dynamic nature. Any node may join or withdraw at will. While join of a new node is handled by admission control protocol, withdrawal affects availability and overall reliability of a network against query processing. Considering planned withdrawal only, when an ordinary peer wishes to withdraw, it informs its super-peer and the super-peer in turn updates its local DHT. Other members of the cluster are also informed about this withdrawal. If the same node wishes to join again to the same cluster, the admission control protocol considers its earlier trust value in its overall trust computation. However, withdrawal of a super-peer needs a more elaborate process. If a super-peer withdraws itself, all the ordinary peers under it automatically get disconnected from the network. In order to prevent such a situation, each cluster maintains more than one node having sufficient resources to provide the service of a super-peer. Whenever a system becomes a super-peer in a cluster, it elects a back up super-peer. This back-up super-peer is also shielded from the actual P2P environment at the super-peer level. This redundancy has been introduced to improve availability and to provide resilience against DNS attack. All data relevant to the P2P network, and other information like DHTs, are replicated to the backup super-peer from the actual super-peer. Any activity of the super-peer is also reported to the backup. It ensures that, if the actual super-peer has to withdraw, the backup super-peer can easily takeover and continue P2P service to the network as well as to its own ordinary peers. In case of any DNS attack from any other super-peer in the network, the victim can always withdraw itself from the network. The backup super-peer of the affected cluster takes over and informs all its trusted neighbors and also the ordinary peers of the cluster. The trusted neighbors are also informed about the DNS attack revealing the identity of the culprit (IP address of the attacker). Similar to search, this event is also propagated through out the network. This causes reduction of global trust value of the adversary. The new super-peer also puts the attacker in the black list and inhibits any future communication from it. The next important job of the new super-peer is to elect a backup super-peer. After recovery, the old victim of the DNS attack will join the cluster as an ordinary peer. Detail of the DNS Resilience protocol is yet to be worked out.

2.5   Query Processing

Query generated by a node is always forwarded to its super-peer. If it can be resolved locally, the super-peer does it using its local DHT. Otherwise, the query is forwarded to the trusted neighbors. This way the query travels through the network till some node finds an answer in its global DHT. It then communicates the IP addresses of each other to the query originator and the possible responder. There can be more than one responder to certain query. The originator and the responders then communicate among themselves. Any possibility of DNS attack in these communications, triggers the DNS Resilience protocol. This query processing technique ensures two-way anonymity. When a super-peer forwards a query to the P2P environment, it shields the identity of the ordinary peer that actually raised the query. The answers to a query are also collected by the super-peer, and then collated. The necessary query commit protocol is also executed at the super-peer level. Later the super-peer communicates the final result of the query to the actual originator at the local level within the cluster. Thus the identity of the originator always remains anonymous to the outer world. Similarly, when a super-peer responds to a query, it may actually get the answers from one or more of its ordinary peers but their identities remain shielded again. So, actual responders also remain anonymous. This query processing technique is also free from the blocking problem of two-phase commit protocol. In case the coordinator or the query originating node goes out of order, in two-phase commit protocol, the responders or the participating nodes have to wait indefinitely for the recovery of the coordinator. However in this case, if the originator fails, the backup super-peer takes over and reestablishes the commit protocol within finite time.

3   Conclusion

This project has proposed a secured Peer-to-Peer architecture that ensures two-way anonymity, resilience to DNS attack and stability against withdrawal of nodes. The present effort is towards developing a simulator for the SPEAR model. The different protocols would then be implemented. Two possible areas of applications have been identified; one is e-Governance and the other is inter-library document access. Both the system being inherently hierarchic, it is envisaged that SPEAR model would be suitable for them.

References

1. http://www.napster.com
2. http://gnutella.wego.com
3. http://www.kazaa.com
4. Daswani N., Garcia-Molina H., Yang B.: Decentralized Trust Management. In Proceedings of the 17th Symposium on Security and Privacy, IEEE Computer Society Press (1996), 164–173.
5. Daswani N., Garcia-Molina H., Yang B.: Open problems in data-sharing peer-to-peer systems. In Proceedings of International Conference on Database Theory (2003).
6. Kim Y., Mazzocchi D., Tsudik G.: Admission control in peer groups. In Proceedings of IEEE International Symposium on Network Computing and Applications (NCA) (April 2003).
7. Saxena N., Tsudik G., Yi J.H.: Admission control in Peer-to-Peer: design and Performance Evaluation. In Proceedings of ACM Workshop on Security of Ad Hoc and Sensor Networks (SASN'03) (October 2003).
8. Stinson D.: Cryptography: Theory & Practicer. 4th.Printing, CRC Press (1999).
9. Theotokis S.A., Spinellis D.: A survey of Peer-to-Peer Content Distribution Technologies. ACM Computing Surveys, **38** 4 (2004) 335–371.
10. Winsborough W., Li N.: Towards practical trust negoitiation. In Proceedings of IEEE 3rd. International Workshop on policies for distributed systems and networks (June 2002).
11. Yang B., Garcia-Molina H.: Comparing hybrid peer-to-peer systems. In Proceedings of 27th Very Large Databases Conference, Roma, Italy (2001).
12. Yang B., Garcia-Molina H.: Designing a super-peer network. Proceedings International Conference on Data Engineering (2003) 49–60.
13. Yu T., Winslett M., Seamons K.E.: Supporting structured credentials and sensitive policies through interoperable strategies for automated trust negotiation. ACM transactions on Information and System Security, **6** (February 2003).

A Web-Enabled Enterprise Security Management Framework Based on a Unified Model of Enterprise Information System Security
(An Ongoing Project Report)

Anirban Sengupta[1], Aniruddha Mukhopadhyay[2], Koel Ray[1],
Aveek Guha Roy[1], Dipankar Aich[1], Mridul Sankar Barik[3],
and Chandan Mazumdar[1]

[1] Centre for Distributed Computing, Jadavpur University,
Kolkata 700032, India
coordinator@cdcju.org.in
[2] Webel Technologies, Kolkata 700091, India
send2ani@yahoo.com
[3] Bengal Engineering And Science University, Shibpur,
Howrah 711103, India
mridul@it.becs.ac.in

Abstract. This paper presents an ongoing research project that is a sequel to an earlier work on the Development of Enterprise Information Security Management (EISM) Tool Suite for different stages like Requirement and Risk Analysis, Policy Development, Infrastructure Advisory Generation, and Testing of the Security Engineering Life Cycle. The present project attempts to develop a set of web-based information security management services using web-service technologies. The study also aims at developing a unified formal model of Enterprise Information System Security and suitable metrics for its measurement.

1 Introduction

The adoption of Information System Security at the Enterprise level and the subsequent adaptation to the changing context require handling of a large volume of diverse classes of data. In order to be precise and useful, this handling of data should be automated by products similar to software engineering tools.

This report begins by defining Enterprise Information System Security as a management problem. It then states the work done and the products developed during a previous project. Finally, the objectives and proposed deliverables of the ongoing project are discussed.

2 Security Management

The complexity of Enterprise Information System Security arises from the dynamic nature of security requirements due to the introduction of new technology

S. Jajodia and C. Mazumdar (Eds.): ICISS 2005, LNCS 3803, pp. 328–331, 2005.

and/or change in the company organization and infrastructure. Also, the technology and social threats to security systems can be quite unpredictable. As such, there is no absolute security and it has to be handled as a management issue rather than trying to find a closed-form solution. In order to be survivable, this management process should be based on a life-cycle concept.

Security management involves identified steps like requirements analysis, risk analysis, vulnerability and gap analysis, policy generation, infrastructure advisory generation, operational management, testing and validation. These steps form the Security Engineering Life Cycle.

3   EISM Tool Suite

The Centre for Distributed Computing, Jadavpur University, has executed a project entitled "Development of Validated Security Processes and Methodologies for Web-based enterprises", funded by the Department of Information Technology (DIT), Govt. of India. The team put forward the idea of Security Engineering Life-cycle [2].

The project work resulted in the following theoretical developments: 1) Security Requirement Analysis Methodology, 2) An XML-based Language to express the Requirement Specification, 3) A Security Risk Analysis Methodology,4) Identification of Baseline Policies, Guidelines and Procedures, 5) Methodology to generate infrastructure advisory, and 6) Methodology to generate the compliance test cases from the Requirement Specification. A major strength of the concepts developed is that all of them conform to the ISO 17799 Standard on Best Practices for Information Security Management System. The team developed a security management suite consisting of the following tools: 1) A security requirement analysis tool, 2) A security policy formulation tool, 3) A security infrastructure advisory generation tool, and 4) An automatic test case generation and penetration testing tool. This suite has been validated in several organizations. The existing suite of tools is based on the Enterprise Security Requirement Markup Language (ESRML) developed in the project [1]. The benefits are rapid development of the policies, comprehensive and detailed risk analysis, control-based infrastructure deployment and automated and integrated testing.

4   EISM as Web-Service

Based on the above study, this ongoing project envisages the rise of a new breed of entity, called Information System Security Service providers, on the Web. The present follow-up project entitled "Development of Web-enabled Enterprise Security Management Framework based on a Unified Model of Enterprise Information System Security", funded by DIT, has the following objectives [3].

4.1   Objectives

Formal models of systems are needed whenever their complexity increases to such an extent that it becomes impossible for human and organizational structures to manage. The security design and management are becoming too complex because of the interplay among technology, management, economics, social issues and the huge volume of data to be managed. The matter is complicated because of frequent changes in all these aspects and in fact, once the design and development is done, the changes in the requirement and environment appear much more frequently than in software systems. There exist various separate models [4] [5] [6] [7] [8] for the different aspects of enterprise security. The major objective of the present project is to integrate these models into a unified model of enterprise information security, so that the different outputs of the tools can be checked for completeness and validity. The second objective is to develop a set of web services to support the different phases of the Security Engineering life cycle. The web service framework will be based on the formal model; the clients will be able to get service from anywhere in the world; the framework will support rapid deployment of newer services to be integrated in the future. The upgradation of the existing servives will also be easier. A third objective is to develop a set of new metrics for risk, assurance, architectural efficacy, operational efficiency, protection capability, protection performance, etc. In summary, the present project is going to bridge a long-standing gap in the Enterprise Security Management area with its two-pronged attack to the problem. With the above objectives in mind, the following management components are envisaged to be developed.

4.2 Components

Enterprise Security Requirement Analysis Component. An enterprise would be able to log in to this web service and enter online, the different components of their security requirement specifications. After completion of this specification, the enterprise would be able to get the control requirement analysis report, the gap analysis report and the initial vulnerability analysis report.

Risk Analysis and Mitigation Component. Given the requirement specification file, the other kind of service, which the enterprise may avail of, is Risk Analysis. This will be done in three phases: Comprehensive Analysis, Detailed Analysis and Risk Mitigation Advice.

Policy Development Component. In the Policy development component, the enterprise will get the customized model security policy manuals for Enterprise-wide Baseline policies, Issue-specific detailed policies, and system specific policies. These manuals will be accompanied by the Guidelines and Procedures manuals for managerial and operational controls. The Policies and controls will be based on the standards like ISO 17799, COBIT, and NIST SP 800-53. The prevailing IT Act and other business specific regulations will also be considered.

Security Architecture and Infrastructure Advisory Generation Component. This service component will identify and assess the technology and tools required to secure an enterprise. An additional service is the identification of the available products and configuration advice for the products.

Security Testing Component. This component will take, as input, the requirement specification and risk analysis files for the enterprise and generate a report containing the list of vulnerabilities and advisories to plug the same. The component will also generate a list of test cases to perform compliance checking and penetration testing.

Training Component. Training for different levels of employees and different functional requirement will be offered as online web-based courses, so that the employees can take up the courses at their own time and pace.

5 Conclusion

The EISM Tool Suite has been copyrighted and already been applied in several organizations. Work is now underway for developing a formal unified model of Enterprise Security. This model will provide the basis for the development of a web-service based framework around which providers will be able to offer EISM services.

References

1. Roy et. al, "ESRML: A Markup Language for Enterprise Security Requirement Specification", in Proceedings of IEEE INDICON 2004, held at IIT, Kharagpur, from December 20-22, 2004.
2. Mazumdar et. al, "Final Technical Report for Project Development of Validated Security Processes and Methodologies for Web-Based Enterprises", 2003.
3. Sengupta A., Mukhopadhyay A., and Mallick A.S., "Preliminary Technical Report on the Development of Web-enabled Enterprise Security Management Framework based on a Unified Formal Model of Enterprise Information System Security", Technical Report, Project WebSecurity-II (CDC-JU), June, 2004.
4. Bell D and La Padula L, Secure Computer Systems: Mathematical Foundations and Model. MITRE Report MTR 2574 v2, Nov 1973.
5. Biba, K.J., "Integrity Considerations for Secure Computer Systems", MTR-3153, MITRE Corporation, Bedford, MA (June 1975).
6. Clark D., and Wilson D. A Comparison of Commercial and Military Security Policies. Proceedings IEEE Symposium Security and Privacy, IEEE Comp Soc Press, 1987, pp 184-194.
7. Sandhu, R.S., "Lattice-based Access Control Models", IEEE Computer, Nov. 1993, pp. 9-19.
8. Ravi Sandhu et. al., "Role-based Access Control Models", IEEE Computer, February 1996.

Development of a Comprehensive Intrusion Detection System - Challenges and Approaches

N. Subramanian, Pramod S. Pawar, Mayank Bhatnagar, Nihar S. Khedekar,
Srinivas Guntupalli, N. Satyanarayana, V.K. Vijaykumar,
Praveen K. Ampatt, Rajiv Ranjan, and Prasad J. Pandit

C-DAC, 67/68 Electronics City, Bangalore 560100, India
{subbu, pramod, mayank, nihar, srinivas, satya, vijay,
praveen, rajiv, prasad}@ncb.ernet.in

Abstract. Key challenges in the area of Intrusion Detection are the reduction of false alarms, event correlation & attack prediction. As a part of DIT, MCIT, Govt. of India supported project to carry out research and development in the area of Intrusion Detection System (IDS), we have developed N@G (Network at Guard). While developing N@G, we faced various challenges pertaining to performance, accuracy, analysis, survivability, adaptability and standards. In this paper we discuss these challenges and share our experiences, bringing out our approach towards solving them.

Keywords: Challenges in IDS, IDS Architecture, IDS Standards.

1 Introduction and N@G Architecture

N@G is a hybrid IDS having capabilities of both a Network IDS (NIDS) & a Host IDS (HIDS). We have devised a comprehensive architecture (Figure 1) encompassing N@G sensor (network & host), threat profiling, event correlation and incidence analysis. The communication interface is through IDMEF (Intrusion Detection Message Exchange Format) [1], an evolving IETF standard.

2 Key Challenges and Our Approach

2.1 Key Challenges

Performance
Performance is a key challenge with respect to various components in IDS such as Data Collection (DC), Signature Detection (SD), Protocol Anomaly Detection (PAD) & STATistical anomaly detection (STAT). Performance Challenges with respect to network DC involve; Packet capture rate & protocol decoding at line speed; Signature evaluation: the complexity involved in processing the captured packets; Pattern matching: deciding to choose and implement the most efficient algorithm for pattern matching. With respect to PAD the challenge is in keeping track of states, session and achieving synchronization: utilizing the resources effectively to manage states/sessions. For STAT, the challenge lies in processing load and providing near

S. Jajodia and C. Mazumdar (Eds.): ICISS 2005, LNCS 3803, pp. 332–335, 2005.
© Springer-Verlag Berlin Heidelberg 2005

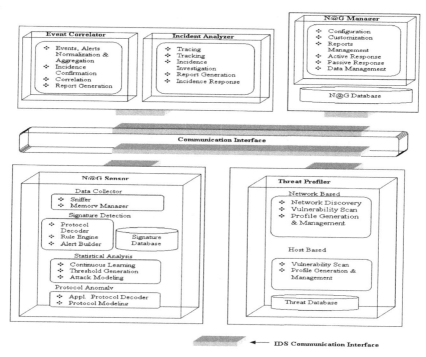

Fig. 1. N@G Architecture

real time response and adopting efficient methods towards the analysis of statistical data.

Accuracy

One of the issues discussed widely in the IDS community is how to handle the problem of "False alarms" including false positives & negatives. The challenge out here is confirmation of an intrusion with 100% confidence. Accuracy issues related to SD emanate due to flawed signature formation, partial signature match, and flaw in pattern matching implementation. In PAD technique false alarms are generated due to the problems of mapping between protocol specifications and implementations. STAT techniques depend on 'correctly' profiling the normal behavior, which cannot be guaranteed thus leading to false alarms.

Analysis

An ideal IDS includes both misuse (signature based) and anomaly based mechanisms. The challenges and issues in SD include; Fastness of matching the packets against signature database and in processing packets at a fast rate; Flexibility in representing a signature; deciding the effective boundaries of signature owing to its impact with respect to false alarm; Signature framing: & customization and Signature chaining which involves identification of a chain of signatures for a single attack.

The analysis challenges in PAD include Protocol modeling: Understanding of a protocol & modeling a normal behavior of the same; Frequent protocol updations;; and widely differing vendor implementations.

STAT is a standard approach wherein the network is profiled using various parameters related to network, protocols, users, hosts, equipments, services etc., The key challenges in this approach includes; Profiling the normal behavior; Building predictive models; identifying the right algorithm, identifying the appropriate model based on domain, traffic pattern, protocols, application etc.; and devising a feedback model for self-correction based on changing behavior of the network.

Survivability
IDS being a security solution are themselves susceptible to attacks and hence survivability of all the entities in the IDS is essential. Building survivable models that allow cooperation & cohesiveness among IDS entities is a research problem in itself. The other issues to be handled by the model are initiation of backup, availability of alternate resources, delegation of responsibility, and isolation during crisis situation, switching among various modes of operations and revelation of the status information about the IDS components etc.

Adaptability
Enabling IDS to become adaptive is a daunting task and it depends on the strength of the learning algorithms, predictive models built within and the ability of the IDS to automatically generate signatures upon confirmed anomaly patterns.

Standards
As more and more security products are available from many vendors, interoperability among them is a key issue and hence standardization is important. There are evolving standards such as CVE [2] (Common Vulnerability and Exploits) and IETF's IDMEF [1]. In spite of the above evolving standards, there are still lots of gaps with respect to standards to address common signature representation and providing interoperability to enable response mechanisms irrespective of vendor implementations.

2.2 N@G Approach

Herein we explain, our approach towards dealing with the challenges and share some of our implementation experiences in designing and developing N@G [3].

The first challenge is in dealing with high rate Network traffic and to process the packets for which static memory allocation was done during load time of IDS. This also has provision to handle traffic overloads. Additionally, the SD engine makes sure that each packet is evaluated with minimum rule comparisons achieved through a rule classification technique, which ensures that only the applicable rules are matched with the packet to be evaluated. Pattern i.e. content matching against the packets has to be done for almost 90% of the rules. This has been implemented using Boyer-Moore-Horspool Algorithm [4].

The STAT module implemented has three phases viz; Initial Learning, Detection and Continuous learning. We use Chi-Square technique. to compute values for identified parameters, setting thresholds and detecting the deviations from these set thresholds. As part of STAT, to evolve our system as a adaptive IDS, we have also implemented the continuous learning mechanisms.

N@G's PAD component currently supports protocol specific models for TCP, UDP and HTTP protocols. Detection mechanisms using RFC based violations for above-mentioned protocols are implemented. For HTTP, detection of header-based anomalies and URL encoding based attacks has been provided.

We have adhered to CVE and IDMEF standards. While implementing IDMEF based communication protocol, the necessity of adding more components to it was noted and has been suggested to IETF [5].

Apart from detection approaches N@G provides a comprehensive GUI based centralized management capability.

3 Conclusion

As the compute and network infrastructure becomes ubiquitous and new applications are evolved, it is imperative that security must be the key concern and IDS research and efficient product solutions have more responsible roles to play. While developing subset of intrusion detection entities is crucial, even more important are the techniques to correlate and make predictions & provide forecast of the threats and attacks. Key challenging issues like reduction of false alarms and building predictive models are interesting research problems for researchers and security solution providers across the globe.

Acknowledgement

Our sincere thanks to the DIT, MCIT, India for supporting our research work and to the Project Review and Steering Group for guiding us in right path and providing valuable inputs.

References

1. H. Debar et al.: The Intrusion Detection Message Exchange Format, http://www. ietf.org/ internet-drafts /draft-ietf-idwg-idmef-xml-14.txt, January 27, 2005
2. Common Vulnerabilities and Exposures (CVE): http://www.cve.mitre.org/about/
3. N@G- Network at Guard, A hybrid Intrusion Detection System: http://www.ncb. Ernet . in/nag/
4. R. Horspool. Practical fast searching in strings. Software - Practice and Experience, 10(6):501–506, 1980.
5. IDMEF Proposed Suggestions: http://www.cs.hmc.edu/idwg/archive/msg00116.html :January 25;2005

A Transparent End-to-End Security Solution
(An Ongoing Project Report)

Shince Thomas, Devesh Misra,
P.R. Lakshmi Eswari, and N. Sarat Chandra Babu

Centre for Development of Advanced Computing (C-DAC),
2nd Floor, Delta Chambers, Ameerpet, Hyderabad - 500016, AP, India
{ksthomas, dmisra, prleswari, sarat}@cdac.in

Abstract. Looking through the past couple of decades in information
security we can say that sophistication and advancements are not limited
to information security solutions alone but also in parallel applies to
cyber exploits and crimes which have grown both in number and in
their capacity to create havoc in cyber space. Originated in the form
of malicious code and unauthorized access, cyber security threats have
come a long way, today posing threats to end systems and applications.
This resulted in an exponential growth in end systems and application
security threats.In this paper we present a new approach to address end-
to-end security issues. This security solution is designed to be transparent
to applications, offering flexibility to deploy any cryptographic algorithm
and also providing features for efficient administration.

1 Introduction

Cyber security surveys in recent past shows that 85% of all the attacks are
launched from within organizations. End-to-end security solutions, which address these attacks, provide security encompassing the entire path from initiat-
ing process to responding process. These solutions need to have the flexibility
to configure encryption and authentication methods to enable the administrator to select the right level of security depending on the application needs [1].
Traditionally many end-to-end security solutions were developed like SSL and
IPSec supporting features of confidentiality, integrity and authentication. SSL
acts above TCP layer in the form of a software library and requires that network
applications directly interface with it [2]. Thus SSL security applies only to applications that have already incorporated this feature. IPSec also provides similar
services, but at network layer, and secures communication between session end
points, regardless of applications [3].

In this paper we present an end-to-end security solution interfacing with TCP,
which is transparent to applications. Since cryptography is computationally expensive, this solution provides the flexibility to control its use for various network applications. To overcome the spoofing attacks a novel approach is used
in authenticating end systems by making use of a fingerprint computed from its

S. Jajodia and C. Mazumdar (Eds.): ICISS 2005, LNCS 3803, pp. 336–339, 2005.
© Springer-Verlag Berlin Heidelberg 2005

hardware and software parameters. This solution is implemented in Windows operating system using a Winsock Layered Service Provider (LSP) introduced into the layered architecture of Winsock, which is a popular network-programming interface in Windows. In Linux the solution is implemented by adding the security functionality to specific system calls at kernel in addition to their normal behavior [5].

This paper is organized as follows: Section 2 describes the architecture. Section 3 explains the testing scenarios and in section 4 we present our conclusions.

2   Architecture

The network protocol stack implementations in various operating systems follow a well-defined layered architecture, which allows incorporation of sub layers between protocol layer implementations. The Transparent Security Solution (TSS) has a Socket Sub Layer component to intercept the communications (Fig. 1. shows the TSS architecture), which exists between the socket API layer in user mode and the socket implementation layer in kernel mode. Depending on the implementation needs we have the choice to implement this Socket Sub Layer in user mode or in kernel mode. Socket Sub Layer passes the intercepted communication stream to Socket Security Coordinator (SSC) for the application of security mechanisms with the help of other sub modules Security Policy Database, Machine Authentication System (MAS), Secure Channel Protocol (SCP) and Cryptographic API. The application of security features by SSC is governed by the security policies set by the administrator through an Authentication Server. Local security policy database of end systems are updated from time to time with relevant policies applicable to them.

Cryptographic API interface provides methods for selecting appropriate providers dynamically after the negotiation of algorithms by end systems that wants to establish a communication session. This framework provides means to dynamically add additional cryptographic algorithm modules through a programming interface. A cryptographic provider database is maintained at all end systems to manage the cryptographic algorithms. End systems need to be registered to the central Authentication Server in order to facilitate the Machine Authentication. This registration is done by computing fingerprint of the machine from hardware and software parameters selected by the administrator and enforced through a registration policy. The end systems that initiate a session exchange their machine fingerprint in a secured manner and get it verified from the Authentication Server. Machine Authentication System (MAS) provides the methods to perform all the authentication related steps.

Secure Channel Protocol (SCP) provides a secure channel for communication between the end systems as well as the Authentication Server. A Cipher Protocol encapsulates a secure payload, which include the encrypted communication data, message digest for integrity and required padding. SCP includes sub protocols, which facilitates the secure communication. All the sub protocols and application protocols are encapsulated in cipher protocol messages. The Network Access

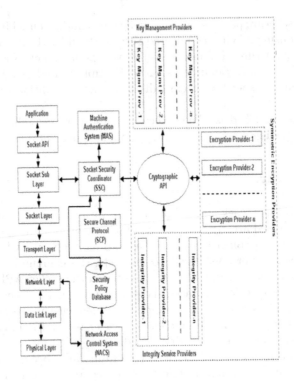

Fig. 1. Transparent Security Solution (TSS) architecture

Control System (NACS) interfaces with the network layer in the protocol stack and filters the communication to and from the host based on the filtering policies in the database.

3   Test Scenarios

3.1   Scenario I: Protection Against Sniffing

Sniffer programs can change the NIC to promiscuous mode, captures the traffic in real-time on the networks and look for anything transmitted in plaintext such as passwords, web pages, database queries etc. An Attacker can use sniffer on a machine in the internal network and gather the user ID and passwords, which are transmitted over the network in plaintext. By installing the TSS in all the critical machines of the network, sniffing of the passwords can be easily defended. As TSS can be configured to encrypt the session of any application, the traffic sniffed by the sniffer programs will be in encrypted form.

3.2   Scenario II: Protection Against Spoofing

IP and MAC spoofing can be used to exploit many applications, which rely on the IP address and MAC address for authenticating and filtering. To perform IP spoofing, an attacker need to first find an IP address of a trusted machine and then modify fields of the packet headers in such a way, so that it appears that the packets are coming from the trusted hosts. TSS has a machine authentication feature, which allows authenticating the trusted hosts with the Authentication Server using a machine fingerprint generated using many other hardware and software parameters of the system other than IP address and MAC address.

3.3   Scenario III: Protection Against the Propagation of the Worms

A worm is a self-replicating piece of code that spreads via networks and usually doesn't require human interaction to propagate and causes denial of services as it consumes network bandwidth and processing power of machines while replicating. Worms replicates itself by creating backdoors running at some port numbers. An administrator can get the early information about the spreading of the worms from security alert news and use the TSS Network Access Control System (NACS) to block the propagation of worms in the network by configuring appropriate rules on the central server.

4   Conclusion

The Transparent Security Solution (TSS) approach is a novel method of providing security features transparent to the applications, offering flexibility to deploy any cryptographic algorithms and features for efficient administration. This solution is designed for windows and Linux environments and is interoperable. Currently we are extending the solution for UDP based applications.

References

1. The Network Security Crisis - A White paper http://www.attrition.org/ modify/texts/security/whtpap2.html
2. Lakshminarasimhan R. and Solworth J.A., End-to-End Network Security, USENIX Symposium '03 http://parsys.cs.uic.edu/ solworth/networkSecurity.pdf
3. Kaufman C., Perlman R., and Speciner M., Network Security - Private Communication in a Public World
4. Nortel Networks, IPsec and SSL: Complementary solutions http://www.nortelnetworks.com/solutions/ip_vpn/collateral/nn102260-110802.pdf
5. Lakshminarasimhan R., Kernel-based Network Security http://parsys.cs.uic.edu/r̄lakshmi/Documents/SecureKernel_latest.pdf
6. Wei Hua, Jim Ohlund, Barry Butterklee, Unraveling the Mysteries of Writing a Winsock2 Layered Service Provider, Microsoft Systems Journal, May 1999.
7. CIPRESS White Paper - "The Network Security and Filtering Layers in the Microsoft Windows NT Operating System Family Environment", Mitsubishi Corporation. URL: http://www.igd.fhg.de/igd-a8/projects/cipress/
8. "Network Security Essentials", William Stallings - Pearson Education

Author Index

Lecture Notes in Computer Science

For information about Vols. 1–3704

please contact your bookseller or Springer